WAKE UP LITTLE SUSIE

RICKIE SOLINGER

WAKE UP LITTLE SUSIE

SINGLE PREGNANCY AND RACE BEFORE ROE V. WADE

ROUTLEDGE
NEW YORK & LONDON

Published in 1992 by

Routledge
An imprint of Routledge, Chapman and Hall, Inc.
29 West 35th Street
New York, NY 10001

Published in Great Britain by

Routledge
11 New Fetter Lane
London EC4P 4EE

Library of Congress Cataloging-in-Publication Data

Solinger, Rickie, 1947–
Wake up little Susie : single pregnancy and race before Roe v.
Wade / Rickie Solinger.
p.   cm.
Includes bibliographical references and index.
ISBN 0-415-90448-X (hardback)
1. Illegitimacy—United States—History. 2. Unmarried mothers—
United States—History.   I. Title.
HQ999.U6S65   1992

306.85′6′097309045—dc20   91-25068
CIP

Contents

For Jim Geiser and Sylvia Zuckerman, and to the memory of Herbert Gutman—my three best teachers.

It is not sexuality which haunts society, but society which haunts the body's sexuality. Sex-related differences between bodies are continually summoned as testimony to social relations and phenomena that have nothing to do with sexuality. Not only as testimony to, but also testimony for—in other words, as legitimation.

Maurice Godelier
"The Origins of Male Domination"

In Peyton Place there were three sources of scandal: suicide, murder and the impregnation of an unmarried girl.

Grace Metalious
Peyton Place

Having babies for profit is a lie that only men could make up, and only men could believe.

Johnnie Tillmon
"Welfare Is a Woman's Issue"

Preface

From the day I began to think about this book, it was first a political project and second an academic project, but always both. The several years I have worked on *Wake Up Little Susie* have not been a time of progress for the issues this study addresses. As of the summer of 1991, the Supreme Court's 1973 decision legalizing abortion, *Roe v. Wade*, is under severe attack in many states. Louisiana and Utah have virtually outlawed abortions, and the recent Supreme Court decision, *Rust v. Sullivan*, will have disastrous consequences for thousands of pregnant girls and women and, potentially, others depending on First Amendment guarantees. Reagan-Bush social policy regarding civil rights, welfare, taxes, education, contraception, health, housing, and programs to assist poor women and children has deliberately eroded past gains in these areas. Women—often especially single mothers—are targets and victims of this federal agenda.

For many readers of *Susie*, the postwar era will be sepia-toned, a time before they were born, or at least very long ago. Some will find the treatment of "unwed mothers" in that era terrible, but almost quaint. But my political project here is to show that the treatment of unmarried pregnant girls and women in the era that preceded *Roe*, a period contemporaneous with the postwar phase of the civil rights movement, reflected a powerful and enduring willingness in our culture to use women's bodies to promote conservative political goals. Without adequate opposition, this willingness *could* outlive the vitality of both *Roe* and the civil rights movement. In the end, while I have tried to be scrupulous, academically, in preparing this study, the final product is addressed to all those who care about justice and equal rights.

As I moved toward imagining this book I was very lucky to have been associated with a number of people who care deeply about *these* social and political goals. Despite the fact that I have already named Herbert Gutman in the dedication, I feel compelled, as have so many of his students and colleagues, to honor his memory by naming him again here, and calling to mind his striking talents as a teacher and an historian. I went to the Graduate Center to study with Herb, and every Monday for several years his class was a tremendously exciting adventure. Though he died before I began this work,

Foner
Gutman
Berkin

Brinkley

I count a number of his stern injunctions as the foundation material of *Susie*. I slipped into the Graduate Center in time to study with Eric Foner, as well, whose teaching inspired me then, and whose work continues to inspire me today. A special thank you to Carol Berkin who tried to teach me to exercise restraint, and in some ways succeeded. Carol also deserves thanks for helping out Herb Gutman's students after he died; without her the landscape would have been forbidding. I have thanked Alan Brinkley several times in private for his involvement with this project. In public I'd like to add that this man is a natural-born mentor.

Beyond the institution, most of my thanks go to my women friends and colleagues who have read all or parts of this book while it was in progress, or have supported my efforts in general. I thank the WIT group in New Paltz—Lee Bell, Amy Kesselman, Eudora Chikwendu, Elisa Davila, and Lily McNair—for providing five different and wonderful models for what it means to be a serious scholar. Now in Boulder, I likewise thank Martha Hanna, Lee Chambers, Polly Beals, and Barbara Engel. Nancy Hewitt has been encouraging and kind to me since the first day we met, and I appreciate her comments on various parts of the manuscript. I also appreciate Barbara Omolade's careful reading of *Susie* and her very helpful suggestions. Deborah King's meticulous and incisive comments helped me to improve key aspects of the book. I consider my chance meeting with Eileen Boris in the corridors of the National Archives a fortuitous occasion; more than she knows, her proselytizing for CGWH-CCWHP structured *Susie*'s fate. Amy Kesselman and Lee Bell both read every chapter, as each one was written, in an amazingly timely and helpful way. I depended on both of them enormously, as they must know. (More than once, I have been the grateful beneficiary of Lee's skills as a secret pal.) Thank you also to Elizabeth Baker, who has been a thoroughly steadfast friend since the beginning, always interested in my work, and usually willing to go off with me to archives and conferences. A newer friend, Patti Gassaway, not only eagerly read the whole manuscript, but makes me laugh almost every day. Finally, in this category, I'd like to name my oldest friend, Susie Lerner, with whom I spent most days in the fifties. The title and the era of this book make me think of her.

I am very pleased to thank others who have helped me toward *Susie*. Gerald Sorin was among the first to support my decision to study history seriously. Margaret Halsteadt in Interlibrary Loan at SUNY/New Paltz procured many important materials for me, and the research staff of the Sojourner Truth Library often turned me in the right direction as I began the study. In Boulder, the Norlin Library ILL staff has been welcoming and efficient, especially Regina Ahram and Linda Kraft. I received wonderfully professional help from everyone I dealt with at the National Archives; Judith Johnson at the Salvation Army Archives was a serious, interesting, and helpful guide. My stay at the Social Welfare History Archives in Minneapolis was sociable as well as academically fruitful, thanks to Dave Klaassen, a superb archivist. I also appreciate very much the institutional accommodations that the Women's Studies Program at UC Boulder has provided me. Thanks also to the National Women's Studies Association and the Elizabeth Cady Stanton Foundation, both of which chose to support my work. Cecelia Cancellaro approached me early and most warmly about *Susie*. Her reputation and her spirit would have been hard to resist. I'm glad I didn't.

I cannot write here that my children, Zachary and Nell, ever suffered because their mother would not come down from her writing room. I came down. I had to because I love living with them so much. Being mother to these two has deepened my life profoundly and has touched my scholarship as well. Sylvia and Irving Zuckerman visited often as I worked on this book, but never often enough. I am forever deeply grateful for their confidence in me. Finally, as is customary, I end with the most heartfelt thanks to my husband, Jim Geiser. Jim works more days of the year than anyone else I know, with more intensity, but still thoroughly earned the dedication I've given him. He always made it possible and likely that I would write this book. After ten years, he remains the perfect mate for me.

Introduction

Female and Fertile in the Fifties

Sally Brown and Brenda Johnson both became pregnant in 1957. Both girls waited desperately for periods that never came. Both worried about angry parents, disloyal boyfriends, and the knowing looks of classmates. Within the year, Sally and Brenda both became unwed mothers. There were limits, however, to what Sally and Brenda shared. In fact, the two girls were separated by race most effectively and more enduringly than by the private burdens of their unwed pregnancies.

Short case histories of Sally and Brenda's pregnancies show the profound commonalities and extreme differences in the experiences of black and white single pregnant females in the United States in the decades after World War II. Sally's story, so familiar to readers of women's magazines in the 1950s, goes like this:

> In 1957, Sally Brown was 16. Just before Thanksgiving, she missed her period for the second month in a row. She concluded, in terror, that she was pregnant. Sally was a white girl, the elder daughter of the owners of a small drycleaning establishment in a medium-sized city in western Pennsylvania. The Friday after Thanksgiving, she told her mother. Mrs. Brown told Mr. Brown. Both parents were horrified—furious at Sally and particularly at her boyfriend, Tim, a local "hood" they thought they had forbidden Sally to date. In October, Sally told Tim about the first missed period and in November, the second. It was obvious to Sally that Tim's interest in her was dwindling rapidly. She felt heartsick and scared.
>
> Mr. Brown, a businessman for twenty years with deep roots in his community, was bitterly obsessed with what the neighbors, the community and their friends at church would say if they knew about Sally. He proposed a sensible solution: to send Sally away and tell the townspeople that she was dead. The Monday following Thanksgiving, however, Mrs. Brown put her own plan into action. She contacted the high school and informed the principal that Sally would not be returning for the second half of her junior year because she'd been offered the wonderful opportunity to spend the Spring semester with relatives in San Diego. She then called up the Florence Crittenton Home in Philadelphia and arranged for Sally to move in after Christmas vacation.

1

Before Sally began to "show," she left home, having spent six weeks with parents who alternately berated her and refused to speak to her. They also forbid her to leave the house.

At the maternity home, Sally took classes in good grooming, sewing, cooking and charm. In her meetings with the Home's social worker, Sally insisted over and over that she wanted to keep her baby. The social worker diagnosed Sally as borderline schizophrenic with homosexual and masochistic tendencies. She continued to see Sally on a weekly basis.

In mid-June, after the birth of a 7 pound 14 ounce boy, Sally told her social worker that she wanted to put the baby up for adoption because, "I don't think any unmarried girl has the right to keep her baby. I don't think it's fair to the child. I know I don't have the right."

On June 21, Sally's baby was claimed and later adopted by a Philadelphia lawyer and his infertile wife. Before Sally's 17th birthday in July, she was back home, anticipating her senior year in high school. She had been severely warned by the social worker and her parents never, ever, to tell anyone of this episode and to resume her life as if it had never happened.

Brenda Johnson had quite a different experience in 1957, and, undoubtedly, in the decades that followed.

In February, 1957, Brenda Johnson was 16 and expecting a baby. Brenda was black. She lived near Morningside Park in upper Manhattan with her mother, an older sister, and two younger brothers. Brenda hadn't had to tell anyone about her pregnancy. Her mother had picked up on it in September when Brenda was beginning her third month. Mrs. Johnson had been concerned and upset about the situation, sorry Brenda would have to leave school and disgusted that her daughter was thinking about marrying Robert, her 19-year-old boyfriend. On the day she discovered the pregnancy, she said to Brenda, "It's better to be an unwed mother than an unhappy bride. You'll never be able to point your finger at me and say, 'If it hadn't been for her.' "

In October, Brenda had been called into the Dean of Girls office at school, expelled and told not to plan on coming back.

At first, Robert stayed around the neighborhood. He continued to be friendly, and he and Brenda spent time together during the first half of Brenda's pregnancy. As she got bigger, though, she felt sure that Robert was spending time with other girls too.

During the winter, Brenda hung around her family's apartment, ran errands and helped her mother who worked as a domestic for a middle-class family downtown. She went for her first pre-natal examination at seven months.

As Brenda got close to her due date, she worried how she would take care of a baby. There was no extra space in the apartment and no extra money in the family budget for a baby. Brenda asked her mother and her older sister about giving the baby up, maybe to her mother's relatives in South Carolina, but her mother told her firmly, "You put your child away, you might as well kill him. He'll think no one wants him."

In early March, Brenda had a girl she named Jean in the maternity ward of the local public hospital. Brenda told the nurse, "I love the baby as much as if I was married." Having no money of her own, and having been offered little help from Robert who she heard had left for Florida to find work, Brenda went to the Welfare Office. There she received a long, sharp lecture about young girls having sex that taxpayers have to bear the costs of. She was told she would have to find Robert if she wanted to get on welfare and that the welfare people would be watching her apartment building for him. The welfare worker asked Brenda if she knew what happened in some places to girls in her situation who got a second baby. The worker told her that in some states, a girl with a second illegitimate child would lose her welfare grant. She also said that some people liked the idea of putting a repeater in jail or making it impossible for her to have any more bastards.[1]

The stories of Sally and Brenda suggest that single, pregnant girls and women were a particularly vulnerable class of females in the post–World War II era. Regardless of race, they were defined and treated as deviants threatening to the social order. Single, pregnant girls and women of whatever race shared the debased status of illegitimate mother: a mother with no rights, or a female who had, according to the dominant culture, no right to be a mother. For Sally and Brenda and the several hundred thousand girls and women in their situations each year between 1945 and 1965, illegitimate motherhood was a grim status.

The stories of Brenda and Sally also suggest that the scenarios prepared for white and black unmarried mothers diverged dramatically. This was, in part, because in the immediate pre–*Roe v. Wade* period, politicians, service providers, the media, and communities constructed the experiences of unwed mothers, black and white, in new ways. By considering the nature of these constructions, we can understand why and how racially specific prescriptions for unwed mothers emerged in the postwar era, took the particular forms that they did, and were institutionalized. In addition, we can explore the major, though still race-based, changes in the ways that black and white single pregnancy were constructed by substantial and influential segments of the public in the United States between 1945 and 1965. *Wake Up Little Susie* provides a case study of the plasticity of the social construction of "unwed mothers" in the United States. In sum, this study of unwed motherhood in the postwar era argues that many politicians and academicians, the popular media, social service professionals, and sizable segments of the public-at-large incorporated unwed mothers into the political arena and assigned them political value by race. In this way, the reproductive capacity and activity of single girls and women in this period were used to explain and present solutions for a number of social problems identified in the chapters that follow.

Being an Unwed Mother

In *The Feminine Mystique*, Betty Friedan identified the socially sanctioned (and presumably racially neutral) career ladder for women in the post–World

War II years: Having a baby is the only way to become a heroine.[2] But consider the response to black and white unwed mothers to see what was really demanded of women in the era of family togetherness. An unwed mother was not part of a legal, domestic, and subordinate relation to a man, and so she could be scorned and punished, shamed, and blamed. She gave birth to the baby, but she was nobody's heroine.

Many unmarried girls and women got pregnant and for one of a number of possible reasons did not get an illegal or "therapeutic" abortion. So many spent most of their months of pregnancy in some or all of the following ways: futilely appealing to a hospital abortion committee; being diagnosed as neurotic, even psychotic by a mental health professional; expelled from school (by law until 1972); unemployed; in a Salvation Army or some other maternity home; poor, alone, ashamed, threatened by the law. If a girl were so reckless as to get herself pregnant outside of a legally subordinate relation to a man in the postwar era, all of society had the right to subordinate her human dignity to her shame.[3]

By taking a closer look at a few of the slim alternatives open to a single, pregnant woman in the two decades after World War II, we can evoke the desperate character of her predicament. We can also see how her capacity to bear children was used against her.

Consider the possibility in the mid-1950s of getting a safe, legal, hospital abortion. If a girl or woman knew about this possibility, she might appeal to a hospital abortion committee, a (male) panel of the director of obstetrics/gynecology, and the chiefs of medicine, surgery, neuropsychiatry, and pediatrics. In hospitals, including Mt. Sinai in New York, which set up an abortion committee in 1952, the panel of doctors met once a week and considered cases of women who could bring letters from two specialists diagnosing them as psychologically impaired and unfit to be mothers.[4]

By the early 1950s, procedures and medications had eliminated the need for almost all medically indicated abortions.[5] That left only psychiatric grounds, which might have seemed promising for girls and women desperate not to have a child.[6] After all, psychiatric explanations were in vogue, and white unwed mothers were categorically diagnosed as deeply neurotic, or worse. There was, however, a catch. These abortion committees had been set up to begin with because their very existence was meant to reduce requests for "therapeutic" abortions, which they did.[7] It was, in fact, a matter of pride and competition among hospitals to have the highest ratio of births to abortions on record.[8] But even though psychiatric illness was the only remaining acceptable basis for request, many doctors did not believe in these grounds. A professor of obstetrics in a large university hospital said, "We haven't done a therapeutic abortion for psychiatric reasons in ten years. . . . We don't recognize psychiatric indications."[9] So an unwed pregnant girl or woman could be diagnosed and certified as disturbed, probably at considerable cost, but she couldn't convince the panel that she was sick enough. The committee may have, in fact, agreed with the outside specialists that the abortion petitioner was psychotic, but the panel often claimed the problem was temporary, with sanity recoverable upon delivery.[10]

The doctors were apparently not concerned with questions about when life begins. They were very concerned with what they took to be their responsibility to protect and preserve the links between femininity, maternity, and marriage. One doctor spoke for many of his colleagues when he complained of the "clever, scheming women, simply trying to hoodwink the psychiatrist and obstetrician" in their appeals for permission for abortions.[11] The mere request, in fact, was taken, according to another doctor, "as proof [of the petitioner's] inability and failure to live through the destiny of being a woman."[12] If such permission were granted, one claimed, the woman "will become an unpleasant person to live with and possibly lose her glamour as a wife. She will gradually lose conviction in playing a female role."[13] An angry committee member, refusing to grant permission to one woman, asserted, "Now that she has had her fun, she wants us to launder her dirty underwear. From my standpoint, she can sweat this one out."[14]

For many doctors, however, condemning the petitioner to sweat it out was not sufficient punishment. In the mid-1950s, in Maryland, a doctor would almost never agree to perform a therapeutic abortion unless he sterilized the woman at the same time.[15] The records of a large, midwestern general hospital showed that between 1941 and 1950, 75 percent of the abortions performed there were accompanied by sterilization.[16] The bottom line was that if you were single and pregnant (and without rich or influential parents who might, for example, make a significant philanthropic gesture to the hospital), your chances with the abortion committee were pretty bleak.

If a girl were white and broadly middle class, and failed to obtain a therapeutic abortion, or never sought one, there was a pretty fair chance her parents would pack her off to a maternity home just before she began to "show." Her destination was terrifying and likely out of town, but the silent interval before the departure was equally chilling. A woman, in her late fifties, remembers the freezing day in 1952 when she stood alone, outside, at the top of the majestic stairs of the law school where she was a student. Certain that she was pregnant, she considered throwing herself down the icy steps because, "You just couldn't have a baby."[17] A Radcliffe student in the same era needed to tell someone about her pregnancy. Jean chose a close male friend who'd been her pal for years, a "regular guy." But hearing the news, he became so aroused that he attacked her sexually. Horrified, Jean rebuffed the attack and faced the young man's petulant anger: "You're pregnant, aren't you? So what's the worry, let's have some fun." Jean felt that she had "gotten herself pregnant." She thought, "I wanted to die, but he was right. I got what I deserved."[18]

It is important to understand why it was so easy for young white women to blame themselves. Many aspects of the culture supported such feelings, but two were explicitly and immediately to the point. A single, pregnant woman was expected to take responsibility for violating norms against premarital sex and conception. Plus, she was expected to acknowledge, as a condition of changing herself, that her pregnancy was a "neurotic symptom." The experts— social workers, psychologists, psychiatrists, clergy, and others—insisted that unmarried girls and women got pregnant willfully and spitefully, if unconsciously. Professionals particularly stressed that the young woman was determined, through her pregnancy, to get back at her domineering mother. The blame was out there, authoritative and easily internalized.

Once a girl or woman entered a maternity home, there was safety and protection of a sort. Many residents appreciated the protection but felt they paid a very high price. Among some young women, it appeared to be a toss-up whether the loneliness or the lie were worse. Karen, at a Salvation Army home in California in the early 1960s said, "I think the worst part of it has been the damned loneliness. I've adjusted pretty well to the hiding and the lying to the outside world, but I've just never gotten used to being all alone inside." A recent arrival in the same Salvation Army home, angered by a moment of good-spirited camaraderie among the girls, expressed her frustration. "We're all in here to have babies we don't want. We're hiding it from the world and we'll leave here pretending it didn't happen. I hate those lies— and you just laugh."[19]

One experience that the overwhelming majority of maternity-home residents, and many white unwed mothers who did not make it to these homes, did share was the experience of giving their babies up for adoption. In the years before *Roe v. Wade*, the experts were, again, pretty unanimously agreed that only the most profoundly disturbed unwed mothers kept their babies, instead of turning them over to a nice, middle-class man and woman who could provide the baby with a proper family. Leontine Young, the prominent authority on social casework theory in the area of unwed mothers, cautioned in 1954, "The caseworker has to clarify for herself the differences between the feelings of the normal [married] woman for her baby and the fantasy use of the child by the neurotic unmarried mother."[20]

For complex cultural, historical, and economic reasons, black, single, pregnant women were not, in general, spurned by their families or shunted out of their communities into maternity homes, which usually had "white only" policies in any case. For the most part, black families accepted the pregnancy and made a place for the new mother and child. As one Chicago mother of a single black pregnant teenager said at the time, "It would be immoral to place the baby [for adoption]. That would be throwing away your own flesh and blood."[21] In contrast to the very large percentage of white girls and women who gave up their babies for adoption, about nine out of ten blacks kept theirs. In a postwar New York study, 96 percent of blacks keeping their babies reported deep satisfaction with this decision eighteen months later.[22] Yet welfare and social caseworkers persisted for years in their claims that the only reason why blacks kept their babies was that no one would adopt them.

Social workers and other human service professionals claimed repeatedly that black single pregnancy was the product of family and community disorganization. Yet in comparing the family and community responses among blacks and whites to out-of-wedlock pregnancy and childbearing, it is striking how the black community organized itself to accommodate mother and child while the white community was totally unwilling and unable to do so. The white community simply organized itself to expel them. Still, black girls and women who became pregnant while single faced a forceful array of prejudices and policies threatening to the well-being of poor, minority, single mothers and their children.

Most women in this situation felt that lack of money and adequate housing were their biggest problems, but many got hassles and worse from the agencies meant to help them. One black unwed mother said, "When I needed financial assistance, all Welfare did was to give me a hard time. They wanted me to place the baby and go to work to support myself. Also they made matters worse for me by trying to drag the baby's father to court. I probably would have been able to work if there had been a daycare center where I could have left the baby." A young woman in New York who needed a place to live with her baby said, "Well, I think maybe the Housing Authority could let an unmarried mother apply for an apartment. I am not going to hurt anyone if I get into a project." Another, seventeen years old, described the death of her education. "I wanted to finish my commercial course, but when the truant officer came to see me after the baby was born, he said, 'I suppose you're NOT going back to school,' and he gave me such a dirty look I felt bad and decided not to go back."[23]

A black woman in her twenties summed up the public treatment she and others faced: "I don't know. I feel that wherever you go or whatever you do, if they find out you are an unwed mother, you've had it! Like when you go to Welfare, I know they would treat you like you were nothing. I bet if I went to look for another place right now and they know I wasn't married and I had a kid, they'd refuse to even talk to me. It's just in little ways that you're looked down upon and that's what really begins to work on you."[24]

Howard Osofsky, an obstetrician in Syracuse devoting his career during this period to improving services for poor single mothers, described the attitude of his colleagues who use "anthropological and cultural data to equate [the nonwhite unwed mother] with the savage who must be protected by the more capable and learned members of society."[25] A young, black, single, pregnant teenager showed how her sensitivity to this attitude shaped her expectations when she reported to a social worker, "I don't need nothing from nobody. I don't want nobody messing around my life. I just want to be left alone."

But in the late 1950s and early 1960s, there was a burst of activity in numerous state legislatures that reflected a determination not to leave single, poor, mostly black, unwed mothers alone. In every section of the country, state legislators either passed or tried to pass laws mandating substantial fines and prosecution, incarceration, and sterilization of women who "persisted" in having children without being married.[26] There was enthusiastic public support among some whites in every region for these legislative efforts because they explicitly tied illegitimacy to such concerns as the "population explosion," crime in the cities, welfare costs, and integration.

The Population

The unwed mothers whose experiences form the basis of this study do not necessarily stand for all unwed mothers in the United States during the twenty years following World War II. The experiences of poor whites, middle-class blacks, and well-to-do whites are absent or not central to this study, although Chapter Five, particularly, focuses on the experiences of lower-class white girls and women. But the study *is* based on what was undoubtedly considered, by a wide range of experts and nonexperts, as the racially specific *representative* experiences.

The issue of unwed motherhood was a growing concern of various professional and academic communities, government agencies and foundations, and the community-at-large during the period of this study. As these various constituencies worked to account for the rising rate of illegitimate pregnancy and to address the need and costs for services to unwed mothers, members of these groups relied on race- and class-defined stereotypes of single pregnant girls and women as they structured their particular missions. The representative white unwed mother—the one described by academic studies, government officials, agency personnel, and the media as typical, was, in general, broadly middle class, in the sense that she was perceived as having resources of value to her credit. That is, she was perceived as having parents who could and would, in her behalf, negotiate with helping institutions and underwrite their daughter's care. She had, despite her unfortunate sexual misstep, the likely potential to become a wife and mother in the postcrisis phase of her life. And most important, she was in the process of producing a white baby of value on the postwar adoption market.

The representative black unwed mother, according to the same influential groups, was a poor, Aid to Dependent Children grant recipient who kept her illegitimate child or children. This unwed mother was most often perceived as bereft of resources. She was, rather, perceived as burdened by her illegitimate child, by her financial dependency, and by the social and cultural pathology allegedly infecting the black population in the United States.

In the postwar era, the site of the problem afflicting the typical white unwed mother was relocated from her body to her mind. The white unwed mother was no longer a genetically flawed female, as she would have been in the Progressive and prewar eras. She became, instead, a treatable neurotic. While there had been no solvent for the biological stain of illegitimacy, psychologists and social workers believed that the neuroses of illegitimacy responded to treatment. The biological stain, however, remained affixed to black unwed mothers, who were often portrayed by politicians, sociologists, and others in the postwar period as unrestrained, wanton breeders, on the one hand, or as calculating breeders for profit on the other.

These stereotypes of unwed mothers occurred so often, so predictably, and uncontestedly in postwar studies and commentaries on single pregnancy that they came to stand for *naturally occurring*, racially specific subjects. In addition, the stereotypes were so pervasive, inclusive, and powerful that the public discussion of unwed mothers at this time routinely conflated race and class, despite the fact that some white single pregnant girls and women had no resources in the sense that policy makers and social service professionals defined these, or came from communities that did not disparage or eject single pregnant girls and women and their babies. Likewise, the stereotypes were not undermined by the fact that some black single pregnant girls and women were neither poor nor ADC recipients, and some did not want to keep their illegitimate children.

In fact, it must be emphasized at this point that politicians, social workers, and others who addressed or responded to illegitimate pregnancy in the postwar years distinguished between blacks and whites, but not between rich, poor, and middle class. Thus the difficulties and options before, for example, an upper-middle-class pregnant high-school senior in Scarsdale, New York, and a pregnant, white working-class girl from Mobile, Alabama, were not publicly distinguished from each other by government officials, social workers, psychiatrists, educators, or clergy. This was the case, in part, because anybody's white baby had become valuable in the postwar era. With the rise of the psychological explanation of white single pregnancy and the decline in the belief in the genetically flawed illegitimate mother and child, white babies were born out of wedlock not only untainted but *unclassed* as well. Thus, the salient demographic fact about white unwed mothers was that they were white. The salient demographic fact about black unwed mothers, then, was that they were not white.

To a significant extent, class, like gender, indeed, amounts virtually to a given in *Susie*, although even this given divides by race. The vast majority of broadly middle-class white girls and women who sought help from agencies, shared certain class-defined needs. For the daughters of this class, a sexually tainted crisis like out-of-wedlock pregnancy was not strictly family business or a private affair. Unlike the daughters of the very rich or of the very poor perhaps, unmarried pregnant middle-class daughters could not look to their families alone (if at all) for protection because the shame of illicit sex and maternity was tremendously threatening to the social standing of the whole family.[27] The very need for protection from an outside agency was the mark of middle-class standing as well as an indication of the fragility of that standing and of its partial dependence on the family's ability to sustain the appearance of raising chaste daughters. It also suggests one more way that kinship functions in the white middle class became attenuated at this time.[28]

In midcentury, the agendas of the agencies that served white unwed mothers were set to facilitate an unwed mother's reconstruction, a specific process that was necessary for the girl or woman to undergo if she were to go forward in life with access to normative, adult, female roles. By allying themselves with these agencies, white unwed mothers and their families acknowledged their ties to gender and class codes of behavior, and systems of redemption mandated by middle-class status.

For the black girls and women considered in *Susie*, class is an even more certain given. This is true both because race and class were very nearly identical categories for blacks in postwar America, and because the sources for the sections on black unwed mothers in this study were often associated with welfare or other basic services agencies whose clients were particularly lacking financial resources. These girls and women were often defined as if their class were embedded in the meaning of their race.

The agencies serving unwed mothers, and their clientele, were class-defined, respectively, by the nature of their services and their intentions, and by their needs. Neither the agencies nor unwed mothers typically commented on the issue of class, which it seems they took for granted. But agencies and social service professionals were fundamentally concerned with the issue of race, and unwed mothers themselves made choices (in part because of social, economic, legal, and institutional constraints and in part because of community mores) that were thoroughly race-specific. Thus, while class was an implicitly important factor determining the treatment and experience of unwed mothers and excludes some from consideration here, race was an explicitly important fact and far more inclusive.

The particular historical era covered by this study is one in which race, or rather the place of blacks in American society, was emerging as a vital, pressing social issue. In the post–World War II era, as the United States was becoming a society in the throes of racial consciousness and tension, racial distinctions—including the distinction between black and white unwed mothers—had special meaning and special functions that are discussed throughout this study. Suffice it to say here that these race-specific distinctions were one way of justifying race hierarchy at a time when that hierarchy was threatened.

In the postwar decades, American society, particularly large segments of white society, began to perceive itself as experiencing the opening of an era of sexual liberalism.[29] Concern most often focused on the weakened mechanisms governing the social and sexual regulation of white girls and women.[30] As D'Emilio and Freedman have pointed out, this perception "raised issues [concerning] the maintenance of sexual order. . . . [H]ow could legitimation of heterosexual eroticism remain within 'responsible' limits?" How was it possible to prevent turning the new freedom to license?[31] D'Emilio and Freedman argue that the white middle class used black sexual mores—including, and especially, relatively high rates of black illegitimacy—"as a convenient counterpoint" to white sexual behavior, thus sustaining a kind of group image of white sexual propriety, in contrast. In this case, race and sexuality—old bedfellows—combined again to bolster fraying systems of dominance and subordination.

Two other potentially meaningful demographic facts were ignored by professionals chiefly interested in race. As suggested above, social service workers and policy makers did not distinguish between a white unwed mother in Scarsdale and one in Mobile when they considered the causes and consequences of her illegitimate pregnancy. Nor did they make distinctions between the causes and course of a black unwed mother's pregnancy in Chicago or Tupelo. While regional mores, regional race relations, and regional political climates (in many cases influenced by black migration, for example, from the southeast to the urban midwest) may have, indeed, shaped the experiences of these unwed mothers differently, the experts whose work this study draws on did not refine their analyses with reference to regional considerations. For them, white girls had one set of experiences, black girls another.

The third demographic fact eclipsed by the overriding interest in race—although somewhat less so than class and region—was age. Following the conventions of postwar experts, the present study mixes the experiences of teenagers with the experiences of women in their twenties and thirties, and sometimes simply ignores the age of a particular unwed mother. The postwar convention of minimizing the importance of age reflected the fact that during the period covered here, the most common age bracket in which single pregnancy occurred was between twenty and twenty-four.[32] Many experts recognized that teenage illegitimacy was becoming more common, but diminished its importance in comparison with the incidence among older women.[33] Moreover, very high rates of teen marriage in the 1950s encouraged parents, clergy, teachers, and social service professionals to blur distinctions between teenagers and slightly older girls and women. A seventeen-year-old could get pregnant and married, or not, in 1957, just like a young woman in her midtwenties. Most important, whether a single pregnant person was sixteen or twenty, or even older, the agencies that dealt with her situation felt perfectly entitled to treat her as if she were a child, a daughter, especially a dependent.

In short, all black unwed mothers were widely assumed to be like the black stereotype; all white unwed mothers were assumed to possess, to a high degree, the characteristics of the white stereotype. Undoubtedly, many girls and women, black and white, succeeded in constructing experiences for themselves outside of the scenarios shaped by the prevailing stereotypes. This study, however, chiefly (but not exclusively) considers the experiences of girls and women caught by these stereotypes, which captured and satisfied some powerful social and institutional interests of the postwar era that *Susie* explores. For these reasons and others discussed throughout this study, race occupies the foreground of the study.

The Public Record

The "case histories" of Sally Brown and Brenda Johnson obscure several aspects of the sources on postwar unmarried mothers. For the most part, quantitative and qualitative data on whites were captured *during* the pregnancy by maternity home staff, national organizations, and the governmental agencies that gave financial, research, and ideological support to shelters and treatment programs for white, single, pregnant girls and women. Since the black community adjusted itself to accommodate single pregnancy and since most maternity homes discouraged or refused admittance to blacks, the circumstances of these unmarried mothers were most often documented *after* the pregnancy, when the black girl or woman was a recipient of some form of public assistance.

In the sources, therefore, a white unwed mother was almost always in a state of potential motherhood. She was described and evaluated in psychological terms as she prepared for the institutional abortion of her maternity via the adoption process. The black unmarried mother, on the other hand, was institutionally defined as a sociological and economic disaster, and evaluated as a supplicant-dyad: a mother-and-child.

The largely institutional sources are skewed by age and class as well because of differences in clientele. An academic analyst of unmarried pregnancy in the pre–*Roe v. Wade* era noted these distinctions:

> Charitable agencies (such as the Salvation Army) tend to select or be selected by very young adolescents with limited education, possibly from lower socio-economic strata. Private agencies (such as Youth Consultation Services) tend to serve older adolescent and college students from established middle class homes. Physicians in private practice . . . tend to be chosen by older, well-established middle and upper-class women who are financially able to afford their services. The public welfare agencies then take up the slack. Indigent single mothers of whatever age and Negro clients will be over-represented in their caseloads.[34]

While this analyst distinguishes clientele using various types of agencies by class, it is important to note that race remains, even within his schema, the important variable. Charitable agencies such as the Salvation Army, private agencies such as Youth Consultation Services, and private doctors, all chiefly serving whites, shared priorities: sequester the unmarried girl or woman; treat the psychiatric problems her pregnancy suggested were present; separate mother and child at birth and place the baby for adoption. While public welfare agencies did serve both white and black indigent unwed mothers, "Negro clients" were assumed to resort to these agencies. The foremost interest of welfare workers was often described as determining the eligibility or ineligibility of unwed mothers for money grants.

The contemporary public perception as well as the historical analysis of single pregnancy in the pre–*Roe v. Wade* era draw disproportionately on the institutional experiences of younger, poorer, white girls and minorities. Older girls and women, and those from more well-to-do families, were able to obscure their illegitimate pregnancies from the public record then and now. Since illicit sex and illegitimate pregnancy were at issue, history's most typical and consistent first-person informant—white, educated, socially and economically secure—is nearly silent.

As specialized as the documented population is, in fact, some experts estimated in the late 1950s and early 1960s that perhaps as few as one-third of all unwed mothers were receiving services from public, private, or voluntary agencies.[35] The characteristics and experiences of a large majority of unwed mothers were not known to those institutional employees who did so much to create, preserve, and—as is suggested here—to shape and constrain the experiences of unwed mothers.

In 1957, for the first time, the official number of illegitimate births in the United States broke 200,000.[36] As high as this number was, most people who found it meaningful considered it a serious undercount.[37] It was common knowledge that many white unwed mothers had the resources to conceal their pregnancies, often by traveling far from home to have their babies, to states that didn't record illegitimacy on birth certificates. Whatever the precise number of babies born out of wedlock, statisticians, policy makers, and service providers acknowledged that the illegitimacy rate (the percent of women of childbearing age who had babies out of wedlock) had tripled between 1940 and 1957, and the number of illegitimate births had increased by 125 percent since World War II began.[38] Experts further acknowledged that while black women, far more often than white, had babies without being married, the illegitimacy rate for white girls and women was rising faster than for blacks.[39] In this context of the rapidly increasing incidence of nonmarital childbearing, new distinctions between black and white single pregnant women emerged. Government policies and the agencies charged with carrying them out supported different meanings of black and white sexuality, pregnancy, and motherhood, meanings that justified, even demanded, different treatment of black and white single, pregnant females. The study of single pregnancy in the pre–*Roe v. Wade* era demonstrates quite clearly the reciprocal relationship between ideology and public policy—how the former infuses the latter, and how, in turn, public policies create outcomes that strengthen the bases of ideology.

It is important to note here that to a certain extent, I have allowed the "public record" to guide my choice of terminology throughout the book. I have used words such as "unwed mother," "illegitimate baby," and "putative father" —all heavily burdened with intended prejudicial meanings—in order to convey the flavor of public discussion of these matters and these individuals in the postwar years. I trust it will be obvious that my use of period language does not reflect negative moral judgments on my part. My occasional use of the word "bastard" is a bit more complicated. This word is a technical term, and also, of course, a profound derogation. It is rarely found in the record of public discussion of single pregnancy during the period of this study, although sometimes a politician did not choose to bite his tongue in time. But as I uncovered the public and private fear and rage that structured the treatment of single pregnant women in this era, I sometimes felt that "bastard" was the only word that expressed the meaning intended by my sources.

Recasting Unwed Mothers

Wake Up Little Susie demonstrates how the idea and the experience of unwed motherhood were socially constructed at midcentury. It must also consider why older, prewar responses to single pregnancy were no longer attractive or effective after World War II, and why postwar responses took the form they did. In the context of rising rates of illegitimate pregnancy for both blacks and whites, why did the treatment of white girls "soften" and the treatment of black girls "harden"? Why were white girls no longer pressed to keep their illegitimate babies? Why were sociology and biology no longer regarded as able to provide explanations for both black and white single pregnancy as they had in the past?

An unmarried white pregnant girl looking for help in the early decades of the twentieth century—after illegitimacy had become a "traumatic event . . . not only for the girl, but for families and communities at most levels of society,"[40] could only have found specialized, institutional protection in an evangelical rescue or maternity home.[41] These were usually located in cities and staffed by sternly religious matrons and their assistants. In general, the mission of these homes was to prepare ruined girls and women for lives as service workers and as outcast but caring mothers.[42] Probably a very small percentage of white unwed mothers actually entered such homes and stayed for the months or even years required. Still, these programs incorporated the culturally sanctioned intentions for white unwed mothers before World War II.

Innovations after World War II included preparing white unwed mothers to relinquish their illegitimate babies and grooming them to resume the roles of normative young womanhood—coed, coquette, and bride. Throughout the late 1940s and the 1950s, institutions eased out staff imbued with religious fervor and handed over authority to professionals steeped in psychological theory. In many cases the institutional settings had not changed physically, but within a brief period, their programs, and the expectations for the white unwed mother, had changed very substantially.

Wake Up Little Susie argues that in three major ways, all interrelated, the context in which white single pregnancy occurred and was handled had changed by the end of World War II. First, annual rates of white unwed motherhood began a steady increase in the mid-1940s and continued to climb throughout the period of this study. The demographic facts of single pregnancy were changing. As nonmarital sex and pregnancy became more common (and then very common during the later postwar period), it became increasingly difficult to sequester, punish, and insist on the permanent ruination of ever-larger numbers of girls and women, as later it became difficult to label rapidly growing numbers neurotic. In addition, in the postwar period, a growing proportion of the population in the United States assumed an affiliation with the "middle class." Many unwed mothers were also the daughters of this engrossing segment. Again, it became increasingly difficult for parents and the new service professionals, with middle-class affiliations themselves, to sanction treating "our daughters" as permanently ruined.

Secondly, the Florence Crittenton or Salvation Army maternity home may have looked the same in 1950 as in 1935, but in many ways the institutional setting for handling unwed pregnancy had altered significantly. Its postwar program was largely secular; its staff dominated by professional social workers; its funding drawn partly from community sources.[43] Postwar maternity homes sustained the rescue homes' innovation of serving the private and individual needs of their clientele, but were, at the same time, increasingly beholden and responsive to the interests of the community. Many communities began to expect maternity homes to offer an attractive option to white unwed mothers who might otherwise turn to alternatives that parents, government officials, clergy, doctors, psychiatrists, and other service professionals did not sanction: illegal abortion, black market adoptions, or motherhood.

Finally, the ideological context in which illegitimacy occurred changed radically after the war. During the Progressive Era and throughout the 1930s, social science commentators and social service professionals explained female sexual deviance, which included illegitimate pregnancy, as the result of poisonous interaction between environmental conditions and moral degeneracy. These factors, characteristic of urban slums, were said to produce young women predisposed to sexual misadventures in part because together they stimulated (or some thought, were predicated upon) a biological incapacity to resist seduction.[44] A typical assessment of white unwed mothers in the late 1920s found them to be "from the economically inferior strata of the population," "excessively equipped sexually, but lack[ing] ordinary normal inhibitions." The author described the average unwed mother as "a young moron . . . [who] as a child . . . had inadequate home training, due to the ignorance, poverty, and alcoholism of her parents." This investigation of eighty-four unwed mothers found "a definite causal relationship between [the girl's] weak inhibitions and her intellectual level," and thus identified "a high correlation between mental defect and illegitimacy."[45] Here, illegitimacy occurred at the intersection of negative sociological and biological conditions and was an expression of an inhering, unchanging, and unchangeable "physical" defect.

By the mid-1940s, medical and social work professionals disdained this explanation. They accused its proponents of depending on the pessimistic view that the individual unwed mother, or potential unwed mother, was at the mercy of harmful environmental and other "forces" that had the power to determine her fate. The postwar, modern alternative claimed that illegitimacy reflected a mental not environmental or biological disorder and was, in general, a symptom of individual, treatable neuroses. An episode of illegitimacy was contingent upon the mutable mind, rather than upon fixed, physical entities—the city or the girl's body. The girl could undergo psychological treatment; she could change. She could escape being permanently defined by her error. With professional help, in a triumph of individualism, she could prevail over her past, her mistakes, her neuroses. This more positive and forward-looking postwar explanation suggested that the American environment was not culpable, nor was the female *innately* flawed. Reliance on the psychological explanation redeemed them both.

The psychological model also offered, of course, an alternate view of sexuality. Early-twentieth-century commentators believed an unwed mother had indulged in intercourse and become pregnant because she was "subnormal," suggesting an identity between mental degeneracy and the degeneracy of sex. The postwar analysts, however, accepted the neo-Freudian view that sex "expressed one's deepest sense of self."[46] Thus, even though an unmarried girl who had coitus and became pregnant was, perforce, maladjusted, it was not her relationship to sex that was the basis of the diagnosis; it was her psychological inability to form a sanctioned relationship to a man that proved her anormative. Under these conditions a girl or woman could transcend her maladjustment simply by marriage, or by preparing herself for a marriageable future.

These more optimistic views of society, the individual, and sexuality included a paradoxically more expansive and restrictive view of the family with significant implications for the unwed mother. On the one hand, the typical middle-class white family was depicted as no longer beleaguered or threatened by economic depression or war. Families with access to postwar resources defined children as a desirable asset; in fact, culturally, "family" now required two parents and at least that many offspring. On the other hand, this postwar definition of family strongly suggested a new definition of motherhood—that it could not be achieved without a husband, outside of a properly constructed family—as postwar "womanhood" could not be achieved without a man.[47] Both constructs insisted on the centrality of the male to female adult roles, an idea that offset the postwar concern that women were aggressively undermining male prerogatives in the United States. At the same time, then, in an environment where white illegitimate babies could be a resource for childless couples who wanted to achieve a proper family, unwed mothers became not-mothers. Further, the experts insisted that by accepting themselves as not-mothers, unwed mothers were contributing to their own rehabilitation. This prescription, again, suggested a triumph of individualism, and a triumph of American society in which even the lowly unwed mother was generously offered the option of the second chance.

The postwar recasting of white illegitimate mothers offered these girls and women a remarkable trade-off. In exchange for their babies, they could reenter normative life. A very high percentage accepted the neo-Faustian deal, suggesting that the postwar female and family ideals were powerful constructs, indeed. It also suggested that a white unwed mother in the middle decades of the twentieth century understood that not-mothers who tried to be mothers anyway stood to suffer too much. Perhaps having internalized this, or perhaps in a self-protective act of obedience, she could relinquish her baby.

An unmarried black pregnant girl looking for help in the early decades of the twentieth century could probably have found assistance only within her own family and community. Most maternity homes excluded blacks; most of the few government assistance programs that existed excluded unmarried mothers. In any case, black families and communities did not typically require each other to expel their unmarried pregnant daughters, as white families and communities did.

The combination of this and several other factors ensured that the experience of the black unwed mother was not the concern of white policy makers, taxpayers, or social service professionals before World War II. Single pregnant black women did not look beyond the boundaries of family and community for help. Thus, black single pregnancy and childbearing cost white America little, and few whites felt they had a vested interest in the subject, which, until the late 1940s, mainly stimulated the commentary of anthropologists and sociologists. Moreover, high rates of black illegitimate pregnancy supported century-old and older white beliefs about the uncontrollable sexuality and promiscuous childbearing of blacks and the source of these alleged behaviors in biologically determined inferiority.

Herbert Gutman's pathbreaking work on the black family includes a careful review of most nineteenth- and twentieth-century studies of the "matriarchal family," defined as a poor compensation for the normative, patriarchal American family. These studies tied the difficulties of the black community to the matriarchal family form.[48] E. Franklin Frazier, like his predecessors and successors, both black and white, explained the problematic black family system during Reconstruction and into the twentieth century in these terms: "Marriage as formal and legal relation was not a part of the mores of the freeman."[49] It was, indeed, a truism among observers of the black family, well into the second half of the twentieth century, that for black girls and women, unmarried pregnancy and motherhood was normal and typical.

The 1940s marked a turning point in public attitudes about black single pregnancy because during this decade, for the first time, public money became available to substantial numbers of unmarried mothers and their children through the Aid to Dependent Children program; many potential recipients were black. The white public's commitment to expenditures of this type was at best ambivalent, and during succeeding decades, with the emergence of the civil rights movement, some politicians, taxpayers, and social commentators in every section of the country mounted campaigns of resistance against black unmarried childbearing women. These campaigns were implicitly or explicitly tied to the larger, related campaigns of resistance against tax-supported welfare programs for blacks and against civil rights for blacks. Some policy makers and segments of the public drew on an interpretation of culture of poverty theory that constructed black unwed mothers as a key symbol in the middle decades of endemic black pathology. They became bearers of syndromes for which white society could not be blamed and for which it should not be forced to assume responsibility. While the plight of black males, some conceded, could be tied to hiring and firing policies in industry, for example, the behavior of black women was often defined as simply and completely biologically determined and thus beyond remedy. By the mid-1960s, many politicians, taxpayers, and social analysts had become willing to locate the genesis of problems in the black community—and many problems that threatened the white community—in the wombs of black unwed mothers.

Wake Up Little Susie explores the relationship between race and unwed motherhood in order to demonstrate that gender subordination is not a single phenomenon that depends on the biological characteristics and capacities of females. This study argues that biology derives social significance, in this case, by its association with race, in a context in which race-specific meanings are attached to the breaching of social rules governing sexuality and maternity. Thus this study of illegitimacy maintains that race was a centrally important factor in constructing two different sets of strategies of female subordination.

The central point, finally, is that race had a special salience for these girls and women in the United States. Race, in the end, was the most accurate predictor of an unwed mother's parents' response to her pregnancy; of society's reaction to her plight; of where and how she would spend the months of her pregnancy; and most important, the most accurate predictor of what she would do with the "fatherless" child she bore, and of how being mother to such a child would affect the rest of her life. With the centrality of race to the experience of single pregnancy at its center, *Wake Up Little Susie* aims to present and analyze the thoroughly race-specific public policies, professional practices, community attitudes, and family and individual responses to single pregnancy that prevailed in postwar America. The intentions of *Susie* are to shape a feminist analysis of the social and political uses and meanings of this variant of female fertility and to suggest that the race-specific public and private responses to single pregnancy, between 1945 and 1965, have profoundly influenced the race-rent politics of female fertility into our own time.

To see how unwed pregnancy was cast in the recent past helps to understand more about contemporary political responses to issues related, directly or indirectly, to female fertility. This study aims to argue most forcefully— both implicitly and explicitly—that politicians and others in the United States have been using women's bodies and their reproductive capacity for a long time to promote political agendas hostile to female autonomy and racial equality.

This book describes the postwar background of welfare and abortion politics in the Reagan-Bush era. These administrations and the social critics who share their goals have consistently built social policy in the 1980s and 1990s upon the racist and sexist assumptions that structured the experiences of unwed mothers in the earlier period. To this day, these policy makers and social critics regularly ascribe poverty in black communities to the wanton breeding of black women. The Reagan-Bush administrations have designed— or defunded—social programs so as to discredit the needs of these mothers and their children, and to dismiss the revelance of economic and social discrimination against both black men and women to poverty, single-parent households, and illegitimacy. The Reagan-Bush abortion agenda, dedicated to denying all girls and women the right to decide whether and when to become mothers, is most often promoted in religio-ethical or scientific terms. But at its heart, as social policy, this agenda yearns to reproduce a society in which all "illegitimate mothers" are in disgrace and in danger, without male protection.

Chapter One

The Stick and the Carrot: Public Meanings of Black and White Single Pregnancy in the Pre–Roe v. Wade Era

Race-specific explanations and experiences of single pregnancy in the postwar era shored up evidence of difference and hierarchy of race. They also affirmed a different degree and kind of sexuality in black and white women. In addition, racially specific ideas about single pregnant women supported similar ideas, policies, and practices regarding the babies born to these women. This chapter argues that public discourse assigned black and white unwed mothers strikingly different meanings, meanings that justified differential treatment of the girls and women involved and of their children. Thus the chapter—in fact, this entire study—demonstrates that the reproductive capacity has contributed to the oppression of women in the United States in variable ways. Public policies and community practices enforced racially distinct lived experiences of black and white unwed mothers in the postwar era, despite the fact that all of these girls and women experienced the same biological events.

The different treatment of black and white unwed mothers emerged during the postdepression, postwar era that privileged the white family imperative, or what is now called the "family agenda." Then as now, fertile women were designated prime agents in a central portion of this project. To satisfy the family imperative required then, as always, a high degree of conformity and traditional behavior among white women, in particular, their willingness to marry, to bear and rear a number of children, and their willingness to perceive themselves and act as consumers for the household. In the public discourse, the nature of the unwed mother's violation was expressed in racially specific terms, and in terms that suggested that unwed mothers were not simply violators of sexual or gender norms. In fact, they embodied a threat to key elements of the family agenda. Large segments of the public, policy

20

makers, and service providers felt justified in responding to nonmarital pregnancy as a subversive activity, as a threat to the healthy, procreating, consuming family, the bedrock of postwar society in the United States.

Unwed Mothers and the Postwar Context

Until the late 1930s, cases of illegitimacy were generally handled by child-centered agencies charged with making sure that children born out of wedlock were accorded care as nearly equal to other children as possible, mainly by ensuring that illegitimate children remained with their birth mothers.[1] To this end, a handful of states, led by Maryland and Minnesota in the World War I era, legislated state-enforced breast-feeding for six months. Such laws were meant to enforce the state's and the agencies' intentions that illegitimate children and their mothers would not be separated.[2] While such policies may have been coercive in some cases, they were not race-specific. All unwed mothers were expected to keep their bastard children, an expectation that could be enforced by law, by the pressure of social norms, or by choice.

The postdepression, postwar social agenda—including the new, race-specific responses to unwed mothers—gave a prominent role to the family and thus to female conformity. It was implemented during the famous, quiescent fifties, an era, in fact, of widespread lawbreaking and anormative behavior, such as very high rates of illegal abortion, public evidence that females were assuming new degrees of sexual and social license, and the law-defying behavior of blacks associated with the emergent civil rights movement.

During this period, considerations of the family and gender relations were dominated by charges against "Momism" and the "Matriarch."[3] These attacks, targeting white and black women respectively, demonstrated a deep concern about the postwar capacities of adult males to sustain their traditional role of dominance in the family and in the culture at large. The concern for masculinity, however, was expressed in terms that condemned women. Those who attacked women insisted that all contemporary forms of "social disease," from juvenile delinquency, to homosexuality, to unwed motherhood, to henpecked husbands, were caused by "women's misplaced sexuality," which meant her reputed unwillingness to be subdued within the family.[4] A woman's assertion of self was equated with perverse and dangerous sexuality.

A potent subcategory of the attack was aimed at single women. Elaine May discusses the postwar family imperative and notes the "widespread fears that single women might not be willing to settle down into domesticity once the war ended."[5] She ties the cultural uneasiness about single women to the independence many women had experienced during the war, usually by force of circumstances. The public associated independence of mind or action among single women, as well, with dangerous sex or unsubordinated "sex on the loose." A good woman participated in sexual acts that "contributed to a man's power and enjoyment without threatening him."[6] Bad women—

including ball-busting wives (practitioners of Momism, and black matriarchs), potentially all single women, and certainly all unwed mothers, participated in sexual acts that reduced men to "biological accessories."[7] The sexual lives of these women, many claimed, contributed to nobody's power and enjoyment but their own, perversely.[8]

Among single women, unwed mothers were most vulnerable to this strain of public opinion partly because they had violated multiple rules concerning femininity and sexuality, marriage and maternity, and were thus a powerful testament to the wages of uncontained female sexuality, dangerous as a threat to the integrity of the family. In explaining society's response to the single pregnant female after the war, Sara Edlin, the director of a large maternity home in New York wrote, "[Society] regards illegitimacy as an inroad on the family's stability and permanency, and repels it by ostracizing the unwed mother."[9] Edlin might have added that like most groups of pariahs, unwed mothers tended to be badly in need of multiple social services.

A second line of attack against these antisocial behaviors took the form of defensive racism. As the civil rights movement was gathering force and focus, particularly in the south, various states attempted to legislate sanctions against blacks to buttress segregated society against the transformations intended by integrationists and other civil rights activists.

Many of these efforts were directed against black women, specifically against unmarried mothers. Soon after states began to extend Aid to Dependent Children (ADC) grants to some children of unmarried mothers in 1939, including some black children, states mounted campaigns of resistance for the first time.[10] "Surveillance" laws were passed in a number of states after 1947 to establish special investigating units to ferret out unwed mothers consorting with men. Such women were to have their ADC eligibility rescinded. In 1951, Georgia became the first state to legislate the practice of denying welfare grants to more than one illegitimate child of an unwed mother. This was a postwar innovation: the formal, legal status of racist policies directed against procreating black women. Throughout the 1950s states were able to resist federal interference with their discriminatory policies largely because the federal government was not disposed to interfere. Policy makers at that level recognized that using taxpayers' money to support illegitimate children and their mothers was an incendiary issue better left to the states.[11]

By the early 1960s, state and local attacks were even more ambitious. In 1960 the Louisiana state legislature moved to deny public assistance to twenty-three thousand illegitimate children, affecting the households of more than six thousand unwed mothers. Eighteen other states attempted the same strategy. A number of other state legislatures, including those in California, Connecticut, Delaware, Georgia, Illinois, Iowa, Maryland, Ohio, Tennessee, Mississippi, North Carolina, and Virginia, had majorities that supported preventative, punitive actions against women who might in the future conceive another child defined by these states as "unwanted." These states enacted or attempted to enact laws mandating imprisonment or sterilization of women who had more than one illegitimate child.[12]

Civil rights organizations associated these state policies directed against women with an interest in containing the threat to the traditional order represented by the growing number of black activists. A 1960 Urban League memo widely circulated to civil rights and social service organizations criticized the media for a lack of attention to these racist measures and called the overall public response to them "weak and fitful." The memo claimed that what looked like a "morals bill" in Louisiana was actually "an act of reprisal or of intimidation against a Negro population which has been insistently pressing for an end to racial segregation in education and other areas of living." The memo also pointed out that the bill directed against unwed mothers and their children was included in a segregation package prepared by the legislature.[13] The triple vulnerability of black women, defined by their race, their gender, and their childbearing age, created a climate of viciousness and danger for them even more than for white unwed mothers who were pariahs in their own communities.

A discussion that analyzes both the internal assumptions of public policy and public policy's threatening intentions toward individuals has to contend with a dangerous, double-edged question: does this study depend on notions of conspiracy among governmental elites and their agents, and a complementary vision of females as victims? In fact, this study assumes and provides evidence of a social consensus about the different meanings of black and white single pregnancy among policy makers and service providers around the country in these years. A conspiracy connotes the secret intentions of the few who believe they hold sufficient resources to accomplish their ends. Social consensus, however, implies broad agreement among many, in this case an agreement that was not effectively challenged in any collective sense during the period under consideration. Relative to the other part of the question, there is no doubt that between 1945 and 1965, many girls and women did not have the power to define the meaning of pregnancy for themselves. So, many became victims. Yet, in the pre–*Roe v. Wade* era, millions of women in each decade resorted to law-defying behavior to gain control of that meaning. And, just as important, many of the unhappily pregnant women who for one reason or another did not have access to illegal abortions took steps, within the constraining circumstances constructed for them, to protect and assert their own interests. This chapter, however, focuses on the ways that public policies and practices tended to disempower black and white women who were of childbearing age and unmarried.

Fallen Women and Bad Girls

Race-specific policies and practices regarding unwed mothers emerged and were institutionalized in the 1940s, along with the shift from child-centered agencies to woman-centered agencies to manage the outcomes of illegitimate pregnancy.[14] It was at this point that public and professional attitudes about *who was a mother* emerged as racially variable. Women-centered social agencies introduced casework treatment for white, single, pregnant girls and women, with the effect of redefining illegitimacy for this population as a psychological rather than a sexual issue.[15] Maud Morlock, the Children's Bureau Consultant on Services to Unmarried Mothers, shared this perspective with her colleagues in 1950: "We used to think that illegitimate pregnancy was a sex problem, but now we recognize that all human behavior is purposive. . . . Life is a chain of events for all of us and illegitimate pregnancy is a result of the mother's life experiences starting in the cradle."[16] Consistent with postwar attitudes about single women, white unwed mothers became, by definition, unfit mothers, in fact, not mothers at all. By professional definition and diagnosis, white unwed mothers who wanted to keep their babies were diagnosed as particularly immature, or more usually, mentally ill.[17]

In sharp contrast, politicians, social workers, and others continued to define black single pregnancy as the product of uncontrolled, sexual indulgence, the product, in fact, of the absence of psyche. Leontine Young, a highly respected social work theorist in the area of illegitimacy who was often hired as a consultant to federal, state, and local governments, and who served on national boards of organizations addressing the problem of unmarried motherhood, associated this population of unwed mothers with the "psychological wastebasket," and asserted, they have "no personality structure."[18] For midcentury commentators concerned about population growth among blacks, about rising welfare costs, or about black challenges to white supremacy, biological determinism was a useful explanation of the behavior of black women, in part because it explained behavior as "natural," that is, preordained by nature. Biological determinism justified punitive responses to black single pregnancy as the only effective means of behavior modification.

Public and private agencies and government policies viewed both black and white women as breeders, but with a major and consequential distinction. The former were viewed as socially unproductive breeders, constrainable only by punitive, legal sanctions. Proponents of school segregation, restrictive public housing, exclusionary welfare policies, and enforced sterilization or birth control all used the issue of relatively high rates of black illegitimacy to support their campaigns.[19] White unwed mothers in contrast were viewed as socially productive breeders whose babies, unfortunately conceived out of wedlock, could offer infertile couples their only chance to construct proper families.[20]

In order to support this distinction between black and white women and to justify resulting racially distinct policies and practices, the moral conditions of black and white illegitimately pregnant women were distinguished as well. White women in this situation were defined as occupying a state of "shame," a condition that admitted rehabilitation and redemption. The pathway was prescribed: casework treatment in a maternity home, relinquishment of the baby for adoption, and rededication of the offending woman to the marriage market. The conditions of success are illustrated by Marilyn, interviewed by her Florence Crittenton caseworker six months after she was released from the agency's Boston maternity home. "Marilyn reported a deep satisfaction for the time she had had with her baby and regretted that it had been necessary for her to give him up, but not for the decision that she herself had made. She now wanted to find a husband who could and would enjoy sharing parenthood with her."[21] White illegitimacy was generally not perceived as a "cultural" or racial defect, or as a public expense, so the stigma suffered by the white unwed mother was individual and familial.

Black women, illegitimately pregnant, were not shamed but simply blamed, blamed for the population explosion, for escalating welfare costs, for the existence of unwanted babies, and blamed for the tenacious grip of poverty on blacks in America. There was no redemption possible for these women, only the retribution of sterilization, harassment by welfare officials, and public policies that threatened to starve them and their babies.

Helen Perlman at the University of Chicago, who wrote frequently about social policies regarding unmarried mothers in the 1950s and 1960s, took a clear-eyed view of the differences between black and white illegitimately pregnant women in 1963. She remarked that in truth, the more than five hundred "sisters who each day become unwed mothers" are essentially the same. "The immoral act [which caused illegitimate pregnancy] isn't different [for blacks and whites] in purpose or kind." It was simply that some girls and women were luckier or more careful, and certainly some could avoid welfare.[22] Embedded in public policies and practices dealing with unwed pregnancy, however, were postwar critiques of women, and racism. These were combined with a stiff allegiance to the era's white family imperative, and the mix ensured that the definitions and the outcomes of illegitimate pregnancy were substantially different for black and white women.

Black single pregnancy and white single pregnancy presented different problems or opportunities in the context of the postwar family agenda. In general, public policies and practices regarding white girls and women transformed the threat of independent, sexual power suggested by nonmarital, white, female sexuality, into a condition of pathetic powerlessness. This was a powerlessness that justified policy and agency decisions on the white, single, pregnant woman's behalf, for example, decisions regarding the disposition of her baby. It protected her from responsibility for her condition and maintained her in readiness for a legally subordinate relation to a man in her marriageable future.

Public policies and practices addressing black single pregnancy defined a woman out of the moral universe and justified her exclusion from maternity homes, from welfare benefits and other fundamental rights as a woman and a mother. Both black and white unwed mothers had a role in the postwar campaign to apotheosize the family. Girls and women of both races were targeted among the family's worst enemies, for attack and marginalization. This process transformed the family's nemeses into its best friends by providing a population of visible, vulnerable nonconformists, punishable and punished for their sins against the family.[23]

Unwed Mothers and Postwar Demographics

Nonmarital childbearing was treated as the most profound violation of postwar population goals.[24] These goals constituted a midcentury variant of traditional eugenics: vitalize the white, middle-class family and, at the same time, curb childbearing among minorities.[25] Cultural proscriptions against premarital sex and particularly nonmarital childbearing remained strong for all girls and women, but black and white unmarried mothers fit into the government's demographic calculations in radically different ways. If one can derive the intentions of policy from its outcomes, then it seems clear that white unwed mothers were designated as contributors to the white, family imperative in a double sense. They could provide babies to infertile couples, and then afterward, having been rehabilitated, go on to form proper families of their own.[26] A few social service providers in the postwar period critiqued the system that mandated relinquishment of white babies on an every-case basis,[27] but the vast majority, including officials of the United States Children's Bureau, the leadership of the Salvation Army, Florence Crittenton Association of America, and Catholic Charities, psychologists, psychiatrists, and clergy were largely in agreement that white unmarried mothers must, for the sake of their own futures and the future of the illegitimate child, put these babies up for adoption.

Maud Morlock of the United States Children's Bureau, in charge of overseeing programs and services for unmarried mothers across the nation from the late 1930s through the late 1950s, wrote optimistically in the early postwar era of a time in the near future when, with the help of properly trained caseworkers, the unmarried mother "will be in a better position to decide on the best plan for the child. This probably means . . . less guilt and [less] compulsion to keep the babies. They [will be] free to make a more objective and realistic decision on what is best for them and what is best for the baby."[28] During the postwar decades, adoption *was* established as the rule for white unmarried mothers.[29] Government funds—on the state, county, and municipal levels—became available to pay for maternity home care and medical costs for white, single women who planned to relinquish their babies. Ruth Pagan of the Salvation Army noted that public assistance "for bed and room and medical care are only made contingent upon a girl's willingness to surrender the child in adoption." Pagan cited Georgia as a state in which a girl had to sign away her unborn child before the state would "undertake to pay for her care."[30] Public and private agencies exerted pressure in this direction as well. A maternity home administrator wrote to the Children's Bureau:

> When occasionally we have a mother who would like to keep her child it has been our experience that she is not served by the social agencies quite like any other client. Consciously or unconsciously pressure is put upon her by the caseworker and she accepts the established point of view, namely that adoption is best for the baby and therefore also for her, or she is asked to remove her child from the care of the agency.[31]

A Children's Bureau report to the House Appropriations Committee in 1962 detailing what individual states were doing to improve their programs and services for unmarried mothers showed that over 50 percent of the states reporting focused exclusively on bolstering their adoption services.[32]

In contrast, black unwed mothers, assigned a negative role, demographically, were put by their childbearing in a triply dangerous position. They had a child in poverty, they were vulnerable to harassment by welfare workers, and they were targeted for attack by public officials. In the mother-blaming mode of the postwar decades, many analysts identified the black single mother's alleged hypersexuality and immorality, her resulting children, and the public expense as traceable to the source: the Negro woman who gave birth, as it were, to black America, with all its "defects."

These black women, of course, kept their illegitimate babies. Whether they did so because there were no other options or because black people love babies was a source of debate among many social service policy makers and providers in these years.[33] Whichever argument prevailed, the mandate for a black woman to keep her child was so strong and enforceable that when a black unwed mother tried to put her baby up for adoption in Cook County, Illinois, in the late 1950s, the court charged her with desertion.[34] A report on the Chicago Family Court, prepared in the early 1960s by the Ad Hoc Committee on Service to Unmarried Mothers in that city, raised the question of the role of the State Attorney's office in relation to black unwed mothers. According to the report, welfare officials "pointed out that the previous attorney had carried the role of prosecutor, frequently not permitting young women who had worked out careful adoption plans with an agency to give up their children, threatening them with charges of child abandonment."[35] Ursula Gallagher, Maud Morlock's successor at the Children's Bureau, reflected on this mandate in the late 1950s: "In some courts it is almost impossible for a Negro unmarried mother to give up her baby for adoption. The general interpretation of this is that the courts believe the girl should be *made* to support her children and should be punished by keeping them."[36] Social policy could protect white women from the consequences of their sexual experiences. For black women, social policy functioned to affirm their mother-hood and then punish them for it, as criminals.

Ironically, the Children's Bureau, the federal government's designee in this area, promoted "community planning" as the most effective way to deal with unwed motherhood in the postwar era, and yet it supported policies that were implicitly or explicitly inimical to the community's stance toward nonmarital childbearing. White communities ejected single, pregnant females, but the public and private agencies handling white unwed mothers provided a measure of secrecy and protection for these girls and women that raised a question for some professionals: "Are we communicating to young people, both male and female that by helping to keep the secret of their pregnancy, we are in some way saying this is acceptable?"[37] On the other hand, the black community organized itself to accommodate single pregnant girls and women, morally and logistically, even without adequate economic resources.[38] The agencies charged with responding to these women, however, trampled the community's response with a series of stigmas imposed from outside the community.

The demographic interests shaping the different treatment of black and white unmarried mothers were tied most closely, of course, to the different social meanings attached to black and white illegitimate babies. Ursula Gallagher wrote to a colleague about this issue in 1959: "In general, throughout the country there are certain problems that play a part in developing attitudes toward unmarried mothers in influencing restrictive action in regard to them. There is a difference in attitude on the part of the public toward the unmarried girl who delivers a child who is sought after for adoption and the mother of a child who might need public support."[39] Black illegitimate babies, like their mothers, aroused the anger and racism of the white, taxpaying public, while white illegitimate babies, if not their mothers, aroused the public's compassion and their interest in seeing these children well placed.

It was, indeed, a common observation among policy makers and service providers that it seemed difficult to keep the agency's attention focused on the white pregnant single girl or woman when the adoptable baby was so near at hand, promising the social worker and society such a rewarding project. Maud Morlock, writing to the Children's Bureau Child Welfare representative for the southern states in 1951, described the seductiveness of the available white infant to social workers: "One of the things that impressed me in reading the report on the Tennessee Children's Home Association . . . is that the emphasis was focused almost entirely on adoption and that practically nothing was said about the importance of getting services to the mother."[40] Leontine Young, a very active consultant to programs and policy makers concerned with unmarried mothers, cited "the tendency to regard [white] unmarried mothers as breeding machines, means to an end. As individuals . . . they are overlooked, and popular support tends to concentrate upon securing babies for quick adoptions."[41] Throughout the 1950s, this attitude prevailed. At the end of the decade, Miss Gallagher spoke to a group of social workers in New Orleans: "A source of satisfaction to me was the emphasis placed [by this group] upon the unmarried mother herself . . . instead of on the baby, which is certainly contrary to what I have been finding in many parts of the country."[42]

Unwed Mothers in Consumerist America: Buyer's Market and Seller's Market

The treatment of unmarried mothers was also conditioned by the postwar commitment to consumerism. Single pregnant women had not conformed to the mandate for family formation, so they were vulnerable to attack for violating the prescribed, productive relationship between marriage, motherhood, and the market. In postwar America, as wives and mothers were being groomed and glorified as consumer experts, both the state and business interests stepped up campaigns to make women's bodies—and their children—into commodities.[43] The issue of unwed motherhood was thrust into the middle of this process. A special set of tropes that associated unwed mothers with the marketplace, especially with regard to the "value" of the child, became useful in classifying the violations of both black and white unwed mothers.

Black unmarried mothers were frequently construed as "women whose business is having illegitimate children."[44] A Philadelphia judge, recommending jail for women who had more than two illegitimate children, explained his stance: "It becomes apparent that childbearing has become a business venture to collect relief and benefits."[45] Thomas B. Curtis, a delegate to the House of Representatives from Missouri, testified to this effect before the House Ways and Means Committee in 1956:

> [T]hrough the programs as we now set them up we actually are encouraging illegitimacy. . . . And certainly where we have specific cases—and I know of them; incidently a lot of work I myself have done in my own community has been on the board of a number of these agencies, where we have unwed mothers who have had . . . not just two but several illegitimate children. And actually that is their livelihood. It is not a great burden on them to have another, and as a matter of act it brings in addition money.[46]

This illicit "occupation" was portrayed as violating the most fundamental consumerist principles, including good value in exchange for a good price, for a product that, in general, benefits society. Black unmarried mothers, in contrast, were said to offer bad value (black babies) at a high price (taxpayer-supported welfare grants), to the detriment of society demographically and economically. The behavior of these women—most of whom did *not* receive Aid to Dependent Children grants for their illegitimate children—was construed as meeting only the consumerist principle that everything and anything can, potentially, be a commodity. Those who accused black girls and women of having babies in order to be eligible for larger welfare checks assumed that these females were treating their reproductive capacities and their children as commodities, with assigned monetary values. From this perspective, black unmarried mothers were portrayed as "economic women," making calculated decisions for personal, financial gain. In 1951, the Georgia state welfare director, making an argument for denying Aid to Dependent Children grants to mothers with more than one illegitimate child, noted that "Seventy per cent of all mothers of more than one illegitimate child are Negro. . . . Some of them, finding themselves tied down to one child are not averse to adding others as a business proposition."[47]

The precise economic principle most grossly violated by these women was, according to many, that they were getting something (ADC) for nothing (another black baby). Entering into this scam made single black mothers into chiselers, determined to cheat the public with a bad sell. The fact that it was, overwhelmingly, a buyer's market for black babies "proved" the valuelessness of these children, despite their expense to the taxpaying public.[48] White babies, of course, entered a healthy seller's market, with up to ten couples competing for every one adoptable infant.[49]

Spokespeople for this point of view believed that black unmarried mothers should pay dearly for the bad bargain they foisted on society, especially on white taxpayers. Governor Orville Faubus complained in 1959 that, "By taxing the good people to pay for [ADC], we are putting a premium on illegitimacy never before known in the world."[50] Many felt that rather than paying for their sins, black women were being paid, by ADC grants, an exchange that could encourage further sexual and fiscal irresponsibility. One of a number of readers responding irately to *The New York Times*'s editorial position in support of giving welfare grants to unmarried mothers wrote to the *Times,* "As for your great concern for those careless women who make a career of illicit pregnancy, they should either bear the expense or be put where they can no longer indulge their weaknesses."[51] According to this analysis of the motivations behind black single pregnancy, society was justified in criminalizing or otherwise punishing black unwed mothers. Extreme sanctions were appropriate for this variant of prostitution, and only they would curtail the rip-off.

The attempts to pass legislation permitting the sterilization of women who "persisted" in having children out of wedlock were premised on another economic metaphor. The black unmarried woman, willing to trade on her reproductive function, willing to use her body and her child so cheaply, earned the state's equal willingness to regard her childbearing capacity cheaply and take it away.

The ironic truth was that ADC benefits were such inadequate support (and employment and childcare opportunities so meager or nonexistent for black unmarried mothers) that some policies had the effect of causing, not responding to, black women's economic calculations that might lead to pregnancy. For example, the average welfare payment per child, per month was $27.29, with monthly averages less than half that amount in most southern states.[52] In many cases, maternal and child poverty created the boyfriend-as-economic-necessity. The famous Greenleigh Associates study of the Aid to Dependent Children program in Cook County, Illinois, published in 1960, asserted strongly that the impossibly small money grants to unmarried mothers were directly responsible for increasing these women's need for male companionship and whatever financial assistance male friends could provide.[53] The following case is a striking and typical illustration of the nature of the relationship between illegitimacy and economics, from the woman's point of view—a relationship born of poverty and maternal concern rather than personal greed or "careerism." "When the case analyst visited the family, the little girl came in with a new dress and shoes. The mother explained that it was the last day of school and the child had begged for new clothes like the other children had. She got them, but the mother's comment was, 'I hope that dress does not cause me another baby.'"[54]

In Florida, the assumptions of welfare officials and legislators concerning the "business" intentions of black unwed mothers received a jolt in the early 1960s when mothers withdrew from the ADC program rather then risk having their children sent away from home, to the homes of married relatives, for example, under the state's "suitable home" law. "At least some [social workers] anticipated that among Negro families, the 'extended family pattern' would ease the pain of separation and rarely generate resistance to placement. But as one mother said, 'People give away puppies and kittens, but they don't give away their children.'"[55] In the face of the persistence of nineteenth-century southern plantation owners' mentality among Florida's welfare professionals and legislators, and the commodization of children this view supported, black women demonstrated their adherence to a value system that placed their children and their bodies outside of the economic nexus, as far as the government and the welfare system were concerned.

Since white unmarried mothers were supplying a seller's market, the policies shaping their experiences had an altogether different thrust. Unlike policy intentions for black women, public and private efforts for whites were designed to mitigate their treatment and their fate. Clark Vincent, a leading theorist in the area of single pregnancy in the postwar era, observed that black unmarried mothers were censured more heavily than whites,

in part [because the] censure of white unmarried mothers was tempered in the 1940s and 1950s [since] at that time they represented the largest single source of adoptable infants and served a useful social function by enabling childless couples to have a family. As physicians, lawyers and social caseworkers can testify, many of the estimated one million involuntarily childless couples in this country a decade ago would have been highly displeased had this major source of adoptable white infants disappeared.[56]

There were, however, two personal decisions a white woman could make that would queer her relatively protected status. She might decide to forgo the sanctuary and services offered by the maternity home and adoption agency in favor of an independent adoption, as approximately 39 percent of all unmarried mothers did in the late 1950s and early 1960s.[57] If she chose to pursue this route, guided perhaps by her obstetrician or a lawyer, she would be entering into "black market" dealings.

Social service providers, encouraged by Children's Bureau personnel and policies, devoted an extraordinary amount of time and effort to dissuading white women from this course while championing state legislation to outlaw black market adoptions. The concern of many professionals about improving the standards of community care for white unwed mothers was supported by a belief that this was the only way to induce some women to go the prescribed route. Katherine B. Oettinger, head of the Children's Bureau, cited the black market in white babies as one of the main concerns of the Bureau in the late 1950s: "The unmistakable fact is that the unwed mother needs help. . . . And until she can get and use these services anywhere in the country, the black and grey market placements of children for adoption will continue."[58] A Seattle program begun in 1951 was designed specifically as an antidote to the allure of the black market. New and higher-quality services were provided to unwed mothers in order to protect those "who now get into wrong hands and who are encouraged, indeed obligated to give up their babies in order to pay their own freight."[59]

When a woman made a black market deal for her baby, she was paid money to cover her prenatal care and living costs, her delivery expenses, and an additional sum, in exchange for the baby. The efforts of policy makers and social service providers to curb the black market appear to have been motivated by a sincere interest in eliminating cash, or market values, from transactions involving human life. In addition, there was an implied concern with keeping white women free of the taint of economic, market-driven involvement. As this group had been relieved of sexual responsibility, relieved even of having engaged in sexually meaningful behavior by psychiatric explanations of the illegitimate pregnancy, so it was important that white unmarried mothers be sustained as economic innocents. After putting the episode of illegitimacy behind them, these girls and women could reenter the marriage market with a socially constructed cleaned slate, sexually and economically. These were, of course, important conditions for postwar American brides.

Beyond these considerations, Children's Bureau and social service professionals were interested in stamping out the black market because its existence undermined the most basic intentions and the jobs of maternity home personnel and adoption caseworkers. If an unmarried mother were lost to the black market, the maternity home/adoption agency apparatus would lose the opportunity to shape her rehabilitation. The system would also lose the ability to select the appropriate parents for the illegitimate baby. An article in *Cosmopolitan* argued in 1956, "The 20,000 or more babies sold each year on the black market should be made available, instead, to deserving couples who have applied through legitimate channels."[60] Both of these losses seriously compromised the redemptive social benefits the white unmarried mother could have provided society, if she had adhered to public policy prescriptions.

The second damning personal decision a white, single, pregnant woman might make, and many did, was to keep her illegitimate child. There are not reliable statistics regarding how many white unmarried mothers kept their babies in the postwar period since only three states had laws requiring a hospital to notify a state agency of the mother's plan for her illegitimate child. A 1957 study in Wisconsin, one of these three states, estimated that between 40 and 60 percent of white unmarried girls and women kept their babies. Nationwide, the proportion seemed to be closer to 30 percent.[61] The white woman who kept, was, like black unmarried mothers, violating consumerist principles. She was robbing society of the payment her deviance required. Policy makers, buttressed by the psychiatric position equating refusal to relinquish with severe mental illness, took a dim view of this position.

Segments of the public, however, found it morally satisfying to extract the only payment possible: the woman who kept her child had to pay with her reputation and with community ostracism. A white unmarried mother from Pittsburgh described her payment and her resulting social status this way:

> I am an unwed mother who kept her child. And I fear no hell after death, for I've had mine here on earth. Let no man or girl deceive herself—hell hath no punishment like the treatment people give a "fallen woman." The heartache, tortured thoughts, recriminations, fear, loneliness could not be put on paper. Neither can the scorn, insult and actual hate of self-righteous and ignorant people.[62]

The white unwed mother who did relinquish her baby according to prescription preserved her relationship to a marketlike transaction. She paid for her pregnancy by providing the child, and she received good value in return: the opportunity to complete her rehabilitation in preparation for the second chance.

One longtime observer of the treatment of unmarried mothers observed in 1965:

> The argument that financial remuneration fosters and encourages unmarried mothers to become pregnant repeatedly reveals [a] facet of society's attitude toward the problem. Only social workers and other professional people working with unmarried mothers are concerned about repetitious pregnan-

cies if the babies are not given in adoption. This suggests either that the social order does not resent or deeply disapprove of the woman's behavior, but objects to the fact that it costs money; or else society covertly approves of a grey market in babies, since so many childless couples wish to adopt children.[63]

Unmarried Mothers As a Threat to Postwar Stability

The postwar interest in preserving or restoring social stability, or at least slowing down social change, also conditioned the treatment of unwed mothers. In this regard, single pregnant girls and women became key symbols of the potential for race and gender insubordination. Simply by implementing a two-tiered service system, coercive and humiliating to white and black women, but particularly threatening for blacks, politicians, service professionals, and community spokespersons sanctioned the theory and practice of difference and hierarchy of race. There were not effective challenges or initiatives from within interested government circles or among service providers to the notion that "adoption services of good standards, with flexible policies, and an adequately financed ADC program are the two prime requisites for any community."[64] Children's Bureau personnel and other professionals who approved the two-tiered approach felt they were recommending what "reality" demanded. They were also supporting the argument that black single pregnancy was different from white because for blacks, "birthing a baby may be less of a disgrace than giving the baby to someone else." Professionals regularly used this argument to justify the lack of services for blacks.[65] Ironically, the same professionals who justified their neglect of the needs of black unmarried mothers by arguing that black women loved and welcomed all babies, whatever their birth status, later supported Daniel Moynihan's contention that all problems in the black community stemmed from single mothers heading "matriarchal" households.[66]

The many attempts of state governments to legislate criminalization of black illegitimate pregnancy and childbearing reflected a willingness to use the law innovatively against blacks. It shows, as well, that legislators could make a facile association between black women, sexuality, and crime while assuming their constituents would agree. These attempts to degrade black women, their children, and the black community, in general, functioned as one of a number of effective ways to reassert white dominion at a time when many whites were feeling threatened. In the late 1950s, a Pennsylvania judge expressed his frustration about the limits of the law in controlling black procreation and his anger about the financial rewards given black unwed mothers. Most forcefully, he expressed his disgust at the boldness of these women who would not submit to the humiliation intended for them by the bar:

State money is being handed out to unmarried mothers who stand before the bar with smug faces despite the fact that some of them had ten or eleven illegitimate children by ten or eleven different fathers. There was once a time when a young girl or woman who found herself in the unfortunate situation of having an illegitimate child would stand in court with her head bowed and contrition in her heart.[67]

Public policies directed at black unmarried mothers were designed to redress that boldness.

Gender insubordination was equally threatening at a time when many social commentators perceived the gender caste system as badly frayed. As some politicians in every segment of the country defined black single pregnancy as an affront to white taxpayers and as a display of wanton, racial disobedience, so single pregnancy, in popular culture, was often defined as an affront to established male social and sexual prerogatives. The deviance labeling of unwed mothers in this era conforms to Edwin Schur's observation that, "It is the perception of a threat [to dominance] regardless of whether that perception is well-founded, that triggers the efforts at systematic devaluation."[68]

A common finding in studies of illegitimately pregnant women in this era was that they had had short and meaningless relationships with the "putative fathers."[69] This supported the charge that single women were using males as "biological accessories" to their own scripts, psychological or economic. In both cases, women were engaging in a costly form of role reversal. The traditional expression "he ruined her," archaic by midcentury, had been meaningfully replaced by "she got herself in trouble." Postwar females were described as taking a dangerous degree of social and sexual license that challenged their traditional, subordinate role. Unwed mothers were offered as a prime example and as a warning about the wages of this challenge.

The New York Times, considering causes for the upswing in illegitimacy in the 1950s, cited a report prepared by the North Carolina Conference for Social Service that "suggested that a new spirit of female boldness might be . . . responsible for the rise in illegitimate relationships."[70] Philip Wylie put a particularly gruesome cast on this new "spirit" and its effect on would-be suitors: "Young men . . . bounce anxiously away from their first few brutal contacts with modern young women, frightened to find that their shining hair is vulcanized, their agate eyes are embedded in cement, and their ruby lips casehardened into pliers for the bending of males like wire." Soaring rates of illegitimate pregnancy were proof that young men were eventually ensnared by the "gynecocracy."[71]

The evaluation of unmarried mothers that stressed role violation fit well with a common evaluation of American matrons after the war. It was not simply that daughters, particularly single pregnant daughters, were taking cues from their frustrated, domineering mothers. Social work theorists and practitioners claimed that such a mother was determining her daughter's fate—her failure to make a "gratifying heterosexual adjustment"—because of the mother's own like failure.[72]

The theoretical and practical work produced in the postwar era concerning single pregnancy gave tacit protection to the "putative father." He remained the unexamined phantom at social work conferences, community councils, and in the consulting rooms of psychiatrists and social workers. Early in the 1950s, Maud Morlock, whose Children's Bureau office was a clearinghouse for materials on unwed parenthood nationally, remarked, "I regret that little material comes to me on the unmarried father. It is almost an unknown subject, and . . . there has been little research."[73] Not much had changed by the end of the decade when another Children's Bureau employee noted, "For the most part, all men seem to be forgotten men in studies of illegitimacy—with the possible exception of boy babies. Another forgotten man is the unmarried mother's father who would probably repay some attention."[74] Aside from these occasional expressions of dissatisfaction, the Children's Bureau did not exert effective leadership efforts to direct significant attention to "putative fathers."[75]

The girl or woman who "got herself pregnant" was the locus of blame, the target of treatment programs and punishments. In fact, however, the male in question could be instrumental, by his absence or his presence, in the implementation of sanctions against the offending female. Certainly states that required unwed mothers to "produce" the alleged father before she could collect ADC benefits were putting an additional onus on already burdened girls and women which the male regularly escaped. One prominent consultant to policy makers noted that, "Frequently [an agency's] offer of help becomes interlaced with hints at legal action if the unmarried father should fail to respond to the agency's overtures. The result often is that what was supposed to have been a reaching out with an offer of help may turn into a threat. . . ."[76] One commentator reviewed the situation this way:

> If the presumed father refuses to sign a paternity acknowledgment, then the girl, to receive public assistance must permit the Department of Welfare to institute paternity proceedings in the Court of Special Sessions, which if the defendant insists, will order blood tests. If he loses the case, he is legally bound to support the child. Something like nine hundred such cases come before the Court of Special Sessions in New York City each year. "Taken as a group, the girls who go through all this are the most pathetic of all," [the social worker] said.[77]

Often, even if the father did agree to contribute support, his willingness could turn out to be a liability to the unmarried mother. Public assistance agencies deducted from the mother's grant the amount the father was to contribute. If the father defaulted, the unwed mother would have to wait up to a number of months, in dire financial straits, for the public assistance office to reconsider the size of her grant.[78]

A state's interest in minimizing public assistance expenditures could be implemented through a strategy that protected men while punishing women. For example, in the 1950s in Georgia, eligibility for public assistance depended on the mother's ability to establish paternity and her ability to give evidence that every resource had been exhausted to require the father to support the child. For a mother to demonstrate that she had gone to all necessary lengths, she had to negotiate a punitive, and often impossible obstacle course, which included swearing out a warrant and sending letters to the state's solicitor general and foreman of the grand jury. In some counties of Georgia, initiating a warrant cost the often destitute, unwed mother between two and five dollars. On occasion, a justice would refuse to hold a paternity trial—all prior steps having been taken—unless the client had legal counsel. These provisions ensured that impoverished, mostly black, unmarried mothers would not receive ADC benefits.[79] In 1950, the *Chicago Sun-Times* argued that such laws, which protected the male and punished the female, came "from a society which still believes the woman is a sinner."[80]

In one state, if the unmarried mother wanted to put her child up for adoption, she had to get the father to sign his agreement, or she had to publicly state on the record that she had no idea who the father was or what his name was, thus "confessing" in open court that she was promiscuous. Unmarried fathers could also impugn the morality of unmarried mothers in court, by producing witnesses friendly to himself to testify, rightly or wrongly, that they also had intercourse with the female in question.

Robert Viet Sherwin described paternity suits—"popularly considered a hopeless trap for innocent males," in this era—as actually "devastatingly rigged against women, [their] requirements barbaric in terms of consideration for human dignity." He explained how quite often when a single mother was forced into court to obtain paternal support for the child, she was made to describe, "in open Court in very explicit terms, how, when, and where the male defendant's penis entered her vagina. The entire procedure implicitly indicates that the Court regards her as a whore, and that the Court listens to her at all only for the sake of the taxpayers."[81]

As courts sometimes took special steps to subdue sexually disobedient and socially unassimilated females, so did some in the medical profession. Many doctors who sat on hospital abortion panels and created hospital policy regarding therapeutic abortions were particularly retributive toward unmarried, pregnant girls and women. A prominent psychiatrist, reflecting on the prevailing logic of these committees, observed, "The very fact that this girl [petitioning for permission to get a therapeutic abortion] was single of itself means that a recommendation for the interruption of her pregnancy, at least for psychiatric reasons, would most probably be rejected even if her emotional status had been such that for a married woman the same recommendation might conceivably be approved."[82] An unwed mother, breaking the links between femininity, marriage and maternity, could be scorned and punished for the violation.[83] The fact that there were so many more of these girls and women after the war than before was justification for governmental and other institutions to take steps to reinforce women's reasons and their will to conform to traditional female norms.

Conclusion

The racially specific approaches to black and white single pregnant girls and women in the postwar era had powerful and long-range effects. They reinforced white male authority, partly by reinforcing institutional authority over female fertility. In addition, responses to single pregnancy in the immediate pre–*Roe v. Wade* era tightened the wedge placed by a racist society between black and white women. The state- and community-enforced, racially distinct experiences of these women helped sustain the feeling (and the reality) that reproductive issues facing black and white women were different and incompatible. Public policies of the pre–*Roe v. Wade* era conditioned the lives of individual women profoundly, often in ways that forestalled additional acts of "disobedience" and curbed an awareness of women's collective interest in reproductive freedom.[84]

The idea that black and white women had different degrees and kinds of inborn sexuality was useful to some who wanted to justify white domination over blacks, and to some desiring to justify a two-tiered public policy response to black and white single pregnancy. It was also useful to some who wanted, first, to protect the reputation of white womanhood, statistics demonstrating high rates of nonmarital pregnancy notwithstanding, and to others concerned with proving that the childbearing practices of black girls and women were determined by hypersexuality.

The most fundamental assumption about black and white female sexuality shaping the treatment of unwed mothers was that for both races of women, nonmarital sex was not really sex, or alternately, was "only sex." And nonmarital childbearing did not constitute maternity in the culturally sanctioned sense. The treatment of these girls and women reinforced the notion that legitimation of sexuality and maternity were the province of the state and the community and were not the rights of individual girls and women. In the case of white unwed mothers, the community (including the mother, herself, and her family) with government support, was encouraged to efface the episodes of illicit sex and maternity. Outside of marriage neither the sex nor the resulting child had "reality" in the community. They became simply temporary mental aberrations. In the case of black unwed mothers, sexuality was brute biology and childbearing its hideous result. State legislatures, with the support of other institutions, could deface the black single mother's dignity, diminish her resources, and even threaten her reproductive capacity. In both cases, the policies and practices that structured the meanings of race and gender, sexuality and motherhood, for unwed mothers were tied to social issues—such as the postwar adoption market for white babies and the white taxpaying public's hostile identification of ADC as a program to support black unwed mothers and their unwanted babies—which used single pregnant women and unwed mothers as resources and as scapegoats.

Postwar public policies and community practices also failed profoundly to influence the reproductive histories of millions of women in the United States. At the end of the period considered in this study, the rates of nonmarital pregnancy were higher than ever for younger-than-ever females, and some state legislatures were poised to legalize abortion. In short, in the years just before *Roe v. Wade* millions of women began to take control over their own fertility and answer for themselves the question "who is a mother?" It is possible that an ironic outcome of the state's institutionalization of the "who is a mother" distinction in the late 1930s and early 1940s helped define the way for women to make their own decisions, once one definition for all had been set aside. There is no question but that the state's authoritarian, postwar attitudes and policies toward single, pregnant girls and women stimulated thousands of women in the 1960s and 1970s to construct reproductive freedom as a feminist issue.

The state's failure to reverse the upward trends of nonmarital pregnancy and childbearing in this (and our) era, was, in part, the result of its determination to deal with these phenomena from a rigid ideological position. This was a position that justified the state's role in managing female fertility as a national resource, the deployment of which was of vital interest to the state's white, male-supremacist definition of a healthy society. As a consequence of the government's adherence to such a stance, which often ignored or fantasized about the life conditions of the women involved, the state was, and remains, unwilling to address issues such as why poor women either want to or are forced to have their babies without being married; why black men so often do not marry the mothers of their children; how the cultural, legal, and economic endurance of male domination in American society structures the reproductive histories of American women, white and black. The state's past and current commitment to an ideology that blames females for sexual "mistakes," blots out its own role in protecting the life of the vicious cycle which binds the outcomes of female fertility to the social construction of the man-as-economic-and-social-necessity.

In the postwar period, whether a single woman was perceived as pregnant to satisfy psychological or economic self-interest, the state's response to her was conditioned by its response to her issue. The meaning assigned to the child's existence shaped public policies that distinguished between unwed mothers by race, as socially productive or socially unproductive breeders. As long as the state could define women as the machinery of reproduction, it felt justified in subjecting female fertility, and particularly the unwed variant, to regulation by state policies. Only after *Roe v. Wade* was the state's ability to regulate compromised.

The state's view of white unwed mothers as desirable reproducers, which supported and in part created the postwar adoption craze, is closely related to the views of some in the antichoice movement today. Following the initiatives of the late 1930s and 1940s that declared white unwed mothers to be unfit mothers, policy makers and others, drawing on notions of woman-as-breeder, proposed an innovative plan for the disposition of babies: assign them to socially assimilated, middle-class wives and their husbands. Today many antichoice activists want state policies that will protect fetuses until they are adopted at birth by deserving families.[85] In promoting this strategy as the resolution of unwanted pregnancy, antichoice proponents draw on the same view of women that shaped public policies in the pre–*Roe v. Wade* era.

The period of this study ends in the years just before the first, national legalization of abortion. As the history of the postwar era reveals, the pro-choice struggle that peaked in the Supreme Court's *Roe v. Wade* decision in 1973, was fought by feminists and *others*. Among those others were people for whom the legalization of abortion represented a new way to meet old goals, particularly the goal associated with strengthening the middle-class family in America through population control. Perhaps the alliance between those struggling for reproductive rights as part of the feminist agenda and the population controllers was, in the long run, even more dangerous than it might have seemed at the time. For one thing, prominent voices in the alliance emphasized the notion that unwed mothers and their illegitimate babies were the cause of social problems in the United States.[86] By focusing on the need to curtail the fertility of unwed females, these analysts obscured the fact that the multiple and race-specific meanings assigned to unwed mothers rendered them rich cultural resources and enormously vulnerable. This potent combination sustained the dilemma of the unwed mother in the United States and helped block a broad and enduring association of female fertility and female autonomy.

Chapter Two

The Making of the "Matriarchy": The Persistence of Biological Explanations for Black Single Pregnancy

In the 1958 legislative session, Mississippi State Representative David H. Glass proposed House Bill 479, "An Act to Discourage Immorality of Unmarried Females by Providing for Sterilization of the Unwed Mother Under Conditions of the Act; and for Related Purposes." At the time, David Glass explained his thinking about the usefulness of sterilization. He wrote, "During the calendar year 1957, there were born out of wedlock in Mississippi, more than seven thousand Negro children. . . . The Negro woman because of child welfare assistance [is] making it a business, in some cases, of giving birth to illegitimate children. . . . The purpose of my bill was to try to stop, or slow down, such traffic at its source."[1]

The proposed legislation was not enacted, although the issues it addressed remained provocative—politically stimulating and sometimes profitable—for many white politicians and taxpayers in the south and all other regions of the United States throughout the 1950s and 1960s. David Glass's efforts to curb the fertility of black women provides an example of one form racism took during the period of this study. It illustrates, in particular, that the bodies of black women became political terrain on which some proponents of white supremacy mounted their campaigns.

This chapter will raise questions about why, at this time, the postwar brand of defensive racism discussed in Chapter One relied anew on body-centered attacks against blacks, and why women's bodies, especially, were targeted, specifically their reproductive function. The chapter will explore how black illegitimacy was used to support both arguments about the biological bases of black inferiority and antiblack public policies. It will also explore how arguments centering on culture and cultural difference to explain black illegitimacy in the 1950s and 1960s were unsuccessful in countering biological determinism because proponents of the former often incorporated the premises of the latter, sometimes on purpose, sometimes not. The failure by 1965 of various attempts to uncouple black illegitimacy and biological inferiority attested to the durability and appeal of this association in the postwar United States. Finally, this chapter considers attitudes within black communities toward illegitimate pregnancy and unwed mothers. It identifies some community strategies for responding to these situations and cites personal responses of black girls and women themselves.

Illegitimacy and Biological Determinism in the Postwar Era

One of the salient facts of domestic politics in the postwar years was the rapid and sharp increase in public welfare costs. The welfare cost most uneasily borne by many localities, and according to some polls, by the public-at-large, was the bill for Aid to Dependent Children grants for the maintenance of illegitimate children and their unmarried mothers.[2] Despite the fact that by 1960, a growing percentage of white unwed mothers and their children required such aid, and despite the fact that most black women with illegitimate children did not receive ADC, ADC was, in the public consciousness, a black-identified program. The ADC issue became politically compelling in part because opponents of aid to black unwed mothers suggested a direct association between the sexual behavior of these women and the money it cost the (white) taxpaying public. Drawing on an alleged biological condition of black womanhood—their irresponsible hypersexuality—opponents of ADC revived an old connection—black women, sex, and money—to stir up a new resentment. For many white Americans, black women had historically suggested an association between sex and money, as procreating slaves and as prostitutes, profitable or pleasurable for white men. Now some politicians represented the association of black women, sex, and money as a direct financial loss for whites. As white unwed mothers were portrayed as a threat to the moral integrity of the family, black unwed mothers were often construed as an economic threat to the same white family. The money to pay for the consequences of their sexual behavior came out of the white family's wallet, some politicians argued, and seriously undermined its economic security. The fact that ADC expenditures and illegitimacy rates continued steadily upward throughout this period convinced many white politicians and taxpayers that the ADC program was a doubly dismal failure. It was unable to promote traditional, disciplined work and family life among its recipients.[3] In addition, the most persistent charge against ADC was that these benefits were incentives for black women to have illegitimate children. In short, some white politicians and taxpayers claimed that black women used their bodies in ways that were morally and fiscally destructive to the nation.

The campaigns against black unwed mothers and their alleged abuse of the ADC "opportunity" took place as black communities were organizing, nationally and locally, their own campaigns against white supremacy. As this system was challenged and its viability compromised, whites in many localities felt pressed to reassert their domination with renewed vigor. These efforts sometimes took a violent form. A number of studies of the civil rights movement have cataloged retributive physical attacks on black men and women who engaged directly in struggles for black rights.[4] It is important, as well, to take note of the supplementary forms of attack, physical and otherwise, enacted, in this case, against childbearing women, whose persons, whose bodies, came to be portrayed as one challenge to the security of the white community.

Jacqueline Jones, Barbara Omolade, and others have described the central role of women, collectively and individually, in movement activities in the 1950s and 1960s. This new, public female assertiveness was dangerous for individual women. For example, Jones points out that, "To deprive an 'uppity woman' of her livelihood was as easy [in these years] as it was common. . . ."[5] It was dangerous as well for black women, collectively, who were promoting resistance against white authority while lacking access to resources to protect themselves from the consequences of such activities. Relative to black childbearing, the construction of black women as unrestrained, wanton breeders, on the one hand, or calculating breeders for profit, on the other, could raise the moral and fiscal hackles of white communities all over the nation, and did. These body-centered attacks on childbearing black women as proxies for a race resisting white supremacy, became, in part, a public relations strategy and a practical plan for preventing black women from claiming the means to physical sustenance that the federal government, via ADC legislation and allocations, had deemed their right. Some in the campaign against black childbearing women claimed to propose a punishment that fit the crime: black unwed mothers used their bodies in violation of the nation's standards. Their actions should be met with responses directed against their bodies, to abort their behavior, as the Mississippi legislator put it, "at its source."

Definitions of black women, particularly black unwed mothers, as innately biologically flawed by hypersexuality became useful in the postwar era for other reasons as well. The prevailing definition of white single pregnancy as a psychological rather than a sexual phenomenon was bolstered by the definition of black single pregnancy, in distinction, as purely sexual. For some analysts, white girls were the products of complex, cultural patterns, refined community and gender mores, and traditional family structures. Aberrations within any of these entities, particularly the last, could cause psychiatric problems, such as unwed pregnancy. Black girls, on the other hand, were, according to this view, products of no such higher-order structures. Their behavior, in contrast to whites, was unmediated, natural, biological. The postwar responses to white single pregnancy represented, in part, a thirteenth-hour attempt to contain white nonmarital female sexuality. Some commentators drew on the white tradition of projecting free sex norms onto black women, thereby (as if "sexuality" could be submitted to a zero-sum equation, racially) desexualizing unmarried white mothers by contrast.[6]

Whether the basis for response to black unwed mothers was economic, political, or cultural, analysts of the subject had behind them a tradition in which white masters used the black's body as a target in the service of racial control.[7] In addition, strains of American tradition sanctioned the regulation by whites of black sexual behavior and the practice by some whites of misconstruing African women's sexuality for their own purposes.[8] These traditions were grounded in a racial, biological determinism that was still compelling for some in the midtwentieth century.

In fact, in the post-World War II era, an unusually broad spectrum of whites—lay, professional and political—had reasons to draw on biological determinism to explain the childbearing behavior of black women. This explanation of illegitimacy justified policy initiatives, or their absence, to address postwar social, economic, and political concerns. For demographers interested in promoting white, middle-class reproduction while curbing minority population growth, biological determinism justified the use of measures to interrupt the fertility of black women. Concerning postwar hopes for a robust consumerist society, the biological explanation for black illegitimacy argued against the usefulness of extending social services to black girls and women, and thus implicitly argued for preserving the resources of taxpayers for consumerist activity. The state's interest in slowing social change was compatible with racial, biological determinism, which could define unwed black mothers as permanent victims of their sexuality. This being so, the intentions and visions of social change promoted by civil rights activists could be cast as hopeless.

Biological determinism, or body-centered racism, directed against black unmarried mothers, by its nature superseded and canceled out the historical and social context of black childbearing. Its proponents were not compelled to face the contradictions or ironies inherent in their midcentury response to black illegitimacy. For example, commentators did not have to square the white master's response to black female fertility in the 1850s with a prevailing white response to the same phenomenon in the 1950s. Herbert Gutman quotes the chancellor of the University of South Carolina, William Harper, regarding white responses to black illegitimacy during slavery:

> The unmarried slave mother was not a less useful member of society than before . . . she has not impaired her means of support, not materially lowered her character, or lowered her station in society; she has done no great injury to herself, or any other human being. Her offspring is not a burden, but an acquisition to her owner.[9]

An ex-slave remembered that slave owners "would buy a fine girl and a fine man and just put them together like cattle; they would not stop to marry them. If she was a good breeder, they was proud of her."[10] Barbara Omolade, reflecting on the black woman's body as a profit center during slavery times, has written, "Her vagina, used for his sexual pleasure, was the gateway to the womb, which was his capital investment—the capital investment being the sex act and the resulting child the accumulated surplus, worth money on the slave market."[11] While black women may or may not have retained childbearing practices from the era of slavery, the attitudes of many whites toward the fertility of black women changed entirely between the midnineteenth and midtwentieth centuries.

A related issue concerning illegitimacy that was not addressed publicly in the postwar years was the fact that the biological events that led to an illegitimate pregnancy were common to all girls and women, black and white. The biological determinists did not address the fact that what made the experience of a white girl different from the experience of a black girl was the environment in which the biological event occurred, including the public attitudes, policies, and practices that responded to the biological event of her pregnancy.

Black Women's Bodies as Political Terrain

The argument that the biological and moral constitution of black girls and women created their propensity to have illegitimate babies became a factor in large questions of national life and public policy in the postwar era. Proponents of school segregation, restrictive public housing, and exclusionary welfare policies, for example, all pointed to relatively high rates of Negro illegitimacy and the example of individual Negro unwed mothers to support or reinforce their campaigns.

The New York Times, reporting on congressional hearings regarding the desegregation of schools in the District of Columbia, observed, "The prevalence of unwed mothers among black school girls was an immediate rallying cry for Southern segregationists, and the House sub-committee majority triumphantly wrote its report recommending that segregation be restored."[12] During these hearings, held in the early fall of 1956, in the second year of desegregation, the superintendent of schools, his assistants, building principals, and teachers appeared and assessed the impact of desegregation on schools in the nation's capital. The active members of the Subcommittee to Investigate Public School Standards and Conditions, and Juvenile Delinquency in the District of Columbia, were Representative James C. Davis of Florida, the chairman of the subcommittee; Representative John Bell Williams of Mississippi; and Representative Joel T. Broyhill of Virginia. Counsel to the subcommittee was William Gerber of Tennessee, and its educational consultant was H. M. Roland of North Carolina. The subcommittee's charge was "to make an investigation of juvenile delinquency and alleged and reported low standards in the District public school system."[13] During the nine days of hearings, southern congressmen directed the attention of their witnesses again and again to the connection between the presence of black students in previously "white" buildings and the deterioration of the educational climate, standards, and performance in the schools.

One area of particular interest to the subcommittee members was the sexual conduct of black girls and their resulting pregnancies. Following is a typical exchange, this one between the representative from Mississippi and a junior high school principal:

Mr Williams: Mr. Storey, you mentioned . . . that you had five cases of pregnancy in 1955. Could you tell us how many cases, if you recall, you had of pregnancy in 1954?

Mr. Storey: I do not know the exact number. We might run one or two, something of that kind . . . before last year.

Mr. Williams: Do you recall having had any such cases in 1953?

Mr. Storey: No, I do not remember the data for that. We would occasionally get a pregnancy.

Mr. Williams: You would have an occasional case of pregnancy?

Mr. Storey: Yes sir.

Mr. Williams: But am I safe in assuming that since integration there has been a sharp upswing in pregnancies in your school?

Mr. Storey: This last year's figure represented an increase over what it had been.

Mr. Williams: And that would be an increase of several hundred percent or would it be a small increase percentagewise?

Mr. Storey: Well, if I knew exactly the figures of the year before, if we were running one or two cases every year, then it would be an increase of 150%, if it were two, and 500% if it were one.[14]

As each teacher or administrator appeared before the committee, he or she was asked, "Have you had any pregnancies over there?"; "Miss Davis, did you have any sex problems while you were there?"; "Mr. Smith, did you have many pregnancies over there in your school last year?"; and to an administrator who claimed to have no increase in disciplinary problems after integration, "You had no sex problems?"[15] *The New York Times* reported that, "This one-sided investigation helped convince segregationists that one of their most potent arguments [for resegregation], because based on a kernel of truth, was that of Negro illegitimacy."[16]

Elsewhere, as well, those opposed to school desegregation drew on the differences between black and white illegitimacy rates to justify the separation of the races. Southern newspapers such as the *Richmond Times-Dispatch*, the

Charleston News and Courier, and the *Nashville Banner* played up this angle frequently.[17] A 1957 editorial in the *Richmond News Leader* was direct:

> During the span of twenty-one years covered by this [annual] report from the Bureau of Vital Statistics, vast improvements occurred in the social and economic growth of Negroes in Virginia. The period was marked by spectacular advances in income, in educational opportunities, in improved housing. None of this appeared to make any difference [regarding the illegitimacy rate]. There are the sobering and unpleasant facts. . . . The "mere statistics" tell an eloquent story of promiscuity and behavioral standards; the figures underlie one of the more significant reasons for the South's resistance to integration of the schools.[18]

Upon receiving news of the Supreme Court's 1954 school desegregation decision, the North Carolina welfare director anticipated hostility against black unmarried mothers and directed John R. Larkins, the Consultant on Work among Negroes, to "step up his campaign against Negro illegitimacy."[19] The Louisiana state legislature, repeatedly willing to target black unwed mothers in the early years of federal desegregation orders, passed a bill in June 1960 that made it a crime to have more than one illegitimate child. This bill was part of a successful package of thirteen designed to reinforce Louisiana laws "to counteract racial integration."[20]

Another arena in which black unmarried mothers became vulnerable targets and political fodder in the postwar years was public housing. Public Housing Authorities in a number of localities excluded or attempted to exclude or evict single pregnant girls and women and unwed mothers from publicly subsidized facilities. These efforts were portrayed as exclusions on moral grounds, but they functioned as a threat against the black community and as a warning about the power public agencies had to punish childbearing women. The practice was widespread in the 1950s and 1960s. In 1959, for example, the Chicago Committee on Services to Unmarried Parents (CCSUP) obtained a letter sent by the Altgeld Gardens Murray Homes Management Company to all their tenants who had had one illegitimate child. The letter warned these women that they would be evicted if they had another such child. After the Chicago Housing Authority acknowledged that sending this sort of warning letter was an "unwritten policy," the CCSUP, the NAACP, and the Chicago Welfare Council became involved in a long campaign to pressure the Housing Authority to stop this practice.[21] In the same year, the California attorney general found that local Housing Authorities all over the state were exceeding their powers by evicting unwed mothers.[22]

In one community in a southeastern state, the policy of the public Housing Authority mandated the eviction of all unwed mothers, including first-timers, if they kept their babies. Despite widespread protests in the community to make an exception in the case of a pregnant fourteen-year-old girl whose parents wanted to keep her with them, the Housing Authority refused to relent. Similarly, in a midwestern community, the Housing Authority wrote a policy to evict "unmarried women who make it a habit of having babies."[23]

An extensive study of the aftermath of illegitimate conception for unwed mothers in New York City in the early 1960s found that because she was not married, the black unwed mother and her child were "automatically ineligible for public housing . . . [and had] no resources with which to test the legality of this restriction. . . ."[24] Dr. Jean Pakter, chief of the Bureau of Child Health's Maternity and Newborn Division, deplored these exclusionary tactics employed by the New York City Housing Authority and said they "condemned unwed mothers to a vicious cycle of squalor and depravity."[25] The New York study revealed, in fact, that 20 percent of the mothers, each living at the time of the study in New York City with her eighteen-month-old illegitimate baby, had no bathroom or kitchen facilities. Most of these were blacks.[26]

A single, pregnant black woman from Richmond, Virginia, who wrote to the president of the United States for help, revealed how lack of housing aggravated the desperation of many black unwed mothers. She wrote,

> [My boyfriend] promise me if I would have intercourse with him that he would marry me so I did and got pregnant . . . and now he won't marry me and wont help me and I am not able to work. Got no home. The law in Virginia said because I ben married before that they are not nothing I can do about it.
>
> My boyfriend want me to destroy the baby but I wont do that for I dont want to murder my baby and I don't think it right. . . . So please try to help me Mr. Truman and I go for 3 or 4 days I don't have nothing to eat at all. I don't have no money to see a doctor with or anything are they any way you can make him marrie me . . . a friend saw him last night with another woman. . . . So let me know at once if you can help me for I am in trouble Lord.[27]

These problems were not peculiar to black unwed mothers in the south. The nursing supervisor of obstetrical services at Harlem Hospital (New York) described the consequences of homelessness for some of the black unwed mothers she met, and for their babies:

> [The problems of unwed mothers] frequently give rise to boarder babies and also to mothers spending many days in the hospital, even though previously discharged. This is costly for the Department of Hospitals. In some instances, the mother is unable to provide for the infant, since she has no home herself. In other instances, she is not interested in keeping the baby, and as a result, leaves the hospital without establishing contact. Caseworkers must therefore make arrangements for the infant's placement without the family's participation. The infants, for the most part, are waiting for placement through the Bureau of Child Welfare of the Department of Welfare.[28]

Dr. Pakter in New York identified what was for some the central argument concerning society's responsibilities, including providing a place to live, for black unwed mothers rendered bereft by their situation: "If unwed mothers have decent housing," Dr. Pakter said, "that will help to make a productive citizen rather than a reproductive citizen."[29]

As "reproductive citizens," black unmarried mothers became the concern of taxpayers, politicians, and social service professionals worried about rising welfare expenditures and their ever-escalating cost to states and localities responsible for 49 percent of the bill. These women seemed a natural locus of concern, even anger, as the bearers and caretakers of children many of them were unable to support without public assistance. In the context of the postwar years, particularly by the late 1950s, taxes were becoming a sharply perceived burden to white, middle-class families, the tax bill for social services an especial anathema. The emergent civil rights movement was frightening to many middle-class, taxpaying whites, many of whom claimed not to understand why blacks should be accorded the full rights of productive citizens, if they were not.

In the mother-blaming mode of the postwar decades, many analysts assigned black childbearing women the responsibility for what was wrong within the black community. The alleged hypersexuality and immorality, the resulting children, the public expense were all traceable to the source: the black woman who gave birth, as it were, to black America, with all its "defects."[30] In this vein, Julius Horwitz characterized the black unwed mother and child:

> We know that the damage to the infant takes place long before he sees the dirt, the drunks, the drug addicts, the spilled garbage of the slum; the damage takes place when the unavailable mother brings her child home from the hospital and realizes she hates him for being alive.[31]

The identification of ADC as a black program in the public mind created a racial dimension to welfare opposition that many found appealing, but did not represent the reality of the ADC picture. Despite the increase of illegitimate births by two and a half times between 1940 and 1957, the proportion of ADC cases receiving aid due to unmarried parenthood rose by only one-third between 1948 and 1958, and was the same 20 percent in 1958 as it had been in 1953. The percentage of white ADC families receiving aid because of unmarried motherhood rose slightly between 1950 and 1960 (6.0 percent to 6.1 percent) while the percentage of nonwhite ADC unmarried-mother-recipients declined from 25.0 to 19.1 in this period.[32] Still, the higher rate for blacks remained the salient fact during the period. A government official wrote in the late 1950s that "There is reason to think that [because of the racial differential] much of the venom in the current attacks on ADC is directed against the latter group."[33]

Many localities simply refused to offer welfare assistance to black girls and women or made it virtually impossible to obtain. A black in Philadelphia wrote to the president in Washington:

> I am a girl expecting a baby . . . an unmarried girl. And I have been to Public Assistance here also Municipal Court and Public hospital and they wont help me and I want to know if you could write them . . . because I need help bad and can not work because I'm not well and every time I go to them, they tell me to found my friend and I dont know where he is and can't found him and I dont have any one to help me at all. Please write them right away and see that they can help me because that is their job public assistance for the public.[34]

Maud Morlock of the United States Children's Bureau, part of whose job was to monitor programs and services for unwed mothers nationally, was keenly aware of local practices that in effect excluded black unwed mothers from welfare assistance. In 1949, when *True Confessions* published an article about unwed motherhood and listed the Children's Bureau as a source of information, Morlock's office was flooded with letters from girls and women like the letter writer from Philadelphia. Morlock called them "pathetic letters" and described them further to a colleague. "Many [writers] were adolescent girls. Many said that they had no money, or that they had no medical care. Some were Negro, and you know what that means in the availability of services and care. It taxed our ingenuity to answer them constructively."[35]

One woman who taxed Morlock's ingenuity was the mother of a black unmarried pregnant girl in Norfolk, Virginia in 1948. The mother described her daughter's situation in a letter to the Children's Bureau:

> Please inform me of the address of the home for unwed mothers as I have a daughter that wish to be admitted to there if possible to have her baby as I have heard of the kind treatment and the best that they receive at this home. my city doesnt have one for (colored) people so please let me know if it is any way possible for my daughter to be admitted to this one and also let me know of the fee and how to get there. . . . We are very poor people. My daughter is working now but will stop as soon as she knows whether she can be admitted to the home. I have 6 other children besides her and havent any husband now, been divorced so please help me to get my daughter in this lovely place where she can have the best of care.[36]

A year later, a woman from Greenwood, Mississippi, also seeking a maternity home that would accept blacks, appealed to Morlock:

> I'm ill but I'd be willing to work, cant find a job in fact nobody wants to hire a person that will faint any minute or if I stand in 1 place 10 minutes at a time. So madam if there is a maternity home that a colored girl can birth her child in peace, will you please let me know. I dont care if it happens to be in Chicago because down here in Mississippi I dont have a possible chance to get help because my face is Black.[37]

The Mississippi woman's desperate search for peace and services was echoed by a young black woman from Baltimore who was forced to write to Morlock a second time, since Morlock's first response provided advice this pregnant woman could not use.

> Perhaps I better tell you now that I am a Negro girl, and the Crittenton home only accepts white girls. Isnt there any place at all for unwed Negro girls? . . . I really don't know [what to do] unless I commit suicide . . . . Is there any place for me or not please tell me right away unless there isnt I will just kill myself. There is no other way.[38]

The fact was that Morlock had virtually no alternatives in most cases but to refer black single pregnant girls and women to their local welfare office, despite what she knew about local practices,[39] since in 1951 there were only seven black maternity homes in the United States, and a handful of others that accepted a very limited number of blacks.[40] Sometimes Morlock wrote ahead to the welfare office about a particular girl from whom she had received an appeal for help, thus providing an impressive letter of introduction for an otherwise destitute young woman. Yet this Children's Bureau employee was only an army of one. A young black girl from New York spoke for many when she complained, "I don't know. I feel that wherever you go or whatever you do, if they find out you are an unwed mother, you've had it! Like when you go to Welfare, I know they would treat you like you were nothing."[41] A study of black unmarried women receiving ADC benefits in Philadelphia in the late 1950s revealed that the unwed mothers felt that "telling [Welfare of their pregnancy] is a necessary evil, something that sooner or later must be done, but that it is well to put it off as long as is feasible."[42] The researcher observed, "None of this points to any concept of the Agency as a resource." In fact, 30 percent of this study's subjects managed to conceal their condition throughout the pregnancy.[43] One said, "I didn't want [the welfare worker] to know; she'd have a whole lot to say. . . ."[44]

By the 1950s, numerous states and localities were moving beyond simply sanctioning informal welfare practices that denied or harassed black unwed mothers and were instituting formal policies to do so. For example, in 1962, the Illinois Public Aid Commission passed a resolution mandating that mothers on ADC relief be warned that they faced jail if they had an illegitimate child.[45] A report issued in Erie County, New York, in 1957 warned that "Complacency in the face of increased illegitimacy . . . must be replaced with a severe [welfare] program involving penalties . . . [because] subsidized immorality in the Erie County (Buffalo) social welfare program could undermine the entire community."[46]

In Cook County (Chicago), Illinois, for an unwed mother to be eligible for ADC benefits, she had to show proof that she had been a resident of the county for one year; that she maintained a suitable home; that she had bona fide financial need; and that she was ready and willing to take legal action against the putative father.[47] The second condition was often exclusionary since an unwed mother, by definition, was considered to provide an unsuitable home. A social worker described the logistics of the last condition, from the woman's point of view. The woman's task involved,

> [I]dentifying the father, becoming involved in a determination of the extent to which he is a financial resource to her now, beginning steps looking toward obtaining support for the baby from him (with action in the Women's Criminal Division of the Municipal Court possibly involved), attempting to locate the man if he is no longer in touch with her. All this activity touches her in painful ways, and then there is the additional fact that the result can be lowering, interrupting or even terminating the grant, if it is determined that the man is a resource or if she refuses to make available necessary information for this determination."[48]

The point of these welfare policies, and the shifting focus, in welfare offices across the nation, to issues of eligibility instead of modes of service, was to save money, the difficulties of black unwed mothers notwithstanding.[49] Georgia Governor Herman Talmadge, for example, declared himself in the early 1950s to be "willing to tolerate an unwed mother who makes one mistake but not when the mistake is repeated three, four or five times." Talmadge worked with the Georgia state welfare director to devise welfare policies to "save the state $440,000 a year mainly by limiting aid to children of unwed Negro mothers."[50]

Included in economy-minded state and local welfare policies were provisions for sterilization and for midnight raids on the homes of unwed ADC mothers. Both provisions, of course, allowed for the violation of the personal safety and physical integrity of the black woman's body. In North Carolina, local public welfare superintendents were "forthright . . . on the savings to be achieved through sterilization of the [Negro] unwed mothers among their charges." An observer commented, "These superintendents were neither petty autocrats nor fanatics, but they generally agreed on the value of eugenic sterilization in reducing both general relief and ADC payments. Since Negroes accounted for a disproportionate share of illegitimate births subsidized by ADC, the racial aspect of the superintendents' intent was clear enough."[51]

Across the United States in these years, welfare personnel took part in midnight raids seeking men in the houses of unmarried mothers on ADC.[52] If one were found, the family would be disqualified from receiving benefits, as the presence of a man, any man, indicated to the officials the presence of unreported financial support.[53] Welfare rules in Phoenix, Arizona, for example, provided that the welfare recipient had to allow agents into her home at any time, day or night, to check for a man, or she would jeopardize her welfare allotment. One Sunday morning in May 1962, Phoenix welfare officers invaded thirteen homes, beginning at 4:30 A.M. In the press, the mission was referred to as a "pre-dawn safari" to emphasize the African connection. One agent was posted at the backdoor of the dwelling, one at the front. The safari turned up little, to the surprise of the officers. No arrests were made. The journalist reported that "each visit was a business-like interview. The women did not seem surprised at the early morning check. Many had been through it before."[54]

One of the thousands of more "successful" raids was described by Richard Briggs, appointed by the Oneida County, New York, welfare commissioner to "ferret out welfare chiselers." Briggs reported his visit to one woman who was receiving welfare aid for herself and her children and [said] that he had found a man hiding under blankets in the apartment. According to Briggs, the man had been living with and supporting the woman. She was removed from the rolls.[55]

In 1967 the Supreme Court declared midnight raids unconstitutional, but not before thousands of women, an untold but surely disproportionately large number of whom were black, had been punished by welfare officials in this way. According to welfare policies and practices, women's sexualized bodies were the source of the crime against welfare and the appropriate target of punishment. The nature of the crime was complex. Black unwed mothers were guilty of being without a man, thus in some sense independent, or at least "on the loose" in a way that violated gender norms. At the same time, they were guilty of being too dependent, their lives sustained by public assistance. In this way, they violated the ethic of self-reliance. They were guilty of having been extramaritally sexual, again a violation of gender norms, but were also guilty of being mothers, the ultimate postwar gender role fulfillment. In the context of the postwar climate of fiscal conservatism and white racism, black unwed mothers were an easy mark, due to their poverty, their race, their gender, their motherhood, and the absence of a man's public protection. Thus they could be guilty of all these crimes at once. Hodding Carter reflected in 1958 on attempts to legislate against black illegitimacy as a crime of "racial misbehavior." He cited the "widespread sentiment for some means of coping with the fantastically high number of illegitimate births. They do add," he suggested, "an onerous burden and provide a readily employed argument as to asserted Negro inferiority."[56]

The Reproductive Capacity of Black Unwed Mothers As Political Terrain: the Sterilization Solution

However the nature of black unmarried mothers' crime was explained, the result of the crime was a child many white taxpayers and politicians defined as an unwanted public expense. Going to the "source" meant ceding power over the fertility of these girls and women to the state in order to curtail the conception of unwanted babies. In fact, the proposals for state control of the fertility of unwed mothers, via sterilization legislation, were actually a postwar addition to an already functioning set of laws and public practices that had taken a great deal of the control of fertility away from women for decades. These included, of course, laws banning abortion and birth control. In the postwar era a number of state legislatures expressed the will to add to the state's pronatalist interest in fertility—an interest that outlawed the means to curtail female fertility—a racially specific antinatalist policy that mandated the mechanisms to curtail the childbearing capacity of black women.

It was, to be sure, a schizophrenic set of practices that aimed to regulate black fertility at this time. For example, in Chicago, in the same state that threatened women on welfare with jail sentences if they had a child out of wedlock, in the same city where unwed mothers were threatened with eviction from their homes, social workers in the Department of Public Welfare were forbidden to refer their clients to Planned Parenthood clinics. Moreover, the director of the Cook County Hospital where about five thousand illegitimate babies were born each year in the early 1960s, justified the absence of a birth control clinic in the hospital on the grounds that "busy doctors could not take the time to give the necessary education in contraception," despite the fact that the hospital's clients begged for this service. One woman, reflecting on the effect on her life of the hospital's policy, said, "So, every year here we are again, back with another baby."[57]

In Syracuse, New York, and elsewhere, public health clinics, with a high proportion of minority clients, generally refused to dispense birth control materials to unmarried girls and women. Policies of the city Welfare Department exacerbated the problem in several ways. A woman trying to prevent pregnancy was told that all "nonessential" prescriptions, which included birth control pills, required the approval of the welfare commissioner, an approval that often took many months to find its way through the bureaucracy. Even when the okay was obtained, the pills would only be dispensed—often along with a lecture from the pharmacist—month by month, because government reimbursements were so slow.[58]

At the same time that public institutional policies were obstructing the efforts of black girls and women to control their own fertility, a substantial segment of public opinion and representatives to a number of state legislatures were becoming convinced that the state, and only the state, could effectively manage the fertility of girls and women producing illegitimate babies. A Gallup poll in 1965 asked Americans, "Sometimes unmarried women on relief continue to have illegitimate children and get relief money for each new child born. What do you think should be done in the case of these women?" About one half of the respondents believed such women should be ineligible for relief money; one out of five believed that unwed mothers on relief who had additional illegitimate children should be sterilized.[59]

The public response to the attempt by the city manager of Newburgh, New York, to terminate welfare benefits for those he called "the dregs of humanity . . . [coming in a] never-ending pilgrimage from North Carolina," suggested that many Americans supported state control of fertility. Meg Greenfield, writing in *The Reporter*, analyzed the response: "It is clear from the letters that have flooded local newspapers . . . that [Newburgh City Manager Mitchell] has tapped a deep reservoir of popular emotion that extends all across the nation. Among the 'Thank Gods' and 'God Blesses' there have been many demands for further humiliation of welfare recipients."[60] These included many calls for the sterilization of black illegitimate mothers.

In the 1950s and 1960s, many Americans were concerned that the extension of public monies to the undeserving poor constituted the expensive act of an inappropriately activist government. Often these were the same citizens who believed the state had the right and responsibility to take an activist role in managing black female fertility. They found their consistency in the fact that curtailing fertility would reduce the mass of undeserving poor and thus reduce the government's misguided welfare expenditures, maybe even deflect attention from the "Negro problem" if there were fewer blacks in the population.

A willingness to sanction state activism in order to promote a restrained state, however, required a complex justification. Proponents of state-managed programs to control black women's fertility justified such state activity with reference to what Theodore H. White called the crisis of "biological anarchy." While White did not himself write in behalf of sterilization legislation, the analysis he offered of the black community in *The Making of the President 1964*, might have supported this sort of law. White described the appalling black "pattern of mating and breeding without responsibility" in "zoological tenements" and "loveless breeding warrens." He pointed to such facts as, "Today Negro women bear children in the big city at a rate 40% faster than white women; and the differential between them is composed almost exactly of children born out of wedlock." White raised the specter of a less-white America by citing growing minority populations in major urban centers and by stressing that "When Kennedy was elected in 1960, one in ten Americans was non-white. When Johnson's Presidency ends in 1972 [sic], one of eight will be non-white; of infants under a year, one in six is non-white."[61] These visions supported the construction of the reproductive capacity of black women as the culprit.

Those who publicly promoted the state's right to terminate the fertility of unwed mothers (explicitly or implicitly acknowledged as black) typically drew on four salient conditions of postwar American life. First, proponents of sterilization drew on and stimulated white racism. North Carolina State Senator Luther Hamilton, for example, argued the case for sterilization on a higher ground than fiscal concerns. "We are," he said, "breeding a race of bastards."[62] A minority report issued by the Commission to Study Problems Relating to Children Born Out of Wedlock in Virginia in 1959 decried the Commission's opposition to sterilization. In attempting to keep alive interest in the sterilization solution that created the committee, the authors of the minority report reminded the Virginia General Assembly,

> [T]he data in the report show clearly the race in which the problem is greatest, and that the number of illegitimate births has been increasing quantitatively and relatively among the Negro race. The proposals of the majority will do little to stem this tide which can be expected to increase and become even more aggravated.[63]

During the floor debates on House Bill No. 180 in the 1964 session of the Mississippi state legislature, Representative Stone Banfield stated, "When the cutting starts, they'll [blacks] head for Chicago."[64]

Secondly, sterilization was often presented as a balm to the insecurity of white taxpayers. As City Manager Mitchell of Newburgh declared to the Economic Club of Detroit, "We challenge the right of social parasites to breed illegitimate children at the taxpayers' expense."[65] In virtually all states in which sterilization legislation was discussed or debated, including California, Illinois, Louisiana, Maryland, Mississippi, North Carolina, and Virginia, the boon to the taxpayer of curtailing black fertility was a central consideration.[66] As Frank Breul wrote in 1962, the unwed ADC mother is made into "the scapegoat for much of the frustration of those who resent their tax dollars being used to support others."[67]

Proponents of state control of female fertility, thirdly, presented this policy option as one in the spirit of preserving American democracy, threatened in the postwar world not least by illegitimacy.[68] An Illinois Public Aid Commission member who advocated sterilization of women and men producing illegitimate children asserted, in explanation of his advocacy: "We simply need respect for the law and the basic morals that underlie the law if we are to continue as a free people."[69] The implication was that, concerning illegitimacy, the American system was in jeopardy, not at fault.

Finally, advocates of sterilization drew on and stimulated hostility toward women, especially black women. Legislative debates, the media, and politicians typically referred to them in terms such as "immoral," "amoral," and "promiscuous," and described black unmarried mothers as using their bodies for profit. William Rutherford recommended to the Illinois General Assembly that "all persons convicted of being prostitutes should be sterilized." Within the category of prostitutes he included persons who bear more than one illegitimate child and, going a step further, defined women who had obtained an illegal abortion as equal to bearers of illegitimate children, and thus to prostitutes.[70]

A 1957 sterilization bill in the North Carolina legislature had an interesting fate that suggests the specificity with which women's bodies and their fertility were targeted. In the course of the debate, Senator Edwin Lanier introduced an amendment to the bill that would make all provisions of the bill apply to men as well as women. Lanier justified including men this way, "What's fair to the goose ought to be done to the gander." The amendment was adopted, but the bill's sponsor immediately tabled the whole business.[71] As Jewell Handy Gresham has recently pointed out, the racism and sexism involved in such social policies are inextricable.[72]

The efforts to legislate punitive sterilization of black unwed mothers were largely unsuccessful and many of the attempts drew substantial negative publicity, nationally. Most Americans did not favor compulsory sterilization of black unmarried mothers, on welfare or not. Still, the many attempts, apparently supported by only about 20 percent of the American public in 1965, suggests how far, and in what direction, biological determinism could be pushed in the postwar era.

Even without state laws or a national, public mandate for sterilization of black women who had illegitimate babies, the practice of this form of population control remained a part of the de facto race-specific population policy of some states, particularly in the south.[73] Fannie Lou Hamer created a big stir when she was quoted in the *Washington Post* to the effect that "six out of every ten women were taken to Sunflower City Hospital to be sterilized for no reason at all. Often the women were not told that they had been sterilized until they were released from the hospital."[74] But she was never effectively refuted.

Black Illegitimacy, Motherhood, and Biological Determinism

Black unwed mothers in general kept their babies; in 1958 only 9 percent of all adoptions were of nonwhite babies.[75] Yet the motherhood status of these girls and women was as thoroughly challenged as the motherhood of white unwed mothers, the majority of whom placed their babies for adoption. As one observer put it, "Those who look on the birth of any baby as a natural event—many many Southern Negroes—may pass the child along as a 'gift child' to whoever wants it."[76] The challenge was different but equally direct. The public popularity of biological determinism as an explanation for black illegitimate pregnancy translated into a public perception of black unwed motherhood shaped by the same concept. Black unwed motherhood was often treated, publicly and politically, as a status devoid of affective, traditional, cultural, or historical dimensions; it was simply a biologically determined fact. According to this perspective, the relation between mother and child was less important to the woman than the sex urge of which the child was merely a by-product. Alternately, the relationship was described as less important than the nineteen or twenty-six dollars the mother received per month in welfare payments for having conceived the child. White policy makers felt justified in defining and redefining the status of illegitimate children in part because they did not fully believe in the legitimacy, not only of the child, but of the mother-child dyad. For example, in 1957, the Illinois state legislature considered House Bill No. 155, which provided that "the second or subsequent illegitimate child born after July 1, 1957, of the same mother shall not be considered a dependent child." The stated purpose of the bill was "to reduce irresponsibility and abuses of the Public Assistance code."[77] The legislature was interested in defining the meaning and status of this class of children because it assumed an unlawful degree of willfulness on the part of their mothers that was at odds with traditional maternal norms as well as expensive to the state.

By 1960, twenty-three states had some form of "suitable home" law enacted to reduce welfare expenditures by disqualifying mainly black women from eligibility for ADC benefits.[78] These laws defined unwed mothers as immoral by definition. They created an association between public money, unsanctified sex, and illicit motherhood that suggested and sometimes explicitly defined the mother as a criminal. For example, in 1960, the Louisiana state legislature passed a law making it a crime punishable by imprisonment to conceive or give birth to a second illegitimate child. A New Orleans attorney, State Senator Adian Duplantier, who led the unsuccessful opposition to the law, expressed his disapproval: "This [law] makes motherhood a felony, gentlemen. This will force a boom in criminal abortions. Fornication is a sin but this is not against the sin. This law is against the miracle of birth—an act of God—I cannot vote to make God a felon . . . no civilized government in history has ever done that."[79]

Outside of the legislative chambers, black unwed mothers were not necessarily viewed or treated as immoral or criminal. In the welfare office, they might typically be defined and treated in other ways that slighted their maternity. An experienced social worker and professor of social work, Helen H. Perlman, described what she observed as the most prevalent "obstacle to the social worker 'knowing' the black unmarried mother." She said, "This woman has been defined and viewed not in her role as a mother but in the role of 'relief client.' " Perlman added, if the welfare worker were actually able to perceive the girl or woman as a mother, "then a wholly different kind of content would shape the communication."[80]

Attitudes such as these toward black unwed mothers, constructed of race, gender, and class prejudices, shaped by fear of high welfare costs and supported by convictions about the biological bases of black behavior, led some to a harsh conclusion: if black women had babies without the sanction of legal or religious institutions, that strongly suggested that these women were normless and immoral. These observers did not imagine alternate codes or systems of morality. The *Detroit Free Press*, for example, asserted, "There's nothing wrong with telling flagrantly illegitimate mothers, 'One more strike and you're out.' "[81] The North Carolina Commission to Study Public Welfare Programs took a similar position in 1962. One of the recommendations in the Commission's report to the governor made the birth of a third child out of wedlock a rebuttable legal presumption that the mother . . . is an unfit person for the rearing of her children and . . . made this "unfitness" the basis for removal of one or all of the children from her custody. This recommendation applied to all mothers with three children born out of wedlock, regardless of whether they received public assistance.[82]

The insistence on one standard of childbearing and maternity for all women, based on an ideal version of white, middle-class behavior, created extreme difficulties for some black girls and women. Sometimes institutions forcibly imposed white normative behavior on black girls and women because staff defined them as otherwise anormative and antiinstitutional.[83] In a post-war tour of programs for unwed mothers in Kentucky, Maud Morlock of the United States Children's Bureau heard a story from an administrator for Family Services in Louisville that she was told was a typical example of the treatment of black unwed mothers by the Juvenile Court. The administrator, Esther Taylor, told Morlock about a thirteen-year-old pregnant black girl who

> was told by the probation officer that she could return to her own home if her mother signed the statement permitting her to marry the boy. The boy [involved in the incident that led to the girl's pregnancy] had delinquency · records—drug addiction, rape and larceny. . . .The [boy] that the probation officer was insisting the girl marry was of low mentality. The family agency, to whom [the girl's] mother appealed, knowing the attitude of the court, suggested that perhaps they could reach an agreement if the girl was placed in a foster home temporarily. This was agreed to by the mother on Wednesday. Unbeknownst to the agency, the court hearing occurred on Saturday and the [girl] was practically compelled to agree to marry.[84]

Culture Challenges Biology

Throughout the period of this study, there were people who challenged biological determinism as an explanation for the incidence of black illegitimacy and as a justification for the treatment of black unwed mothers. Despite its persistent, recurrent appeal as an enduring judgment against the black community, and against black women in particular, some social scientists, government workers, and service providers tried again and again over the years to deflect focus in various ways from the racial, biological imperative. Again and again, the challengers attempted to redirect the biological determinists with considerations of black culture. For many the task was to undermine the use of the relatively high rate of black illegitimacy as proof of a predominantly biological basis of human relations as against a higher order, affective basis for whites.

The postwar challengers often drew inspiration and analytical categories from the work of sociologist E. Franklin Frazier. His 1939 book, *The Negro*

Family in the United States, made Frazier a hero and a beacon to those attempting to counter racial biological determinism.[85] One of Frazier's central intentions in *The Negro Family* was to address, and then undermine, charges of the "inherent moral degeneracy of the Negro" and the reputed natural link between this trait and biological degeneracy.[86] Frazier aimed his environmentalist argument against the work of leading proponents of black biological and moral inferiority, including Frederick Hoffman (*Race Traits and Tendencies,* 1896), William Hannibal Thomas (*The American Negro: What He Was, What He Is and What He May Become,* 1901), and A. H. Shannon (*The Negro in Washington: A Study in Race Amalgamation,* 1930). Frazier's analysis of the black family, and of unwed motherhood in particular, was especially notable at the time because he constructed it from the popular concepts of mainstream, modern sociology.

In explaining the causes of the relatively high rates of black illegitimacy, Frazier insisted that an analysis of power and race relations in the south and in the northern city was central. For example, in refuting A. H. Shannon's argument that black illegitimacy in Washington, D.C., was an outgrowth of blacks' false sense of equality there, Frazier asserted, "What we know of racial mixture in the South, the social and economic subordination of the Negro has been more fruitful of illegitimacy than the enjoyment of equality."[87] He specifically tied black illegitimacy to "the sexual exploitation of the subordinate race by the dominant race."[88] Following the work of Georg Simmel and Robert Park, Frazier used "the city" in his analysis as a dynamic agent of social and personal change. In particular, he focused on the city as a negative influence on the "simple peasant folk" migrating to northern slums from the rural south.[89] It was "the poverty and disorganization of the city slums [which] constantly re-creates the problem of unmarried motherhood."[90]

Frazier's assumptions were powerful. By lifting the burden of culpability for black illegitimacy from the bodies of black women and placing it outside, in the ravages of the city, he made a strong, memorable case for the proposition that the same social laws and sociological principles govern the lives of blacks and whites. Similarly, by demonstrating that black behavior and the meaning of that behavior changed over time and place, Frazier argued that his people had a dynamic history and culture, like whites. This pair of claims could only be viable and visible when the focus was shifted off the black woman's body, away from biology.

Frazier's conclusions denied the alleged undertow of hypersexuality and focused attention instead on the black woman in dynamic relation to her environment. His strongest finding, therefore, was that black illegitimacy rates were a reflection and a measure of inferior living conditions, but emphatically not a proof of moral or biological inferiority. The worm in Frazier's analysis turned out to be the idea that different environments encourage, even produce, different cultures. In a racist society, difference has always connoted hierarchy.[91]

In the postwar era, the escalating rates of illegitimacy among both blacks and whites provided part of the stimulus among academics, politicians, and policy makers to distinguish and catalog distinctions between these two "cultures" in American society.[92] Once "culture" was introduced into the discussion of illegitimacy, the concept was usually used interchangeably with "race." Most postwar analysts ranked black culture beneath white and ascribed black behavior regarding, for example, sex norms, to "cultural lag." In the postwar United States, illegitimate pregnancy was defined as a white woman's violation of her culture, caused by her individual neuroses. This maxim assumed that whites lived within a unified culture, and one with wholesome standards. It assumed, as well, a complexity and responsiveness of mind in white girls and women. The focus on mind rendered white illegitimate pregnancy essentially asexual. White women got pregnant without husbands due to higher order, psychological causes. Finally, professional intervention was useful for white unwed mothers. Psychiatrists, psychologists, and social workers simply had to help individuals; they didn't have to transform a culture.

In contrast, the use of "culture" to explain racial difference in the rates of illegitimacy suggested that blacks had a unitary culture as well, but one that was unwholesome. For one thing, it provided no institutions to restrain black behavior. Without the benefit of cultural institutions as mediators, the sex behavior of black females was constructed as a natural expression, once again, of biological urges. Professional intervention to assist individuals was essentially futile or unnecessary, since it was the culture at fault, and the "basic personality patterns" it spawned.[93] In sum, unlike white culture, black culture subsumed all individuals. It was impenetrable, unchanging, biological. White culture, in contrast, was permeable, supportive, institutionally flexible, and responsive: democratic. The white culture and the white environment as well was portrayed as protective and benign; failure was an individual matter. Black culture and the environment in which it was expressed, was pictured as aberrant and dangerous. The failing here was collective.[94]

In these ways, the use of culture, suggested in part by Frazier's work, became a dignified cover for biological racism. Culture as an analytical concept and category sounded respectful and holistic. It aimed to include and pay attention to all aspects of a people's lives. But as "culture" was used in the postwar era, in particular to explain the racial differences in rates of illegitimate childbearing, it was so inclusive and so comparative an abstraction that many began to draw on "culture" to support a distinction between a white culture of the mind and a black culture of the body. All racial differences in the experience of illegitimacy flowed from this distinction.

Many postwar social service professionals who dealt with black unwed mothers or the issue of black illegitimacy were deeply concerned about institutional practices that denied services to black girls and women and about community attitudes that justified the denial.[95] Some tied these outcomes to the misuse of the concept "culture" and especially to the fact that biological determinism remained embedded in the current use of the term. A black social worker, Annie Lee Davis, the Consultant on Services to Children in Their Own Homes at the United States Children's Bureau, worked with great intelligence and persistence during these years to redefine the term "culture" so as not to exclude black unwed mothers, by definition, from services offered to whites. While her vision and strategies may seem, in some ways, limited today, in the postwar era Davis's colleagues—black and white—considered her a foresighted authority and relied heavily on her judgments and advice.

Davis's first line of attack was to emphasize that culture was not an inborn trait.[96] She wrote, "[T]oo often when we think of culture, we view it as something that is innate with certain groups of people; rather than viewing culture as the result of the interaction of people and the social forces with which they are surrounded."[97] Davis stressed repeatedly in speeches and in her correspondence and visits with many practitioners across the country that black unwed mothers *were* individuals, not simply undifferentiated expressions of a culture: "Each girl must be seen as an individual, and her unique, emotional, social and economic problems must be understood in the light of her cultural heritage."[98] A central part of Davis's project was to insist that her colleagues approach a black unmarried mother with the expectation of meeting a girl with intelligence and a psychological dimension to her dilemma. To this end, she directed one colleague to the work of Maurine Boi LaBarre, a social worker who had written, "While the cultural patterns and ideals are significant, it is primarily the way that the differences are used psychologically in the [clients'] emotional development through their relations with their parents that is important rather than the specific culture."[99]

Throughout the 1940s and 1950s and into the 1960s, Annie Lee Davis labored to redefine "culture" especially in relation to black illegitimacy. As an ardent integrationist, Davis believed it was essential to convince policy makers, service providers, and the general public that a black unwed mother was, first of all, an American, as American as her white counterpart, "with the same basic heritage."[100] In fact, Davis argued that black girls were often more American than many ethnic whites because [white] girls have had more direct and recent contact with their European backgrounds than any American Negro girl could have with African culture."[101] Davis criticized an "expert" who described " 'Negro culture' as if blacks were entirely separate and apart from the total American culture and its variation." She stressed her own perspective: "Negroes have lived in this country since 1619 and . . . the importation of large numbers of Africans to the United States ceased in 1808. Therefore for 142 years American Negroes have had no contact with African culture."[102] To Davis, it was necessary for whites to view blacks as Americans, in order to shift the focus, historically, biologically, and culturally, off their slave past. In this regard, colleagues of Davis's observed that when black illegitimacy is ascribed to slavery, we are "Leaning too much on the slavery crutch [which] prevents us from moving more quickly toward sounder understanding and practice."[103] Reference to blacks' slave past functioned as a means of condemning and demeaning black unwed mothers, Davis felt, and a way of effectively placing them outside of mainstream American culture.

Arguing that black unwed mothers were essentially the same as white unwed mothers involved a proof that illegitimacy had the same meaning in the black community as in the white, and thus carried the same kind and degree of stigma for offenders of both races. Davis argued that shame was not for whites only. In this aspect of the discussion, guilt became a hallmark of culture—of American culture—so proof of its presence was important to the opportunities available to black unwed mothers.[104] Bess Williams, one of Davis's Children's Bureau colleagues warned a professional group in San Francisco to be wary of "Fallacious, generalized statements about the pregnant girl from some minority group [who] presents no social problem to her family." Williams stressed that this information was false and that the pregnancies of nonwhite girls were as troubling and embarrassing to their families as a daughter's unwed pregnancy would be to a white family.[105] Ten years later when the famous Greenleigh Report on the Cook County ADC program was issued, it was still important to emphasize this aspect: "Contrary to most literature on the subject of Negro cultural patterns, illegitimacy was not found in this study to be without stigma to the mother and child. Most mothers of children born out of wedlock expressed great feelings of guilt and were fully aware of the stigma in the Negro and general community."[106]

In the effort to place black illegitimacy within American culture, it was also important to establish that black girls and women were not simply baby breeders or baby lovers, or chronic dependents. They had other goals and intentions for their lives, as did whites. An important study of fifty unwed black mothers in Indiana in 1957 found that almost two-thirds of the girls' families were bitter and punishing toward their erring daughters and that most of the unwed mothers described their illegitimate children as unwanted. Many had unsuccessfully sought abortions and, failing that, adoptive placements for their babies.[107] These findings continued to be meaningful into the 1960s to counter the findings of other investigators who stressed that the black unmarried mother was an extreme outsider in American society who began her "career" of illegitimate childbearing with low self-esteem and low intelligence. One study described her plight this way: "Although she does not like it, she is not really surprised that she continues to bear illegitimate children. She sees it as an act of fate. In fact, there is a strong likelihood that her most important sense of identity is that of being an unwed mother," a status which the investigators likened to the identity of a psychotic person as a "mental patient."[108]

Davis and her colleagues also pleaded with the social work establishment to recognize stratification within the black community. They were convinced that such awareness would make agencies more willing to offer services to some black girls. Perhaps just as important, an acceptance of the fact of socioeconomic stratification within the black community would signal a will-ingness to perceive this community as a complex, "advanced" entity, more like the white community. This perception would provide a major rebuttal to the contention that the behavior of the black people, as a race, was driven by the biological imperative. In one such effort, a black professional active in national and local service organizations for unwed mothers, Patricia Garland, railed against the lack of attention, in the literature and among service agencies, to black middle-class unwed mothers: "It is unconscionable for the profession to use fragmented, unrepresentative, and incomplete data as the basis for its assumptions, policies and administration of services [for black unwed mothers]."[109]

In the context of the postwar era, Annie Lee Davis understood that "culture" was a loaded term. When used, as it so often was, to ascribe apparent racial differences to inhering qualities, blacks stood to suffer for having a culture of their own. In 1950 she wrote to a colleague in Chicago, "I know that adequate services and resources for Negro unmarried mothers and their babies cannot be developed as long as we cling to the belief that this behavior is a part of the Negro cultural pattern."[110] Consequently, Davis defined her most pressing task as the resurrection of a Frazierian analysis of illegitimacy, which primarily ascribed the high incidence of black childbearing out of wedlock to the quality of the environment in which American blacks were forced to live. Again, she wrote,

> What appears to me to be needed is general information that will give understanding of Negro people in terms of the circumstances under which they live; how these circumstances affect their attitudes, ideals and group standards; the effect of the conflict between the democratic ideals and philosophy that they inherit along with all other Americans and the restrictions that they face because of their lower status in the total social structure.[111]

In the 1940s and 1950s policy makers, social theorists, and service providers were deeply engaged in constructing perversion and neurosis as individualized conditions with psychological roots. A focus on the environment seemed old-fashioned, out of step with American life. The sex life of the black female, portrayed as a deviation from alleged American standards, might have challenged the psychological model. Throughout the 1950s, however, the incidence of black illegitimacy did not stimulate commentators to draw on the passé, environmental explanation of social problems. During these years social theorists were not generally disposed to subject the American environment to negative assessments or charge it with responsibility for racial difference and racial conflict. Thus, it followed that many observers and professionals ascribed black illegitimacy to a third possible variable: racial, biological inferiority, a condition expressed in black culture.

Where Culture Prevailed

Still, Annie Lee Davis had reasons to feel that her exhortations were not altogether in vain. A number of public policies and service options recognized the individual needs of black unwed mothers in the 1950s, in new ways. For example, despite public sentiment and public policies in many states to the contrary, black unwed mothers and their children had become eligible for public assistance, under federal legislation.[112] When push came to shove in Louisiana, the highest relevant official in the United States government reiterated the state's commitment to providing basic assistance to black unwed mothers, whatever the status of their maternity.[113] The government justified its stance, in part, by reference to a number of studies undertaken in the 1950s specifically designed to find a link, or its absence, between the increase in illegitimacy and in ADC costs.[114] Most often the evidence indicated no link whatsoever.[115] Studies of black unwed mothers receiving ADC in Illinois, North Carolina, Virginia, and many other states confirmed the absence of a relationship between illegitimacy rates and ADC payments.[116]

Demonstrating how psychology had become, for some, a more attractive justification than environmental problems for serving black unwed mothers, James R. Dumpson, First Deputy Commissioner of the New York City Department of Welfare, denied in 1958 that providing unwed mothers with welfare assistance "was aiding and abetting immorality." "Indeed," he added, "aiding these troubled, disturbed mothers is frequently the first opportunity the community may have to get at the causative factors of their difficulties and begin to reverse the patterns."[117]

Davis's call for attention to the individual and psychological needs of black unmarried mothers, including the need for adoption services, all generally considered ridiculous in the 1940s, were heeded here and there in the 1950s and early 1960s.[118] A community project for pregnant unwed black schoolgirls in Washington, D.C., for example, made psychological testing of the clients a central program feature. Tests indicated that the pregnancies were connected with conflicts with mothers, ego problems, and problems of feminine identity, among other psychological causes. The tests also demonstrated that the girls developed "socially acceptable attitudes" toward sex and men over the course of their participation in the program.[119] Moreover, in a radical break with customary attitudes and treatment of black unwed mothers, the program directors strongly advocated that these girls should abdicate the maternal role so that they could pursue appropriate adolescent activities, and particularly their studies.[120] A number of programs in cities all over the country were begun in the 1950s to promote adoption of black babies, thus justifying and facilitating Davis's insistence that "Actual experience has shown that Negro unmarried mothers do give up their babies."[121]

In part because the Children's Bureau and the social service community favored care for white unwed pregnant girls and women in maternity homes,

Annie Lee Davis and her colleagues were persistently interested in making these homes an option for blacks; Davis strongly favored integrated homes and worked with Maud Morlock to overcome "the prevailing idea in the community that 'Negroes just have babies,' and therefore maternity home service for them is an inappropriate expense."[122] Davis countered this attitude with her own insistent vision:

> The chief difficulty in providing maternity home care for Negro girls is the lack of competent and trained personnel, inadequacy of programs, lack of a planned program of interpretation to doctors, teachers, ministers and other community people who have contacts with unmarried mothers, and lack of adequate funds. If a sound program of maternity home care were established for Negro girls and if there were direction in reaching girls who need the protection of a maternity home, the values of the service to Negro girls would be the same as those for any other girls.[123]

In fact, for some years, a number of black maternity homes had been serving their communities; most had been established through the efforts of black women's groups.[124] Many operated, however, under such severe financial constraints that their existence was threatened by the late 1940s. The building that housed the Talbert Home in the Hough section of Cleveland, for example, was condemned by the city in 1951; still, the home continued to serve black unwed mothers until late 1961.[125] The black communities in Kansas City, Topeka, and Little Rock also supported maternity homes,[126] although under straitened circumstances. Partly reflecting her feeling that black girls would not receive the most modern treatment or the most enlightened range of programs in an all-black home, Davis described the Florence Home in Kansas City as serving few girls because it was a "*very* punitive place [where] few wished to go." She regretted the home's decline as, at one time— before integrated homes were even a remote possibility—it "had been a leading provider for Negro unmarried mothers in the country."[127]

The Phillis Wheatley Home in Columbus, Ohio, on the other hand, continued to provide a sought-after service to its community in 1950, during an era when every one of its fifteen beds was usually taken, despite the fact that the home's program and facilities were restricted by the same lack of funds that plagued other black homes, and its code of discipline was very strict. Residents were expected to spend their leisure hours knitting and crocheting, and making gowns and diapers for their babies from material donated by a local club. A volunteer came to the home once a week for two hour sessions to teach the girls sewing skills. Each girl was expected to produce items in this order: first something for the baby, then a maternity dress, then something for the home. The only additional planned activities were religious. Every Friday a deacon conducted a service for the girls featuring a discourse based on a Bible verse selected by one of the residents. The deacon's visits were supplemented by twice-weekly visits by a woman from the community who submitted the girls to Bible quizzes.

The home's mission as a place of protection was reflected by its roster of rules. These were designed to shield the community and the expectant mothers from each other. For example, the home's board—fifteen permanent members, all black—decided that girls must not be permitted to go outside alone. Many came from the neighborhood around the Phillis Wheatley Home, and the board determined that the girls should not be seen in their condition. It is not clear whether the policy aimed to spare the home's residents embarrassment or was the result of the board's knowledge that the neighbors did not want to see the evidence of sexual misconduct, or did not want their children to see. Even spending a sunny afternoon in the yard was considered a problem since the home's small lawn area was open to view from the street. When one girl was seen walking in the neighborhood by a black schoolteacher, the teacher complained to the home's superintendent, whose job indeed included a hefty measure of surveillance. The board expected her to read and censor every letter residents sent and received.

Inside, a visitor found the home "clean and [possessing] a homey atmosphere"; however, all fifteen residents slept in one dormitory room on the third floor. The white visitor reported, "The room was exceedingly hot and the ventilation poor. Beds were close together and suitcases piled underneath. Drawer and closet space was inadequate. The stairs to this floor are narrow and steep." She added, without explanation, "Because of [the] visit, all of the girls were in bed." Perhaps it was a staff decision, or perhaps the girls were embarrassed to be seen. Perhaps they chose not to figure in the white government official's account of the maternity home, which they did not.[128]

Despite the hot attic, the censored mail, and the other shortcomings of the home, some black families, like the mother in Norfolk, Virginia, felt their pregnant unmarried daughters would be better off removed from the family setting, under the care and protection of the Phillis Wheatley Home. The many letters from pregnant black girls and women to the Children's Bureau requesting information about maternity homes, suggest that for a significant number of unmarried mothers themselves, this was an attractive option. The decision to go to the Phillis Wheatley Home did not, apparently, suggest a desire to keep the illegitimate pregnancy a secret, as many residents were from families living in the immediate vicinity of the home and almost all of the girls left the home with their babies, whom—according to the superintendent— they planned to raise. Annie Lee Davis observed that black mothers were interested in maternity homes for their daughters because they "wanted to get them off the street and under supervision" since they were excluded from school because of the pregnancy.[129] Surely many parents, disappointed by their daughter's nonmarital pregnancy, looked to these homes to protect themselves and their daughter from any further missteps on her part. But the Norfolk mother, looking for "kind treatment" and "peace" for her daughter, provides an example of a parent who was not shocked or angry; nor does her letter show disappointment. It is the expression of a mother desiring the best for her girl and, presumably, the best for her grandchild. For her, the maternity home was a "lovely place."

The "lovely place," however, remained a dream for many of these black girls and women and their parents. In the early postwar years, for example, the more than fifty Florence Crittenton facilities served only about 250 blacks annually, and many of these were helped not in the homes, but in affiliated boarding-home programs. The situation for blacks desiring maternity home care in Chicago was terrible. Three of the four homes in that city—the Chicago Foundling Home, the Sarah Hackett Home (which was located in a black neighborhood), and the Florence Crittenton Home (in a white neighborhood)—all refused to serve blacks. Only the Salvation Army Home admitted this population, but in limited numbers, serving eight to ten blacks at a time, one-third to one-quarter of its capacity.[130] The Florence Crittenton Home in Phoenix was pointed in its exclusionary policy. A 1952 visit to the home revealed that this facility "has served Spanish Americans, Indians, Chinese, Japanese, Koreans, and Philipinos [sic], but [the staff] say they don't serve 'colored' which means they really only exclude the Negro."[131] Throughout the early 1950s at least twenty Florence Crittenton residences remained fully segregated.[132] In the *Maternity Home Directory* for 1960, a number of homes explicitly advertised their segregation policies, including the Florence Crittenton Homes in Washington, D.C., Atlanta, Topeka, Baltimore, and Pittsburgh.[133]

During the late 1950s the situation began to change; in 1958 the Crittenton homes cared for six hundred blacks in twenty-four integrated residences and four programs for nonwhites only. Some of this new inclusiveness was due to the success of the integrationist agenda that Davis championed: black unwed mothers should be understood in the context of their environment, and even rescued from that environment for their own protection and rehabilitation, as many white girls were. In addition, the new inclusiveness reflected a white response to the civil rights movement, the effects of which reached even into maternity homes. For example, Robert Barrett, the patriarchal leader of the Florence Crittenton operation, shared his strategic plans for integration with the chairman of the board of directors of the Florence Crittenton Association of America. He wrote in 1954,

> There is a renewal of interest in the work for colored girls in Washington [D.C.] and I have urged the Washington Home to give up their segregation policy. All D.C. schools go on a non-segregation basis this fall. If the Washington Home will do so I would be willing to recommend to our trustees that we grant a liberal contribution to a building fund to take care of increased population.[134]

Even in the face of national data indicating that large numbers of black unwed mothers were not availing themselves of Crittenton maternity home services, when available, and in the face of hostility from southern homes, this organization pushed on, fitfully, toward desegregation, vowing to follow the school integration program.[135] One white southern affiliate, in Tennessee, however, warned the national office, "Like it or not, we must admit that the segregation furor is a tender spot down here, and any action we take must take that into consideration. The wrong move now, or if the entire matter isn't handled with the most extreme delicacy and tact, can have either the Negroes or the whites down on our heads." In reference to a black initiative to build a facility on Crittenton property, the Tennessean wrote, "I do wish I felt sure that their interest is motivated by concern for Negro unmarried mothers rather than a definite step forward in the desegregation problem in Chattanooga."[136]

Often maternity homes' boards of directors, like the Phoenix Florence Crittenton board, were openly hostile to integration. Board members of the Catherine Booth (Salvation Army) Home in Cincinnati, described as "believ[ing] strongly in segregation" despite the Army's integration policy, were expected to object to a plan to solve space problems by arranging for white and black girls to sleep together in one building. The same board even wanted the home to provide separate delivery rooms.[137] In Washington, D.C., the House of Mercy's Ladies' board, a group "responsible for much of the financing of the home," was adamant that "the home accept only white girls."[138] In a number of cities, the Community Chest (an important source of support for most nonprofit human service agencies), whose board members came from the same social stratum as the members of maternity home boards, often shared and cooperated with their segregationist sentiment by making it practically impossible for white homes to support more flexible policies. For example, in the late 1940s, the Salvation Army Home in Louisville, Kentucky, expressed willingness to accept blacks "on a non-segregated basis" in response to concern in the black community about an "inadequacy of facilities for Negro unmarried mothers." But the Army remained unable to offer the new service, as the Community Chest "did not want the home to expand."[139] In some cities the Chest was in a position to exercise its concept of maternity home care as a service appropriate only for whites. This happened in Columbus when the Phillis Wheatley Home wanted to expand its facilities in the early postwar years. The local Chest "replied that this is not the time to do this" and suggested instead that the Home consider closing down.[140]

Where integration did occur, it appears to have been given a push from the white girls in residence when the decision was in the balance. The executive director of the Florence Crittenton Home in Charlotte described how the white girls at the home responded to the idea. "The resident group was accepting. . . .They felt Negro girls needed this service as badly as they did. They were asked for a show of hands on approval of integration and all voted in the affirmative. Then they turned their discussion toward ways they might be helpful since they identified with the lone Negro girl in a white Home."

When, in the fall of 1963, the color line was severed at the Charlotte facility, the staff "chose [the] first girl carefully." She was a twenty-three-year-old teacher and considered a "good choice." The executive director reported that the teacher had been "so well satisfied" by her stay at the home that her only suggestion upon leaving was "one point we had completely overlooked—arranging a place where the Negro girl might press her hair."[141]

Some years before, in the early postwar period, an influential group of local, state, and national social service professionals discussed opening a maternity home for blacks in Charlotte, "the logical location for such a home," and had approached the Crittenton organization about sponsoring this project. Sixteen years passed, however, before black unwed mothers were served under Crittenton auspices, when the schoolteacher was carefully selected in 1963.[142] By this time, far more blacks were receiving care in integrated than in segregated homes, no doubt in part because integrated homes had sufficient philanthropic and Chest support to offer relatively modern facilities as well as educational programs in the later postwar years for pregnant girls still excluded from school. In view of these services, integrated homes may have represented a civil rights victory for the black community, one worth taking advantage of.[143]

The national offices of the two largest maternity home chains, the Salvation Army and the Florence Crittenton organization, had both explicitly adopted integrationist stances by the late 1940s. Throughout the period of this study, the Army was more generally committed and successful in achieving the policy, particularly in its northeastern homes.[144] Jane Wrieden, in the 1940s the superintendent of the Door of Hope, an Army home in Jersey City, wrote to Morlock in Washington, describing some consequences of that home's new practices:

> I want to tell you that since . . . January, when we decided that there would be no limits on admission in terms of color, we have not become, as it was suggested we might, a "segregated" institution. [Morlock, herself, had suggested this to Wrieden.] It has made little, if any difference in the groupings as to color. I have spoken with clarity and firmness, however, when referring agencies seem to use us on a segregated basis—for example, "the white girls can go there, the Negro girls can go to 503" [the Door of Hope's street number]. Sometimes I think it may have irritated people. And when I have had the privilege of going to Rotary, Kiwanis, Lions, Optimists, church groups, etc., I have made one of my major emphases the Salvation Army's policy of inclusiveness. . . . I feel I can write to you freely and frankly about this, and sometimes I want to try to write something about the deepseatedness of our attitudes even when we think we're "inclusive."[145]

Wrieden was also committed to black representation on an advisory board she was forming at this time. She was interested in recruiting outstanding members such as Mrs. Richard Martin, who sat on the boards of the national

YWCA and the Council of Social Agencies in Jersey City, had done "YW" work in Harlem, and had just received a law degree.[146]

Over the years, Wrieden was pleased by the progress the Salvation Army homes made in providing racially harmonious settings in which black and white girls could live out their pregnancies together. Both before and after she became the Army's national consultant on women's programs and thus overseer of all Army maternity homes in the country, she often provided Maud Morlock with examples of good feeling between residents of different races, such as this vignette:

> There has been no problem in the relation between Negro and white girls. [Here is] an example of the feeling between the two groups . . . on Thanksgiving Day only one girl was not able to be downstairs for dinner and she was Negro. Two white girls requested to eat upstairs with her. They arranged to set up a table in the staff living room . . . so that they could be together.[147]

Other Salvation Army staff, however, were not so sanguine. A caseworker at the Booth Home in Cincinnati wrote to Morlock during the same period, in a more skeptical vein:

> I know that you have not been completely happy about the semi-segregated program in effect in our maternity home. I might mention an incident which occurred at our Halloween party at which were present thirty-eight girls, evenly distributed between Negro and white. The usual tub of apples was in the center of the floor, for the traditional "bobbing" for apples. Very few of the the while girls participated because some of the colored girls "bobbed" first.[148]

The Florence Crittenton organization had a weaker relationship with its affiliates than the Army had with its branch homes. In fact, the Crittenton national office, and its charter, considered each of its homes autonomous. While the organization defined its mission as a commitment to "extend the opportunity of shelter and care to needy girls and women of any sect or race," it also asserted that the "national organization is rarely set up as an authority over state incorporated, associated units." Translating to a representative of a southern affiliate, the chair of the national board of directors explained, "This does not say that you have to take them [blacks] in your Home, but it is hoped that every home that had such a requirement would take the trouble to work through your other social agencies to meet the need of such an applicant." In short, the national policy favored integration, but defined this stance as simply a "resource," with no governing power. The chair conceded, "The local home has the responsibility of meeting the local need on the basis of community demand, and in the best way for them."[149] That is, the Florence Crittenton organization recognized and tolerated racial exclusion. In some cases the organization paid for this stance. In Cleveland, for example, the integrated Salvation Army home was often full, while the exclusionary Crittenton facility served only half the number it could accommodate.[150]

In some cities, the Crittenton homes tried to extend services to black girls and women while keeping their facilities segregated. In Little Rock, for example, the black community established a maternity home in the 1950s; by the early 1960s, its program, though not its residential setting, had been brought under the Crittenton aegis. The national Crittenton office assessed the "amalgamation" as a great success: "Service to Negro girls has been upgraded in every way." Actual changes involved assigning responsibility for financing, programming, and staffing the black home to the existing white board that agreed to accept some black members. This was an "outstanding" development according to the national office.[151]

From the perspective of the black members of the board, however, the accomplishment may have had a different flavor. Acknowledging its lack of financial resources to support the Colored Home, the black board voted to dissolve itself in 1961. The vote followed the Crittenton organization's insistence that their own "amalgamation" plan was the only strategy possible for preserving services for blacks in Little Rock. The black board, in return, insisted that its dissolution was provisional; five of its members must be accepted on the white board. The black board members surely knew that mere token representation would not protect their project. It soon became a question, however, whether even five members could preserve the Colored Home, now that its fate was in so many white hands. Immediately following the dissolution of the black board, the white male board members put forward a motion that read: "[I]n recognition of the unacceptable standard of care provided girls in the Little Rock Colored Home, voluntary steps must be taken to assure a correction of this problem . . . and if this assurance is not forthcoming, we recommend to the FCAA Board at its next meeting that the [Colored] Home be dropped from membership." The motion passed.[152]

The Crittenton organization considered that its most successful program for blacks in these postwar years was in Houston. In this thoroughly segregated city, the Crittenton people followed suit. It ran a maternity home for whites only, and a boarding- or foster-home program for blacks. This program, similar to programs in New York, Chicago, and Los Angeles, supported placement of black, unmarried pregnant girls and women in homes where a woman was paid by Crittenton to feed, house, and supervise them.[153] In Houston the program consisted of three boarding homes, licensed by the state board of health. The Florence Crittenton organization paid the boarding-home "mother" ten dollars a week for keeping a pregnant woman, twelve dollars for a mother and child, forty-three cents a day subsidy for vacancies, and a salary for the "mother" of between twenty and forty-five dollars a month, depending on how many girls she could accommodate. In 1948, this program cost the Florence Crittenton organization $15,222, which covered care for 116 unwed mothers and seventy-eight babies, or about $130 per boarding-home resident. The program was managed by two black social workers. One held an M.A. from the Atlanta School of Social Work and the other was trained at the University of Southern California. The social workers recruited unmarried black pregnant girls and women at the prenatal clinic of the County Hospital and referred them to the boarding homes, also run by black women. In the late 1940s, the three foster mothers had been associated with the program for some time; one was a housewife, one formerly boarded children from the Negro Children's Center, and one was the former maid of a social worker. All three boarding mothers were given two weeks' vacation each year during which they received salary.

The Houston foster-care program included some gestures toward helping the unwed mothers prepare for their future. A group worker from a black settlement home met about twice a month with all twelve girls for discussion, and occasionally a white "county agent" visited the boarding homes. Apparently her most notable project was to teach the pregnant girls how to "make things out of sugar sacks."

The recruitment process at the hospital was considered a success by Grace Knox, the director of the Crittenton home in Houston. She explained to a national officer of the organization that the social workers went to Jefferson Davis Hospital (a segregated facility) to give out pamphlets to every unmarried pregnant girl and even "remain[ed] there until every one has gone in order to interview those who might be interested in having some care through our agency." Knox justified this recruitment strategy on the basis that the social service department at the hospital was "not governed by a group of trained medical social workers . . . most of them are political appointments and pretty much just clerk so that we go out of our way to go to the hospital and give the kind of service that is most necessary." She added, probably disingenuously, that the Florence Crittenton offices were in an obscure part of the city, thus "a little difficult [for these black girls] to reach," especially since "the bus drivers aren't very helpful."[154]

The black social workers themselves described the Crittenton effort to reach black unwed mothers differently, displaying a painful sensitivity to the experience of the pregnant girls:

[One caseworker said] that her interviews took place under very inauspicious circumstances. There is no privacy. Others are interviewing in the same room, telephones are ringing, and the room is crowded. If it is the unmarried mother's first admission at the clinic, she must register at 7:30 a.m. This means she has gotten up early, maybe had a long trip to the clinic and no breakfast. Perhaps she does not see the Florence Crittenton worker until noon. By that time, she may be suspicious, antagonistic and the caseworker spends time in calming her. She sees the caseworker as another "meddling Matty." Often the girl is near delivery. The caseworker's approach is to tell her about Florence Crittenton. The girl often says she needs no help.[155]

The all-white board at the Houston home felt content with the scope of their services to blacks. They did not consider that black girls desiring or required to live away from their families during the pregnancy might choose a maternity home situation. Here, the board refused black members altogether and agreed only to send one of its own to attend the Negro Advisory Committee. The white board was openly racist, freely expressing sentiments such as "[These unwed mothers] can all get jobs and they should save. Instead they buy ice-boxes and then are on relief."[156]

The white delegate to the Negro Advisory Committee must have often heard Mrs. Carter Wesley's analysis of Crittenton's segregated programs. Maud Morlock described Mrs. Wesley, the owner of a black newspaper in the city, as "an intelligent person with much leadership [and] an exceedingly busy person." On a 1950 trip from Washington, Morlock met with Wesley. The black woman was direct and highly critical of the Crittenton program for blacks:

> [O]nly the lower income Negro groups are reached by Florence Crittenton. There are other unmarried mothers who need help. Many need training—to learn new skills and how to get on with others. The white girls in the maternity home have this training. The foster mothers are not trained. The girls have to do the housework in the foster homes. There is an emotional adjustment in the foster home as the unmarried mother must take on the pattern of the boarding home. . . .[A]re the girls better off when the case is closed [?] Has there been any real rehabilitation? [157]

Mrs. Carter Wesley spoke for herself and for her colleagues on the Negro Advisory Committee, all of whom were actively engaged in improving services to black unmarried mothers. When Maud Morlock visited Houston, the advisory committee was militant enough to point out that she had not allotted them enough time and to insist that their group be given an additional, private session with the government official. The meeting took place at the church of a community activist, Reverend Moore, and was attended by twenty-five influential activist blacks, among them the chief fund-raisers for black causes and services. This group included, along with Wesley, Mrs. Anna DuPree who had recently donated twenty thousand dollars to build a cottage at the Houston Negro Children's Center. While the participants looked to Morlock as the "national expert" on illegitimate pregnancy and questioned her as the expert, their intention was clearly to get useful information from her which they could translate into programmatic terms, to the benefit of unwed mothers in their community.

Despite its national-level commitment to provide some services for blacks, whether through integration or by supporting segregated programs, many black community leaders continued to consider the Crittenton association an exclusionary white organization throughout the postwar era. When the Ionia Whipper Home in Washington, D.C., for example, faced financial difficulties in the early 1960s, a prominent black member of that program's board rejected FCAA affiliation as a route to improving the home's financial condition. He observed "that the agency would not be interested in membership in the Association because of the attitudes of many of its member agencies toward Negro unmarried mothers."[158]

In the later postwar period, most black maternity homes closed or were amalgamated under sometimes threatening terms, as in Little Rock. Integrated programs served greater numbers of blacks than had ever been residents of the handful of black homes scattered around the country in the 1940s and 1950s. The new black residents included many girls and women with the resources to cover the full range of fees these homes required.[159] By the time that the white homes began to accept blacks, however, the fit was particularly infelicitous. In the 1950s, these homes had become deeply enthusiastic promoters of the postwar adoption mandate for illegitimate babies, while black unwed mothers traditionally kept their babies. Moreover, as one government official observed, even where maternity homes accepted black girls, and even if these girls agreed to place their babies for adoption, "The placement [adoption] agency still won't accept the baby." The only solution was for "all agencies . . . to change." In the meantime, this Children's Bureau employee stressed the limited relief integrated maternity homes provided for black girls and women, single and pregnant, and suggested that "We should consider problems and lack of total services rather than to think alone of . . . maternity home services for Negro girls."[160]

The civil rights movement's challenges to biological determinism in the late 1950s and early 1960s reshaped the professional response to black illegitimacy. Black unwed mothers, individually and collectively, were now worthy subjects of research. A number of studies conducted at this time went far beyond the question of the relationship of illegitimacy and ADC costs and focused on the individual needs of these girls and women and on the issue of if and how they were being met.[161] In addition, many black communities were making the treatment of illegitimacy part of their larger agenda for self-determination. For example, in 1960 a black physician in Greenville, North Carolina, Andrew Best, formed an organization he called the North Carolina Joint Council on Health and Citizenship, which sponsored training for teachers in twenty-nine counties who were engaged in illegitimacy prevention in their schools.[162] In Richmond, Virginia, the black community held a series of meetings in 1962 to develop strategies for combating white attacks on welfare grants to black unwed mothers and their children.[163] Interest in desegregating maternity homes, adapting maternity homes to the needs of black girls and women, and even scattered interest in building new maternity homes for blacks only was high in a number of black communities.[164] These efforts reflected the black community's determination to recognize the needs of individual unwed mothers. In this sense, the black community shared the assessment of white professionals that the maternity home was the epitome of what could be offered to individual unwed mothers. The efforts reflected, as well, the black community's determination that it could initiate programs, build facilities, and guide policy for its own unwed mothers.

Culture and Biology Merge Again

Ironically, at the same time that black unwed mothers were, for the first time, gaining access to maternity homes and to the treatment rooms of social workers for the neuroses some caseworkers believed caused their illegitimate pregnancies, white theorists, policy makers, and practitioners were beginning to rethink their approach to the etiology of unwed pregnancy. Just as integrationists like Annie Lee Davis were having some success in winning attention to individual cases and in gaining treatment for some black girls that resembled what was offered to whites, the individualistic, psychiatric perspective on single pregnancy was dissipating.[165] The dissipation reflected a number of aspects of contemporary culture and politics in the United States. These included first, the difficulty of labeling such an increasingly vast number of young, white women as psychiatrically disturbed, without reference to the culture or the environment that shaped their behavior. In addition, by the early 1960s, social theorists were becoming less reluctant to analyze the conflict and the complex problems of society in the United States.[166] In relation to analyzing the still-rising incidence of single pregnancy, Clark Vincent called this a shift to a belief in "society as patient."[167] Moreover, at the same time that some integrationists were insisting on attention to individuals, the civil rights movement was exposing the structural, systematic oppression of blacks as a group. One of the outcomes of these competing currents, visible at academic and policy levels in the beginning of the 1960s, was a recasting of the central question regarding the source and the meaning of Negro illegitimacy. Replacing the distinction between the individualistic etiology of white single pregnancy and the cultural etiology of black was an interest in whether high rates of illegitimate pregnancy was a function of race or class. Was the black girl pregnant because she was Negro or because she was poor?[168]

Elizabeth Herzog, an anthropologist and an influential Children's Bureau employee whose work involved research in the area of unwed mothers, wrote to a colleague in 1960, expressing the shift in the terms of the debate:

> There is a tendency, I think, to overrate the importance of ethnic differences and underrate the importance of the socio-economic ones which, in our society, have strong ethnic correlations. It is not that I think the ethnic factors are unimportant, but that to overplay them results in an oversimplification that fosters distortion . . . [and] feeds prejudices. It seems to me that if we ascribe differences solely to ethnic factors, we fail to give due recognition to the extent to which cultural differences in our society are economically as well as ethnically determined.[169]

The distinction Herzog and others was making at this time was sound; however, as with the uses made of Frazier's attempts to explicate "difference" more than twenty years earlier, the newer distinction between the poor and the not-poor was soon used in ways that were not always in the interests of black unwed mothers. The focus on poverty, a culture of poverty—at first, perhaps, in distinction to a culture of race—provided an integrated, inclusive, and astonishingly self-referential explanation and description of the folkways of the poor.[170] Once again, the larger, environmental context was essentially irrelevant. The way the theory of poverty was used, if not always according to the intentions of its authors, accounted for all aspects of the life of the poor, including "biological anarchy." Various forms of degeneracy, high rates of illegitimacy chief among them, were described as endemic to communities in the grip of the culture of poverty. Thus, again in the early 1960s, high rates of illegitimacy were perceived by some as biologically characteristic of a people.[171] Once again, a difference between the inherent levels of sexuality, this time between the poor and the not-poor, was used to explain and justify the disadvantaged condition of a segment of society.

The determination, expressed by Herzog and others, to keep race and class separate in understanding such phenomena as black illegitimacy did not hold. It was not long before class or, more accurately, the "disadvantaged" or the "poor" came to stand for minorities, most often for blacks, in social analyses. This was, of course, a recapitulation of the way "culture" came to stand for "race" in the 1940s and 1950s. Finally, the "biological" essence the culture of poverty ascribed to blacks sanctioned the theory's dismissal of bona fide cultural dimensions in the lives of the poor, the black, its nomenclature notwithstanding. Herzog, whose chief contribution was to the literature of unwed mothers, claimed repeatedly that "Reference to culture has become a 'neo-stereotype' that blurs rather than sharpens the picture."[172] Yet she herself doubted the possibility of "culture" in the black ghetto in 1963. She implied simultaneously that culture and race were inextricable and that slum culture did not generate the sorts of institutions that could refine the unmediated, biological impulse to copulate and breed.

> More substantial [than the also absent, distinctive artifacts and technology] is the lack of the basic core that gives to a culture its identity as a culture: the sense that its members have of belonging to a cultural entity with its institutions, patterns and shared beliefs; a sense of that entity as good—a sense of allegiance as well as identity. . . . This positive aspect of culture, the sense of belonging, with its corollary elements of sharing and of participating, seems to be absent from the so-called culture of poverty.[173]

With the rise of culture of poverty theory, in the context of the early 1960s, a new distinction between black and white single pregnancy became possible, although the new echoed the old. Rising rates of white, premarital pregnancy reflected the fact that many unmarried white girls and women were choosing to engage in unsanctioned sexual affairs because of the greater availability of birth control, because of some apparent relaxation of standards of female chastity, or for others reasons of their own. This was called the sexual revolution. Black girls, on the other hand, were simply, as always, doing what came naturally.[174]

The Limits of Biological Determinism

A practical and theoretical weakness of culture of poverty theory, as it applied to black single pregnancy, was that it couldn't account for the strategies, calculations, and feelings of black girls and women in relation to marriage and children. It couldn't account for their good reasons for devising separate calculations to govern decisions about men and babies, when necessary. Culture of poverty theory could only account for the "bad" reasons, since its purpose as an intellectual construct, as a policy guide, and as a description was to account for the persistence of poverty (and to justify racism) in the otherwise affluent society of the United States.

Studies of black unmarried mothers conducted during the period covered here revealed again and again that many black girls and women were responding to their nonmarital pregnancies from an elaborated, shared, and distinct value system. The studies revealed this even when their authors were uncertain about how to mesh evidence of such a value system with culture of poverty theory which suggested that these females behaved normlessly.[175] Relative to the meaning of marriage, black unwed mothers (and their mothers) often expressed attitudes quite clearly distinct from their white counterparts. For example, a group of women in Washington, D.C., was asked how they would feel if their daughters became pregnant out of wedlock. "The answer was unanimous: They would feel terrible . . . but would not urge the prospective parents to marry unless they really loved each other. 'An unhappy marriage,' they argued, 'is worse than no marriage at all.' "[176] One woman explained how she sorted out her options: "I had a child before I was married. I wouldn't marry his father. I told him I wouldn't have him. I didn't love him. I stayed with my mother."[177] Another mother in Washington schooled her fifteen-year-old daughter, "It's better to be an unwed mother than an unhappy bride. You'll never be able to point your finger at me and say, 'If it hadn't been for her.' "[178] And still another sized up the influence one set of white norms was having on cultural responses to illegitimate pregnancy: "Don't holler marriage so quick! I think that's the biggest mistake society is making."[179] In contrast, among whites at this time, the high bridal pregnancy rate and the subsequent divorce rate among those premaritally pregnant suggested that a large percent of whites believed that an expedient marriage was better than no marriage at all.[180] The author of a Philadelphia study of black unwed mothers remarked, "I got the impression that to be known as 'Mrs.' was of paramount importance only to a few women."[181] This impression suggests that for the subjects of this study, and maybe others, female legitimacy was obtainable in the black community without marriage, even for unwed mothers. Indeed, the women in Philadelphia reported that they were not known at their children's schools as unmarried mothers. The researcher conjectured, "This may tie in with the attitude they have expressed toward their children: that they are 'just as good as married women.' Perhaps we could say that as mothers they feel legitimate."[182]

Possible explanations for this cultural difference, explanations rooted in male unemployment—and the infamous "pathology" of the black family—were offered by the Moynihan Report and by others.[183] Studies of black unmarried mothers themselves confirmed that many perceived marriage as an economic burden on the women rather than as a source of financial support.[184] Well over three-quarters of the unwed mothers in one study identified themselves as the best or their "first choice" as financial supporter of their child. Only about 7 percent identified the child's father as the first choice.[185]

In American society, where black men were often unable to support their own children, 93 percent of the black unwed mothers in a major North Carolina study agreed with the second part of this question put to them by interview: "Do you think that almost all men turn out to be good husbands . . . or do you think that a girl must pick her husband carefully because most men turn out to be no good as husbands?"[186] An unwed mother in Cincinnati "spoke for many," telling interviewers, "If your old man has been like my old man you wouldn't think not having one around was any loss."[187] These pragmatic assessments concerning the problems of associating with boys and men did not mean that black girls and women thought their only recourse was to accept childlessness or celibacy. Like white girls and women, blacks developed strategies and attitudes to protect themselves and to compensate for what males could not or would not offer them. As Herzog observed in 1963,

> If most men are beasts and most women are exploited by them, then a smart woman does not want marriage unless she can find that rare paragon, a really good husband. . . . If she bears a child out of wedlock, that is a social misfortune. But illegitimate children do not necessarily preclude a good marriage, and a lack of marriage does not necessarily preclude sex.[188]

An enduring attitude among white professionals in this era was that unwed mothers, black and white, had had short, relatively meaningless relationships with the "putative father." The attitude was typically expressed in this way: "It is common knowledge that frequently the alleged father has had little real meaning to the mother."[189] Part of the indictment that accrued against the girl or woman for having participated, sexually, in this alleged meaningless relationship was that she had become a mother without having demonstrated that she was "capable of establishing a mature love relationship."[190] This rendered her womanhood and her motherhood assailable, even deniable, if necessary.

Contradicting this prevailing attitude among professionals, however, was some convincing evidence that some black unwed mothers had quite meaningful relationships with the fathers of their babies, even despite the odds and despite the fact—confusing for white professionals—that the relationships often did not lead to marriage. Studies of black unmarried mothers in Cook County, Illinois and Marion County, Indiana,

> reveal[ed] that for the majority of mothers of illegitimate children, the relationship with the putative father had not been a casual or a passing one. Of 616 families interviewed in the Greenleigh [Cook County] study, 50% of the unmarried mothers had "dated" the father for more than a year and an additional 10% for three months or more. For one-third of the cases marriage was out of the question because one partner was married—often the woman herself whose husband had deserted.[191]

It may have been difficult to mesh findings such as these with the popular forms of culture of poverty theory because they implied that rational, though noneconomic, calculations on the part of unwed mothers, as well as emotional ties, shaped their behavior.

In addition, a New York study in the early 1960s provided evidence that black unwed mothers were, as a group, "not economically dependent." Specifically, the authors reported, "Proportionately more of the unwed mothers—64 percent—received at least *some* help from the putative father than . . . from any other source except their own families. At the time of the eighteen-month follow-up, the putative father was the *main* source of support for 25 percent and for 15 percent he was the *sole* source of support."[192] Besides undermining theories about the economic intentions of black women who bore out-of-wedlock children to gain ADC benefits and about "meaningless relationships," these findings suggested levels of responsible behavior on the part of the mother, the father, and the family that culture of poverty theory could not incorporate. They suggested, as well, a complexity of relationship between black unmarried parents which raised the strong possibility that it was more than biological determinism creating all those out-of-wedlock black babies.

Evidence gathered over time indicated that "marriage" was a variable notion, considered by some women as a less-than-blessed institution. Still, white commentators could not generally let go of the idea that the absence of marriage for any woman, and especially for an unwed mother who kept her child, was not just a source of financial and logistical difficulty, but a source of guilt and degradation. A famous study of blacks in Chicago published after the war quoted one unmarried mother in whose expression of frustration with the interviewer, the authors could only detect guilt. She "shouted at the interviewer," "I ain't never had no husband. Haven't you heard of women having babies without a husband? Maybe I didn't want to get married."[193]

As with black women's strategies concerning men, sex, and marriage, white commentators often perceived their strategies regarding maternity as devoid of norms or values. A rare, white social worker in the early 1960s addressed her colleagues, "We cannot assume that [black unwed mothers] view themselves as we view them, that they long to live as we live, that because they do not have our values, therefore they have no values."[194] In fact, this researcher found that for her subjects "good citizenship and social usefulness [were] compatible with begetting and rearing illegitimate children." She defined her own task as describing the "values in family life of these unwed mothers which have not been sufficiently recognized, even by social workers, and which warrant appreciation."[195]

A number of prevalent, readily identifiable attitudes of black unmarried mothers toward maternity distinguished this group from whites. For the most part, these attitudes were cited as proof of the casualness with which black women viewed their maternity and as proof of their deficient quotient of motherliness. For example, in describing the "unhealthy" residential arrangement consisting of mother-and-child that was characteristic of some black unwed mothers, Ellery Reed and Ruth Latimer observed, "This matriarchal setting obviously denies the child the important influence in his life; this is sometimes aggravated by the mother's temporary alliances with men other than the baby's father. . . . It is aggravated further by the unwed mother's attitude toward men in general."[196] In contrast, a study of black unwed mothers in Washington, D.C., found a determination among its subjects "to regard motherhood as a goal in itself, signifying maturity and the fulfillment of the function of a woman, whereas marriage is not so valued."[197] Another study that explicitly contrasted the attitudes toward maternity of black and white unwed mothers found that "Negro girls [feel] that having a baby made a girl an adult; white middle-class girls strongly disagreed." When asked whether a single mother could do just as well raising her baby as a married mother could, the blacks generally said yes, the whites no.[198] Attitudes such as these reflected the black unwed mother's assessment of the opportunities and constraints available to her. They also violated white norms associated with maternity, femininity, and gender relations.

Regarding the disposition of the illegitimate baby, white policy makers and service providers occupied a murky terrain as they attempted to guide, or more often, responded to the decisions of black unwed mothers. After World War II, white culture mandated that a good woman gave up her bastard child. The caveat to this maxim was that blacks kept their out-of-wedlock babies. They were, therefore, excluded from the universe of "good women." A white unwed mother was redeemed from her state of sinfulness by relinquishment; however, a black unwed mother was not redeemed by keeping the child with her. Even the parallelism that might have rendered the difference more comprehensible was excluded by white analysis. On the one hand, the decision of the black mother to keep her child could not be understood *in the terms* of white culture. It was an alien and mystified decision for which white professionals and politicians could offer no satisfactory explanation and no effective alternative, either punitive or ameliorative.

On the other hand, in part because black illegitimacy was expensive—demographically, economically, and politically—service providers and politicians constructed and drew on an alternative description of the black unwed mother. It was a description that *could* make her behavior comprehensible in the terms of white culture. According to white culture, having a baby out of wedlock was deviant; black girls and women had babies out-of-wedlock; therefore black girls and women were, by definition, deviant. Similarly, a mother who kept her out-of-wedlock baby was mentally unstable; black girls and women kept their illegitimate babies; therefore they were unstable. From this perspective, white culture could explain the behavior of blacks satisfactorily. By applying the "universal truths" that governed white childbearing and maternity, black girls and women could be found severely wanting.

Neither of these attempts to illuminate the behavior of black girls and women—and it was behavior rather than decision making at issue—could account for the prevailing black belief that "it is immoral to place a baby in adoption, to throw away your own flesh and blood."[199] Moreover, if a black unmarried mother were unable to keep her child, she might give it up to someone she knew, a friend or a relative, so that she herself might retain some control or some involvement in the child's life. This was an additional practice in the black community that challenged the terms of white culture, terms which mandated that adoptive parents remain strangers to the biological mother.[200] These strategies concerning disposition also posed a challenge to culture of poverty theory, as it was popularly presented, in which motherhood was simply incidental to sexuality.

Perhaps most challenging to culture of poverty theory were expressions by unmarried black mothers of their own desires and intentions for themselves and their babies. Sauber and Rubinstein, who interviewed approximately 220 black unmarried mothers in New York City in the early 1960s, found that above all, these girls and women "yearned to be considered with dignity and personal worth"; they "longed for friendship" and wanted "an independent life."[201] While many women had small hopes of achieving these goals, black unwed mothers often had very high hopes for their children, who they wanted to nurture, somehow, out of poverty and dependency.[202] Despite descriptions to the contrary, often these girls and women were not caught by the culture of poverty; they were caught simply by poverty. Sauber and Rubinstein reported that black unwed mother, far from being narrowly culture-bound, had numerous innovative ideas and suggestions to ameliorate their own situations. For example, one said,

I think there should be a place where we could talk and cope with the new experience of having a baby—like setting up a center—like Alcoholics Anonymous—a place where you all go and have the same problems and you talk about it. Then you find out you have something in common and it's not that bad. Some girls are not as strong as others.[203]

In the early 1960s when this woman spoke, many white unwed mothers participated in a group culture to these ends in maternity homes and therapy groups across the states. But in the early 1960s, politicians and public agencies were not often ready to consider the needs or the capacities of black girls and women in this light. The culture of poverty theory, poverty itself, racism, and sexism cast black unwed mothers as simply biologically motivated and mired in the negative behaviors of their people.

Conclusion

Thus, the strategies, calculations, and feelings of black unwed mothers were deemed unimportant or symptomatic of their "culture." Helen Perlman described the white public's attitude toward these girls and women at the time:

The mass of unmarried mothers and their children has been the group least liked, least sympathized with, least identified with by the taxpayers, the legislator, and the learned professions. Social workers have perhaps unconsciously shared this general distaste or have wanted, again unconsciously, to keep their skirts clean of what, as a social problem, has an illegitimate status. Whatever the reason, social work today has less knowledge and less practiced competence with the non-white unmarried mother and her child than with any problem group of comparable size and significance.[204]

Culture of poverty theory aimed to fill in this lack of knowledge of black unwed mothers and of the black community in general. In the context of the postwar era, and particularly in the late 1950s and early 1960s as the civil rights movement gathered momentum, culture of poverty theory appealed because it suggested that black unwed mothers achieved or deserved their fate. As a consequence, it suggested, American culture was absolved of any responsibility for both black illegitimacy and the problems it caused black girls and women and the community in general.

Jewell Handy Gresham has recently written in this vein about the appeal of the Moynihan Report in the 1960s, a document that exemplifies the policy uses of culture of poverty theory in that era:

Whether Moynihan knew his history or not, his report served the time-tested purpose: whenever the system is in crisis (or shows signs of becoming transformed); whenever blacks get restless (or show strength); whenever whites in significant numbers show signs of coming together with blacks to confront their mutual problems (or enemies), the trick is to shift the focus from the real struggle for political and economic empowerment and—in Moynihan's innovative twist—to the "deterioration" of the black family (previously defined as non-existent!).[205]

In regard to black illegitimacy in particular, culture of poverty theory condemned unmarried girls and women for their failure to remain chaste or at least avoid pregnancy. For some white policy makers, taxpayers, and service providers in this era, biological determinism, with both its racist and sexist dimensions, served distinct political purposes. For one thing, as Lynda Birke argues, deterministic theories justify "biological medical interventions aimed at changing underlying biology if that is considered to be at fault."[206] For another, biological imperatives are assumed to have primacy over cultural imperatives or environmental conditions. Thus the invocation of biology, even in the context of a theory of culture, becomes a powerful and primary explanation for, in this case, relatively high rates of black illegitimacy. The biological imperative was a powerful justification, as well, for, in this case, white (rational) control over the Negro (irrational) community.

Between 1945 and 1965, in several different ways, proponents of biological determinism managed to fully subordinate cultural arguments about the meaning of black sexuality and illegitimacy. This process has not, of course, ended. Gresham quotes a speech Ronald Reagan gave as president to the International Association of Police in New Orleans which drew "applause and some whoops of approval." In the speech Reagan debunked "social thinkers of the 1950s and 1960s" who blamed antisocial behavior on "disadvantaged childhoods and poverty-stricken neighborhoods" and dismissed those who believed government-funded programs could help. Reagan argued that there is only one way to diminish antisocial behavior in the United States, presumably including high rates of black illegitimacy: "Only our deep moral values and strong institutions can hold back that jungle and restrain the darker impulses of human nature."[207]

Into and throughout the 1980s, high rates of black illegitimacy continued to be construed by some as the fruits of one such darker impulse. Ken Auletta, author of *The Underclass*, commented in the mid-1980s that in response to black illegitimacy rates, some policy makers were considering "drastic solutions like involuntary sterilization and castration." He said, "These proposals are still in the whispering stages . . . but as this problem continues to grow, apparently out of control, those whispers are getting louder."[208]

The persistence of biological explanations for black illegitimacy rates explains, in part, why it has been so easy to decry the presence of unmarried black mothers in our culture and so difficult to provide resources to meet their needs. Two leading academic analysts of black illegitimacy underscored the consequences of thinking in these terms when they determined in 1970 that "unprotected premarital intercourse involves much greater social risks for the white woman [than for the black]."[209] These analysts were defining "social risks" relative to illegitimate pregnancy in terms supplied by white culture: the risks of social ostracism and loss of reputation. Yet how does one compare the loss of status for a white unwed mother with the loss of education (much more prevalent and enforced in this era for blacks than whites),[210] the increased risk of lifelong poverty, and the risk of legal threats and retribution that black unwed mothers faced between 1945 and 1965, their emotionally supportive communities notwithstanding. One compares these losses only at the risk of fueling divisions between groups of women, and between races, and at the risk of misunderstanding the nature and extent of social cost levied against girls and women whose reproductive capacity was snagged on the hooks of sexism and racism.

Chapter Three

The Girl Nobody Loved:
Psychological Explanations for White Single Pregnancy

Today, public discourse about pregnancy often centers on the biological or religious meaning of conception. When does life begin? When is the fetus viable? In the years between World War II and *Roe v. Wade*, however, public discourse about pregnancy—especially single pregnancy was most strongly characterized by its racial distinctions.[1] Single pregnant women of whatever race shared a debased social status, but the cause of black single pregnancy was portrayed as the strength of black women's biological, sexual urges and their *absence of psyche*; white pregnancy (both single and marital) was discussed mainly in psychoanalytic terms. Psychiatrists argued that a real woman lived to fulfill her destiny as wife and childbearer. When they considered white women who were unhappily pregnant, including white unwed mothers, they asked what disorder or disease accounted for behavior that denied this destiny?

The racial distinction between the motivations, the sexuality, and the offspring of black and white unmarried mothers determined the levels and kinds of responsibility society assumed for these two groups of unmarried mothers and their babies. This chapter focuses on the adaptations of psychoanalytic theory that gained currency in the postwar era as explanations for white unwed pregnancy and explores how these adaptations shaped treatment strategies for white, broadly middle-class unwed mothers.[2] Both the psychological theories and social policies they supported treated individuals in ways that shored up the postwar family agenda: they absolved the male sexual partner of responsibility; rendered white illegitimate babies adoptable by removing any inheritable "taint"; made white unwed mothers marriageable despite the episode of illegitimate pregnancy; punished nonmarital female sexuality; and generally reinforced the containment of females in roles of domestic subordination. The psychological explanations did provide a form

86

of social protection for many white girls and women. But these "diagnoses" were applied indiscriminately and coercively to all white unwed mothers, defining them, both as a group and individually, mentally ill.

Unwed Pregnancy As Mental Illness

Before World War II, single pregnancy in this century in the United States was often explained as the product of mental defects and bad morals bred in a squalid environment. This Progressive Era explanation suggested that negative environmental conditions produced a biological flaw—mental deficiency, for example—which, in turn, created a propensity to moral weakness.[3] In response, communities and institutions treated illicit pregnancy and maternity as proof of degeneracy; institutions developed their rehabilitative efforts accordingly. The girl or woman who had become pregnant without a husband was "ruined." The best that the mostly evangelical institutions sheltering unwed mothers could do for them was to preserve their anonymity, train them for domestic service and illicit motherhood, and through religious teaching, sternly fortify them for life as marginal women.[4]

In the 1940s, psychiatrists began to offer an alternate, ostensibly more compassionate response: the woman is ill. While maintaining the white unwed mother as helpless and vulnerable, they insisted she must be understood, and helped. Their professional intentions were to diagnose, to treat, and to cure her. But the language and the content of the diagnoses, and the course of treatment suggest a moral and political agenda that many psychiatrists, consciously or not, supported and spoke for.

In postwar America, mental illness was considered a universal condition for white unwed mothers, by definition. In 1965, two Harvard University psychiatrists wrote, "Every unmarried mother is to some degree a psychiatric problem . . . the victim of mild, moderate or severe emotional or mental disturbance."[5] Psychiatrists and social workers insisted that their first commitment was to reform the treatment of these unwed mothers by assessing each one as an individual, without reference to stereotypes or generalizations. Implicit in their models, however, was an equally strong commitment to the generalization of psychiatric causality. Jane Wrieden, a leading Salvation Army social worker, administrator, and writer, asserted in 1955 that an unmarried mother is simply "a person with all the dignity of human personality who comes to our attention because she is pregnant out-of-wedlock." She went on, "I do not mean a category or a statistic or a social or psychological phenomenon, or a resource for adoptable babies. I mean a PERSON." Yet her next thought reflects the compelling currency of psychiatric explanations: "She is a person whose psychology is understood in terms of her early childhood relationships carried over to the present, especially the mother/daughter relationships. Her pregnancy is often a purposive acting out of her inner drives."[6] Indeed, a central, underlying certainty in the thinking of psychiatrists and other mental health professionals was that since society reserved deeply punitive responses for unwed mothers, a single girl who flew in the face of certain and severe censure and became pregnant had to be sick. She had, in fact, to be pregnant on purpose.[7] Only a truly sick person could deny reality so radically.

One prominent psychiatrist found in his study of fifty-four unwed mothers that he could label fully one-third of them schizophrenic.[8] The author of a Ph.D. dissertation at New York University in the late 1950s wrote, "My study demonstrated that unmarried mothers behaviorally are overtly dominant, aggressive, narcissistic and bitterly hostile, but are covertly passive, inadequate, and masochistic. The experimental group was found—at both levels of behavior . . . to resemble a hospitalized psychotic control group."[9] Such explanations for a single woman's pregnancy could be profoundly dehumanizing. Psychiatrist Harry Gianakon, in an often-cited article, "Ego Factors in the Separation of Mother and Child," wrote, "The unwed mother has been stripped of the greatest human gift—rational thought—in finding effective solutions for her needs by the very fact that those needs have been exerting their influence in unconscious, irrational, and reality-alien ways."[10]

The psychiatric perspective was remarkably effective because it accomplished so much at once. It defined the unwed mother as helpless and needy, an important first step for transgressing females. Psychiatric diagnoses referred to a condition brought on by forces in the girl's past and beyond her control, usually some form of family dysfunction that produced, inexorably, her out-of-wedlock pregnancy. So, a priori, the single pregnant woman was not responsible; she had been overtaken by something larger than herself—not a man, but a pathology. She could be subjected to an authoritarian process that severely modified her right to self-definition and transformed her into a child, morally, and a patient, psychologically. She had a illness to live up to, and to recover from.

The psychiatric perspective did not remain an abstract, theoretical construct. It was attractive, meaningful, and useful to hundreds of professionals who wrote or adopted public policies and to thousands of service providers in the 1940s and 1950s and 1960s. It inspired psychological studies and structured social work theory and practice. The individual psychiatrists and psychologists who promulgated theories explaining the behavior of unwed mothers were a mixed but influential lot. They held faculty appointments at major universities, including Harvard, the University of Washington, and Adelphi University, and had affiliations at large teaching and general hospitals. Their articles about the psychology of unwed mothers appeared in such respected journals as the *International Journal of Psychiatry*, the *American Journal of Psychiatry*, and the *Journal of Orthopsychiatry*. There is no public evidence that colleagues objected to their formulations or found them out of concert with mainstream psychiatric theory and practice.

Psychiatric explanations of single pregnancy inspired the work of most leading social work administrators and practitioners in the field, throughout the 1950s and beyond. These professionals were in close touch with local, state, and federal agencies responsible for making policy decisions and delivering services to single pregnant women. If you were white, single, and pregnant (and without the opportunity, the money, the know-how, the guts, or the ethical convictions to get an illegal abortion, or to marry), there was a good chance you labored to redeem yourself from the stigma of mental illness.

Psychology Observes the Unwed Mother

Psychologists, psychiatrists, and social workers found "observable" behavior to support the diagnosis of mental illness. They remarked frequently that unmarried mothers got pregnant easily, had few miscarriages, little nausea, no food fads, no moods, and no delivery complications, and exhibited an unusual degree of contentment.[11] These characteristics contrasted with the experiences of married women, who struggled into, through, and out of pregnancy, rewarded by offspring righteously and rightfully theirs in the end, an interesting application of the "no pain, no gain" proposition. Throughout the 1950s, in making these observations, the professionals failed to consider that the pregnant women they had access to had been admitted to maternity homes well after their first trimester, the period when, for example, most miscarriages and nausea occur. These "easy pregnancies" were considered proof that the girl had "gotten herself pregnant" on purpose. The contentment indicated that the pregnancy resolved a girl's conflicts, even while, on the other hand, it brought ostracism and censure.

Some mental health theorists took the fact that the girl hadn't prevented or terminated her pregnancy as conclusive proof of psychological disturbance. Leontine Young, the leading social work theorist in the area of unwed mothers, insisted, "We know that the pregnancy is purposive because the girl doesn't consider contraception and doesn't want an abortion."[12] Helene Deutsch assessed one of her cases this way: "The fact that she expected the man to take full responsibility for contraception shows that here her infantile narcissism won the upper hand over her proud self-reliance."[13] Stephen Fleck, a psychologist who studied one hundred unwed mothers at the Florence Crittenton Home in Seattle in the late 1950s, claimed of his sample, typically, "She wants to be pregnant." He based this judgment on the fact that national statistics suggested that so many abortions occurred that if a girl didn't get one, she was deliberately choosing pregnancy.[14] None of these writers, or others, referred to the legal obstacles in the way of both contraception and abortion. Displaying surprising willingness to expect criminality in girls and women, they were willing, as well, to deepen their blame of the victim by using her law-abiding behavior to justify the diagnosis of mental illness.

Perhaps the most bizarre justification for the diagnosis was offered in 1957 by Edmund Pollock, who, citing the work of a psychiatrist, agreed with the proposition that unwed pregnancy was an unconsciously planned act precipitated by an event that made the girl or woman feel unlovable. She then exercised conscious control over her ovulation and timed intercourse to ensure pregnancy.[15] This proof, going as it does far beyond observable behavior, suggests the single, pregnant woman as witch.

Psychiatrists, psychologists, and social workers saw a number of presenting symptoms of mental illness when they interviewed these girls and women, most of whom were incarcerated in maternity homes at the time of their individual diagnoses, in a state of ostracism and shame that could indeed have contributed to—or, just as likely, created—mental disturbance. Personality and character disorders discovered by the professionals included masochism, sadomasochism, severe immaturity, psychopathic tendencies, homosexual tendencies, schizophrenia,[16] delinquency, and chaotic personality structure.[17] Whether the experts understood these disorders as the causes or the wages of unwed motherhood, the implication was clear. Females who violated gender-determined sexual norms were routinely designated as formally ill. One observer found so much frigidity that it was not even worth cataloging.[18] Several different studies noted that the worst off among single pregnant females were the high achievers, the most intelligent, the ones who refused to marry the "putative father," and those most richly endowed with emotional capacities.[19] One can easily believe these findings, without feeling any relief for other unwed mothers.

Why Did Disturbed Girls Get Pregnant?

Psychiatrists were most interested in considering why these girls and women had engaged in proscribed sexuality and become pregnant. The professionals asked, first, what was so terribly wrong with their lives? And second, how did pregnancy address and even solve the problems they faced? The answers were complicated and disturbing. Girls and women were driven into sex and pregnancy, professionals determined, as a result of both gender dysfunctions and family dysfunctions.[20]

A number of the theorists located the etiology of single pregnancy in the confusion of sexual identity.[21] Pollock, in his study of unmarried pregnant girls, found that they "perceived themselves consciously to be friendly-conventional as they viewed their mothers to be, but behaved narcissistically and aggressively like their fathers."[22] This finding offers rich insights about gender roles and family relations at midcentury but suggests an unproven causality. Another investigator, who identified "marked rebelliousness" as a governing attitude of his subjects, found "a lot of latent homosexuality . . . coupled with contempt for men" as a pervasive cause of single pregnancy.[23] A study of one hundred Jewish unwed mothers found the majority of the subjects to be conflicted about their masculine and feminine drives.[24] Jane Judge, in 1951, cited the case of Miss Grey, an unwed pregnant girl who was "boyish in appearance and seemed to have adopted behavior which was symbolic of her unconscious conflicts. In all her activities—work, recreation, sports,—she was aggressive, almost as if she denied her femininity by redirecting her sexual energy. . . . Her pregnancy seemed to represent a breaking through of unconscious wishes, hostility and striking out at her family."[25] Mental health theorists and practitioners often looked for evidence that girls and women assumed male prerogatives, sexually, aesthetically, and otherwise. Such searches reflected a deep concern about the postwar capacities of adult males to sustain their traditional role of domination in the family and in the culture at large.

Family dysfunction was found to be a central cause in nearly all cases of white unwed motherhood. According to the experts, the difference between girls who got pregnant and girls who didn't was that the former had parents who did not offer appropriate models of sex roles or gender characteristics.[26] Mothers were assigned the lion's share of the blame for driving their daughters toward sex and pregnancy. Fathers, though, came in for their portion as well, both directly, because they did not fulfill their paternal role correctly, and indirectly, because they were unwilling or unable to curb and correct their wives. Dr. Cattell found a disproportionate number of passive fathers and women "who wore the pants of the family."[27] A 1958 study of residents in the Los Angeles Florence Crittenton Home found "dramatic evidence of severe emotional deprivation. Absent relationships with fathers appeared as a rather routine finding. In the Draw-A-Person Test almost all depicted the male parent as faceless with detached feet."[28]

One study, published in 1949, asserted that personality, economic, and social-cultural factors contributing to illegitimate pregnancy all paled as explanations, compared with the psychological condition of the parents. Out of thirty families studied, twenty-three revealed one parent or both who suffered from neuroses, psychoses, psychopathic tendencies, or feeblemindedness. Specific examples of parental disorders included five overly passive fathers, six mothers who exhibited excessive narcissism, four who were excessively aggressive, and four who were sadomasochistic. All were found to reject their daughters.[29]

The most typical patterns appeared to be a weak father and a hypochondriacal and controlling mother, or a strong but neglectful father and a frustrated mother. Within even such a broad range of possible parental temperaments, the mother was consistently described as dissatisfied and, by implication, not appropriately deferential to her husband. In response to these family pathologies, the unmarried pregnant girl constructed "a neurotic base

. . . a symptom of an unresolved love-hate parental relationship, originating in early childhood."[30]

The question of the effect on the daughter of the poor quality of the family's emotional life was given consistent, although confusing attention. Babette Block, a prominent social work practitioner in Chicago, on whom the United States Children's Bureau relied for both theoretical explanations and model programs, labeled the unmarried mother "the girl who has never been loved."[31] Conversely, another social worker explained to Ursula Gallagher, the USCB's consultant on services for unmarried mothers in the late 1950s, that "girls who have been loved are prone to get into trouble. They can't distinguish between mature love and the sex act." In addition, she said, these girls use their pregnancy to "take the spotlight."[32] Psychoanalytic theory and its application by practitioners could incorporate any girl and any family configuration that produced undesirable behavior. During the postwar period, concern was intense among many professionals about the preservation of traditional gender roles and power relations within the family. A daughter's out-of-wedlock pregnancy became evidence that these dimensions of family life had gone awry. Often such a family event was ascribed to a wife's "misplaced sexuality," that is, her reputed unwillingness to be subdued within the family.[33]

Whatever the specific content of family pathology, the pregnancies of these daughters, it was alleged, revealed a "compulsive necessity to act out infantile fantasy," usually in order to strike back at their mothers.[34] One psychiatrist cited the case of Ruby, a seventeen-year-old only child, to demonstrate how illegitimate pregnancy could be purposive. "She was struggling intensely to escape from her mother's over-protective dominance and almost consciously chose to become pregnant in order to achieve this."[35] Leontine Young identified the syndrome of the "mother-ridden daughter," who was much worse off than the "father-ridden" girl. For example, the former much more frequently than the latter made the "putative father" into a "biological accessory," the ultimate gender-role violation.[36] In line with prevailing psychiatric attitudes about the wages of insufficiently deferential wives, the daughters of these women, it could be predicted, would use males for their own distorted purposes.

Social workers, drawing on psychiatric and psychological theories about frustrated, controlling mothers and linking these women to the postwar outbreak of single pregnancy, defined a compensatory role for themselves. Jane Goldsmith's formula was simply, "where a mother fails, the caseworker can prevail."[37] Babette Block and others bestowed surrogate maternity on the social worker, who, she wrote, "should be the guiding mother." The caseworker's focus should be on "supplying the deficiencies in the client's own mother."[38] Even more explicit was Frances Scherz: The caseworker should "become a parent substitute, a substitute mother, an amended, loving mother." It is the caseworker's central task, she argued, to demonstrate to unloved, pregnant daughters that mothers can be loving.[39] In the face of family—and particularly maternal—pathology, the professionals aimed to construct a functional surrogate family for the unwed mother. Social workers could supply the mother element, supported by the shadowy presence and expertise of the psychiatrist father.[40]

The labeling and ostracism suffered by unwed mothers functioned in a number of ways, including as warning to other girls considering sexual relations. In the same way, the mothers of unwed mothers suffered labeling that cautioned all mothers of America, often in women's magazines such as the *Ladies' Home Journal*, to redouble their commitment to the virtuous and vigilant maternal round.[41] Aggression, frustration, hypochondria, and the other chief alleged disabilities of the postwar mother were not simply unpleasant for father and kids to live with, they were dangerous.[42] The disproportionate focus on "bad mothers" as the source of pregnant daughters worked to deflect consideration of the role of good or bad fathers, a fact that undoubtedly contributed to the suffering of both generations of females in the family. Marcel Heiman, a prominent psychiatrist, viewed out-of-wedlock pregnancy as, at once, "a biological act of creativity, of neurotic acting out and of delinquency . . . [that] could be called the doomed-to-failure rebellion of the immature." Heiman linked the girl's mother closely to the rebellion, and asserted, "The pregnant girl and her mother must both be given a decisive 'No!' The girl's mother must be dealt with as if she is a child herself."[43] She could be denounced as a mother and dismissed as a woman.

In postwar America, a child in trouble was not a private sorrow. This child was a public humiliation, evidence of parental, especially maternal, failure in the form, for example, of the latchkey kid heading toward juvenile delinquency or the unwed mother. One unwed mother in a Denver maternity home observed, "[Before my pregnancy] I'd been the living proof that they were good and successful parents. No matter how I tried to make up for my mistake in the future, their life together would always be clouded by a feeling of failure."[44] The public and professional insistence on the centrality of the maternal role to white, middle-class culture rendered mothers extraordinarily vulnerable, since success in the role depended on embracing—all at once—such a high degree of self-denial, self-mortification, and responsibility.

How Was Unwed Pregnancy a Solution?

Having explained the personal and family dynamics that led girls and women into premarital sex and pregnancy, psychiatrists were left with the question why did these problems manifest themselves in pregnancy—how was pregnancy a solution? The range of answers was, again, complicated. Yet few theorists doubted that self-punishment was at the heart of the matter. Heiman suggested that in cases of out-of-wedlock pregnancy, it "appears that the girl is using her body, particularly her reproductive organs as the tool with which to hurt herself."[45] Dr. Viola Bernard viewed sanctions against the self as only part of a complex set of unconscious needs that illegitimate pregnancy satisfied. These needs included "regressive dependence, narcissism, prestige, defiance and self punishment."[46]

Single pregnant women and girls were theoretically motivated to punish themselves in repetition, in confirmation, and in justification of the punishing rejection they had suffered from their mothers. Heiman suggested, "Out-of-wedlock pregnancy should be looked upon as the means by which a girl tries to prove she is in control. The girl reestablishes feelings of omnipotence by creating the lost love object [her mother] by herself, within herself, through pregnancy."[47]

A number of theorists determined that pregnancy accomplished the troubled female's central purpose of giving a baby to her mother, a woman who, by definition, was dissatisfied with her own life and procreative efforts. The "gift" of the illegitimate child was sometimes offered in bitterness, sometimes in love.[48] On the other hand, the pregnancy also gave the girl a baby "without a father," one belonging, happily, "only to her."[49] Helene Deutsch referred to aggressive, masculine women who exercised their "parthenogenic, puberal fantasy" by asserting, "I have a child born of me alone. I am its mother and father. I do not need or want a man for the begetting of a child."[50] The psychiatrist, speaking here for the unwed mother, illustrates the most socially and psychiatrically unacceptable expression of a female's willingness to eclipse the male.

Treatment

Given what psychiatric and psychological theory posited as the etiology of out-of-wedlock pregnancy, what did the professionals recommend as treatment? Essentially, the cure for the white unmarried mother required three steps: remorse; relinquishment of the infant for adoption; and renewed commitment to fulfilling her destiny as a real woman.

To this end, unwed mothers from the group with whom psychiatrists, psychologists and social workers were familiar—white and broadly middle class—went to maternity homes, no longer considered by the professionals as merely "a place to hide."[51] In the postwar years there were maternity homes in all but four states and at least one in most large cities. Life in the homes was often bleak.[52] By the mid-1950s, a great many of these residences provided social casework services, which many professionals considered the cornerstone of the rehabilitation process for unmarried mothers. The caseworker worked on the front lines of service delivery, bringing psychiatric theory into the lives of white, single, pregnant girls and women all over the country. They typically met the unmarried mother with the idea that her "wish to have a baby without a husband is neither an adult nor a normal desire."[53] The treatment was successfully completed when the client had demonstrated readiness for "a heterosexual adjustment on a realistic basis."[54] Local, state, and federal agencies, and voluntary organizations hired and paid social workers as well as psychological and psychiatric consultants to regularize the lives of these women and girls who had violated important social and sexual norms.

Public statements about "understanding" and "compassion" notwithstanding, most homes took as their mission the rehabilitation of fallen girls and women, even into the 1960s. As long as these females had no control over their reproductive lives, they were subject to the will and the ideology of those who watched over them. And the will, veiled though it often was, called for unwed mothers to acknowledge their shame and guilt, repent, and rededicate themselves to achieving the proper goals of American womanhood. The professionals, and the community that expelled the unwed mother from its boundaries, affirmed that the cure could best be accomplished under conditions of modified incarceration and isolation. It is notable that maternity homes considered it a central part of their mission to groom girls for the second chance. Psychiatric theory "redeemed" girls and women who in the American past would have been social discards. Because it focused attention on the mind instead of on the genitals, or even the womb, unwed mothers could be "cured" and "rehabilitated" instead of "ruined."

For white girls and women illegitimately pregnant in the pre–*Roe* era, the main chance for attaining home and marriage—a normative life—rested on the aspect of their rehabilitation that required relinquishment of the bastard child. More than 80 percent of white unwed mothers in maternity homes came to this decision in the immediate pre–*Roe v. Wade* era, acting in effect as breeders for white, adoptive parents, for whom they supplied up to nearly 90 percent of all nonrelative infants by the mid-1960s.[55] While motherhood as a state of being was apotheosized by the culture at large in the postwar years, only "good" and properly married mothers were inviolate. For the others, "mother" was an honorific that could be bestowed or denied by the judgments of professionals.[56] Unwed mothers were defined by psychological theory as not-mothers. Many internalized this perspective. A single pregnant girl in a New York maternity home explained that her baby would be adopted because "I don't think any unmarried girl has the right to keep her baby. . . . I know I don't have the right."[57] Another girl, one who had just delivered her illegitimate baby in a California maternity home, expressed the way she came to terms with herself as not-a-mother this way:

> When it was all over I felt like laughing and dancing, and yelling from the roof tops for all the world to hear that I am a mother. . . .There is a brand-new little boy and his family is waiting for him. He is no longer a concern of mine. I have served my purpose. So I couldn't be a mother for you, little boy, but you will have a mother. You will be loved very much. You have helped me, but someone else will meet your needs now.[58]

Leontine Young explained the psychological process and value of adoption in terms of the theory that the illegitimate baby was the girl's gift to her rejecting mother: "We need to see that we do not take the baby away from the mother as we did when punishment was the motive, but that, on the contrary, the girl gives the baby to us. In essence, the caseworker becomes the substitute, the good mother that the girl has been seeking, not the punitive mother she fears. And by giving the baby to us, the girl can complete a drama of deep psychological meaning to her."[59] Again, the drama could incorporate all of the motives for having an out-of-wedlock child. The relinquishment, justified by psychological explanations of white single pregnancy, could bring them all to *dénouement*.

In all cases, however, the baby, which many agreed was important to the girl's intentions in becoming willfully pregnant, was posited as simply an object of its mother's psychological disturbance. Young dismissed the unwed mother's relation to her child in no uncertain terms. "The caseworker has to clarify for herself the differences between the feelings of the normal [married] woman for her baby and the fantasy use of the child by the neurotic unmarried mother."[60] Professionals belittled the meaning of the relationship, as they actively engaged in separating the one from the other on an every-case basis.

Relinquishment involved a psychiatric paradox for the unwed mother. According to one condition of the theory, by giving up the child, she was embracing, as a worthy female, the ultimate act of renunciation and self-denial. She thereby earned credentials as a redeemed woman and prospective wife. According to a second condition, by renouncing her child, she was cutting off her experience of motherhood, which had affirmed, irrefutably, that she was a woman. With the act of relinquishment, she became more and less a woman at once. The resolution of the paradox was in the hands of a man willing to marry her. With a husband, she could call on her proven capacities of self-denial in order to reconstruct herself as a legitimately pregnant mother and wife.

Similar paradoxes surrounded the connection between femininity and dependency. A consulting psychiatrist at the family services agency in Cincinnati suggested to Maud Morlock of the United States Children's Bureau in 1949 that

> unmarried, pregnant girls are dependent people and that's the reason they got pregnant—to stay in a dependency situation. . . . So an agency working with unmarried mothers shouldn't offer maternity home or other assistance too quickly. If the unwed mother is relieved of her anxiety in these matters too quickly, she continues her feeling of dependency, which complicates treatment.[61]

On the other hand, mental health professionals often found unwed mothers too independent, aggressive, and masculine, and considered it the goal of casework treatment "to bring out [the girls'] feelings of envy towards men

. . . and to assist [them] to move from this to a consideration of the positives of the woman's role and to a more feminine identification."[62]

In the postwar decades, most maternity homes were actively engaged in training unwed mothers to intensify their feminine identification. Most homes offered courses or workshops in the feminine arts of grooming, glamour, charm, beauty, sewing, cooking, handwork, and flower arranging before they offered courses with vocational or educational content.[63] Maud Morlock, for many years the Children's Bureau consultant on unmarried mothers, visited St. Faith's Home in Tarrytown, New York, in 1948, and her notes on the visit capture the flavor of this home's intentions. The staff, she wrote, "aimed to teach [their] girls personal attractiveness." A woman from a New York modeling school came to St. Faith's every other week.

> She formerly had acne and became interested in how people could improve their appearance. She, herself, is a very well-groomed person of 49, but looks younger. She sees each new girl individually. Afterwards the other girls assemble and hold a sort of clinic using each other as models. They do make-ups, hair-dressing and other things related to good grooming. . . . The President of the Board said her daughter who is at a private school, was having much the same kind of course.[64]

Despite the defilement with which the girls entered St. Faith's, the intention was to send them out as ladies. Even in the homes where it was possible to get school credits while in residence, restoring marriageability was considered more important than education. To the extent that maternity homes served as training schools for wayward girls, both working and middle class, the training was in femininity, not, as it would have been in the past, in menial work skills suited to sustain a (ruined) single woman and her child in poverty.

One additional idea for treatment of unwed mothers was offered by Dr. William Masters in a paper called "What Does the Physician Desire for the Social Agency by Way of Service to the Unmarried Mother?" The essay is a brief for a "positive action program" of medical care designed to forestall a girl's desperate turn to an abortionist and thence, according to Masters's evidence, to sterility and suicide. Although the paper does not deal directly with psychiatric matters, it ends with a startling recommendation, richly steeped in psychiatric concepts: if medical care has been good, Masters writes, "by the third trimester a major emotional transference will have occurred. The physician will have assumed a position of all-abiding, paramount, masculine importance in the girl's life. . . . In short, the physician should have assumed the husband's role."[65] Prevailing ideas about the super-suggestibility of pregnant women supported Masters's and other professionals' optimism about the likely success of their strategies.[66]

In whatever functional sense Masters meant this, his proposal suggests willingness to manipulate the unwed mother, using her vulnerable status, for moral and political ends determined by the doctor. In addition, it illuminates, quite specifically, how temporary the status of "unmarried mother" was con-sidered to be. The doctor could be an effective "husband" stand-in because the run of the play was so brief. Once the adoptable infant had been delivered, both husband and baby ceased to be factors in the mother's life. Masters held with his colleagues that an unwed mother was not equipped or situated properly to be a satisfactory mother to her child. The experts agreed that only the most profoundly disturbed unwed mothers wanted to keep their babies.[67]

Dr. Masters's application of transference meshed with the prevailing view of the American female's development after adolescence. It was widely believed that the proper progress for a young woman was to move smoothly from teenage dependence on her mother to dependence on a husband in her early twenties.[68] Deviations from this pattern might be a matter of psychiatric concern. The final goal of diagnosis, treatment, and cure was to improve the girl's likelihood of achieving this transition, the early derailment notwithstand-ing. Caseworkers and administrators, citing "success stories," often drew on letters from former maternity home residents that included sentiments akin to those expressed in a letter sent to the director of the Lakeview Home on Staten Island: "You know when I used to say that I didn't care about home and marriage, I was only pretending; at the bottom of my heart, it's what I always wanted."[69]

Challenges to the Psychological Explanations

By the mid-1960s, the relationship between psychiatry and white unwed motherhood had been supported by government funds and had guided the government's policy decisions for a generation. Of course, many single, preg-nant women and girls refused to enter into this relationship. Hundreds of thousands obtained illegal abortions each year. Some, playing a swifter but only slightly less grisly game with psychiatrists, got letters diagnosing them as psychologically impaired and unfit to be mothers. Women and girls presented these letters from psychiatrists to hospital abortion boards, and rarely, but sometimes, were successful in getting permission legally to terminate their pregnancies. And even among those who were trapped by psychiatric diagno-ses, there were some who made up their own lines. Consider Shirley, who "looked like a cherub and swore like a longshoreman." She could recognize a con job when she saw it. Shirley explained what she would say when the psychiatrist, fishing for neuroses and pathologies, asked her how she got pregnant. "I will say, how do you think?"[70]

Rose Bernstein, a social worker and administrator in Boston, who some-times did consulting for the federal government on issues relating to unwed pregnancy, wrote with unusual insight and sensitivity about the treatment of white, middle-class, unwed mothers.[71] Sizing up the treatment and the cost involved in producing "successes," she wrote,

> With casework services, psychiatric consultation and treatment, psychological testing and group psychotherapy and the like, some maternity homes are taking on the character of small psychiatric centers; a few are providing practice training to psychiatrists. . . . The climate of illness such an approach generates, the continuous focus on self which it encourages, and the image of the unmarried mother which it tends to project, raise some doubts as to its universal helpfulness. . . . We have a proliferation of services to a small segment while much the largest segment is scarcely receiving basic services.[72]

At first, the protests of Rose Bernstein and of Elizabeth Herzog, an employee of the United States Children's Bureau who was particularly concerned with defining a distinct etiology of black single pregnancy, were respected and largely ignored.[73] This attitude began to change when federal antipoverty funds became available in the 1960s for demonstration projects to build services for single pregnant women, usually minority group members, in the inner cities. At this point, designers and facilitators of such projects struggled through questions about the differences between white and black single pregnancy and began to construct multicausal explanations.[74] In the course of this transition, theorists and practitioners ran into public concerns about the "population bomb," the "sexual revolution," the civil rights movement, the women's movement, and the complex and changing abortion agenda. Psychiatry no longer dominated ideas about white single pregnancy. But the control that psychiatry had exercised, and the ends to which its theory had been used in constructing the life experiences of young women in the postwar United States, suggests one way that psychiatry was used to support the postwar family agenda, an agenda that depended on the subordination of fertile females.

The Uses of Psychological Explanations

The adoption of the psychological explanation and a psychiatrically oriented cure for white single pregnancy had a number of social functions. First, it spared the putative father from social opprobrium and responsibility—in fact, from professional attention of any kind. As Leontine Young wrote in 1954, "In the truest sense, [the unwed mother] is a victim, not of a seducer, but of herself."[75] If single pregnancy was simply a sign and symptom of mental illness, then the sexual partner was absolved of all responsibility, except for that of having helped make manifest what was festering destructively all along. The psychiatric explanation of white single pregnancy spared the male as it punished the female. Second, it rehabilitated the image of the illegitimate baby; the baby was rendered adoptable and the adoption market was served. Third, it likewise offered rehabilitation to a girl or woman who had been sexually active, even pregnant. A central goal of the psychiatric project was to replace sexual with psychological explanations for unmarried female sexual activity and pregnancy. This transition reduced the stigma, identified and associated the unwed mother with American women in general, and, in the process, restored her marriageability, if not her sexual purity.

Ironically, the compassion that psychiatric theory brought to the diagnosis of the unmarried mother depended to some degree on dehumanizing her: the single pregnant girl had gone "on automatic"; she had sexual relations with a male because the inexorable force of her past, not sexual interest or arousal, had impelled her. In fact, the theory and the treatment plan clearly skirted the issue of female sexuality altogether. This was possible because of the implicit belief in the idea that the single pregnant woman had not engaged in sex exactly. Rather, in spreading her legs, she was engaging in a family form of psychological warfare.

But beyond what the diagnoses and the labels accomplished in treating the individual, they had powerful uses for the culture at large. An episode of social ostracism warns the community to toe the line and reminds its vulnerable members of the power held by authorities. In this way, the label of illness—along with the virtual expulsion from the community—experienced by white unmarried mothers warned like women everywhere to keep their commitment to marriage and motherhood strong, in that order, and reminded them—indirectly, but powerfully—of the wages of unsanctioned sexuality.

Psychological assumptions and treatment reinforced the subordination of women in the family. The white, unwed mother in the pre–*Roe* era was the daughter and the variant of the debilitated American mother who caused such concern among psychiatrists and family relations and child development experts in the postwar years. Professionals feared that married women who failed to adjust to their roles as wife, mother, and woman were threats to the fabric of American life. Maladjusted wives and mothers undermined the possibility of the harmonious nuclear family, threatened the natural leadership capacities of their husbands, and therefore spoiled what would have been the next generation of physically and psychologically healthy citizens.[76] White unwed mothers exhibited the same distinctive, distorted behavior as married women. But without husbands, whose masculinity they could impair? Without children, whose future they could disrupt?[77] Who, then, were they hurting? Why did the experts make such drastic diagnoses, and why did they seem so deeply concerned—even angry—about these girls and women?

Psychiatric theory had always assumed a subordinate, domestic, maternal role for women. It was well suited to arbitrate issues associated with the implementation of the postwar "family" agenda, which mandated marriage and domesticity for women. Psychiatrists had a professional tradition and a body of theory to draw on in responding to working mothers, mothers of "troubled" children, "over-educated" women, women seeking abortions, and unwed mothers—all females who seemed to violate the psychiatric model of the good wife.[78] A great many psychiatrists in the 1950s earned their livings and their reputations by adjusting women to accept prevailing "family" norms.

These doctors provided the public with disturbing explanations for the behavior of those who were not "homeward bound,"[79] explanations that were readily institutionalized. During this period, the state situated "the family"—the white, middle-class family, in particular—as the cornerstone of its political, economic, and demographic postwar goals. By constructing the unwed mother as mental patient, psychological explanations of white single pregnancy provided a powerful testament to the wages of uncontained female sexuality, which they interpreted as a major threat to the middle-class family.

From a more positive standpoint, expelling the white unwed mother from the community rewarded each woman who behaved herself and didn't get inappropriately pregnant. The professions and the community sacrificed the unwed mother, a symbol of both the failure and the violation of "family." The sacrifice was part of the larger campaign to preserve, protect, and valorize this institution.[80] Out of the sacrifice came the unwed mother's chance for a new life. She "acquiesced" in her banishment from the community for a period of self-mortification and self-denial in the maternity home. She "agreed" to deny her motherhood by relinquishing her child so she could return to the community recertified as good material to assume the status of American wife and mother.

It is important, particularly in the 1990s, to be clear about what was at issue for single pregnant women and their interpreters. To what extent were unmarried mothers victims of their own desire for sexual freedom? To what extent was what we now call "reproductive freedom" an issue for them? The fact that the rates and ratios of single pregnancy were escalating steadily in the postwar years and that the yearly number of illegal abortions was estimated to be so high is evidence that females were taking more sexual freedom than previously, albeit in a culture which, as strongly as ever, privileged male domination.[81] It was this taking of sexual license that so troubled psychiatrists and became so consequential to the young women themselves. These females hadn't sought to have babies, nor were they agitating to keep their babies (or to have "reproductive freedom"). But they were subject to laws and policies that constructed their postcoital experiences for them.

These psychiatric responses to white unwed mothers constituted a late, long lament from mainstream professionals against premarital sex for females. The white, broadly middle-class unmarried mothers who became the subjects of the studies cited here had engaged in sex without procreative intentions, outside of a legally subordinate relation to a man. While the white American wife had come to be recognized, in a rather contorted sense, as a person with sexual needs and interests, the white American teenage girl and single woman had not.[82] Sanctioned, recognized sexual life for a female still began in the nuptial bed. Only after marriage could a white woman's sex life be variably evaluated and diagnosed: good or bad, healthy or sick. Before marriage, a white girl or woman with a sex life, or a baby, was, according to the psychiatric mainstream, simply sick.

Unwed pregnant girls and women were implicitly cast as sex offenders. They had transgressed against female norms of purity and passivity by engaging in sex without marriage, a patently male pursuit, and they were to become mothers without a man's love, a perversion of female destiny.[83] The experts who constructed or drew on psychiatric theory to deal with the growing number of white single pregnant women in America after World War II shared race and class with this group. Thus, as the severe tone and content of their diagnoses suggest, in containing unmarried female sexual license, they had before them a personal as well as a professional task.

White unwed mothers in the pre–*Roe v. Wade* era suffered because they had sex in the ill-timed moment in the twentieth century when large numbers of white unmarried females began to take some increased latitude in sexual decision making, without any legal access to control the outcome of this decision. These women suffered and complained under psychiatric judgment, but not yet in political terms or forms. Psychiatric theory helped unwed mothers see their plight as an individual, not a collective, concern.

This material, retrieved twenty-five and more years later, is clearly relevant to abortion debates today. The material strongly suggests that whether the public discourse about the meaning of female reproductive capacities is conducted in the terms of biology or economics or religio-ethics or psychiatry, those who draw on these disciplines to structure women's social options and to curb women's reproductive freedom are serving an interest in governing the reproductive capacities of women. Biologists, psychiatrists, and religio-ethicists have promulgated the concepts and the language to support this end.

The field of psychiatry had an expansive role in postwar America. Its theorists and practitioners were charged with, or assumed, the task of establishing baselines of normalcy and devising labels, explanations, and cures for the legions whose behaviors were "different." The encounter between psychiatry and single pregnancy was similar to psychiatry's encounters with many other forms of "deviance" in the 1940s and 1950s. Yet there are special legacies of the psychiatric explanations of single pregnancy in the pre–*Roe v. Wade* era. Certainly, even into our own time, the labels of illness affixed to unwed mothers have added a layer of entrapment for women struggling toward sexual and reproductive freedom.

Psychiatric explanations extended a twentieth-century practice of drawing on "science" to illuminate illegitimacy. The generation before World War II had used the sciences to determine that unwed pregnancy was the consequence of mental defectiveness. The application of psychiatric theory to single pregnancy further legitimated the use of science to punish women for their unsanctioned sexual experience and to limit their control over their own bodies and their own children. Psychiatrists demonstrated again that science could be used, implicitly or explicitly, to protect the traditional roles and functions of women in American society. The record of this effort cautions us to subject the public, social uses of science to rigorous questioning.

Chapter Four

Behind the Fence: Maternity Homes, 1945–65

> Unwed mothers at that time, at the time Sheryl joined their ranks, were a specific group; they fell somewhere between criminals and patients and, like criminals and patients, they were prescribed an exact and fortifying treatment: they were made to disappear.[1]

The world of maternity homes in postwar America was a gothic attic obscured from the community by the closed curtains of gentility and high spiked fences. The girls and women sent inside were dreamwalkers serving time, pregnant dreamwalkers taking the cure. Part criminal, part patient, the unwed mother arrived on the doorstep with her valise and, moving inside, found herself enclosed within an idea.

Rosalind Petchesky's description of her girlhood contact with the maternity home in Tulsa captures—and extends—the gothic flavor of these institutions at midcentury.

> When I was growing up in Tulsa, Oklahoma, the local home for unwed mothers was as shrouded in horror and hysteria as an asylum or leper colony. Located outside of town in a field off a rural highway, unmistakably "institutional," it drew my fascination by the lifelessness outside its walls and the miserable types I imagined must dwell within. The windows always seemed closed. There were stories of unknown origin that circulated in our high school about a hatchet-wielding killer named "Sparky," a crazy man who haunted the outskirts of town in search of innocent girls or couples who parked on deserted roads to hack to pieces. Somehow the two symbols of lost innocence and the terrors of sex—Sparky and the "home"—became closely connected in the dark shadows of my mind.[2]

Throughout the period of this study, maternity homes in the United States had a robust physical reality. Approximately two hundred licensed homes were scattered across forty-four states, over two-thirds of them operating under the auspices of the Florence Crittenton Association of America, Catholic Charities, and the Salvation Army. About twenty-five thousand unwed mothers each year spent the final trimester of their pregnancies behind the fence.[3] That is, of the two to three hundred thousand girls and women illegitimately pregnant in an average postwar year who didn't marry or abort, only about one in twelve took up residence in a maternity home, or one out of five or six white unwed mothers.[4]

Among the several hundred thousand unwed mothers each year who didn't marry or abort, the vast majority coped with their pregnancies alone or with the support of relatives, friends, or other social service agencies. Many of these were black girls and women. A large number did not have the resources—the information, the money, or the know-how to enter maternity homes. Some unwed mothers were excluded from homes by race or because they had been pregnant out of wedlock more than once, or for failure to meet other restrictive admissions criteria. Indeed, the sort of protection maternity homes offered was not of interest to some single pregnant girls and women from families or communities that did not require the sequestering of unwed mothers or provided alternate means of doing so. But maternity-home care was the option of choice and was widely promoted for all unwed mothers by the United States Children's Bureau, many social service agencies, the National Association on Services to Unmarried Parents, and its local affiliates all over the country in the postwar era.[5] The maternity home option became increasingly popular during this period, often more popular with professionals, parents, and pregnant girls than it was accessible.

The popularity of maternity homes in the postwar era can be understood in part by considering how prevailing ideas about femininity and motherhood, particularly for white girls and women—the primary clients of maternity homes—fit with other notions current in American society in midcentury concerning personal identity and personal destiny.

First, it is important to note that in the postwar period, both femininity and motherhood as cultural concepts were simultaneously strictly fixed and unusually elastic. The values and behaviors associated with femininity and motherhood were relatively uncontested. Articles such as "Where Do You Rank on the Femininity Scale?" affirmed an objective certainty about the ingredients of femininity: "Scientists in leading universities and research foundations have been putting femininity under the clinical microscope. . . . They can tell you how to find out just how feminine you are, and how your status in this department will affect your personal life."[6] A complementary standard of motherhood was formulated and promulgated, as well.[7] It was not particularly startling for the culture to produce such standards, but the postwar version was innovative because of the scientific and psychiatric expertise behind the prescriptions, and because media treatments were so powerfully pervasive.

On the other hand, the pathway to attaining, or appearing to attain, femininity and normative motherhood had become unusually branched. A mapping of women's routes to these states would have shown a new variety of byways, educationally, occupationally, and sexually.[8] Girls and women with widely varying antecedent experiences ended up assuming lives that had fiercely mandated, similar contours and content. The example of the white unwed mother demonstrates how the maternity home in postwar America could neutralize the unorthodox preparation of many women for the orthodox practice of female adulthood in the United States.

The white girl, single and pregnant, led by her parents, turned to the maternity home because it offered secrecy and protection. It also promised something new: personal revelation and transformation. Supporting this promise was a relatively new cultural belief in the fluidity of personal identity. This was not simply the old American doctrine of mobility, upward, downward, or geographic. In the past, a broadly middle-class, unmarried, pregnant girl would have been permanently marked by the illegitimate pregnancy. Now, unwed mothers could find a repaired or reconstructed identity through the program of the maternity home. The psychological assumptions governing these programs promised to provide a girl with the opportunity "to find herself" there.[9] In the maternity home, the "self" was a newly protean entity, which, properly conditioned, could be reshaped to override the biological, moral, or psychological missteps of the prior self. While in other eras, religious-based redemption or transformation was available to such transgressors, this mode never promised the deniability of the sin, as the midcentury program in the maternity home did. Joan Jacobs Brumberg has described the intentions of homes in the early-twentieth century in this regard:

> [E]vangelical pedagogy offered each girl the opportunity to recast her life and compensate for her sin rather then ever truly erase it. The underlying assumption of the institution was that the girl and her future child were marked and that isolation from the world in a moral institution might head off the worst aspects of the social stigma.[10]

Coupled with the new, postwar notion of the fluidity of personal identity was a matching ideal concerning the attainability of middle-class status for whites. The fate of white unwed mothers who passed through maternity homes tested the power and inclusiveness of this ideal, and validated it, even for these girls and women who had committed what looked like a fatal, exclusionary error. In fact, by midcentury, neither loss of virginity nor non-marital maternity disqualified them from a place in the middle class, despite the violation of genteel femininity these acts represented. Nor could illegitimate birth disqualify their children. Via the offices of the maternity home, sexual misconduct could be overcome, its wages effaced.

In the postwar era, the maternity home became a social agency designed to pull a girl off the wrong branch of the road, to correct her course toward femininity and motherhood. Its mission was fortified by the almost magical notion of the malleable self and by the discovery that the gatekeepers of the middle class would just as soon admit a reconstructed female as a natural one, or none at all.

The unwed mother, valise in hand, who stood in the doorway of the maternity home in Topeka, in Louisville, Los Angeles, San Antonio, Cincinnati, Chattanooga, or Jersey City, understood, to one degree or another, that her only hope was to submit to the transformative program inside and that submission meant going underground, as it were, disappearing to reemerge looking exactly like herself, but different. She had been reconstructed.[11]

It was, to be sure, a dramatically reconceptualized maternity home that promised so much to an unwed mother and her parents in the postwar era. For nearly the first halfcentury of their existence, the homes' impulse was typically charitable and punitive. A United States government document of the 1940s distinguished the old from the new:

> In the early years of maternity homes . . . illegitimate pregnancy was viewed solely as a moral problem. . . . The whole life experience of the individual was overshadowed by this one episode. Repression was the formula for cure; the approach to the young women was moralistic. She was expected to keep her baby.[12]

Far from expeditiously shepherding erring girls and women back to or into the normative life of potential middle-class wives and mothers, homes in the past often kept unwed mothers for as long as four years and trained them to be cooks and parlormaids.[13] At the turn of the century, a home in Elmira, New York, kept unwed mothers, on average, for twenty months. The home's rules warned prospective residents, "No girl can enter this institution who will not promise to remain for training and instruction as long as the trustees think it for her good as this institution is especially to reform and save, not to encourage sin."[14] These facilities did not intend to *trans*form their ruined charges. The best hope for the prewar maternity home resident was that she would redeem herself spiritually by dint of hard work and the dutiful rearing of her illegitimate child. The typically church-affiliated personnel suggested there was room for the unwed mother in the spiritual fold, and only there. Elsewhere she was an outcast. Unlike her postwar sister, she wasn't part criminal, part patient, with the possibilities of rehabilitation associated with both of those statuses. She was simply an outcast, an undone woman who might seek redemption, but not rehabilitation. After a period in the home under the right religious influence, she was sent forth with a simple admonition: "Go and sin no more."[15]

In contrast, the new, postwar maternity home often aimed to provide a rest cure of sorts, conducive to changes of heart, mind, and persona. Maud Morlock, Consultant on Services to Unmarried Parents at the United States

Children's Bureau from the late 1930s through the mid-1950s, described her idea of the benefits of maternity home care to a colleague at the Salvation Army in 1955: "It can bring perspective, relaxation, companionship, physical comfort, regularity of hours, good meals, and peace of soul. It should provide physical care and comfort that every pregnant girl needs."[16] Morlock counseled practitioners in Buffalo, in Birmingham, and across the nation to move beyond the old concept of maternity home as isolated shelter. She advocated policies of greater flexibility, professionalism, and respect for the needs of the individual girl who must be prepared to return to the community and to a normative life.[17] For Morlock and many who provided maternity home services after World War II, the unwed mother no longer looked stained, just soiled.

Reform of the maternity home did not take place rapidly or uniformly; the ragged transition was reflected by a writer for the *Ladies' Home Journal* in 1947:

> There are some two hundred [maternity homes] throughout the country . . . some [are run] on modern social work lines, some still in the days of the Scarlet Letter, some on religious policies. . . . It is only recently that the birth of a baby to an unmarried woman has been considered an economic, social and emotional problem as well as a moral one, and the problem of the baby's future life as a separate individual considered independently of its mother's "mistake." And despite this change, the moralistic atmosphere of most maternity homes is accentuated by—as is true in so many institutions currently—a lack of skilled personnel; and by the dour, ancient quality of most of the buildings themselves, set in isolated areas, walled off, and cloistered in confidential secrecy.[18]

On a 1951 visit to a Florence Crittenton Home in Delaware, Morlock found many empty beds. She tied light use of the facility to the home's backward, unreconstructed ways. These included an unenlightened board of directors whose members were elected for life. She wrote, "The home has been a law unto itself . . . [its] policies moralistic and punitive." For example, until the late 1940s, the medical staff wouldn't allow anesthetic during delivery. In addition, the home accepted only white girls, took no repeaters; no one could enter after the seventh month; no one was offered casework.[19] Morlock and her colleagues at the Children's Bureau were unrelenting counselors and prods to staff at laggard institutions like the one in Delaware, urging them to respect the value of humane practices, the value of unwed mothers, and the value of their babies.

The remainder of this chapter will consider the postwar purposes of the maternity homes and how unwed mothers felt about being residents. It will also present a view of the "home culture" as constructed by those in charge of the institutions, and of the alternate "home culture" constructed by the society of unwed mothers inside.

This chapter contains more "voices" of unwed mothers themselves than any other chapter in this study for three reasons. As institutions, maternity homes kept written records of their activities; these records often included statements, poems, and other material produced by the residents. Second, the government's promotion of these homes as the best treatment plan for white unwed mothers ensured that their programs and their pregnant charges would be documented by government officials and other observers. Finally, large segments of society found stories about maternity home residents interesting—heartrending, titillating, perhaps compellingly disgusting. Women's magazines and other mass circulation media ran articles on this subject often. The authors almost always tried to capture the flavor of life behind the fence by including the voices of unwed mothers.

The Disappearing Act

> Two weeks went went by. They dragged at a snail's pace. Day was joined to day like links in a heavy chain which coiled around me and dragged wherever I walked. . . . I lifted heavy weights. I jumped from the height of a table to the floor until I didn't have the strength to climb back on the table again. At night I sat in hot mustard baths and slept with my head pounding from the effects of quinine. I drank tansy tea and swallowed capsules of turpentine until all I wanted to do was retch out my insides and die. I thought of dying. With all my heart I wanted to die. As the time went on, I wanted to more and more. When I didn't come around during the second month, I was desperate. My face became gaunt and haggard. My eyes sank deep into their sockets. My clothes were always damp with sweat. "I'll kill myself," I would murmur into the darkness at night. "I'll take poison and kill myself."[20]

This girl was terrified and desperate as she imagined her parents' response to her pregnancy. Her experience reflected the fact that the white family system, and the white community, typically could not deal calmly with a daughter in a crisis of this nature.[21] The rending of the myth of the sexually pure daughter and the virginal bride often provoked parental disappointment to the point of rage. A sixteen-year-old girl wrote to President Truman telling that she let "a very horrid boy take me home from a party, thinking I could trust him, and [then he] attacked me." She said her "quick-tempered father . . . would just as soon kill me" if he found out about the pregnancy.[22] This teenager felt her father would find pregnancy sufficient grounds for death. Another father found it grounds for simulating his daughter's death. A caseworker noted this man's plans when he applied for assistance for his daughter at a Salvation Army maternity home.

> Mr. Higgins is middle-aged, a small business man. . . . He has been in business twenty years in a small California city with his roots deep down in the community, prominent in both civic and church activities. His sixteen

year old, Jane, is unmarried and pregnant. Mr. Higgins stated that when the story became known to [the] family, their whole world seemed to crash about them. . . . What seemed to Mr. Higgins as a sensible answer [was], "We will tell them all that Jane is dead."[23]

A third father, a particularly typical one, found the pregnancy simply grounds to deny his daughter's existence. This man refused to see his daughter once he learned that she was pregnant because, he said, he "could not look upon her in this disgusting condition."[24]

Mothers' responses counted, too. Some girls imagined murderous mothers: "I can't tell my mother because she would kill me. I know she would because she already told me if anything happened to me, she would."[25] But often mothers' responses were more complicated than brute aggression or bald denial. Many mothers, consistent with the mother-blaming practices of the postwar era, took the responsibility for the girl's pregnancy on herself. One said, in typical fashion, "Part of the fault must be mine. . . . Maybe I gave you too much freedom."[26] In contrast to many fathers who aggressively threatened or willed the disappearance of their pregnant daughters, a mother frequently effaced her daughter more quietly by denying the girl ownership of her own life.

In anticipation of parental panic, many unwed girls did not tell their parents at all. In 1963, Executive Director of the Florence Crittenton Association of America, Mary Louise Allen, estimated that about one half of the Florence Crittenton residents nationally refused to tell.[27] These daughters often recognized themselves as the family's most vulnerable member. Many of them believed that in bringing evidence of their sexuality to their parents, they ran the risk of losing more than face. That is, many single pregnant girls described their feelings about themselves, particularly in relation to their parents, in terms that suggested a fading sense of vitality and personal identity. Jean Thompson, a pseudonymous resident of a California Salvation Army Home, simply said, "I am nothing."[28] Another, heading for a Denver maternity home, explained,

> I dropped out of school at the close of the first semester. Mother told the principal I was anemic. She answered all my phone calls after that, telling my girlfriends I was resting. After a while they stopped phoning. When her friends came to visit, I had to hide in my room. I began to feel like somebody who had no right to be alive.[29]

Aside from the family, the central social institution in the lives of almost half of all unwed mothers who became maternity home residents was the school.[30] Along with many parents, school officials could not tolerate the presence of unwed pregnancy. Consequently, throughout the period of this study, tens of thousands of pregnant girls each year were expelled from school. Morlock reported in 1947 that in Chicago the schools were adamant. "The

Board of Education tries to exclude any unwed mother from further attendance."[31] Morlock's successor at the Children's Bureau found a similar policy
intact in San Francisco fourteen years later. The "general policy" there was
"to exclude a pregnant girl . . . as soon as the pregnancy becomes known,
whether or not it is noticeable."[32]

School personnel worried that the "rebelliousness" of unwed mothers
might be contagious. Officials in San Francisco felt "that the non-pregnant
girls should not be exposed to a girl in this condition and that [the pregnant
girl] would be likely to flaunt her condition."[33] In Washington, D.C., school
administrators and the media peddled this story to justify exclusion:

> It may well be pointed out in one instance where a young teenager who
> had a baby kept showing snapshots of her offspring to her close personal
> friend, an eighth grade pupil, until she created such a strong desire in this
> girl, who had never been pregnant, that she determined to duplicate the
> feat of her friend. After having intercourse with a number of young males
> and not getting pregnant, she has developed a definite psychosis.[34]

If schools were primarily concerned with the infectiousness of out-of-
wedlock pregnancy, what were the girl's parents primarily concerned with?
Why did so many participate so wholeheartedly (and brokenheartedly, at the
same time) in the disappearing act that led their daughters into maternity
homes?

Parents embraced of the idea of maternity homes partly because in the
postwar decades, parents themselves needed protection as much as their
erring daughters. For white, broadly middle-class parents, gross proof of
an unmarried daughter's sexuality, such as an out-of-wedlock pregnancy,
represented perhaps the ultimate public violation of parental authority and
thus constituted hard proof of their failure as parents.[35] The violation was too
awful to admit or to reveal in the community. As Mr. Higgins, Jane's father
in California, asked in horror, "What would the neighbors say? What would
the community think? What could they say to their friends at church? How
would their relatives react?"[36] Since he could not face the answers to his own
questions, he wished his daughter dead and sent her to a maternity home.
For many parents, a daughter's unwed pregnancy was a dire threat to their
vision of their own future as well as to the vision they'd constructed of the
girl's life.

For many parents, their daughter's disappearance into the maternity
home satisfied a need to deny the horror of her revealed sexuality. If the girl
disappeared, the problem disappeared with her. Maternity homes also met
parents' need to cope with or manage the practical issues of the crisis. The
maternity home promised to take care of this aspect, too. The response of
thousands of white parents each year to a daughter's pregnancy provides one
measure of the meaning of parenthood in the postwar years. The existence
and the promises of the homes suggest that, at least in the case of unsanctioned,

youthful, female sexuality, society was willing to offer parents and daughters a safety net to back up its rigorous but increasingly unrealistic intentions for parenthood and for the sexual purity of unmarried females. The postwar maternity home, above all, promised to take on the girl and efface her problem using psychologically oriented casework and adoption. Having undergone this program, the girl would be free to walk away from her past. Everything could go back to normal—or better. In this way, the reconstructed, unwed mother, having passed through the maternity home, embodied a central 1950s ideal.

But in the meantime, the unwed mother was still out on that very thin limb, sometimes along with her bewildered parents, sometimes alone. She was rarely in the company of the person social agencies referred to as the "putative father." A very typical plea for help, a plea "to know that someone shares this nightmare with me," came from Esther in Illinois in the early 1950s:

> I am in trouble. I am living at home but can't stay any longer. . . . I have planned on coming to Chicago to live. This way my parents would never know of the difficulty I am in. The main thing is that they must never know. I am almost two months pregnant now. I find that the man who was to marry me is already married. He knows of my condition but won't see me or answer at all when I call his home.[37]

Another girl in a typical position reported that "her boyfriend with whom she has been keeping company for six years has denied paternity."[38]

In the process of self-effacement undergone by many single pregnant girls, perhaps most painful of all short-term losses was the lost boyfriend. His rejection was not surprising considering the cultural construction of the white unwed mother as a female who ought to disappear. When several hundred teenage boys were asked, in the mid-1960s, to write their descriptions of an unwed mother, the most common words they used were "gullible, unintelligent, ugly, street-walker, 'pick-up,' one who uses abusive language and low moral character."[39] It is not unthinkable that among these several hundred were at least a few who would find themselves "putative fathers."

The state of altered reality that closed around many single girls and women in the early months of their secret pregnancies left many of them with a sense of having absolutely no resources to call on. Without boyfriends, and especially those cut off from their parents, they were truly bereft. One woman in New York said, "When you first realize you're pregnant, you're so scared and desperate you really can't face things." She went on to describe the details of this limbo:

> I kept tying to pretend in the daytime that everything was all right and went on wearing tight girdles and telling people brightly that Jack and I had parted the best of friends. When I got home to my apartment at night, I

would sit and try to think what to do, but there seemed to be no way out. I had only forty dollars in the bank. I'd spent everything else on a small trousseau. I'd felt that mother must never find out. She's had a tough life, and her respectability and her pride in her children are all she has left. Sometimes I would long for company . . . or I'd sit right through a movie three times till the theatre closed.[40]

Many pregnant girls and women across the country were reduced to pinning their hopes for help on the kindliness of national leaders or on a faceless agency worker in Washington. One girl wrote to the president from San Francisco:

I am in serious trouble, I must have some desired and most needed information at once, but please you must keep this matter most confidential—You see, my parents are respectable citizens back East, and they must not hear of this miserable state of affairs I am involved in. About two months ago I was raped. . . . I do not know what to do or where to go. What would you suggest? . . . What free clinic, home or hospital do you happen to know in this city where care and delivery of unwed mothers is given? . . . Please let me hear from you.[41]

Another, in Cleveland, wrote, "I am a girl in trouble two months pregnant. . . . [M]y parents don't like me because I'm not beautiful like my two sisters. . . . Please help me."[42] A third wrote, "To whom it may concern" in Washington. She explained, "I am writing this letter to get some information on where I can find out the name of a home I can go to and have my baby. . . . I'd like it to be out of Pittsburgh as my relatives would all shun me if they knew. Please answer this letter as I am five months pregnant. . . ."[43]

Sometimes it was a girl's parent who turned to the president or the Children's Bureau, lacking other sources of information or help. One mother wrote, heartrendingly:

I am a self-supporting widow and have just this one child. I work at housework and my salary is around $25.00 a week, plus $5.00 for a room I rent. My daughter works in an underwear factory and makes $26.00 a week if she gets full time. . . . I could borrow money on the furniture to finance the [maternity home]. We are Protestants. We are poor but respectable folks, and I hope you can at least advise me what I can do.[44]

Scores of letter writers addressed their desperation to the Children's Bureau in response to the active outreach program Maud Morlock championed in the 1940s and 1950s. Morlock worked with editors of mass circulation and romance magazines on stories about unwed mothers. She encouraged the insertion of the name and address of her agency in each article, thus inviting single pregnant girls and women to contact her. Morlock often felt gratified about the results. When girls who responded to information from articles on services for unwed mothers were asked what they would have done if they hadn't seen the article, Morlock reported to her colleague, social worker Leontine Young, that "the reply was that they were at their wits end and didn't know what to do."[45] Other organizations had the same experience. The National Association on Services to Unmarried Parents received three hundred letters and many phone calls after being mentioned in a romance magazine article. The Child Welfare League of America got eight hundred letters in just a few months from the same source. An administrator described these pleas: "Every letter [was] an anguished appeal for immediate help."[46]

A typical letter writer, this one from Des Moines, said, "I don't know exactly how to write this letter. I am so ashamed to write. . . . I am an unmarried girl and have sinned so must pay the price. . . . I am so grateful for your article in the magazine without it I hate to think of what I might have done. . . ."[47] A young woman in Connecticut wrote,

> I have just finished reading the story of "The Terrifying Ordeal of an Unwed Mother." Because, you see I am in the same trouble. I don't have any money, no place to go, and no one to help me. I am desperate for need of help. I am about 4 1/2 months gone. The reason I am writing to you is that I saw your name in *True Confessions*, and I thought maybe you could help me in some way. I am 21 years old. I just don't know what to do, so I am hoping you will be able to advise me as to what to do. I am living in a boarding house now even unable to pay my rent. And not eating enough. Please won't you help me.[48]

What seems extraordinary today is that in addition to carrying out all her other complex duties, Maud Morlock personally answered this and every letter from an unwed mother that was sent to any government official or government office in Washington. Even more astonishing is that each letter writer received a response sympathetically tailored to address her particular request. Morlock referred each girl to an agency geographically convenient to her. She often offered her help as a letter of introduction to a specific friend or colleague whom the girl could consult. She began each letter with the same reassuring words: "I'm so glad you wrote to me." If Morlock assumed the writer were white, she gave information regarding nearby maternity homes, and only maternity homes.

The Institution

The government's embrace of maternity homes, together with the appeal these institutions had for parents and other pillars of the community such as ministers and doctors, contributed a lot to the steady increase in the use of homes during the postwar decades.[49] There is some evidence that use was down during the war, but by 1945, the Los Angeles Salvation Army Booth Maternity Home and others, were packed.[50] A maternity home social worker wrote to Morlock right after the war that "We are more than busy these days, have a long waiting-list and have had twenty-eight babies in the last twenty-seven days (an all time high)."[51] Ruth Pagan of the Salvation Army reported in 1949 "that maternity homes were springing up in the West for the sole purpose of getting control of the babies. Three or four such places have been developed near Spokane."[52] On the other coast, Inwood House in New York increased its capacity soon after the war. Throughout the 1950s, civic leaders lobbied for expansion of shelter care for unwed mothers.[53] In growing cities in the west and southwest, the needs were apparently enormous. In Dallas, the maternity homes expanded as Dallas did.[54] A girl in a Salvation Army Home in southern California in 1960 recorded the fact that "All the dorms are filled to capacity and we hear that girls are on waiting lists outside. Miss O'Connor [an administrator] told me that there are girls in the Salvation Army shelters and in rented rooms waiting to get in."[55] In the same year, the Florence Crittenton organization reported that it had more applications than it could accept and that, in fact, 38 percent of the applications received couldn't be accepted, often because of lack of space.[56] Two years later the situation was worse, the Florence Crittenton Association of America straining to meet what the executive director referred to as "an ever-increasing number of applicants." She explained that "our member agencies are striving to keep up with the accelerated pace of referrals, but the demand exceeds the supply of beds available."[57]

Jennie Phelps, head nurse at the Denver Florence Crittenton agency described the crush there. By the mid-1960s there was always a waiting list, even though the home was willing to squeeze in as many unwed mothers as possible. Girls slept on couches and on the tables in examining rooms. While the home had delivered 145 babies in 1945 and 190 in 1950, by the mid-1960s there were more than four hundred deliveries a year, sometimes as many as four in one night.[58] The ex-director of a home in Seattle described a similar situation: long waiting lists and overcrowding. She reported that in her region, entry to the homes was being delayed typically two to four months because of lack of space.[59]

This run on maternity homes proceeded even though services did not come cheaply, especially for girls from poorer families. The data that survives suggests that in the mid-1960s possibly one-third of maternity home residents came from families whose income was below $5,499 and two-thirds had incomes below $8,500.[60] Over 80 percent of these families had at least two children; over two-thirds had three or more children to support.[61]

In the early 1950s, homes typically charged about two dollars a day for prenatal residence, a hospital fee of $85 to $130, plus postpartum costs for mothers and baby.[62] Charges did vary depending on whether the mother was a resident of the county or the state in which the maternity home was located. For example, a Cincinnati home charged a package fee of $100 for county residents and $150 for others. This home took in many girls from Florida,

Indiana, and Kentucky, as well as applicants from the greater Cincinnati area.[63] A typical Salvation Army fee structure in the early 1960s indicated increased costs since the early postwar years. Maternity home care was $3.73 a day, delivery $67.08, and postpartum hospital care $22.75 a day. For the baby in the nursery, the Army charged $12.45 a day, and as long as the mother stayed in the home after the birth, she paid $3.73 a day. With an average maternity home stay of seventy-eight days, the total bill could easily exceed six hundred dollars.[64]

Many homes tried to subsidize the cost of services as much as possible. For example, the executive director of the Florence Crittenton Home in Washington, D.C., reported that her facility had a minimum charge of 50 percent of the cost of service for an average seventy-four-day stay, or four hundred dollars. She said, "If a girl cannot pay the amount and is ineligible for the Public Welfare grant or procedures involved are socially destructive, she could apply for the amount needed from [the home's] Special Fund."[65] As this director indicated, fees covered only a portion of operating expenses, so homes adopted a variety of practices to make up the difference. In San Antonio, for instance, if a girl stayed for eight months, contributing her labor to running the home after her baby was born, she was not charged a fee; if she stayed only four months, she paid one hundred dollars.[66] Similarly, at the Maple Knoll Home in Cincinnati, all residents worked eight hours a day. If the girl could pay her fare, she stayed at the home for fourteen weeks. If she hadn't the money and she was a resident of Hamilton County, she was required to remain an additional six weeks, and an additional twelve weeks if she was an out-of-county resident. At St. Anne's Maternity Home in Columbus, Ohio, if a girl couldn't pay her bill, she would stay for two or three months to work off each hundred dollars she owed.[67]

In the 1940s some homes took in delinquent girls under the auspices of the Juvenile Court to augment their revenues.[68] The Florence Crittenton Home in Phoenix raised money this way until the state Department of Welfare strongly recommended against the practice. A home in Delaware took in delinquent girls whose work in the home's laundry service brought in considerable income. Despite Maud Morlock's disapproval of the practice of running these facilities for mixed populations, the Delaware home's board of directors were reluctant to lose this source of income. Morlock told the board, "There may be little difference in the behavior of a young war bride, an unmarried mother and the girl committed by the court," but maternity homes should not try to meet the needs of all three simultaneously.[69] In a home where delinquent girls were mixed with unwed mothers, Morlock found deplorable conditions, the building

surrounded by a high wire fence, the gate of which was kept locked. The whole atmosphere was restrictive . . . [and without] educational or recreational programs for unmarried mothers as the two groups had such widely different interests that the unmarried mothers wouldn't remain in the living rooms. They withdrew entirely to their bedrooms.[70]

By the early 1950s, most homes received annual allocations from the Community Chest, although some were reluctant to accept such semipublic funding because with acceptance, the home might be pressured to forgo some of its restrictive entrance requirements, such as those based on race.[71] In the early 1950s, for example, the Pittsburgh Florence Crittenton Home wanted to remain free of Chest requirements. Instead of accepting its assistance, the home held three major fund-raising events during the year, "Donation Event" in November, Tag Day in the Spring, and a card party in January, and many minor events.[72]

Ambitious fund-raising strategies were managed by extensive cadres of volunteers, mostly middle-class matrons devoted to community service in general and to the rehabilitation of unwed mothers in particular.[73] St. Anne's in Columbus supported thirty-two guilds with four hundred volunteers who raised money for the home.[74] In Washington, D.C., nine hundred women comprised thirty-one "circles" supporting the Florence Crittenton Home. One of the projects of circles was to raise money for the Mary B. Robertson Fund, established in 1952, to help girls in the home who couldn't pay for their care. The fund received about two thousand dollars a year from the Florence Crittenton Bazaar. Circles also provided the decor for maternity home bedrooms, hosted the Silver Tea Open House, a tour of the maternity home open to the public; fashion shows, card parties, cocktail parties, and the annual Fountain of Flowers Ball.[75] The circle coordinator in Washington reported that there was a waiting list of women who wanted to join a circle.[76]

In Los Angeles there were forty-three such circles; in 1959 they added $7,589 collectively to the Crittenton Home's operating budget. One circle raised $265 at its Casino Night to redecorate a bedroom. In San Francisco a fashion show raised $4000 in 1959; by 1964 the eleven volunteer groups, with 615 women involved, raised $25,000 for a home in that city. In Terre Haute, an annual breakfast raised $300 and a candy sale $90.[77]

Despite such vital and vigorous support, maternity homes were always strapped for money, and many unwed mothers had none.[78] While homes often advertised that they would turn no one away, many distraught, unwed mothers sent letters to the Children's Bureau indicating that, in fact, the homes were often forced to hold out for girls who could pay. One young woman who wrote after reading about a maternity home in a romance magazine told the story of frustration:

> I . . . went to see Major Wrieden in Jersey City and she offered to help but suggested I try Booth Memorial in New York since I wasn't a Jersey resident. That was a joke to me. New York all but said I had to be a millionaire. I note that the girl in the story didn't mention any money at all. . . . The total sum [at Booth] came to almost $270.00. Did the magazine state the

government was trying to help girls in my condition? Most of the married friends I have pay under $200 to go through the same thing. Sure I have a job, but no bank account or rich friends.[79]

A Boston girl wrote a second time to Morlock, to tell her that the advice from the Children's Bureau was too expensive: "I wrote to Hastings House [Maternity Home] in Jamaica Plain, Mass. . . . [and] received a reply a few days ago—it seems [financially] impossible for me to go there.[80]

Morlock was worried about maternity homes turning away such girls because she believed all should be accommodated, one way or another.[81] She wrote about her concern to a home in Tennessee preparing its publicity materials:

> What concerns me, and we have had several illustrations of it recently, is the girl who writes to the maternity home for admission and gets a letter back stating the fee charged. She does not have this amount and therefore thinks that the door is closed to her. Is there any way to include a brief statement that the home takes some responsibility for trying to see that some plan is made or that the girl is encouraged to write again.[82]

Others at the Children's Bureau were more fiscally minded. Morlock's superior, Mildred Arnold, who often took over the letter-answering duties while Morlock was touring maternity homes across the country, had a different style of communicating with unwed mothers and a different set of priorities. A young woman from Kentucky was one of many who had the misfortune to write while Morlock was away. Arnold's answer to her plea for help was rather chillingly composed: "We note your finances are limited. As we are sure you recognize, it costs money to run a maternity home just the same as it costs money to run your own home."[83]

Morlock and some of her colleagues wondered frequently whether many of the girls they referred, by letter, to maternity homes made it there. The results, it seems, were mixed. But the commitment to maternity homes of the social work establishment and other community-based helpers reflected the fact that the postwar cultural climate had upped the ante for white girls and women in a peculiar way. On the one hand, radio, TV, magazines, and school curricula delivered messages about the intense pleasures available to normative women as middle-class wives and mothers.[84] On the other hand, the pervasiveness and insistence with which the prescriptions for females were hammered home suggested that girls and women were more vulnerable than ever to missteps in a society in which "sex and sexuality increasingly entered the public sphere and became part of the definition of youth."[85] As American culture lumbered toward an accommodation with the facts of female sexuality, particularly in the context of the white, middle class, the maternity home provided white girls and women who experimented with sex, a sort of underground finishing school at a time before the law or the community sanctioned other alternatives.

The Arrival

> As we drew near Tarrytown [the maternity home], Frances grew increasingly nervous. She asked [the social worker] for a cigarette and, when it was lit, blurted out, "I want babies of my own some day, but not this way! I want to have babies of my own with a *real* father! Oh, Miss Black, it's all so terrible!"
>
> "You're going to be all right, Frances," Miss Black said, soothingly, "What you need right now is a good bath and lunch, and we'll see that you get them. Come, dear, powder your nose. We're almost there."[86]

Once the maternity home option had been selected by young women or their parents and the date of admission arrived, unwed mothers constructed a personal approach to the ordeal. This was not an easy task, since for many it meant synthesizing the horrified disappointment and anger of their parents, the soothing reassurance of the social worker, the forbidding appearance of the maternity home, their own fear, and their own relief to be safely out of the censorious community. Jean Thompson recorded her journey to the Salvation Army Home where she would have and relinquish her illegitimate baby. Alone, thousands of miles from friends and family, she walked up a broad hill and was pleased to see the large house perched on the top, "surrounded by park-like gardens with large old trees and brilliant flower beds along winding paths." Four and a half months pregnant, her step not so light, Jean trudged to the front door of the old mansion, tried the door, and found it locked. In a minute the door was opened "by a woman with a tight, pinched face . . . as if she'd been waiting for me . . . without a word she held it open so I could walk in and then locked it behind me again, and I couldn't help feeling trapped."[87]

Sometimes staff were sensitive to the fearsome quality of the discarded mansion they'd inherited. The director of the Helena, Montana, Florence Crittenton Home recognized that her facility seemed an almost formidable adversary and asked herself, despairingly: "How does one change a doughty old matriarch into a warm-bosomed friend? What effect had the former mansion with its wide, austere reception hall, the rosewood staircase, the slow movement of the pendulum of the grandfather clock, upon the frightened girl?"[88] Indeed, frightened girls entering the homes were struck by the severity of these facilities. Remembering her own arrival, one girl wrote, "My first impression was of a prison because of the fence," and another observed that to her, from the outside, "it appeared to be a stockade or cattle corral." A third recalled, "I was scared stiff. I felt I had died and gone to Hades and nobody cared." One girl's first impressions included what would become a considerable source of solace for many inside: the society of unwed mothers. She said, "When I drove up to the Home the fence and big house looked like a prison. I didn't like it, but the girls were nice." Gidget, in a Florence Crittenton Home in Cleveland, took one look at the old mansion on Euclid Avenue and said simply, "I was glad, under my circumstances, to be here, rather than at home."[89]

The physical plants of maternity homes suggested a metaphoric congruence with their residents. Created both to contain and project the promise and the image of "the family," these mansions were now used and cast off. In their second lives, many occupied the borderlands of the city, neighborhoods in which old, genteel residences were mixed with shabbiness and commerce. In their second lives, the mansions were refurbished, outfitted for matronly service. The fate of these "doughty old matriarchs" was not unlike the fate of unwed daughters.

Gidget's sanctuary in Cleveland was on "one of the busiest thoroughfares in the city and in a neighborhood that [was] in a residential section but with business places moving in." Like many of the homes, this one was the former residence of a wealthy family and imperfectly suited to the need for privacy of sequestered girls. The large "house [took] up most of the ground space so that there [was] little opportunity for the girls to be outside."[90] The Salvation Army Home in Cincinnati also occupied the former residence of a well-to-do family, this one in an area that was occupied, by midcentury, almost exclusively by blacks. When Morlock visited the home in 1949, she found the intact woodwork and other appointments lovely and spotless, but the house cheerless and lacking in privacy.[91] Here, as at the Salvation Army's Door of Hope in Jersey City and St. Anne's in Columbus, the girls slept dormitory style, in crowded upstairs spaces with as many as sixteen to twenty to a room. A girl coming to the Door of Hope was instructed to bring as few possessions with her as possible, as each girl was allocated but one drawer. Morlock regretted the lack of privacy here and lamented the fact that "the whole place has an air of being used."[92]

The rooms designated for leisure in many homes were grim, at least throughout the 1940s and 1950s. In a Texas maternity home, Morlock found the

> recreation room . . . on the third floor . . . so situated that it would be hot in summer. It is cheerless and unattractive. An old sewing table, small radio and electric player and books stacked on a table were some of the furnishings. [The director] said the girls spent considerable time in their rooms. They do little reading.[93]

In Kentucky, she found that "the recreation room where the girls . . . spend much time, is unattractive and poorly furnished. It was crowded, the furniture drab and there seemed to be a predominance of jig-saw puzzles. They have a radio and record player for this room, but it was out for repairs."[94]

By the mid-to-late 1950s many homes were promoting themselves as genteel, attractive, and homelike; indeed, many volunteer circles and guilds contributed materially to the effort to refine and redefine the look of maternity homes. A home for white girls in Natchez, Mississippi, described itself in the 1950s as a "two-story colonial residence that has been recently re-decorated. [I]t provides an attractive, home-like atmosphere designed for the maximum comfort and happiness of girls while there. The Home provides complete privacy, both in the home and in the garden and recreation area that overlooks the Mississippi River from the backyard."[95] In 1959 the Florence Crittenton Association of America generalized about the organization's aesthetic and intentions concerning the interior decoration of their fifty homes: "In every case . . . Florence Crittenton Homes strive for a homelike atmosphere which has orderliness and beauty as prime requisites to effective service."[96]

Among the thousands of girls and women who entered this refurbished world each year to undergo their own refurbishing, were many who came with what might be called a suspended identity. Greeting a new arrival at the home, an old-timer of several weeks' tenure introduced herself using an alias and gave her hometown as a city a thousand miles west of the truth: " 'I'm Jean T. from Chicago due in March.' . . . The [new] girl nodded slightly and said, 'I'm Marion C. from Norfolk, Virginia.' I recognized her New England accent and wondered if she was from Boston."[97] Later when the old-timer said good-bye to a new friend from inside who was leaving the home, she reflected on the impact these suspended identities had on the possibilities for authenticity inside, and later outside.

> There was a wide gulf between us and nothing to bridge it with. I think we could have been good friends on the outside, too, but Karen never told me her real name or where she comes from, and I never told her mine. If we ever meet again, it will be by accident—and we may not even want to admit we ever knew each other.[98]

Maternity home personnel encouraged or at least supported the practice of submerging a girl's true identity during her stay. Conceivably it worked in somewhat the same way as the self-abnegating practices of military boot camp. At the same time, it offered an unwed mother the practical protection that the culture insisted she needed. In the Denver Florence Crittenton Home, no visitors were permitted in the hospital area of the home, a policy that protected the anonymity of all the girls. For years the home's medical records used first names only. The head nurse there explained the home's attitude: "We were all trained that we didn't ask questions—about family, about boyfriends. There was so much emphasis on confidential care, you just didn't pry."[99] In addition, homes set up elaborate schemes to postmark and reroute the mail of the girl in a maternity home in one city who wanted her friends to think, for example, that she was vacationing in another city. One seasoned practitioner observed, "Often the staff is more vigorous about concealing the residents' identity than are the residents themselves."[100]

One observer described how girls protected themselves when they had to go from the home to a nearby hospital for delivery:

> They usually enter the hospital under their own names with a "Mrs." added, but sometimes it would just cause too much suffering for a girl to use her own name, and in that case she uses a fictitious one—even here at [the maternity home]. . . . From start to finish, these girls face a lonely time, and their stay at the hospital is no exception. They make up all sorts of stories to explain to the other patients why their supposed husbands aren't around—that they have just been drafted, or are off on a business trip, or whatever. . . . The nurses who generally size up the situation pretty quickly, seem to feel there's something romantic about such girls, and give them a little more attention than the usual maternity patient gets.[101]

The pact that unwed mothers entered into—with parents, care givers, and often friends and relations who tacitly agreed to deny what they knew—had a powerful impact on the young woman who went inside. "Rosa," an unwed mother staying in an Atlanta home, wrote a poem she called "The Shore at Night" which suggests how deeply submerged the girl wished and perhaps willed herself to be. The girl here is "free" but invisible. The home provided, at once, the haven of protective custody and the means of full self-effacement.

The Shore At Night

Listen to the waves
  break on the shore
The warm breezes muffle my hair
The stars seem to shine
  forevermore—
I am alone without a care.

Free, to splash in the dark waves,
  to run along the sand.
Free from the tongues of waves
And the eyes of suspicious man.

Nowhere else is there such peace
Nowhere on the face of this earth
Where I can find such release
From man and his cynical mirth.[102]

The Rules

We can't go out on a pass till after lunch and the time drags. I can walk through the hall pretending I've got an errand somewhere but when I get there I don't know what to do and I turn around to go somewhere else. I see other girls do the same; we drift listlessly through the house.[103]

Throughout the first two postwar decades, maternity homes were, in general, trying to improve their "leisure time" programs and relax their formidable systems of house rules.[104] These efforts reflected an intention to align the girl's experience at the home with the evolving philosophical or ideological changes in attitudes toward unmarried mothers and the purposes of maternity homes. The changes were doubtless also designed to satisfy the preferences of their clients, both the parents and their daughters.[105] By the early 1950s, many maternity homes had moved from the prewar emphasis on austerity, punishment, and training unwed mothers in menial skills, to teaching femininity, and then, in some cases, to using the girl's residence to enforce or reinforce her self-concept as a regular girl who was simply on a minor detour to regular American womanhood. Again, the changes were not always easy to institute. Many homes resisted liberalization or stumbled along governed by a code of punitive gentility. Some modified the punitive dimension over time; it was, however, rarely absent.

The rules at a San Antonio maternity home in 1950, the Texas Home and Mission Training School, reflected the ragged transition from an emphasis on punishment to one on femininity, with exaggerated gentility as the constant. This home did not keep a girl if she didn't "cooperate." Cooperation involved agreeing to "leave men alone." If a girl defied this rule and went out with a man, she had to leave. She had to be neat, prompt at meals, and have lights out by the required time. All girls took assumed names. All had to be in residence at least four months before delivery because "the philosophy of the home is that the girl cannot be rehabilitated in less than four months." The home's "training program" entailed chapel, cooking, sewing, home nursing, and "how to be a hostess." Each week "one acts as a hostess at a table while the others are guests. They teach them etiquette and hymns."[106]

The punitive mode could represent a heavy dose of home-brewed medicine, a purgative to cleanse a befouled system. It also represented the attempt of home personnel, *in loco parentis,* to be tough on the girls for their own good by helping them internalize standards of behavior that the pregnancy demonstrated were lacking. A few years after the war, Admiral Robert Barrett, the patriarchal leader of the National Florence Crittenton Mission (the precursor of the Florence Crittenton Association of America), expressed his approval of the all but passé policy that called for staff to open and read the mail of all residents. He approved the observation of the superintendent of the Los Angeles home who argued that reading the mail "gave her so much understanding of the girls." Barrett was shocked to learn that in the San Francisco home, girls could come and go as they pleased and pointed out sternly that "in his own home his daughters hadn't this freedom," especially the right, as they occasionally did at the home, "to be away at meal time."[107] Whether restrictive rules were infused with medicinal or patriarchal intentions may not have constituted a significant distinction for residents who simply had to obey.

Unwed mothers in the homes were expected to obey rules concerning when they could leave the building and where they were permitted to go. In a Columbus, Ohio home the rule was firm: "Girls were not permitted to go out alone except to the corner and then only if their condition is not too obvious." In general in this home, no privileges of any kind were granted until a nonpaying girl had worked off her bill or until she returned to the home as an employee.[108] At St. Mary's maternity shelter in New York, girls could only leave the building under supervision between 2 and 5 P.M.[109]

In response to a discipline crisis at the Home of Redeeming Love in Oklahoma, Maud Morlock counseled her colleague to remember that things were changing and, indeed, had changed. She stressed that "modern practice" meant not depriving a girl of her liberty; a girl had to experience growth in a respectful context.[110] In line with this perspective, many homes monitored their girls closely while providing a kindly modicum of latitude. For example, in the Denver Salvation Army Home, girls could go out unattended two afternoons a week.[111] Another home described its policy: "girls go unattended to the community [but] we exercise our judgment as a staff, in selecting the girls who have this privilege."[112] Major Wrieden's description of policy at the Door of Hope showed how some home directors wanted a new degree of liberty for their charges: "The girls can go out on Thursdays and Saturday for 2:00 to 4:30 after getting permission from the officer of the day." She added, "[I]t is rather ridiculous that [the rules] say these are the two days when the girls go outside as permission is freely granted when it is requested so it virtually amounts to a flexible policy."[113] In Kentucky, one home made an interesting accommodation to liberty:

> Formerly the girls were permitted to go to town one afternoon a week. This was discontinued as they all flocked out together. They are now permitted to go out at any time that they wish, especially to shop but not in a group. They are expected to let it be known where they are going and when approximately they will return.[114]

The newer emphasis on the superintendent as a caring maternal figure guiding her charges to safety is illustrated by Morlock's description of postwar practices at Inwood House in New York City:

> They are free to go out any afternoon and can stay out to dinner until 8:00 pm. They tell the nurse and the house mother that they are leaving the building. When I inquired how this was done, Mrs. Pratt said that she could answer as she often sat in the office and had heard them come in to do this. It is a very natural procedure and without any strain. They usually ask whether they may go to the P.O. or whether there is any errand that needs to be done. Mrs. Leavitt said that they prepare them in the intake interview

for such a procedure and it is put on the basis of what any young person does in her own home who has a good relationship with her parents. They have had very few abuses, such as a girl saying she was going to the movies and then being out with boyfriends.[115]

Maternity home staff grappled with rules about the comings and goings of their unwed residents and also struggled to maintain the right tone and the right type of girls in the facility. Most had definite ideas about the sort of genteel young woman who had strayed but who would benefit from maternity home guidance and find her way back to normative life. The Volunteers of America, who ran several homes in this era, collected extensive information on each girl to confirm her "normality"—educationally, intellectually, medically, and emotionally—before admission. They desired only girls who were seeking care and seclusion as their first priority.[116] In the early 1950s, the obstetricians on staff at the Ingleside Home in Buffalo argued strenuously against accepting girls or women in the home who had given birth to a previous child.[117] That attitude was shared by staff at the Catherine Booth Home in Cincinnati and elsewhere.[118] In 1964, a board member of a Florence Crittenton Home described policy in her facility: "We never accept repeaters. We are not so sympathetic with the problem of 'He ain't done right by Nell twice.' "[119]

Major Cox, in a Salvation Army Home in California, was explicit about the type of girls she felt were appropriate residents: she "liked to help the younger ones [but] did not like to take the sophisticated type and found it very difficult to work with Negro girls who are amoral instead of just immoral."[120]

In most homes, girls who passed through the critical filter still had to meet home requirements and had to accept the full program offered if they themselves were to remain acceptable. The Florence Crittenton Home in Seattle dismissed a girl if staff discovered she was planning to place her baby through an independent (nonagency) adoption.[121] A Wisconsin home, even as late as 1959, felt it was dangerous to allow employed girls to live at the home. They would not benefit from a "planned treatment program" and would merely be "hanging their hats" in the home and looking for no further help. "In addition, the goings and comings of these girls might well cause unrest among the . . . girls who are there full time."[122] Part of the fortifying treatment in many homes involved insisting that girls had no contact with the "putative father."[123]

It was not a simple matter to carry out such a full and stringent regimen of rules. This was especially true given the subtle context in which the rules were implemented. Boards of directors and experienced home administrators often expressed how difficult it was to secure staff who could portray the right balance of strictness and respect toward the unwed mothers. An administrator in Chicago wrote about the difficulty encountered in finding enough mature, kindly women who are interested in caring for unmarried mothers and who are not condemnatory of illegitimate pregnancy and who will not be impatient with the disturbed behavior sometimes manifested by these girls.[124]

Girls in the Cincinnati Salvation Army Home complained that attendants treated them badly, were domineering, and counteracted the orders of the more sensitive nurses.[125] In Frankfort, Kentucky, the housekeeper, who also was the home's cook, was a source of extreme difficulty to the director and the residents, but considered irreplaceable, nonetheless:

She is said to be a very punishing person, and a poor cook. . . . If they buy excellent ground steak, the cook holds it under the hot water faucet and thoroughly washes it before it is cooked. She sounded like a disturbed person, but Miss Jasper has not discharged her as she is apparently fearful that she could not get anyone to replace her.[126]

Some girls left homes where the rules were too rigid or too strictly enforced, even though "conditions [were] awful in their own homes."[127]

In the early 1950s, a Chicago administrator cautioned her colleagues about the cruel practices still prevailing at some homes:

The maternity home may provide a place for the unmarried mother to stay but usually not until her seventh month of pregnancy. If she can manage somehow until [then] she may be admitted, or she may be rejected because it's her second pregnancy, or because she isn't religious enough, or because she doesn't look strong enough to do her share of work or because she hasn't any money. These [observations] may sound querulous and hypercritical, but they are, in cold fact, all things that may happen to the unmarried mother.[128]

About fifteen years later, a physician who came into regular contact with maternity home personnel complained that they wanted to punish illegitimately pregnant women. He charged that staff felt things were being made too easy for the girls in the home, while they should be made to "learn from their mistakes." According to this doctor, maternity home officials set themselves up as judges and behaved as if they were empowered to "burn . . . witches at the stake."[129]

Nevertheless, by the later 1950s and early 1960s, in the heyday of maternity homes, many had recognized the virtues of flexibility. This innovation reflected in part an interest in establishing the homes as suitable facilities for girls and women to whom no permanent stain would adhere. The resident population was now simply in a state of social transit; in order to offer a desirable service, the homes had to accept this perspective and treat clients accordingly. The listings in the *Directory of Maternity Homes* for 1960, which contained descriptions of over 150 homes, demonstrated the diminished authoritarian focus of the homes.[130] Jennie Phelps of the Denver Florence Crittenton Home remembered that by the late 1950s, the home never imposed restrictions on the girls' coming and going. She said, "It was much like living in a dorm."[131] The restrictions, according to Phelps, were all self-imposed by the girls themselves. Local girls, for example, did not like to go outside because they were concerned about running into someone they knew.

Whether maternity homes remained bastions of strict social control or tried to relax their rules, most were situated throughout the period in the midst of communities that found their presence repugnant. Often neighbors trained such eagle eyes on the nearby home—while deploring its proximity—that flexibility inside the home was the result of rigid attitudes outside. In the late 1940s, the director of the Door of Hope in Jersey City decided to allow her girls to smoke in the building. This decision followed the complaints of neighbors who regularly reported to her that they saw girls smoking outside the building. When Major Wrieden herself walked by the home on a rainy day and saw two girls, one Negro and one white, standing under an umbrella, smoking, she devised the new policy.[132] Often neighbors objected to seeing the girls at all. In Youngstown, the president of the board of the Florence Crittenton Home reported that, "It came to our attention that some of our neighbors objected because the girls were seen in the neighborhood shopping plaza and movie, and were annoyed at the way they (to quote) 'flaunted their disgrace.' "[133]

The issue became particularly fraught in the community when a maternity home proposed a new facility in a residential area. In the early 1960s, the Salvation Army wanted to expand its facility in Boston, which meant moving into a new neighborhood. In response to this plan, "vocal elements in the community . . . fought the move as vigorously as if the Army were trying to relocate a leprosarium."[134] Neighbors were especially irate that "thousands of children [would] see the girls." Neighborhood leaders shepherded their cause through a series of public hearings, an appeal of that hearing, a further appeal to the State Superior Court, and finally to the Massachusetts Supreme Court. One educator involved in the attempt to enjoin the Army from building a new facility remarked, "Why reward these girls [with a new home] for the problems they have brought upon themselves and society?"[135] Similar campaigns were mounted by community leaders in Louisville and elsewhere.[136]

When a Chicago social service agency attempted to interest middle-class women in providing boarding-home care for unwed mothers in lieu of placing them in a maternity home (some of the girls were black and therefore excluded from the homes), the agency failed completely.

> Many in the community felt that this program would serve only to encourage delinquent sexual behavior since the care to be given would pamper the girls and . . . in the their minds, implied condoning their behavior. Instead they wished to have the girls punished by depriving them of any pleasures or comforts which would in turn prevent further social promiscuity.

This feeling was so strongly held that an officer of a women's club in a middle-class area refused even "to have the problem and the proposed program discussed with her membership since she knew their neighborhood did not want bad girls."[137]

This club officer's constituency, the Boston group, and some elements in most communities sustained purely punitive attitudes toward unwed mothers long after the attitudes of maternity home personnel became more complex. While some continued to construct single pregnant females as sexual sinners, most professionals began to understand them as psychiatrically disturbed and curable, psychiatrically. At the same time, the thousands of middle-class women who formed circles and guilds to support the rehabilitation of unwed mothers perceived the girls as deserving of their efforts, in whatever way they defined the nature of the illicit pregnancy. But these charitable women, along with their punitive matron neighbors, held strongly to the belief that the community and the girls needed to be protected from each other. When homes all over the country held their annual open houses, "to show the public where their charity money was going," the circle members and board members who hosted these events took care that every girl left the home for the afternoon.[138] Throughout the period of this study, what held these groups together was a shared belief that the unwed mother "had gotten herself pregnant" in large part because she was insufficiently feminine. If efforts were to be expended in the girls' behalf, training in femininity represented resources well allocated.

The Program

The commitment by homes after the war to "teach" femininity reflected a new belief that the girls inside were educable. They could be transformed. Before the war, homes largely offered girls the opportunity to acquire menial skills so that they could construct lives outside in congruence with their moral standing in the community. Programming efforts based on teaching femininity and its attendant skills and graces was a first significant step beyond "training." In the early postwar years, feminine skills were often taught as a bridge between the old attitudes and the new. On the one hand, learning how to do "fancy work," for example, could prepare a ruined girl for earning a living in her ignominious future. On the other hand, it could be part of an attempt to prepare the unwed mother for housewifery. In the late 1940s, Jane Wrieden, the director of the Door of Hope, believed many of her charges should be readied to assume their role as matrons. In addition, she felt that teaching girls to excel at handwork was valuable because, "A girl learns creativeness and perhaps there is peace of mind that comes from doing something with the hands. It can also serve as a wholesome interest when she leaves the home if it is not too costly, [if it is] attractive and something that causes her a feeling of accomplishment."[139]

Throughout the 1950s, homes in every region of the country featured courses, classes, and workshops in the domestic arts. Topeka's Florence Crittenton Home advertised its courses in homemaking and personality development. The Zoar Home in Allenson Park, Pennsylvania, made home economics classes "available" along with games and parties, but the Sophia Little Home in Englewood, New Jersey, required its girls to attend "home ec" course five days a week. In Lynchburg, Virginia, maternity home residents took "specialized courses in sewing, meal planning and preparation and serving."[140] The Dade County Crittenton Home created a weekly schedule for its charges that suggested preparation for life as a middle-class matron:

Monday	Sewing
Tuesday	Bridge
Wednesday	Knitting
Thursday	Enamel on Copper
Friday	Clinic day for examinations
Saturday	Sketch Class
Sunday	Relax and Religion

Girls in residence at these homes and many others might anticipate either employment or marriage after completing such programs.

The other component of femininity, and arguably the more important, was personal attractiveness, an attribute unwed mothers were often assumed to lack. The hundreds of new courses in grooming and charm in maternity home programs after the war was a sure indication that residents were being groomed to go back onto the dating and mating market. Today's unwed mother could expect to be somebody's wife tomorrow. In the fourteen homes in Texas, for example, there were almost no activities offered beyond Bible studies and beauty culture.[141] The House of Mercy Home in Washington, D.C., offered its girls TV, piano, canasta, and ceramics for leisure-time activities, but placed its chief emphasis on good grooming. In Los Angeles, the Florence Crittenton Home was particularly proud of its beauty parlor with up-to-date equipment and its emphasis on beauty culture. "Each month volunteers from the Los Angeles Beauticians' Club [gave] several hours helping girls with their hair styling, instructions in skin care and grooming."[142] St. Faith's Home in Tarrytown, New York, aimed to attract residents by highlighting the fact that its girls had access to "the regular services of a personal grooming teacher."[143] Girls were schooled in improving their looks, and in learning how to use them. Many homes offered courses in "how to win a man" and stressed the genteel skills that many believed could help a girl to keep him.[144]

Homes ran into difficulty while trying to set up programs because often staff was convinced that the girls were without any interests. A Salvation Army matron was doubtful about offering the girls any sort of program since she felt they "couldn't sustain interest" for more than a couple of hours. Staff despaired in Cincinnati after the girls showed little interest in the Junior League's classes in sewing and cooking, and "especially in making layettes." The San Antonio Salvation Army Home gave up classes in current events and the skills necessary for applying for a job, maintaining only handcraft and sewing.[145]

Nevertheless, by the mid-1950s, a substantial number of homes had taken one further step toward assuring the regularization of their residents' post-maternity home lives: they offered tutoring or accredited academic courses in the homes. The courses could be transferred discreetly and count toward junior high or high school graduation. Since approximately half of all girls in maternity homes had to interrupt their schooling because of the pregnancy, such programs addressed the present needs as well as the future concerns of residents.[146] Many homes began to offer full-scale educational programs because of the new way that boards of directors and staff had begun to assess their charges. Many felt that the teenage girls they harbored should not fall behind their peers. Now girls would expect and be expected to fit back into their family, social, community, and educational lives upon release. It became very important in the short run to minimize at least the educational interruption. Since the pregnancy and maternity home experience was now simply an unfortunate detour for broadly middle-class girls, it was equally important, in the long run, that she complete the level of education appropriate to her social class. That way she could attract an appropriate husband.

Educational programs in maternity homes were not exclusively a postwar phenomenon. In the 1930s Isabelle Walters, who directed the Florence Crittenton Home in Toledo for many years, went to the school superintendent of that city and informed him that there were more than ten girls at the home, so the school board had to supply a teacher. Over the years, Walters got a full-scale program: teachers, volunteers, a family life education program, and specialists to work with parents.[147] The Toledo program, however, was an exception. Even after the war, most homes moved slowly in this direction; a number did not follow at all. In the 1950s, before one Texas home began to have a board of education teacher in two times a week to offer tutoring, the only educational program consisted of a monthly series of eight lectures delivered by a public health nurse on such topics as venereal disease, TB, cancer, contagion, and fire hazards. As soon as the nurse finished the cycle of lectures she would begin again.[148] An unpublished study in 1965 found that "the majority of homes provide no education [programs] whatsoever," although a substantial number did have programs two to five days a week.[149] The United States commissioner of education, Lawrence Derthick, noted in this period that community attitudes constituted a powerful roadblock in the way of providing educational opportunities for unwed mothers. In his review of the situation, he found that "In many districts, a girl can't earn credits for work done during her pregnancy, or if she can, she can't hide that it was [done] in a maternity home."[150] An educational administrator for the state of New Jersey explained that in his state, educators were negative toward the idea of school programs for unwed mothers. They were confident that "some of these girls have become mothers deliberately for the purpose of escaping school."[151]

Despite these attitudes, the trend was definitely toward eradicating the contradiction between the statuses of "unwed mother" and "student." By the late 1950s the Bureau of Attendance for the New York City schools had policies and practices in place that allowed unwed mothers to continue their education four and a half days a week in a maternity home, if that was where they were. The boards of education in Chicago, Detroit, St. Paul, Los Angeles, and San Diego had partially removed obstacles to education as well.[152] In Denver, the Florence Crittenton Home built a separate educational building in the early 1960s and offered a complete high school program for the girls inside. At the same time, however, Jane Wrieden, who had recently become the Salvation Army's chief consultant on programs and services for unwed mothers, sought help from the Children's Bureau. She asked Mildred Arnold, the director of the Division of Social Services, if the Bureau could be of help in lobbying state Departments of Education to provide educational services to girls in maternity homes since so many boards of education refused.[153]

Educational programs inside represented one increasingly acceptable way to help an unwed mother maintain a concept of herself as a regular American girl who had made a mistake with temporary repercussions. An even more popular way to achieve that goal was to provide the unwed mother with the services of a psychological caseworker. A study in the early 1960s revealed that fewer than half of the maternity homes offered accredited educational courses to girls under fifteen; about 40 percent provided schoolwork for girls between fifteen and seventeen. But 86 percent provided casework services for their residents.[154] Still, when queried concerning the unmet needs of girls in the homes, staff most often identified the need for even more casework.[155]

As with the other postwar innovations in homes—such as promoting adoption, liberalizing rules, and providing educational opportunities—the trend toward casework was clear and pervasive. Still, like the others, casework was quickly accepted in some homes and sternly resisted in others, at least at first. In the early postwar years, a number of boards and administrators agreed with Mrs. Lee ("a 73 year old cardiac," according to Maud Morlock), who ran the Florence Crittenton operation in Columbus, and the president of her board, a physician and psychologist at Ohio State University, who were "very hostile" to social work. Mrs. Lee considered casework simply "interference." Her intentions were to protect the girl and provide good medical care; all else was "incidental."[156] At the same time, a conflict was raging in the Cleveland Crittenton Home over the use of casework; services were spotty and not professionalized in Pittsburgh; and they were thoroughly accepted in Los Angeles.[157] The state administrator in charge of licensing homes in Texas remarked that homes in the state were not interested in casework or any other services; they were concerned only about meeting minimum requirements and securing more babies to put on the adoption market.[158] By the end of the 1950s, almost all Florence Crittenton, Catholic Charities, and Salvation Army homes provided this service, except for some in the south.[159]

Caseworkers and their administrative sponsors in the homes believed that by working with a social worker, the unwed mother could be helped to achieve new insights about herself and, as a consequence, helped to change herself. This belief was predicated on two deeper assumptions. First, the girl had decent and yielding resources within herself to draw on. Second, the girl was worthy; she deserved understanding, and she deserved another chance. The maternity homes that did not accept these notions generally stuck to the older belief that the out-of-wedlock pregnancy revealed the girl's innate badness. Perhaps this quality had seeped in by way of a bad environment, or unsuitable companions, or a genetic flaw, but once revealed through the pregnancy, there was no denying it, and no cure.

Caseworkers agreed that the pregnancy revealed some inner condition, some essence, of the unwed mother. They equated pregnancy not with simple badness, but with confusion, unhappiness, and the internalization of poor family dynamics. A social worker in the maternity home setting generally held that the girl's "environment"—formerly the neighborhood, the community, the city, even the culture—was now simply equal to and embodied in the family. In addition, the formerly direct relationship between environment, badness, and pregnancy could now be mediated and then broken by "understanding," the caseworker's understanding of the girl and the girl's subsequent understanding of herself. The mind of the individual girl became a more powerful and determinative force than environment, constitutional predilections, or sex. The most fundamental and necessary assumption in the caseworker's repertoire was that the unwed mother did not understand herself when she landed in the home. That being so, the girl could be transformed through the gift of self-knowledge.

An experienced administrator explained the value of casework this way: "By talking with her social worker, a girl comes to accept the fact that she is an unmarried mother and arrives at a better understanding of herself, so that she can make something constructive of the experience instead of passively resigning herself to the role of outcast."[160] Most caseworkers worked to bring to unwed mothers the recognition that out-of-wedlock pregnancy was not like married pregnancy, the final step toward maturity for a female. It represented, on the contrary, both the expression of "hostile, resentful feelings toward her parents" and an inappropriately chosen mode for "struggling for emancipation" from bad parents.[161]

Isabelle Walters in Toledo, always a front-runner, wrote to Maud Morlock in 1949 that she was taking care of "first things first" now that the home was showing a series of psychologically-oriented family life films, under the direction of a psychiatrist who led the postscreening discussions. Walters wrote that according to family life experts, the film *Feelings of Rejection* and others in the series should only be shown with a psychiatrist present, "as [they] are filled with dynamite if not handled properly." The explosive potential of such programming aside, Walters, and many of the mothers of her residents, judged the series a success, as it addressed the caseworker's central goal: "We are getting at the roots of this problem in helping the girl to find herself."[162]

By the mid-1950s, Morlock felt maternity homes across the country were "making great progress" in developing casework services and integrating them into their programs.[163] This was, in no small measure, an accomplishment Morlock herself could take some credit for.[164] Still, it is hard to imagine that even this avid champion of casework could have foreseen the extent to which casework would come to dominate the program content of maternity homes in the decade after her retirement in 1957. A large maternity home in Detroit, for example, which accommodated sixty girls, had on staff a psychiatrist, clinical psychologists, and social workers. In the late 1950s, the home added a group therapist, whose goals were to help girls gain "insight into why [they] became pregnant, develop greater ego strength, provide support in facing up to [their] problems, and to help with social readaptation." The decision to hire the group worker reflected a certainty about the "universality in the problems presented by a maternity home's clientele. . . .The girls' very presence indicated that they have common symptoms, common problems and common needs specific to an unwed pregnancy." It also reflected a certainty that casework was the optimal method of addressing these matters.[165] In the early 1960s, the Crittenton Hastings Home in Boston, whose residents received a full complement of casework services during the day, were now required to attend a social-work-oriented lecture-discussion program in the evening as well. This series covered topics such as: the Challenge of Returning to the Community; My Baby and Me: Hello and Goodbye; Problems in Selecting the Right Man for Me; Changing What I Do That I Don't Like; and Prevention of a Recurrence is Not Birth Control.[166]

Many unwed mothers enmeshed in such rounds of social work services became unsettled by the pervasive casework emphasis on adaptation, adjustment, and accepting reality. The reliance on these key concepts implied that unwed mothers needed to take exclusive responsibility for their predicament and their "cure." In the Boston home, in fact, residents were "quite outspoken about their confusion concerning the intentions of all the caseworkers they were required to see."[167] When Jean Thompson finally agreed to see the caseworker to whom she'd been assigned, she went in forewarned, with her own associations firmly intact: "Mostly I noticed that she isn't pregnant, her office is a tiny cubicle, almost like a cell."[168]

Many if not most social workers in the postwar decades were most concerned about facilitating the reentry of unwed mothers into society. Still, in the context of the maternity home, the concern became embedded in an institutional commitment to the psychiatric etiology of unwed pregnancy. Often the only way the social worker had to express her helpful intentions toward a single pregnant girl was to assess the case in the narrow, rigid terms that constituted the common parlance among staff.

A 1957 article in *Harper's* recognized this tendency for social workers to lose sight of the individual as they met institutional priorities: "Helen R. Wright, dean emeritus of the Chicago University School of Social Service Administration, disclosed that a [maternity home] had slammed its door on an applicant who was seven months pregnant because 'they did not take girls after six months of pregnancy; they had found that they could not do good casework with them unless they came earlier.' " Such policies reveal that in transferring their interest to the girl's mind, some maternity homes had gone to extremes. They had become more interested in full access to the malleable minds of unwed mothers than they were in helping girls through their shameful pregnancies.

In addition to criticizing social workers who accepted institutional policies of this sort, the *Harper's* article faulted them for the tendency to assess the individual completely out of social context. The author advised that social workers "might lift their eyes from the trees of individual behavior to the woods full of social problems."[169] In the case of the unwed mother, the social worker's assessment often had the effect of magnifying the issues involved while shrinking the particular girl until her attributes as an individual were invisible. A typical case record demonstrates how psychology allowed a practitioner to lose sight of other, perhaps larger issues in the case of a teenage girl who had been raped:

> She would not talk about the father of the baby. She had gone out with him to amuse herself. He was tender and sweet and did not make sexual demands on her except in a laughing casual way. Then one night he became very passionate and she could not defend herself. She became a passive object and could not say "no."

> Here we see a girl who having lost parental love, continues to search for love and her primary motivation became centered in getting her dependent needs met. She took the man's sexual interest as love and an opportunity to be loved by somebody.[170]

The social worker, in typical fashion, flattened out both the social context and the individual here and was interested only in the relevant syndrome. The syndrome had explanatory force because it simultaneously validated the prevailing cultural views of females and could account for rape and unwed pregnancy.

The Home Culture of Unwed Mothers

When an unwed mother arrived on the doorstep, she came to join a society of mostly young women, all in a similar predicament. They were all subject to social stigma; they had caused their parents extreme difficulty; and most had been rejected by the boys or men with whom they'd had sex. The shared stigma was powerful. Many unwed mothers felt that they had been removed from society and sent to homes during their pregnancies because their parents, their schoolmates and friends—the community in general—viewed them as criminals, or slightly more gently, as patients. It was difficult for an unwed mother to escape internalizing the notion that she was some sort of felon, incarcerated for committing an act of aggression against society. A girl in a maternity home that she was eager to leave "now and again got aggressive with the matron" because she was so restless. "The matron would [respond to these episodes by saying]: 'Katie, [we] are investigating your case. You can't expect people to do everything for you overnight.' [Katie wrote,] 'It made me feel like a criminal. And a prisoner.' "[171] One young woman, called Virginia, demonstrated in her plea for help how the pregnancy shaped her view of herself:

> I am in need of help and did not know what to do until I read the article in *Woman's Life*. It gave me a little hope as to what should be the right thing for me to do. I was so desperate I almost tried to lose my baby, but I guess one's conscience is really one of God's divine gifts. I could not murder my baby, even though my sins are a black as any murderer.[172]

A schoolteacher from Seattle living in a New York City maternity home described her predicament and its effect on her.

> Only a short time before, the future had been bright and certain. She was engaged to a young lawyer; they had tentatively picked out a house, even started choosing furniture. Now she sat twisting her ringless hands in her swollen lap, her view of her future pinched into the hope that she could keep her secret from her socially prominent parents. Shattered by her fiance's rejection when she told him of her pregnancy, she had fled three thousand miles to New York. "I know what people think," Ellen H. said. "A mistake like this stamps you for life. It's like being a criminal."[173]

This unwed mother did not say she was a criminal, only that other people would think so, enduringly. She did not refute this public judgment or suggest that she could escape it. A Minnesota lawyer who had extensive professional contact with unwed mothers offered his perspective on these matters to a U.S. Senate committee in 1956:

> Throughout her pregnancy the [unwed] mother can avoid further humiliation and embarrassment only by keeping herself confined to a maternity

home . . . Her presence in such a place is not only a poorly kept secret, but the mental shock of the semi-imprisonment and her untouchable social classification is fully equivalent to a jail term among felons. Menial employment is assigned to her as a means of contributing towards her keep. Subsequently she leaves the institution with a heavy burden of debt despite the fact that she may not keep the child.[174]

The director of a maternity home affirmed the pervasiveness of the criminal experience, despite the many postwar reforms that softened the treatment of girls inside.

Even today girls dread coming here. To them an institution is synonymous with a place of punishment, an exile to which they are banished. They look upon their coming as if it were a jail sentence even though the real reason they are sent away from home is usually a sincere desire on the part of parents to protect them from the gossip of neighbors.[175]

The good and protective intentions of parents notwithstanding, society and complicit mothers and fathers insisted that pregnant, broadly middle-class white girls be institutionalized and rendered invisible. Many girls were confused about the reasons for this. Did the home protect them from the cruel social forces that the sight of their pregnancy would unleash? Was removal to the home simply part of the punishment for disobedience and sexual misconduct? Or was the maternity home a psychiatric treatment center for all these girls and women whose unmarried pregnancies demonstrated emotional illness? Many came up with answers that mixed all three intentions, but finding such answers seems to have been a difficult matter for all residents who were thrust into the invisible society of unwed mothers. Perhaps the most painful part of entering the home was this aspect; yet sometimes, even inside, the girls weren't invisible enough. One girl described what it was like to sit through a performance in the home, along with members of the home's ladies' auxiliary: "It's the sort of thing they make funny scenes of in the movies, but it wasn't so funny with fifty or so pregnant girls sitting on rows of straight-back chairs while a small group of well-dressed matrons sat in a corner whispering and stealing glances at us during the performance."[176] On the other hand, the home was a safe haven. When Jean Thompson ventured out, to browse through the racks at a local maternity-clothes store near the home she was staying in, she saw a pregnant woman who was "trying on a very elegant-looking maternity cocktail dress. . . .[She] looked like one of those ads in a woman's magazine (pretty as can be—mother to be). She was chatting with the saleslady about the baby, and I wanted to say, 'Hush, someone might hear you.' "[177] The unwed mother's perception that pregnancy required protection was powerful.

Some girls were acutely sensitive to the fact that all were sharing the same experience. One, who was described by the director of the home where she was staying as an "extremely disturbed girl who couldn't face or accept reality," felt quite competent to speak for herself and her peers:

> You who are an observer, can you ever know what it means to be an outcast, to have no corner to hide in, and to have no hand held out freely to aid you? . . . We come here . . . bewildered, in all frames of mind, from all walks of life; the college student, the nurse, the shop girl, the children barely out of high school, all with our stories, all with our hidden emotions. We come here antagonistic to society, hurt and helpless. We live here, and have our babies, and though to all this is a haven, to some it is a prison as well, because we are not here of our own choice. The situation makes us angry at the world in general and at the visible symbols of the society that proclaimed us unfit to live within the world. I wish to leave as I have never wished anything in my life. And yet, though the door stands open, I cannot go for here is protection and here must be home until once again I can say to society, "I am now ready to return, and obey your dictates and rules."[178]

Many girls inside shared the experience of feeling they had been put away by angry, disappointed parents. Directors of maternity homes witnessed parents who dumped their daughters on the doorstep of the homes. They also knew plenty of stories about the "small-town girl's family tak[ing] the course of simply dumping her on the nearest big town."[179] One director characterized parental responses to pregnant daughters this way:

> By and large, even though a mother rejects her daughter, she never entirely drops her . . . but sometimes antagonism between them is so fierce you almost wish she would. Fathers visit less often than mothers. Some of them are driven wild by the sight of their daughters pregnant and just remove themselves from the whole business.[180]

Another, confirming the distance fathers put between themselves and their pregnant daughters, said, "We didn't see very many fathers—whether they were angry or embarrassed, they didn't come."[181] One father of a single pregnant girl who did not remove himself from the situation, wrote to the director of a midwestern maternity home, revealing family priorities. He wrote, "As concerned as we are with the mistake of [our daughter] and as anxious as we are to give her all the help we can, we do have a problem in the financial end. I have a son going to the University. . . .[The maternity home] is all going to be something of a financial burden."[182] The father, who expressed extreme concern with confidentiality, was inquiring if it would be acceptable to the home if his daughter took up residence there at the last possible moment, to save money.

A director remembered that if "Mama came along" to the intake interview, the girl would be "all tears."[183] Another related what she considered a typical story, one that showed how the girls were generally handled by distraught parents:

While they were in my office, Frances just kept her face buried in her hands and cried, while her parents went right ahead making all the decisions for her. They wanted a shelter out of the city, one where Frances could be with girls near her own age, and, of course, they had decided that the baby should be adopted. [Concerning whether Frances would marry the putative father,] Frances' father said shortly, "Utterly impossible! I had him investigated. He's beneath my daughter's intellectual and social status."[184]

The society of girls inside shared the status of disgraced daughter; most were also the castoff sex partner of putative fathers. A girl's presence in a maternity home, rather than in a newlywed's garden apartment, strongly suggested a boyfriend's rejection. The postwar decades saw rapidly escalating rates of teen marriage and bridal pregnancy. In this era, a girl's life could be defined by who was willing to marry her. Thus, a girl in a maternity home signaled a girl rejected, a loser. The route to this ignominious status was more complicated after the war than it had yet been in the twentieth century.

In the late 1940s and the 1950s, premarital sex was increasingly common, as was teen marriage, bridal pregnancy, and abortion to deal with the consequences. The pervasive example of peers entering into sexual relations and dealing with the resulting pregnancies emboldened boys to ask for intercourse and may have provided girls with some sense of safety. The public sanctioning of teenage marriage, for example, could have made marriage seem more reassuring and more accessible than a diaphragm. Yet in some ways, these cultural trends increased the dangers facing a girl or young woman deciding whether or not to go "all the way" with her importuning boyfriend. Without legal access to birth control or abortion, in the context of pervasive public insistence on male dominance—at home, on the job, and elsewhere—most girls who engaged in sexual intercourse were not safe. In addition, the same elements of the culture that championed male dominance and protected the male prerogative to be sexual at any expense, including female suffering, also protected the traditional male prerogative to be free from blame. These elements sanctioned placing full responsibility for sex that led to pregnancy, but not marriage, on the girl or woman. Many who became pregnant understood that society considered it their responsibility to regulate sexual activity, and many accepted the blame for their condition. The story of a girl from Wisconsin was typical of many who believed they had gotten themselves pregnant: "At first I wouldn't let him touch me, but he said, 'If you love me you'd let me.' I used this means to hold the guy I was crazy about. . . . I blame no one; I have only myself to blame."[185]

The boyfriend of another girl had no qualms about making sure that the girl understood where the blame lay. A girlfriend might be convinced to have sex with you, but only a slut got pregnant.

I didn't want to tell Joey, but finally I couldn't stand it anymore. I told him after class one day. He was drinking an orange soda. It's silly to remember

that now, but he changed right from that minute. . . . Right then all he said
was "Oh, God, no" and then we walked back to his apartment. We didn't
say anything for a long time. I felt I just couldn't reach him anymore. Finally
I made him tell me what he was thinking, and he said, "I'm sitting here
being ashamed of you. God help me, I'm ashamed of you."[186]

The fact was that once most girls entered the maternity home, they had
no further contact with the boy or man by whom they'd gotten pregnant. A
study of 1,130 residents in eight Salvation Army Homes in 1953 showed that
only thirty of them, or 2.5 percent were receiving financial assistance from
the fathers. Only about half of the putative fathers acknowledged paternity.[187]
It was, of course, very painful for a young woman to be bereft in so many
ways at once. A social worker described how one unwed mother, preparing
to give her baby up for adoption, "spoke of the father of the baby, his desertion
of her as soon he knew the baby was on the way, and her feeling that she
never wanted to see him again. This young woman said, 'It hurt me more the
way he done [me], than it did about the baby.' "[188] The hurt often turned to
anger. One young unwed mother in a home after she'd been expelled from
school remarked bitterly, "You never say, 'Oh look, he's an illegitimate father.
He made this girl pregnant. He's a bum.' "[189]

One observer noted,

> The crash of the American dream for the unmarried mother, bred to believe
> in the magic of movie stars and the right brand of toothpaste, is so loud
> that it often leaves her with little sense of personal worth. "Does a girl in
> my position have the right to pray?" a desperate West Virginia girl recently
> inquired in a letter to a Government official?

"You grow up," said a bitter unmarried mother, "believing that if you buy
the right bra happiness is sure to be yours. Well, I tried it. . . ."[190]
When unwed mothers came together in the maternity home, they had
to deal individually with personal shame and blame; rejecting parents and
boyfriends; disillusionment, hurt, and anger, along with the pregnancy, the
impending birth, and the disposition of the baby. How did they deal with
this crushing array of feelings and events? Sometimes girls moved into a
private world in which the difficulties dissipated, a world that could sustain
images of romance and love. Linda, in an Atlanta maternity home, wrote a
poem in this vein.

> I have defended not you, but my feelings for you.
> I have stood up against those I had once thought wise,
> And when they told me things, I screamed "all lies!"

> I have no thought or hope of your return
> I know not well the thoughts you have of me,
> But something deep within does sometimes swell
> And something greater than the spoken word says "it shall be!"

I have slunk off in corners to regard
Each precious moment that I spent with you.
There is no man of title—is no bard
That can tell me just what I feel so true.
I chalk it up to love, and that will do.[191]

Some girls entered into a world of grief from which it was very difficult to emerge. The parents of fifteen-year-old Ann refused to allow her to marry the boy who had gotten her pregnant, despite the fact that Ann described herself as "desperately in love" and eager to marry. The boy, however, passively accepted his parents' decision that he must cut off the relationship and go to school in a distant state. "Ann was angry, hurt, as well as heartbroken." When she got to the maternity home, she "cried for over two weeks and would not respond when spoken to."[192]

Some girls alternated between the world of romance, the world of grief, and the equally solitary world of defiance. Yet for most, eventually, the world of the maternity home offered the opportunity for a collective experience in which the girls together built a spirit of élan, humor, and hope. One director remarked, "They get along astonishingly well together, considering that they are often from many different social and economic levels."[193] When a group of unwed mothers in a home were asked, "What is your opinion about living with a group of girls sharing the same experience [of single pregnancy]?" one of the most common answers was positive because "everyone is equal."[194] The leveling experience of single pregnancy meant that status differences that had meaning outside and would have separated girls from each other were meaningless in the home. The girls were defined inside, as outside, by their pregnancy, but inside, it could be a source of sharing, solidarity, and inspiration.

When one girl in a California home couldn't put the pieces of another girl's story together into a believable whole, she concluded that the girl was probably lying. "We all lie in here," she wrote. That was a given, and not particularly a source of dissonance. Lying fit, almost gracefully, into the life inside, which consisted of the "waiting, the laughing and joking and being together, sharing each other's lives—a little."[195] The factual details of the past were pale, fluid, and not essential compared with the intense but suspended reality of the present. A girl in a home in the mid-1950s said, "You don't worry as much when you know others have the same trouble," when all the girls are "sharing a world."[196] Maud Morlock expressed her sense of how maternity home residents derived comfort from sharing:

> At home the girl's pregnancy has been conspicuous because she's the only guilty one and because she must remain in hiding. They relax in the maternity home physically and psychologically. They are at the "gang" age. Pregnant girls who don't live in the maternity home but get services at the pre-natal clinic are called "outside girls" by the girls in the maternity home—that expresses it.[197]

Morlock did not write about the more complex responses of many residents: solidarity and inspiration. Jean Thompson (the *nom de plume* of a Salvation Army Home resident), acknowledging this dimension, said, "We're all in this together and the girls act as if somehow we can work together and find a way out, too. This feeling of solidarity in a crisis is real enough to touch."[198] When Thompson considered the impact of one of the girls on the rest, she said, "Diane seems so alive in here, where most of us are walking around pretending we are just dreaming or something. . . . She's shaking up the finely-balanced equilibrium we're all trying to preserve."[199]

A girl's strength of character could be an awakening for others; so could another girl's helplessness. An older girl, observing a younger one, said, "I want to reach out and take her pain and fear away, and I get hot with anger when I think of the jerk who forced his way into her childlike world."[200] Another resident observed, "I drew strength from the others who seemed to bear up. [The group] gave me more confidence in myself."[201] In general, Thompson, a superb chronicler of life in the home, and of home culture, derived enormous strength and inspiration from "these poker-playing girls with their bellies full of what most . . . would call babies conceived in sin."[202]

Some staff who did perceive the feeling that was passing between the girls did not approve. Jane Wrieden of the Salvation Army explained, "Some social workers regard these . . . aspects of group living, such as identification, companionship, and discussion with others—particularly about keeping or giving up babies—as reasons for not using a maternity home."[203] This was an old complaint about the homes, one heard much more often when unwed mothers carried an explicit moral stain into the home. Ruth Reed raised the issue in 1934:

> [T]he withdrawal from family and social ties of these young women involves their segregation and close association during the period when they are under the care of the institution, and . . . these conditions permit the exchange of confidences and the forming of new and dubious friendships, comparable to those formed in institutions of correction, with effects for the individual equally harmful.[204]

Like many attitudes toward unwed mothers, this one did not die out all at once. It lingered on, causing staff in many homes in the postwar years to look suspiciously at the girls inside who seemed, to an undesirable degree, to be creating their own experience, together. The director of the Sheltering Arms Home in Philadelphia wrote complainingly to Morlock in Washington after the war about how the girls in her place were conspiring about their plans for their babies, against the interests and plans of the home. She described this as just one "instance of the disadvantage of grouping, under one roof, girls who have little in common except the problem which brings them together."[205] Similarly, in the early 1960s, educators in the city of San Francisco resisted the idea of providing classes on a group basis for unwed mothers, for example, in Continuation School, due to "fear that girls would learn from each other in a way that might be undesirable."[206]

Indeed, the problem that brought these girls together often provided a strong basis for girls to learn from each other. Inside they shared stories about parents, boyfriends and sex. Many girls participated in bull sessions in which unwed mothers expressed their interest in sexuality in ways that were altogether culturally unsanctioned for broadly middle-class white girls. Thompson recorded the following such exchange:

> *First girl:* I got so drunk at a party I don't even remember when it happened. I wasn't even sober enough to enjoy it.
>
> *Second girl:* For me it was wonderful. . . . I knew what I was doing. There couldn't be anything between us—marriage, I mean—but I don't regret it. . . . We had one wonderful week together—it was worth every bit of what I'm going through now.[207]

The ideas that premarital sex was enjoyable for girls, and that it was more powerful than social sanctions, undermined the rehabilitative purposes of the home. It also made the home into an agency facilitating the transmission of subversive ideas about female sexuality, as some in the social service professions had always feared. In the same way that prisons have always functioned as schools for crime, maternity homes offered underground, continuing education in sex. The parents and home administrators may have been focusing sharply and tightly on the issues of the pregnancy and the disposition of the child; the girls had had sex, and they talked about it.

Not surprisingly, there were numerous other ways that residents defined their own desires or interests as distinct from the intentions of the home staff. Sometimes expressing their own interests meant that girls flaunted home morality and rules, such as when girls in a Wilmington, Delaware home persisted in climbing down the fire escapes, in groups, in the middle of the night.[208] Sometimes the expressions of desire for self-determination were subtler. When one maternity home gave girls the opportunity to help plan the meals, "They always plan[ned] the heavy desserts the day after weigh in." These girls found a way to indulge their desire for sweets and protect themselves against the weight-conscious disciplinarians on staff.[209]

Some group expressions were institutionally sanctioned, but still gave voice to the shared concerns of the girls. Most Florence Crittenton Homes encouraged their residents to put out newspapers in this era. Few survive, but a reading of those that do suggests that to some degree the girls were permitted to express themselves and speak to each other in the pages of *Great Expectations* (Boston), *Crittenton Capers* (Norwalk), *Monthly Delivery* (Denver), *From the Home Front* (Atlanta), *Behind the Fence* (Cleveland), and others.[210]

In the more progressive homes, when a group of girls suggested new programs or policy improvements, the group was sometimes heeded, and sometimes even congratulated for taking the initiative. In Seattle, for example, on the request of the girls, the home began to offer a series of group meetings for the parents of residents, to discuss "common problems, questions, and anxieties."[211] In another home, girls got together and urged home staff to allow them to buy their own movie tickets and choose their own movies. In one place girls themselves transformed the home's long, wide corridors into functional spaces "so it would be less tedious to mop them." Sometimes the girls' initiatives were honored and then transformed to meet the goals of the home. For example, one group of girls got together and produced a play. The home staff encouraged this enterprise, then nudged the dramatics group to use its interest in presentation to work on diction, poise, posture, and clothing, the stuff of genteel femininity.[212] Sometimes girls were able, collectively, to deflect home staff from their unrelenting intentions to make the girls over in the image of ladies. A social worker described what happened when she tried to "set up a series on grooming." She reported,

> Nancy interrupted, "Well grooming is OK, but what about the special activity, a party in February?" The girls laughed and teased Nancy for being "a party kid." Jacky picked up on this and asked the group what they wanted to do first, and there seemed to be now a feeling that it would be a Valentine party, since that was the closest holiday available.[213]

When residents in one home were "stung" by the way that unwed mothers were being portrayed in magazine articles, they got together and produced an alternate description, one which did not compromise their dignity. The girls wrote:

> The majority of the girls here are not from broken homes and have not been exposed to backgrounds which seemingly produce the problems suggested in these articles. Most of the girls are attractive and have dated for several years, but have not married for one of many reasons. The reasons are as varied as the girls themselves.[214]

Together the girls could devise support systems that demonstrated group pride and gave honor to the individual girl passing through one of the rituals associated with unwed pregnancy in the maternity home. For example, girls devised home rituals to mark the arrival of a new girl, the onset of labor, the birth of a baby. In each case, the group honored one who elsewhere was shamed and cast out. The most elaborate and attenuated ritual in the postwar years was the one associated with the girl's preparation to appear in court to arrange for the relinquishment of her illegitimate child. This event marked the end of the ordeal. The home ritual was "a celebration" in honor of the girl's new, unencumbered future. "For the girls it was almost a fetish," with various ones overseeing the new mother's selection of clothes, hairdo, and makeup.[215] Each time the ritual was enacted (as it was for about 80 to 90 percent of maternity home residents in these years), all the girls remaining in the home could affirm for each other that there was life after illicit pregnancy, that relinquishment was a significant event, that the group and the individual served each other in this setting, and the girls knew it. A journalist touring a Westchester home in 1951, stopped to visit one girl in her room. Their conversation was interrupted by the sound of many voices in the grand entrance hall of the Victorian mansion.

> "That must be Vera leaving," Carol said. "Will you excuse me while I say goodbye to her?" She hurried out of the room. Mrs. Gould and I went and stood at the top of the stairs, looking down on the scene below. At the door with [the social worker] beside her, stood Vera, in her hat and coat and carrying her baby in her arms. Her face was flushed. Gathered about her were the other St. Faith's girls. One by one, they kissed her goodbye, with fervent wishes of Good Luck! Finally, amid a chorus of farewells, Vera hurried out the door, followed by [the social worker] whose car was waiting at the curb. The girls ran to the windows and waved until the car drove away. Then they slowly subsided again into little groups here and there about the lounge. It was very quiet in the old house. . . .[216]

The group culture had a great deal of meaning to these girls and young women. Like all populations coercively sequestered from society, their care was contrived largely with reference to an ideology, not to their needs as individuals. The group, on the other hand, understood and, to some extent, could honor the needs of an individual girl. Beyond that, collectively the society of unwed mothers could often construct an alternate analysis or alternate experience of life in the home. For example, most homes had strong religious affiliations and based their work with unwed mothers on religious doctrine—to save the sinner, to instill moral values in those who had stumbled. With the group behind her, Jean Thompson could offer a vision of the corny and coercive religiosity of the impulse in her maternity home. When one of the officers in the home, the "Major," spoke to the girls about "Hidden Sin" one evening in chapel, Thompson reported, "It almost made me laugh out loud." Another time,

> Lieutenant Stewart was holding the service, and while the girls sang "Throw out the lifeline, thrown out the lifeline," she threw Life Saver candy wrapped in paper with printed bible verses on it. After the singing the Lieutenant asked each girl who had caught a Life Saver to stand up and read the bible verse out loud.[217]

Next to instilling "values," homes were often keenest to instill the discipline and regular life habits that an unwed pregnancy suggested were absent. A home in Cincinnati arranged the girls' daily schedule this way: 5:30 alarm, 6:30 breakfast, 11:30 lunch, 5:30 dinner, 10:00 lights out. Every girl worked at a job in the home from 7:00 A.M. to 3:00 P.M. or from 3:00 to 11:00 P.M., and visiting was permitted from 2:00 to 4:00 and 7:00 to 8:00 P.M. daily. Despite the rigidity and rigor of the schedule, the matron, Mrs. Bradley, claimed that her creed was to keep rules at a minimum. She complained that the girls often refused when she offered to take them to the movies; "You'd expect them to want to go, but they don't." Instead, she said, they wanted to read their *True Confessions* magazines, but Mrs. Bradley liked to throw their trashy magazines away.[218] In such an environment, the girls might well look to each other for support.

Home staff expected to change the character of its charges. Yet throughout the period of this study, staff consistently misunderstood their residents (and perhaps the ingredients of personal transformation) while honoring the home ideology above all. It was common, for example, for staff to confuse protection with humiliation. In Salvation Army Homes, a report stated in 1959, "It was nothing to have two or three 'see for yourself' groups [from the community] coming through each week. We cooperate wholeheartedly, keeping the girls in a withdrawn part of the hospital" while the visitors were in the home.[219]

One director, expressing desire for harmony in the facility and for well-adjusted, well-behaved girls, explained the modus operandi of her home: "Where a permissive atmosphere prevails, the expression of rebelliousness can be utilized constructively by tracing it to its emotional source and so eliminating its causes."[220] The route to "understanding" that this administrator prescribed could have functioned as a major stimulus for the residents to depend on each other to find a hearing, and respect. Another staff member remarked, in retrospect, "The girls were too busy to be depressed."[221] This assertion doesn't match the self-descriptions of maternity home residents in this era.[222] A foreign visitor to a California home remarked at the conclusion of her tour that "she was distressed to see so many pregnant girls together." The girls did not seem to be happy; "they didn't smile . . . everything had been done for the needs of the body, but the spirit had been neglected altogether."[223] Without the group experience, many unwed mothers described themselves as "reduced to nothingness," a feeling that often abated in the company of their peers.

The Adjustment

The evidence suggests that the group experience could be sustaining and entertaining for the society of unwed mothers in postwar maternity homes. But there is not evidence that it was transformative. In fact, it was probably less so than the rules and programs sponsored by the homes. There is not evidence that girls used the collective experience to rebel together against the ideology or to reject its rules and regulations, or to resist the version of normative womanhood for which they were all preparing inside. The cultural imperatives outside (and championed by the staff inside) remained the most powerful, salient prescriptions for these postwar girls who had tasted the fruits of nonconformity. The vast majority appear to have agreed to take the offer of the second chance. Jean Thompson recorded an exchange she had with another girl inside who expressed her frustration with the conformity of the others, with their willingness to accept the strictures and the promises of the home.

> *Peggy:* This is a crazy place. . . . I thought the girls in here would be a bunch of rebels like me. . . . I mean they're all having babies and all. And they're not that way at all. . . . These kids are the worst conformists I ever met. They're acting as if they're failures—as if they don't measure up.
>
> *Jean:* But didn't you get pregnant for a reason?
>
> *Peggy:* Sure—I thought I'd try it.[224]

Diane W., a resident at another home, gave advice to her peers that Peggy would have deplored; yet this young woman spoke the language that the majority could understand.

> If we can bend with the wind and follow the rules and regulations with acceptance rather than complaints, our stay will be more pleasant. Many times we may feel that the rules and regulations are petty and laid out to make life more difficult for us. Any establishment requires systematic routine, otherwise there would be disorganization. . . . If we can keep in mind our personal reasons for being here, our adjustment would be easier. If we can remember and try to adjust now, we will have an easier time re-adjusting to life when our stay is terminated.[225]

The life that many girls were planning to readjust to included all the elements of normative middle-class life. While these girls were viewed as rebels or misfits because they had had nonmarital sex and gotten pregnant, it is much more likely that they were part of a horde of unfortunate girl-pioneers who became sexually active in the historical moment just before such behavior was widely recognized as typical and just before they had a chance to protect themselves from the consequences. If they were pioneers, it was only in this limited sense; otherwise, most wanted the same sort of life the majority of white women had. Linda, in a maternity home in New York, spoke for many: "I want a home. I want to be married. I want children I can keep and love. Maybe that's why I'm here. Maybe I just need someone to love."[226] Whether one considers the girls in a Norfolk home who bought imitation gold wedding bands at the ten-cent store, or the freckle-faced girl with glasses in Westchester who received her going-away present from the home's director with deep appreciation, saying, "Oh, Miss Gould, it's just the kind of present you give married people," the evidence is that most girls fantasized about similar futures.[227] A Boston caseworker summed up her profession's hope for their unwed clients when she spoke about the afterlife of a former maternity home resident: "Betsy has found a woman to woman relationship with her mother . . . [and] the happiest of marriages and two of the dearest children ever born. More than this no woman should ask."[228]

Jean Thompson, the remarkable chronicler of life inside, provides us with the most painful account of the adjustment process, most painful because her rendition is so intelligent and perceptive. Jean begins her journey as an unwed mother while a college student, independent, self-assertive, maybe rebellious, in Boston in 1959. She has forsworn marriage and has vowed to remain on her own. By the end of her account, after having spent some months in a California Salvation Army Home, she has learned the value of adjustment and lost her taste for independence. She describes her new self at this point: "I'm not worried about being a fabulous success anymore. All I want is an ability to get along with myself and the world. Stability. How I used to hate that word. Now I want it. Stability—continuity—stick-to-it-ness, not to give up." After it's all over, Jean remembers her father's advice— the advice of a man she had previously considered coldhearted and hardheaded. Now she adopts his advice as her guiding principle: "Happiness comes not from doing what you like but from learning to like what you have to do." Jean reflected on her experience as an unwed mother when she added, "I know that now."[229]

The safe house that harbored Jean and her unfortunate peers was in the process of becoming an outpost by the time Jean married and had children she could keep. Girls who got pregnant without husbands would soon cease to be held captive in these houses of female correction.[230] The period of this study covers the heyday of maternity homes, but their decline and transformation followed soon thereafter. Once white girls and women in vast numbers engaged in premarital sex, and particularly after they gained legal access to birth control and abortion, the efforts at sexual social control of this population had to shift terrain. Relatively suddenly, neither sex nor conception constituted crimes for most white unmarried girls and women. Thus the maternity home in its postwar form was no longer relevant.

A girl in 1951 described what it was like for her when she was driven away from the maternity home that had provided her with such a bizarre mixture of protection and self-effacement.

> As we drove along, I kept looking out of the window and marvelling that everything seemed to have gone on unchanged during these three months when so much had happened to me. . . .Then a car passed us, and I thought I recognized a friend of mine in it. I ducked my head quickly. I looked down at little Jerry sleeping so peacefully in my arms. I was acting like a hunted criminal about the most natural and innocent thing in the world— my own baby—and the realization of it made me sick all over.[231]

By the late 1960s white unmarried females had not attained "sexual freedom" or "reproductive freedom," nor would many of these girls and women have their sex lives in an unfettered context of "choice," even after the 1973 *Roe v. Wade* decision. But one result of the rapid "de-criminalization" of youthful, female sexuality and even of unwed pregnancy between 1965 and 1973, was that white broadly middle-class girls would not be forced to go behind the fence, in shame and disgrace, to serve time for the crime of pregnancy.

Chapter Five

The Disposition of Illegitimate Babies I: The Postwar White Adoption Mandate

The public and private treatment of an unwed mother between 1945 and 1965 was clearly structured by society's disapproval of women who violated female norms of sexual purity and obedience. But throughout this study, ideas about the "value" of the illegitimate baby surface again and again as central to an unmarried mother's fate. In short, after World War II, the white bastard child was no longer the child nobody wanted. The black illegitimate baby became the child white politicians and taxpayers loved to hate. This chapter and the next consider how these racially specific postwar attitudes toward illegitimate babies, and ideas about what to do with them, shaped the experiences of the single mother. The babies themselves will be relegated to the background, a position they rarely occupied at the time.

The central argument of these two chapters is that the "value" of illegitimate babies has been quite different in different eras of the twentieth century in the United States. These changing values reflected and supported distinct experiences for an illegitimate child's biological mother, depending on when she gave birth to the baby. In addition, the emergence of racially distinct public policies and practices regarding unwed mothers in the postwar era included racially distinct policies and attitudes toward the public and private problem of the disposition of the illegitimate child. This chapter and the next consider how prevailing ideas about girls and women, mothers and family, postwar racism and midcentury economic concerns in the United States combined to shape public and private solutions to illegitimacy.

Papers of professionals and institutions serving unwed mothers, black and white, between 1945 and 1965, provide a great deal of the material illustrating the emergence of postwar values of white and black babies and the impact those values had on structuring the choices available to their biological mothers. In general, the material demonstrates that social, cultural, and economic imperatives converged in such a way in postwar America as to sanction very narrow and rigid, but different options for black and white unwed mothers. Black single mothers were expected to keep their babies as most unwed mothers, black and white, had done throughout American history. Unmarried white mothers, for the first time in American history, were expected to put their babies up for adoption. The history of illegitimacy in the postwar era is, in part, the history of the institutional efforts to carry out these expectations. This history of illegitimate childbearing is also, in part, an exploration of how and why different groups of girls and women dealt differently with the issue of their illicit maternity.

It is important to note that neither the social work establishment, nor maternity homes, nor adoption agencies, nor adopting parents, nor black marketeers created the racially distinct responses to unwed mothers or the racially distinct options they offered unwed mothers. These groups, in different ways, functioned as facilitators whose guidance supported and reflected prevailing ideas about white and black women, illicit pregnancy, and illegitimate children.

The postwar white family imperative and the social, cultural, and economic concerns of this period intersected to construct the narrow options available to black and white girls and women faced with the question of what to do with the babies they conceived outside of marriage. This chapter doesn't argue that one solution or another for any biological mother, or all biological mothers, is preferable. It does contend that the options available to these girls and women were narrow and rigid and that unwed mothers of both races were pressured to submit to them, whatever their personal preferences.

Prewar Attitudes Toward Illegitimate Babies and Mothers

Before World War II, an illegitimate child was typically considered a "child of sin," the product of a mentally deficient mother. As such, this child was tainted and undesirable. The girl or woman, black or white, who gave birth to it was expected by family, by the community, and by the state to nurture the child and to bring it up. Rarely did others want a child who stood to inherit the sinful character—the mental and moral weaknesses—of its parent. In 1955, Justine Wise Polier, a justice in the New York City Children's Court, reflected back on the prewar notion of the unwed mother and her child: "In those days, the unmarried mother was viewed as a bad woman who must be punished. Her child was regarded as a child of sin, therefore unfit to be adopted into a decent home. Adoption was a rare and unusual thing, risked only with a brand new, beautiful and perfect baby known to have an excellent family history."[1] Before the war, state laws and institutional regulations supported the mandate for unwed mothers to assume responsibility for their babies, not so much because there were others vying for the babies, as to ensure that the mothers would not abandon the infants. There were other reasons as well. A Children's Bureau publication explained,

> Many maternity homes expect the girl who accepts their care to keep her child. The original purpose . . . was a recognition by those responsible for maternity homes of the moral obligation of a mother toward her child and an expression of their desire to win more tolerance for unmarried mothers so that they could bring up their children under favorable circumstances. . . . Many believed that the child would have a stabilizing effect on the mother.[2]

State regulations in Minnesota and elsewhere required mothers seeking care in maternity homes to breast-feed their babies for three months and more,[3] long enough to establish unseverable bonds between infant and mother. A study conducted in 1940 explored the effect of the Minnesota Three Months Nursing Regulation on unwed mothers. One young woman "had wanted to give her child up but because of the three months period could no longer think of doing so. . . . Her difficulty seemed to be that had she been able to relinquish the baby at the beginning she would have done so; but to give him up now. . . would be very hard on her." Another told the investigator, "You have no idea how great the attachment is that grows up between you and the baby in three months." And a third shared her recognition that "[I]t might ruin a girl's life forever if she gave up her baby after so long a period of acquaintance."[4]

In states without such laws, maternity homes created their own nursing regulations. Many of these were still in place after the war. For example, in 1949, at the Catherine Booth (Salvation Army) Maternity Home in Cincinnati, "the mother was expected to nurse the baby and care for it for six weeks, even if she [planned] to place it for adoption."[5] One observer of maternity homes noted, "Some shelters still require a three or four months stay after the hospital, and sometimes even require that the mothers nurse their babies. We feel that to make a mother do that if she has decided upon adoption is just unnecessarily turning the knife in the wound."[6] Homes throughout the state of New Jersey were urged in 1948 by the state's Youth Consultation Service and Children's Aid Society to enforce the practice that all mothers nurse their babies and remain in the maternity home until the child was three months old.[7] The National Florence Crittenton Mission, with maternity homes across the country, took the position, until after World War II, of encouraging girls and women to keep their babies. Only mothers who did were eligible for Florence Crittenton scholarships.

A "letter" that was passed among girls in Florence Crittenton Homes in the 1930s and 1940s expressed the National Florence Crittenton Mission's official feelings about the unwed mother's responsibility to her child. Called "I Am The Abandoned Baby," it berates the mother who relinquishes her infant. The letter reads, in part:

Just as I had become used to your arms and begun to know your voice and to recognize, in my vague but instinctive way, your movements and your smile you are walking off and leaving me. Whose arms will pick me up from my coop tomorrow? Into what home shall I be consigned and who will give me that bottle you taught me to pull on when you decided that I must stop getting my milk from your rather thin breast?

Anyhow, what have I done to you that you should walk off and leave me like this? I never asked you to bring me into this world. . . . I have done the best I could to be cute. . . . I thought you were going to be with me always, at least until I knew my manners and how to make people love me for myself. I thought I belonged to you. . . .

I think you should have thought about me in the first place—I wish you would try to do something that will prevent this kind of thing—I don't like it at all.
Goodbye and Good Luck. (Signed) The Baby you didn't want.[8]

An experienced observer of obstetric practice in the late 1930s described the degree to which children born out of wedlock before World War II were often unwanted:

The Doctor is sometimes less worried about the survival of the unmarried patient's baby. Contrast the feeling of relief throughout the hospital when an illegitimate child is stillborn with the sorrow manifested when a much desired baby is lost. As [the social worker] points out, "Our culture is actually hostile to the illegitimate child whom it sees . . . as a burden and as a menace to the monogamous family."[9]

These prewar ideas about illegitimate babies and illicit maternity stressed the biological imperative and secondarily affirmed that moral conditions were embedded in and revealed by the illegitimacy. According to studies of illegitimacy and to prescriptive literature before World War II, the biology of illegitimacy stamped the baby permanently with mental and moral marks of deficiency.[10] Likewise, the unwed mother's pregnancy both revealed her innate biological and moral shortcomings and condemned her, through the illicit conception and birth, to carry the permanent stain of biological and moral ruin.[11] The biological experience she had undergone was tied to her moral status in a fixed, direct, and inexorable relationship. Equally important, her motherhood was immutable. While the deficiencies, the stain, and her ruination violated her biological integrity, as well as her social and moral standing in the community, the unwed mother's maternal relation to the child was not compromised. That was also fixed directly and inexorably by the biological facts of conception and birth.

These attitudes reflected, in part, the importance of bridal virginity and marital conception in American culture. Social or cultural determinants of illegitimacy that admitted group or individual variability were not sought to explain an event which, until World War II, had, in general, one meaning.

Specifically, racial distinctions were not useful in this regard. Psychological theories had not yet been generally adopted by social commentators to explain nonconforming behavior. Before World War II, social, religious, and educational leaders did not call for the rehabilitation of unwed mothers or suggest that there were steps many could take to restore their marriageability and their place in the community. What was lost could not be regained; what was acquired could not be cast off.

Consequently, most unwed mothers in that era did not have choices to make about the disposition of the bastard child. Some among the very rich and the very poor may have had opportunities or may have lived in communities tolerating deviance differently from the usual ways. But for most unwed mothers, black and white, through the 1930s, illegitimacy was a shame that carried with it shamed motherhood. It was also a shame managed as a family matter or a personal matter. Unwed mothers did not look to complex networks of overlapping social agencies to meet their needs, which were, in any case, not of interest to the public or in the public interest.

Adoption of Illegitimate White Babies in the Postwar Era

Breast-feeding laws and institutional policies protecting the immutability of the unwed mother's relationship to her illegitimate baby were becoming harder to sustain after the war. A complex set of social conditions made this so. First of all, while birth control and abortion remained illegal and hard to obtain, more girls and women were participating in nonmarital, heterosexual intercourse; thus, more of them became pregnant and carried babies to term.[12] At roughly the same time, psychological explanations for sexual nonconformity were becoming popular among social service providers as well as theoreticians.[13] This development had substantial consequences for unwed mothers (and for many other types of sexual nonconformists) as discussed in Chapter Three. Most relevant here is that by moving the governing imperative from the body (biology) to the mind (psychology), all of the fixed relationships previously defining illegitimacy became mutable, indeterminate, even deniable.

Psychological explanations transformed the white unwed mother from a genetically tainted unfortunate into a maladjusted female who could be cured. The biological stain of illegitimacy had been permanent, but the neuroses of illegitimacy could be removed with help from a caseworker. The white out-of-wedlock child, therefore, was no longer a flawed by-product of innate immorality and low intelligence.[14] The child's innocence was restored and its adoptability established. Central to psychological interpretations of deviant behavior was the notion of cure or rehabilitation. In the case of the white unwed mother, psychologists argued that she could be rehabilitated. A successful cure rested most of all on the relinquishment of the child.[15] A program in a Seattle maternity home was designed so that "Planning for adoption is virtually completed prior to the girl's confinement. . . . This procedure . . . is based on the concept that the baby is symbol, without actual reality to the mother."[16] The white unwed mother no longer had an immutable relationship to her baby.[17]

In postwar America, social conditions of motherhood along with notions about the psychological status of the unwed mother became more important in defining white motherhood than biology. Specifically, for the first time, it took more than a baby to make a white girl or woman into a mother. Without marriage first, a white female was not considered to have achieved motherhood. If she "chose" to have a child out of wedlock, despite this dictum, the experts warned, "She has less chance of receiving further help and less opportunity to meet appropriate men and future husbands."[18] A team of academics researching unwed motherhood in North Carolina suggested that "a cause and effect relationship may exist wherein the desire to keep the child while single most often results in the young woman remaining single longer or permanently."[19]

Unwed mothers, their parents, and service providers understood the problem and took steps to improve the single mother's chances for marriage while sidestepping the diagnoses of pathology attached to the girls who made the "unrealistic" decision to keep.[20] The unwed mother who came to terms with the baby's existence, symbolically or concretely, and relinquished, enhanced her ability to "function [in the future] as a healthy wife and mother."[21]

Release from the biological imperative represented a major reform in the treatment of the many white unwed mothers who desperately desired a way to undo their life-changing mistake and find a way out of trouble. "Miss L." spoke for many when she described the complex but welcome decision she was able to make:

> It was not that I did not care for my little Stephanie, but rather I had to decide to give her a chance for happiness in a family, because I was alone. I was sad, and I still have a feeling of sadness, but I know she will be happy by going to a permanent family. . . .In thinking of this, with time and life going on for me, I know that I did the only thing possible for both of us.[22]

The psychological explanations for the behavior of unwed mothers suggested that adoption was an appropriate solution to the would-be single mother's dilemma. Moreover, the rising rate of white single pregnancy would have created an ever-larger number of ruined girls and women if unwed mothers continued to have no option but to keep their illegitimate children. In postwar society, which glorified couples, marriage, children, families, and conformity, this prospect would not have been a happy one. The option of placing an illegitimate child for adoption became, in a sense, an unplanned but fortuitous safety valve for the thousands of white girls and women who became unwed mothers but—thanks to the sanctioning of adoption—could go on to become properly married wives and mothers soon thereafter.[23]

For this arrangement to work required a sizable population of white couples who wanted to adopt infants and who didn't mind if the babies had been born to unwed mothers. In the postwar era this condition was met. As one agency director put it, "It is good to know . . . that in this Century of the Child there are more people who want to adopt than there are children in need of homes." She added, "It's a curious twist that this has made our task just that much harder."[24] It is not clear that infertility rates were rising in the postwar era or that it had become more socially acceptable to acknowledge infertility at this time. It is clear, however, that the postwar family imperative put new pressures on, and suggested more intense pleasures to, infertile couples who in the past would have remained childless. The availability of white illegitimate babies met an overwhelming demand from white childless couples who wanted to create normative American families. A social scientist in the mid-1950s referred to illegitimate babies as "the silver lining in a dark cloud" because:

> Over one in ten of all marriages are involuntarily childless. Since most of these couples desire to adopt a baby, illegitimacy is a blessing to [them]. Curiously, from their standpoint there are not enough illegitimate births because most of these couples must wait one or two or three years in order to adopt a baby, and some are never able to have one because there is not enough for all who want them.[25]

Under these circumstances, white, pregnant, unmarried women and their babies became market commodities. The armed services recognized the problem at the end of World War II. Even though the various branches expressed a desire to assist unmarried mothers within their ranks, many administrators worried that the illegitimate "babies [were] in great demand," and government social service workers felt helpless to protect mothers and children adequately.[26] The Salvation Army, which had been providing shelter and services to unwed mothers for more than fifty years, noted in the postwar years that "There is an unprecedented bid for the child of the unmarried mother." The army was particularly concerned that their role was being "usurped" by adoption agencies.[27] In the early 1950s, Leontine Young, using what was becoming a popular metaphor, was concerned about "the tendency growing out of the demand for babies to regard unmarried mothers as breeding machines . . . [by people intent] upon securing babies for quick adoptions."[28] Judge Justine Polier in New York, using another apt metaphor, referred to "childless couples hungry for complete family life."[29] In fact, in the early postwar years, 80 percent more children were adopted than in the years before and during the war.[30]

The growing numbers of out-of-wedlock pregnancies and births and an eager population of prospective adoptive parents contributed to creating the postwar conviction that it was best for white girls and women to relinquish their babies. Through adoption, the unwed mother could put the mistake— both the baby *qua* baby and the proof of nonmarital sexual experience— behind her. Her parents were not stuck with a ruined daughter and a bastard grandchild for life. And the baby could be brought up in a normative family, by a couple prejudged to possess all the attributes and resources necessary for successful parenthood.

The weaknesses of the adoption mandate did not concern the many white unwed mothers and their parents who used its provisions gladly. They were the concern, however, of a number of other interested parties. These included white unwed mothers who wanted to keep their babies and found themselves therefore condemned, by definition, as unfit. By the late 1940s, the white unwed mother who kept her baby was classified as a deficient mother because she lacked a husband; she was also found deficient in her own right. Virtually by definition, an unmarried mother who kept her child lacked the maturity to mother it.[31] Mary Louise Allen, the executive director of the Florence Crittenton Association of America in that organization's busiest days of the late 1950s, explained to her counterpart at the Salvation Army, Jane Wrieden, that "most of our Directors of our member agencies would [agree] that some girls are tragically prevented from fulfilling their maternal potential because they would have so much to lose through social and economic ostracism, but I think most feel that given today's climate, it is the girl with less mothering resources who tends to keep the baby."[32]

The climate Allen referred to was friendly to white unwed mothers and their parents who sought release from the stigma of illegitimacy. Indeed, for the first time in the twentieth century, nonconforming white girls and women in the United States were offered a nonmarital, or premarital, way to recon-struct normative lives after bearing an out-of-wedlock child. The Salvation Army, Florence Crittenton, and other agencies were meeting the needs of this population and their parents as they worked within the boundaries of prevailing social mores for whites. In this context, an unwed mother who wanted to keep her baby was defined as immature or irrational because clearly she had an underdeveloped sense of the real difficulties both mother and child would face in a culture hostile to illicit female sexuality and its consequences.

There were others uncomfortable with the pressure for adoption. Some service providers felt the mandate was too coercively and too universally applied to white unmarried mothers. Some also objected that agencies com-mitted resources to adoption exclusively and did not develop other services and programs for mothers who did not relinquish their babies and who arguably had the greater needs. Some worried that a society that mandated adoption without sufficient supporting public and private services made white unwed mothers extremely vulnerable to black marketeers interested only in making money off of them.[33]

Finally, and quite significantly, the adoption mandate applied to whites only. This angered black service providers who felt that racism dictated the exclusion of black unwed mothers from the opportunity to relinquish their illegitimate children. Indeed, the social construction of racially distinct treatment of illegitimate babies brought intense public attention to the "differences" between black and white babies born out of wedlock. Agencies, the media, competing adoptive parents, and black marketeers considered white illegitimate babies valuable and desirable. Black illegitimate babies, in contrast, were bad news to agency workers, taxpayers, politicians, and in the media. The value that the adoption mandate bestowed on white babies, partly at the expense of black babies, exacerbated racism and racial antagonism in the postwar era.

The transition to the white adoption mandate was not always smooth, despite pervasive certainty about the benefits of relinquishment. A great deal of the responsibility for effecting the transition fell on the shoulders of social workers who were not always ready for it. A headline in *The New York Times* in 1944 read, "More Babies Kept by Unwed Mothers/Changed Social Attitudes and Jobs for Women Are Listed As Reasons/Course May Be Unwise/Welfare Workers Warned to Help Those Concerned 'See the Facts' Clearly." The article reported a speech delivered at the annual conference of the New Jersey Welfare Council by Henrietta Gordon of the Child Welfare League of America, who claimed, "It is the duty of social agencies to help the mother to see the facts."[34] Gordon's speech suggests that prior to the war, white women had already begun to put their babies out for adoption, but that wartime opportunities for women allowed them to make decisions, even about their status as mothers, that would not be possible again for thirty or forty years. The speech affirmed, in the wartime language of "duty," the social worker's job of enforcing this new social agenda, an agenda the social worker didn't create but was expected to implement.

There is abundant evidence that it was not a simple matter for caseworkers to change their philosophy and treatment strategies on demand. The administrator of Child Welfare Services in Rhode Island wrote to the Children's Bureau for advice and encouragement in the early 1950s. He explained,

> One of our greatest needs is more clearance of our philosophy and help in developing our plan for the unmarried mother, to sort out her values, her feelings, her relationships and needs of the child. Our key supervisors feel we have not worked out sufficient skills and techniques in obtaining releases. . . . We sense from our staff a fearfulness in being aggressive in securing a release, as I feel, for the best interests of the child, they should be in many instances.[35]

During this period, social workers often complained that it was difficult to facilitate adoptions after an era when professionals insisted that unwed mothers accept their babies. Mary Rall of United Charities in Chicago suggested that "workers with unmarried mothers . . . become overwhelmed by the sense of responsibility to the baby." She spoke to social workers: "We must do something for the baby. We haven't any duty to the baby unless we have power in relation to the baby. We must meet the motive of the mother's need to cling to the baby."[36] A social service administrator in Kentucky reported that some of the social workers under her aegis at family services in Louisville "have a great deal of guilt" when the mother decides to relinquish the baby.[37]

The social workers' task was indeed a complicated one. Workers in maternity homes, adoption agencies, or public welfare offices had to braid unmatched strands into one plan for white unwed mothers. Agency workers were deeply uneasy about separating babies from the one individual historically and culturally designated, until the 1940s, as best suited, no matter what her marital status, to care for her own baby.[38] In addition, the community response to out-of-wedlock pregnancy and maternity in the United States had historically been punitive. Before the war, many experts claimed that keeping mother and child together was simultaneously in the child's best interest and the earned wages of sin for the unwed mother. Until the postwar era, most social workers trained and practiced in this tradition. After World War II, the new ideas about adoption stimulated caseworkers to construct new attitudes toward both the baby and the unwed mother.

Making the transition was confusing for everyone. A study of how residents in a maternity home in Minnesota in the 1940s decided what to do with their babies demonstrated the confusion. One unwed mother "thought the [social] workers tried to force their plans on the girls rather than letting the girls work out their own ideas." Another "referred to her distrust of social workers. . . . She had at first wanted to place the child for adoption; this had been discouraged by the worker. Now that she wanted to keep her baby, no plan she suggested met approval."[39]

After the war, social workers struggled to discard the two most basic assumptions that had previously guided their work with unwed mothers. These girls and women were no longer considered the best mothers for their babies. And they would no longer be expected to pay for their illicit sex experience and illegitimate pregnancy by life as ruined women and outcast mothers of bastard children. Social workers were now to offer unwed mothers a plan that would protect them from lasting stigma and rehabilitate them for normative female roles. Psychological literature supporting the efficacy of adoption in these cases, the interest of many white couples in obtaining newborn babies, and the glorification of family in the postwar period helped the social work establishment accept new ideas about the disposition of illegitimate white babies.

Acceptance often took the form of training caseworkers to take "an active, 'steering role' " in the girl's decision about the baby. Specifically, caseworkers were trained to help the unmarried mother "work through to acceptance" of adoption.[40] A caseworker was cautioned to be wary of the girl's own expression of her desires: "[T]hey don't admit unconscious rejection and the fact that the external life situation, however real, serves as an alibi and a bulwark against recognition of the basic rejection."[41] The worker had, in fact, to recognize that "Realistically [the unwed mother] is in no position to make any kind of decision, to know what her feelings are, to evaluate any plan."[42] Caseworkers were encouraged to take a great deal of latitude as they played the role of the good, "guiding mother" and brought the unwed mother to accept the fact that in the world of "external reality" she was not to be a mother to the illegitimate child, her biological experience notwithstanding. The girl's task was simply and straightforwardly to "be a mother by relinquishing the child."[43]

The social work community, parents of white unwed mothers, school administrators, clergy, and others who were unhappy about the rising number of nonmarital and bridal pregnancies shared these perspectives and shared a certainty that no one was served well when the white single mother kept and raised her illegitimate child. Each of these interested groups took the position after World War II that society was ready to offer an unwed mother and her child the opportunity for normative life. Their task, individually, and as it worked, collectively, was to help the unwed mother, if necessary, to bring her internal feelings into alignment with an accurate reading of "external reality," as expressed by society's treatment of unwed mothers.

Dr. Robert Barrett, a member of the founding family of the Florence Crittenton organization and in the late 1940s, still the paternalistic president of the Florence Crittenton Mission, was not pleased by the national trend toward relinquishment. He had sharp correspondence at this time with the director of a Texas Florence Crittenton Maternity Home, criticizing the way social workers facilitated adoption. He wrote that he respected social work schools, but he added,

> I do not think that all, or even the great majority of social workers (especially young, unmarried women) are competent to handle the problem of the unmarried mother and her child. A Master's degree in social work does not always qualify a young woman to deal with the intricate problems of social behavior. . . .[An unmarried mother] must not be rushed into a decision to give up her baby for adoption until every other avenue has been explored and every other door opened.[44]

By the late 1940s, however, Dr. Barrett's voice was echoing down a one-way street as white, broadly middle-class unwed mothers passed through the portals of adoption agencies in record numbers. By 1955, ninety thousand children a year were being placed for adoption, an 80 percent increase since 1944.[45]

In all parts of the country, public agencies allocated resources and developed approaches after the war to facilitate adoption. For example, in Columbus, Ohio, the Family and Children's Bureau reported to a visiting representative from the United States Children's Bureau in 1949 that the organization had placed few babies for adoption before 1944 and had only recently defined standards for placement. However, the agency administrator noted, in the first eleven months of 1948, 145 unmarried mothers had been referred to family service for adoption services. The administrator was concerned that "Money and staff time were going into case work for unmarried mothers and adoption out of proportion to the total program of the agency."[46] In 1950, the Nebraska Division of Child Welfare developed a form letter to be sent to unwed mothers offering single pregnant girls and women aid in placing their illegitimate children with adoption agencies. The form letter read, in part,

> Many young women in your situation want to provide the baby with a good home where it will have the love and care of both father and mother, because it is difficult for a young unmarried woman to give this care herself. We therefore are enclosing information about the organizations in the state which are licensed to place babies in adoptive homes and which are able to assist you in making these plans.[47]

In some localities, including one county in northern California, public funds became available during these years to pay maternity medical expenses of unmarried mothers who were considering adoption placement.[48] One commentator, taking a national perspective, noted that "In recent years, seeking help from a social agency has become a perfectly respectable thing to do, and the popularity of adoption has undoubtedly encouraged unmarried mothers to use agencies still more."[49]

National service organizations also began to support adoption of white illegitimate babies for the first time. For example, the Travelers' Aid Society, which came into contact with white, single pregnant girls and women seeking to have their babies secretly, away from home, was able to promote flexible treatment of nonresident unmarried mothers in Texas in 1950. Travelers' Aid reported that "Part of the reason for this flexibility on non-residents is that Houston wants as many white children as possible."[50] In the same period the American Public Welfare Association reached out to unmarried mothers, caseworkers, and adoptive parents with a comprehensive pamphlet entitled "Public Welfare Services in Unwed Parenthood and Adoption." Similarly, the Child Welfare League of America prepared guidelines for service providers regarding adoption and services to unmarried parents in the 1950s. Its authors aimed "to intensify stress on adoption."[51] All of these organizations believed that adoption offered the best chance for a viable, productive life for both the unwed mother and her child.

In the 1950s, during Dr. Martha Eliot's tenure as chief of the Children's Bureau, this government agency developed a "strong new focus" on adoption.[52] In addition to assigning personnel and other resources to this area, the Bureau hosted a series of conferences in the 1950s concerned with adoption practices in the United States. Meetings focused on the roles of doctors, lawyers, and social workers in adoptions and tried to define good working

relations between these professionals who often resented each others' participation in making plans for the adoptable child.[53] A major Children's Bureau
conference took place in 1955 and included representatives from forty-two
national agencies concerned with adoption. All agreed that adoption was
desirable.

An interesting Seattle study undertaken in the late 1950s reported deep
disagreement among pastors, school personnel, doctors, nurses, and social
workers about whether or not unmarried mothers should marry the putative
father, and about the purposes of counseling, but all agreed that the girl or
woman should relinquish the child.[54]

The Children's Bureau and other agencies were very concerned, however,
that adoption should be carried out properly, under the guidance of properly
trained social workers and under the auspices of properly licensed agencies.[55]
The Bureau promoted state laws restricting or forbidding independent adoptions such as the one passed in Connecticut in 1957, which mandated that all
nonrelative adoptions be made through licensed public and private child-
placement agencies. Laws such as this one forced unmarried mothers to avoid
black market dealers in babies since no court would approve a nonlicensed
adoption. Still, in the 1950s there was no federal law prohibiting commercial
placement or independent adoption of a child across state lines. In thirty-four
states there was no local law prohibiting the sale of children within the state.
These legal lapses were of serious concern to the Children's Bureau staff, who
worked unceasingly for the cause of regularized adoptions of out-of-wedlock
children.

Leontine Young expressed her own and the Children's Bureau position
about the dangerous relationship between the public's demand for white
babies and the lack of adequate services for unwed mothers when she addressed
her social work colleagues in 1948:

> And what of the Siamese twin to the problem of the unmarried mother—
> adoptions? Here we face tremendous public pressure, the desire for babies,
> the deeply rooted human need for a child. Because we cannot give adequate
> service to the unmarried mother, we do not have enough children to place
> for adoption. Because we do not have the children to place for adoption,
> the public grows impatient and ignores us. Caught between public prejudice
> and ignorance about the unmarried mother and public demand for adopt-
> able children, we can protect neither the unmarried mother nor the child
> except within the limits of our own services. The black market steps in
> without knowledge or scruple to fill the vacuum we have left.[56]

In the early and mid-1950s in some states, including Florida and Delaware, only about one-quarter of adoptions were carried out by licensed agencies.[57] To Martin Friedman, a Duluth, Minnesota, lawyer accused of promoting adoption improprieties, this was no surprise. Mr. Friedman testified before
the United States Senate in 1955 about the negative consequences of the

"uniformity and conformity" supported by the Children's Bureau. Licensed agencies served their clients poorly, he claimed, and they excluded many couples who would make perfectly fine parents. Mainstream services took a "holier than thou" position and "proclaimed theirs to be the only correct method of making placements. . . .They contended that giving assistance to the unwed mother in making placements through facilities other than theirs, constituted a moral wrong."[58] Friedman was describing the basis of his clients' interest in alternative services; he was also justifying his own livelihood as an independent operator at a time when social service organizations were consolidating and extending their adoption services.

Maternity Homes and Adoption in the Postwar Period

In the postwar period, maternity homes created new policies and practices that made it easier for white unwed mothers to relinquish their babies, specifically to licensed agencies. For example, by the late 1940s, the recommended postpartum stay in the maternity home had been reduced, not only because the medical profession was revising its ideas about recovery. A maternity home in Westchester County, New York, set a new policy at this time: "The ideal period for the girl to remain in the home after the baby's birth is three weeks. This is sufficiently short that the girl does not get too involved with the baby."[59] In this particular home, as in many, unwed mothers putting their babies up for adoption would only be taken in if they agreed to use a licensed adoption agency. A home in Fort Worth described its policy: "Preference is given to girls who plan to place the babies through the [adoption] agency. . . . There are no fees when the baby is to be placed for adoption through the organization."[60] Increasingly, services became so streamlined that in many homes, as in the Florence Crittenton Maternity Home in Houston, "Babies go directly from the hospital to children's [adoption] agencies."[61] In this same facility, administrative criteria and intake procedures became more lax in this period because of the demand for white babies.[62]

The issue of whether the maternity home resident would see her baby at all, and if so, under what conditions, was a difficult and important one while there was such focused attention on the mechanisms of relinquishment. An experienced program director in Chicago cautioned, "We have all known mothers who, long after taking the baby, have found the difficulties which faced her overwhelming, and have come to us, saying 'If I only hadn't seen my baby I could have given him up.' "[63] The head nurse at the Denver Crittenton Home observed, "Most girls were influenced by their families to the extent that they did not want to see their babies." The nurse also described how many residents signed permission forms for circumcision in advance of the birth, "so if a girl didn't want to know the sex of the baby, she wouldn't have to."[64]

From one Salvation Army Home, a resident reported the relief of some girls when they learned that "We can ask to be blindfolded during delivery if we don't want to see our baby."[65] In a Florence Crittenton Home in a northwestern state, the event was carefully managed by staff: "If a girl . . . asks to see her baby, this is by plan with the maternity home social worker and the baby is seen briefly as a girl is leaving the hospital with the worker."[66] In New York City, there was at least one hospital to which certain girls were sent: "If a mother does not want to see her child, she is usually referred to Misericordia [Hospital] where they have facilities to make this possible."[67]

In some maternity homes, including the venerable Inwood House in New York, there was a pointed psychological and practical intention behind the staff's management of this issue:

> The unmarried mother does not have to see her baby if that is her choice. However, [the home] has not had a single instance where she has not seen the child. In some instances, where she has decided before the birth of the baby that it is better for her not to see it, she finally asked to do so before she left the hospital. Miss Leavitt thinks it is much better for her to see the child, if only for one glimpse. If she does this, she takes the next step of accompanying the social worker to the adoption agency. In this way, she herself is giving up the baby, rather than the agency taking it away from her.[68]

By the early 1960s, policies and programs in some maternity homes were becoming more sensitive to the variable needs of the mothers, but still stressed relinquishment. At this time, for example, the Crittenton Hastings Home in Boston instituted a mother-and-baby center to which the pair could return briefly from the hospital. The director of the home explained the center's purpose:

> The staff seem[s] to feel that by having this service available we help the girl who needs the intimacy with her baby even though she must separate; the girl who, as one of our residents expressed it, "needs to be allowed to feel grief;" the girl who has glamorized baby care; for any girl who has considered thoughtfully the implications of this experience and feels it is essential for her total experience.[69]

These maternity home practices were shaped by a genuine concern for the unmarried mother's painful situation. Staff were sharply aware of her need to resume her life as unstigmatized as possible, and of her companion need to manage the difficulty of putting the baby behind her. Total disengagement from the baby aided in achieving these goals. In addition, maternity home practices were shaped by the staff's conviction that the unmarried mother should relinquish her child. It was only after the war when relinquishment among maternity home residents became *de rigueur* that these policies and practices became so central to the total program.

Maternity home staff often recognized the complexity of their task. Many agreed that "working toward the mother's interest will be a protection of the baby's interest."[70] This was so, many believed, because the mother's interest was shaped by her status as not-a-mother. Joining a longtime maternity home director, many agreed that when the unwed mother looks at her baby, "clearly she is not a mother longing for her child, but a child longing for her mother."[71] Adequate maternity home services and particularly skillful casework treatment would help the mother toward an agency adoption. Without these, single mothers "will seek other solutions: abortion, or frequently independent placement of their children."[72] The worker had to be careful to focus attention on the mother's problems, partly in order to safeguard the baby. As one practitioner cautioned in a presentation to her colleagues: "If casework is directed [primarily] toward the interests of the baby, the mother may become even more maladjusted than before, and in the case of an adoption, she may return to claim her baby if she is left feeling guilty, misjudged or in need of support."[73] Maternity home staff, indeed, had to face the difficulty of meeting a variety of needs as they accepted and safeguarded the postwar adoption mandate.

Many unwed mothers in maternity homes struggled to come to terms with relinquishment. A poem entitled "Love," written by Donna P. at a Florence Crittenton Maternity Home in 1965, expresses one girl's effort to define herself as a mother while accepting her need to relinquish the baby.

> A mother's love does not grow cold
> But flourishes as she grows old
> Remembering all the while
> Delight received from her child.
> A mother's love will never stray
> Although she gave her child away
> For love and faith were in demand
> To put her baby into God's hand.[74]

For others, the acceptance was more difficult. One unwed mother in the late 1950s expressed the painful transition she underwent: "When I came here I was so stubborn. I was determined to keep my baby no matter what anyone thought. I know now that I was thinking only of myself and what I wanted. Now I think about the baby more and what will be best for him."[75] Another girl, Susan, had a similar change of heart. Susan's caseworker associated the change with a specific event. The girl was chosen as the subject of a weekly case conference in the Boston Salvation Army Maternity Home. These conferences were attended by all staff members, the chief of the home's obstetrics service, the consulting psychiatrist, who in this case was Dr. Philip Solomon of Harvard University, all the professionals from outside agencies working with Susan, and Susan herself. Susan entered the case conference thoroughly determined to keep her baby. As a result of the conference, however, during which she was closely questioned by Dr. Solomon in front of all the others, Susan "began to think and respond more realistically." The caseworker reported that "gradually she began to regard the baby as a separate being, with needs that she could not meet. . . . By the time her baby was born, Susan was certain she would release it for adoption."[76]

The "relinquishment culture" of the maternity home, in which up to 90 percent of the residents placed their babies by the late 1950s,[77] helped many girls, confused about their intentions, to make a decision. Parents and professionals readily supported a girl who envisioned the future—her own and her baby's—in normative, family terms. As relinquishment became the solution for the vast majority in the homes, unwed mothers who were uncertain, or who were determined to keep their babies, tended to keep silent on this score.

It is likely that most maternity home residents were grateful to leave the home unencumbered, ready to reconstruct their young womanhood.[78] The social and cultural canons governing young women in the postwar years did not brook transgressions and nonconformity easily, so many could bolster a personal desire for expiation with their knowledge of how difficult it would be to create life as a single, illegitimate mother. Louise's experience in an Eastern Seaboard maternity home, however, is representative of how some white unwed mothers reacted to a set of professional practices that tended to treat all white unwed mothers alike. Louise's experience suggests how difficult it was for a nonconforming girl or woman to effect a nonconforming solution in this era. Louise's caseworker recorded that her client had had maternity home care, casework counseling and adoption service from a local agency, but "for a number of reasons . . . she was not satisfied with the care she received; [she felt] the worker was more identified with her mother than with her; she was pushed into giving up the baby for adoption."[79]

The Adoption Mandate and Abuse

For the most part, not-for-profit maternity home personnel staff in the postwar period were humanitarian individuals dedicated to the kindly and firm rehabilitation of white unwed mothers and to the best interests of their babies. Their expert advice, which counseled adoption on an every-case basis, however, became a support to some who were not primarily concerned with the welfare and rehabilitation of the unwed mother. Among these were individuals who assumed that the state, its institutions, and private supporting services had the right to determine the quality, the viability, and the righteousness of individual parents.

In the postwar era, issues about the extent of the state's prerogatives in family relations were no more resolved than they are today. Opponents of a broad state role in serving unwed mothers and other needy populations in the 1950s argued, in part, that the postwar return of affluence obviated the need for state welfare programs created in times of economic dislocation.

They also argued that voluntary agencies had always done a good job in this area and could continue to do so if government programs would get out of their way.[80] Others argued that the government did have a legitimate role in providing services to unwed mothers (and others), a partnership role with voluntary agencies. These agencies had roots in religious and charitable organizations and were the traditional and dependable source of humanitarian and rehabilitative impulses, based in the community.[81] For those promoting partnership, the state was a source of funds to augment community collections and a source of legislation designed to protect dependent, vulnerable groups.

A third group argued that questions regarding family matters belonged in the court, where the state could function most efficiently and economically to impose order on an untidy aspect of social relations. For this group, issues regarding the role of social agencies, and public and private funding, were subordinated to assertions of the power of the judiciary. This stance permitted individual biases—in this case, the attitudes of individual judges toward the rights of unwed mothers—to shape the experiences of many girls and women who conceived out of wedlock.

Harry D. Fisher, a judge in the Cook County, Illinois, Circuit Court in the 1950s, who was frequently involved in adoption cases from the bench, expressed this position explicitly:

> Strictly speaking, the old common-law theory of *parens patriae* is still part of our law. The supreme parent is the state. Children are given [by the state] to their parents with the right to care, discipline and educate on the assumption that because of their natural love they will do, so to speak, the best job. . . . These [out-of-wedlock] children are citizens of the state. They are wards of the state and the state operates through the courts.[82]

This judge and many of his colleagues believed it was their right and duty to intercede and terminate the parental rights of mothers whose wrongdoing consisted of bearing a child while unwed.

Harry A. Woodward, Juvenile Court judge of Richmond County, Augusta, Georgia, also felt no responsibility to the single mother. He imagined the unmarried mother whose babies had been taken from her plaintively asking, "Oh where oh where are my children tonight?" His response revealed how a particular moral position could stand in for the law and become the law when white public opinion and white married couples condemned the mother and desired her child, or simply believed in the social and personal value of adoption, for everyone:

> The answer to that [question] was that the children now are in the homes of decent people and honest people of Christianity. That is where her children are tonight. I definitely have a duty to children. I will not let a person who wants to live a life of immorality inflict upon her children, regrettable as it may be, her ways. If she has decided to live that life, I will not allow the children to also do so in her path.[83]

Judge Woodward and a number of his colleagues on the bench in this era drew on their own opinions of decency to shape the experience of single mothers and their children directly. They also helped define "family" for adoptive parents and thus influenced the experience of unmarried mothers indirectly. Woodward described the advice he gave to one man for whose family he had legalized an adoption in the past. "I had advised him at that time, or his wife at that time, that a family is not balanced with one child, no matter how good the foster parents may be. You do a lot of harm when you have such a family. . . . My idea of a family is two children."[84] A judge who offered his opinion, sometimes aggressively like Woodward, became another voice supporting the postwar ideal family, the construction of which depended, for some couples, on the availability of out-of-wedlock babies. For Judge Woodward and many of his contemporaries, no hesitation was necessary concerning their right and ability to determine these matters. While illegitimate pregnancy and an illegitimate baby had, in the past, been a private matter, handled by family, perhaps assisted by charity, by midcentury, these issues had become public business and public concerns.

When the federal government undertook to investigate adoption practices in the United States in the 1950s, the task was assigned to Senator Estes Kefauver's Subcommittee to Investigate Juvenile Delinquency. One of the goals of the subcommittee was to propose federal legislation to control interstate baby selling. Ernest Mitler, special counsel to the subcommittee, instructed the participants that redressing problems associated with the "profit motive" was only one of the concerns of the investigators. A good law, he claimed, must assure the "suitability of the home" for adoptable children, a criterion that could not, by definition, be met in homes provided by unmarried mothers.[85]

By implication, and in practice, white unmarried mothers were defined by the state out of their motherhood. If not by law, then *de facto*, they were not parents. They could not provide a suitable home. As the Child Welfare League of America explained in its influential manual on the care of unmarried mothers:

> In our society, parenthood without marriage is a deviation from the accepted cultural pattern of bearing and raising children. It represents a specific form of social dysfunctioning which is a problem in itself and which in turn creates social and emotional problems for parent and child. . . . It is generally accepted in our society that children should be reared in families created through marriage. The legal family is the approved social institution to ensure sound rearing and development of children.[86]

Friedman, the Duluth lawyer with a great deal of experience with unwed mothers, described how society defined a single mother's life as no longer her own. She was "categorized as a public statistic to be handled by superiors who are contemptuous of any failure on her part to show full appreciation for her getting more than she deserves. [Officials don't want to see] insufficient humiliation [or] an [in]adequate sense of disgrace."[87] Friedman's comments describe the conflict agency workers still felt in the 1950s about freeing the unwed mother from the shame and long-term ostracism that formerly would have been her due. Workers assisting single pregnant girls and women may have also felt that as sexually promiscuous females, unmarried mothers did not deserve the staff's protection. Sexually promiscuous females had forfeited the right to manage their own maternity. A Miami judge, Walter H. Beckham, described unmarried mothers in his city as "ignorant": "They usually come from out of town and they philander until they get into the hands of somebody who steers them to an abortionist or a doctor or a lawyer or somebody that may deal in that sort of business."[88] Again, while psychiatric theory had uncoupled mental deficiency and illegitimacy, the tradition of judging unwed mothers in these terms was not always easy to cast off.

Judgments like these supported various forms of state control over single pregnant girls and women, including, of course, the state's formal and informal proscriptions against birth control for unmarried girls and women, its denial of access to safe, legal abortion, and its tolerance in many places of unsafe, illegal abortions. The state determined what types of agencies and individuals an unmarried mother could deal with in planning for her child, and either suggested strongly or legislated which ones were "morally wrong." The state's attitude toward white, female illicit sexuality and pregnancy facilitated the transition for some individuals from an interest in placing white illegitimate babies for adoption to an ability to abuse and exploit childbearing single white women.

Some proponents of the adoption of white illegitimate babies promoted, wittingly or not, a basic disregard for the individual unwed girl or woman. While many agency workers did serve the mothers well, enthusiasm about the baby sometimes eclipsed focus on the mother's human predicament. The mother's needs and the way these were met were defined partly by social and cultural exigencies. These mandated that having placed her child for adoption, she must return to normal life as quickly and seamlessly as possible after relinquishment. Agencies did not offer follow-up services. The brief adoption-oriented services agencies did offer assumed that the unwed mother could return to normalcy essentially as a result of giving up the child. Some practitioners were uncomfortable with these routines. One wrote, "The present prevailing policies in agencies thoughout the country serving the unwed mothers and adoption do not always stack up against the criteria that 'policies exist to serve people.' Few of us providing these services are happy with the status quo."[89]

In addition, while the state and mainstream institutions sanctioned only properly licensed agencies to handle adoptions, it was a well-known fact that the rich and famous obtained their adopted children via methods made possible by their considerable financial resources. Monsignor O'Grady, the secretary of the National Conference of Catholic Charities, pointed this out at the Kefauver hearings, referring to many of those who adopted children "outside of the regular channels" as "among the most prominent citizens of their communities."[90]

In postwar, consumerist America, institutions promoted services and attitudes to protect the out-of-wedlock child from market-driven deals and to see that it was well placed. On the other hand, these same institutions were behaving in market-oriented ways as they promoted a specific, socially beneficial product: the two-parent/two-plus child family. This double message justified the commoditylike treatment of unwed mothers and their babies by the many individuals interested in profiting from the adoption mandate. These individuals included Charlton G. Blair, a lawyer who handled between thirty and sixty adoptions a year in the late 1950s. Explaining how his operation worked, he denied he ever "paid one red cent" to a prospective mother of an illegitimate child to persuade her to part with the baby for adoption. But in suggesting why the adopting parents were willing to pay up to fifteen hundred dollars for a child, which included the lawyer's $750 fee, Blair defined his sense of the transaction very clearly: "If they're willing to pay three thousand dollars for an automobile these days, I don't see why they can't pay this much for a child."[91]

State laws that made it difficult for nonresident unwed mothers to get financial or other forms of assistance, and the lack of state or federal laws against baby selling, also contributed to the ambiguity. The government was committed to the best interests of out-of-wedlock babies and believed that this interest could be best served by licensed adoption agencies. Yet it was unable to check the flourishing black market in these years, even though the government defined its activities as inimical to the interests of unwed mothers, illegitimate babies, and adoptive parents.

Mainstream Agencies and Adoption Abuse

A number of mainstream public and private agencies in this era often abused prescribed adoption practices. There is considerable evidence that in the postwar era, some—though by no means all—Florence Crittenton Maternity Homes in effect used babies to raise money to support their always strapped institutions. For example, in 1953, Virgil Payne, the first director of the newly reorganized Florence Crittenton Association, was forced to announce a "cautious investigation" of the Columbus, Ohio, Florence Crittenton Home because of the institution's adoption practices which violated the national's policy of placement through licensed agencies. The Columbus outfit was regularly engaging in direct, private placements that involved payments to the home.[92]

In the early 1950s, the University of California Hospital staff was concerned about the "rigidity" of the San Francisco Florence Crittenton director. She refused to discuss with hospital staff the girls' plans for their babies, thus concealing the private arrangements the home was involved in making.[93] A few years before the problem in Columbus became public, Maud Morlock of the United States Children's Bureau discovered on a field trip to Ohio that "many of the girls at the Florence Crittenton home in Columbus never know that there is an alternative to adoption." The superintendent's daughter lived in Dayton and was said to "act as a channel for placement of babies." Morlock was particularly disturbed that the home kept no record of their finances and that there was a great deal of "suspicion that [the home] gets money from the adoptive parents. It is said that they send their unmarried mothers to do babysitting in the home of an attorney and he figures out the adoption," with some financial benefit accruing to the home.[94]

Even into the early 1960s, these shady practices continued. A Children's Bureau employee reported in 1962 that she was "gratified that the Florence Crittenton in Wheeling has changed their philosophy and practice last summer." The changes safeguarded against staff and board participation in adoption activities to the financial benefit of the home. Before 1961, girls admitted to the Wheeling home were considered private patients; social work services were not available to them, and adoptive placements "were arranged by the Superintendent and the institution's attorney." The efforts of "many people" were required to convince the board to vote to alter these practices.[95] The Peoria Florence Crittenton Home changed its adoption practices in the same era after many years of a policy that enabled the staff only "to accept as adoptive parents those who could be generous financially with the Home." The president of the board of the home reported the new policy as of 1964: the adoption fee was now 7 percent of the husband's earnings for the preceding year. Assuming adoption, she said, "We are no longer giving parents a bundle of joy. Rather parents are chosen for our infants. In our Home we like to brag that for every infant placed, we have ten homes which have been screened and approved."[96]

Proceeds from baby selling were probably a budgetary factor in a small minority of not-for-profit maternity homes in the postwar years. But parallel to these homes, which were usually affiliated with church-related national organizations, there were a number of private maternity homes harboring unwed mothers and selling babies for profit. A young woman who became pregnant in July 1954 testified before Kefauver's committee about her experience in such a home in Fort Worth, Texas. This was the Edna Gladney Home, a massive operation in these years. The unwed mother who had been sent to the home by her doctor reported that it received six thousand applications a year. In any one month, there were three hundred girls in residence, 150 babies delivered, and one social worker. The costs to the unmarried mother included a $90 per month charge and $150 for the delivery. Adoptive parents paid $2,500 for a baby. Conditions were pretty rough in the home: "[T]he food was very poor. The girls often got nothing more than a piece of cake and a glass of water for dinner." Still, the home's board of directors, which included "some of the most influential people throughout the United States of America," did nothing about this, or about the dishonest and illegal adoption practices at the home. The young woman told the Senate subcommittee her story, which she assured its members was not unique:

> I had been told . . . that the babies were not placed in an adoptive home until they were four to six weeks of age [although I knew that the institution had no way of keeping babies that long], that there was a six month waiting period before anything was legal or final, and that I had six months in which time I could regain the custody of my child . . . . I left the home when he was ten days old and wrote a letter five days later telling them I was ready to return, to regain custody of my baby. I received a letter telling me I was too late, and that he had already been placed out, that it was up to the court. [The girl brought a writ of habeas corpus and lost.]. . . Also . . . one of the documents, stat[ed] that should anything be wrong with the child, physically or mentally, that the mother has to take him back whether she wants to or not. However, if the child is normal and healthy, according to their court procedure there is no way in which I can regain custody of the child.[97]

The unwed mother concluded her story by pointing out that, according to the home and the court, she was good enough to be a mother only if the child was defective. The testifier found this a bitter irony since a defective child would surely require the highest quality of maternal care. This case demonstrates the direction in which the adoption mandate could be pushed. It also shows the limits of the mandate. Couples with $2500 to spend for a baby deserved a perfect product. Imperfect babies were not recruited for the middle class.

Family and child welfare agencies also provided services to unmarried mothers and arranged for the disposition of the child. These public agencies were chronically underfunded, like most human service organizations. Public welfare workers and social service professionals associated adoption abuses primarily with the gaps in services for single pregnant girls and women.[98] In Kings County, New York, in the early 1950s, a grand jury considered adoption abuse cases for two and a half years and concluded that unwed mothers "were thrust into the black market due to the fact they could not find suitable lying-in pre-natal care or were unable to support themselves during the pre-natal and post-natal period, or to meet necessary hospital expenses."[99]

Others argued that the stigma associated with public agencies caused young women in trouble to avoid their services and turn toward individuals who could arrange independent adoptions. A Chicago lawyer, speaking for his unwed-mother clients explained that these women knew that "if any one goes to a social agency . . . that their name immediately is processed through the Council of Social Agencies which is like a clearinghouse and center of all information."[100]

While expressing concern about the lack of services and the stigma, social service workers rarely criticized the attitudes and practices of their own agencies, which often stretched ideas about the advisability of adoption beyond the point of decency. All over the country, public agencies were functioning in an environment in which the separation of single mother and child had become the norm. In Minnesota, for example, there were two hundred such separations in 1925; in 1949, one thousand; between 1949 and 1955, approximately seventeen hundred each year.[101] To meet the demand and to justify their own existence, agencies not infrequently resorted to questionable tactics.

Martin Friedman, the Duluth attorney, remarked that under pressure to produce babies for white couples, the "Welfare Department seems determined to obtain for itself official endorsement announcing to the world of women in trouble, 'you have no right, or privilege, or reason to go elsewhere with your problem.' "[102] Sometimes agency personnel were high-handed with the pregnant young women they served. A researcher studying agency services in the mid-1950s found, for example, that the "girls are confused about the purpose of casework interviews, and puzzled whether these interviews were to make things easier for caseworkers or for them."[103] The chairman of the Committee on Adoption Law of the Chicago Bar Association, Leon M. Despres, testified at the Kefauver hearings that unmarried pregnant girls were reluctant to deal with welfare or social agencies because of the staff's attitude that it was part of the service to invade their privacy.[104]

Dr. Irene Josselyn, a psychiatrist, offered a vivid account of the attitude many unwed mothers met in the early 1950s upon applying to a social agency for assistance:

> The worker is basically angry at the client. . . . The worker's anger may be related to her own frustrations and her defenses against her own frustrations and . . . impulses. . . . She wishes to punish the client as she would punish herself were she in the same position. The client's adequacy in the situation only goads the worker on to punish her more severely. The client must suffer for her sin is against society. . . . The worker punishes by subtle means at times, but more direct means at others. She offers living arrangements that will give only the bare necessities of life. She makes it clear to the client that she does not have a right to have fun until she has paid for her sin by a period of grim, colorless living. She places her under rules that bind her to a way of behaving that completely ignores her rights and capabilities as an adult. . . . The worker feels successful only when the [girl's] defense is destroyed by overwhelming guilt and repentance.

Josselyn's observations suggest the difficulty many social workers faced as they attempted to square the traditional, punitive attitude toward unmarried mothers—girls and women who had engaged in proscribed sexual affairs—with the contemporary commitment to the social efficacy of rehabilitation and redemption through relinquishment.

Josselyn's experience as a psychiatrist working as consultant to public agencies led her to the conclusion that

> Too often the solution [to the girl's problem] depends on the function of the agency rather than on the needs of the unmarried mother. She may become a social problem, a statistic, a representative of a symptom of emotional disturbance, a resource for babies for adoption, a shameful disfigurement of society to be hidden from the public eye, or a punching bag upon which society can vent otherwise controlled hostility.

In fact, white unmarried mothers served in many of these roles simultaneously. As a class, however, they were not considered mothers. Josselyn cited examples of several unmarried mothers who demonstrated that they could cope with their situations. These included young women who wanted to keep their babies. Josselyn's opinion was that these girls, especially, were met by the worker's resistance and hostility.[105]

Perhaps one such young woman was an eighteen-year-old Texan who wrote to the president of the United States in 1951, seeking advice. She wrote, "I've been thinking of getting rid of it [by abortion], but I don't even have the money to do that, and I may sound foolish but I'd like to keep it even though I knew I did wrong. Does that sound foolish?" This unmarried mother had been taught, whether by family, the media, or social service workers, that she would likely be condemned for the desire to keep.[106]

Public agencies handling these adoptions employed specific policies and practices that sometimes made life even more difficult for white unmarried mothers seeking assistance. For example, Leontine Young, intimately familiar with how agencies functioned, reported in these years that sometimes social workers saw "financial assistance . . . as separate from, and of lesser importance than, help with [the unmarried mother's] psychological needs. If an individual girl fails to agree with this, money may be used as a weapon rather than a service."[107]

Residency requirements for public services became another major stumbling block for unmarried mothers, up to 35 percent of whom delivered their babies away from their home states.[108] A typical story of frustration and humiliation was told by "Miss Williams," a young, pregnant woman, about her experience at the New York City Department of Welfare in 1955. She was sent to the nonresident section, where,

> They started asking me [personal] questions. . . . I told them I did not want to give them my parents' name. The reason for my coming there was because I didn't want my parents to know, and well, it came to a point where they told me I was not cooperating with them. . . . I told them . . . I am asking you people to help me for a month to three months until I can get myself started, and I will be glad to pay you people back . . . and this woman . . . she just couldn't see it my way and told me I was being uncooperative.[109]

"Miss Williams," without the resources to live, ended up trading her baby for her own living expenses during pregnancy. The trade was arranged by a New York doctor who put "Miss Williams" in touch with an unscrupulous lawyer who managed the adoption.[110]

Three letters from unmarried mothers illustrate that some public agencies took direct action to separate white babies from their mothers, even against the mother's will.

A very articulate eighteen-year-old unmarried mother from Minnesota wrote to her governor in August 1950. She said that a welfare worker in her city said she could not keep her baby, "that the baby should be brought up by both a mother and a father." Having gotten no satisfaction, she wrote in frustration and anger to President Truman:

> With tears in my eyes and sorrow in my heart I'm trying to defend the rights and privileges which every citizen in the United States is supposed to enjoy under our Constitution [but are] denied me and my baby. . . . The Welfare Department refuses to give me my baby without sufficient cause or explanation. . . . I have never done any wrong and just because I had a baby under such circumstances the welfare agency has no right to condemn me and to demand my child be placed [for adoption].[111]

Mildred Arnold, director of the Division of Social Services at the Children's Bureau, answered this letter and assured the writer that the "Welfare Board is acting in the interest and for the welfare of your baby." Miss Arnold stressed that all of the workers involved in this case "are interested only in your welfare and that of your baby."[112] One can imagine that the young woman got little consolation from Arnold's assurances, as they were accompanied simply by a referral back to the same agency that had taken away her child in the first place.

A year earlier, a young man living in Sterling, Colorado, wrote to the Children's Bureau about a similar case. In this situation, a young man and woman had conceived a baby out of wedlock. When the man went to the Denver Welfare Department for assistance a few days before the baby was born, he reported,

> I asked them not to ask or let her give the baby up as we wanted to get married and go ahead for we had come to see the mistake [of premarital sex and conception] but seemed they wanted the baby and the girl was deaf girl and they ask and recommended to her to give it to them and they claim to have it already placed for adoption. In her condition and under circumstance she signed relinquishment paper thinking she had a year to get the child. Four days after it was born they took her out of the hospital and to juvenile court when she was in no condition to make any decision and I had asked them not to do that and have tried ever since to get the baby but they just pass the buck and say nothing can be done. . . . We want to get married and have the child. Is there no justice? Are people able to take a mother's own child, if so I have lost all faith and respect for such law. It is ruining

her health and breaking her down. . . . I do hope you will see into this and
help in some way. Surely of all these laws and agencies there are good folks
and justice prevailing somewhere.[113]

This case, in particular, demonstrates key assumptions underlying the
behavior of some agency workers. The young mother here was deaf. As a
handicapped person and as an unmarried girl, her maternity, as well as her
child, was considered illegitimate and could be rightfully terminated by the
authorities. Physically defective women had curtailed rights as mothers just
as physically defective illegitimate babies had diminished opportunities to join
the middle class.

This case also suggests how valuable all white babies had become in
postwar America. The value followed the psychological explanation of white
single pregnancy and the decline of a belief in the genetically flawed mother
and child. Now white babies were born not only untainted but also *unclassed*.
A poor "white trash" teenager could have a baby in Appalachia; it could
be adopted by an upper-middle-class couple in Westport, Connecticut, for
example, and the baby would, in that transaction, become upper middle class
also.

Finally, this case illustrates that agency workers believed that a successful
separation often depended on an early and very quick transaction. This was
noticed by contemporaries, including the authors of the State's Attorney's
Commission on Adoption of Cook County, Illinois, which noted in its final
report the problem that arises when "mothers come into court service division
to sign a consent either on the day they are released from the hospital, or
shortly thereafter [and] are physically and emotionally upset to the extent that
they are not capable of making rational decisions."[114]

In fact, a study of the way one hundred unwed mothers planned for their
babies' futures by the Child Placing and Adoption Committee of New York
City in the early postwar era found that while 96 percent described themselves
as "certain" about adoption at first, 60 percent of these mothers became
uncertain after the baby's birth. Among these, the greatest number made their
final decision between four and six months after the birth. When the agency
allowed such a time lapse, almost one half of those who wavered decided to
keep their babies. The study confirmed the value of the soon-to-be obsolete
practice of giving mothers time to make up their minds. "Many," the study
concluded, "appreciated not having to commit themselves finally during the
time directly after the baby's birth when feelings are strong and physical
strength below par."[115]

The third letter came, in the same era, from Advance, Arkansas, to
the Children's Bureau in Washington. In this case, the unwed mother had
previously written to the Bureau for advice and had been referred to her local
Welfare Department. In this second letter, the woman explained that she had
gone to see the welfare workers, but

[T]hey wont me to let them have the baby. They wont me to move to town. I dont like the city and I have my garden and chickens out here. They sure did not talk very sympathetic to me. They talk like I was the only woman ever happen to this kind of luck. I hate it as bad as anyone. But to late. So why do they haft to ask me to give up the baby. I'll start over when I get through this. I'll never take a nother job from a man again. . . . Why dose that wellfare lady have to talk to me like she dose. After all she don't even have any children. If she did she would understand more how I feel. Now here is what I want to no is can they take the baby if I don't want to give it up.[116]

These cases did not represent exceptional behavior on the part of public workers. Many agencies did meet the needs and desires of their unwed clients who wished to put their babies up for adoption. But some agencies constrained other mothers who had different plans to behave normatively.

One other mainstream entity with a central role in adoptions of out-of-wedlock children was the court. An attorney from Memphis, Tennessee, described some problems with adoptions to the Kefauver Committee. He told how the Tennessee Children's Home Society, a notorious commercial maternity home that trafficked in white babies, obtained these infants. He listed "scouts" sent out through the rural counties of the state, "calling on doctors, telling them if they had unwed mothers as patients [to] refer them to Memphis." He also named hospitals and courts as institutions that provided babies for adoption. The lawyer explained how the adoptions were facilitated by the county courts in a manner he considered patently illegal, principally because the natural mother, the adoptive parents, and lawyers were all absent. The process worked this way: [T]here is just an agent or one of the employees at the home who took a handful of papers drawn up by the Tennessee Children's Home Society's lawyers . . . who took them up, and the judges in the county courts, who are not lawyers, not trained, just signed them indiscriminately."[117] In Augusta, Georgia, the method was even more nefarious.

In many cases mothers were brought into the juvenile court . . . and they were charged with neglect of their children.[118] . . . The children were permanently taken away [and] made wards of the juvenile court. Then, in turn, the Richmond County juvenile court judge, Harry A. Woodward . . . would place the children out with adoptive couples very often in California and in New York and in the bulk of the States.[119]

The special counsel to the Kefauver Committee made an intensive study of adoption practices in Augusta because the use of legitimate institutions there for exploitative purposes were extreme but, he felt, they were also representative of similar practices elsewhere. Mr. Mitler, the special counsel, interviewed hundreds of people in that city and found that "the juvenile court was identified with police power . . . and fear rather than constructive child welfare work."[120]

Judge Woodward in Augusta worked closely with Elizabeth B. Hamilton, the chief probation officer in the Richmond County Juvenile Court. This public official spent a great deal of her time finding and "freeing" white babies for adoption, using her position to legitimize these activities. One unwed mother told of her encounter with Miss Hamilton.

> Several hours after delivery [Miss Hamilton] informed me that my baby had been born dead. She told me that if I signed a paper she had, no one, my family or friends, would know about the situation, and that everything would be cleared up easily. She described the paper as being a consent authorizing the burial of the child. . . . I signed the paper without really looking at it, as I was in a very distressed and confused condition at the time.[121]

This young woman went on to say that "Two years later I was shocked to receive in the mail adoption papers from the Welfare Department in California since I was under the impression that the child was deceased."

In another case, in 1949, a woman had had her daughter taken away from her by Miss Hamilton. Later she became a witness against the probation officer when Hamilton was on trial for kidnapping the baby of another young woman, Mary Green. This first woman reported, "I never got to testify because Mary Green was locked up for perjury before they got around to my testimony, and I thought it better not to say anything because I didn't want the same thing to happen to me." According to this woman's sister, a great many people in town feared Hamilton,[122] although many also protected her and approved of her work. She and her accomplice, Judge Woodward, were still at their posts in the mid-1950s, although public disclosures of their dealings by the Kefauver Committee did chase the pair from office.

The following excerpt of a letter from Hamilton to adoptive parents in California illustrates exactly how the court went about engaging in illegal and deceitful practices and how much trickery and abuse the adoption mandate could support.

> This is for your information and for the information of your attorney: When we send the temporary papers to you Judge Woodward will state that the baby was deserted and abandoned by the mother at the University Hospital, therefore this court took the child as a neglected child, and this court is a legal adopting agency, therefore it is [under] the legal guardian[ship] of the court because it is born out of wedlock, [and the mother's] whereabouts are unknown—that makes it so much easier to get the adoption through in California—if we give the mother's written consent (which we have) [obtained under false pretenses], then the agency there goes to all the trouble to write the University Hospital here where the baby was born, and they ask for a social history on the mother and as the hospital has no social worker to do this work all these letters go to them for investigations and

information *are referred to this court*; so we just stop that in the beginning by saying the baby was deserted and that ends the thing.[123] (italics added)

The Black Market

Illegalities and abuse existed in some mainstream institutions, but a great many of the worst abuses were committed by individual baby brokers—lawyers, doctors, and other persons acting without institutional affiliations. Again, there is no question that for many unwed mothers, the opportunity to place their babies independently often meant that they could get exactly what they needed when they needed it: money to live on, shelter, medical care, and assurances about the placement of the baby, all with no questions asked. These girls and women were often spared the delays, the layers of authority, the invasions of privacy, the "permanent black mark engraved in the files of the welfare department," and spared the pressure to reveal the father's name, all of which characterized the bureaucratic agency approach.[124] These characteristics also demonstrate how difficult it was for institutions to perform simultaneously as agents of social control and as sources of humanitarian assistance for the needy and vulnerable.

Clark Vincent, a leading researcher in the mid-1950s and early 1960s in the area of unwed mothers, refuted the commonly held view that unmarried mothers turned to the black market with their babies in order to get money. His studies in California suggested that middle-class girls shunned agencies. These girls, least in need of money, consistently used independent adoption managed by doctors and lawyers. Poorer girls, he found, were the ones most likely to turn to public agencies.[125]

Indeed, more affluent girls and women, particularly those with cooperative parents, were able to avoid institutional and public services of all kinds. But there were many girls and women with no financial and possibly few family resources who were the prey of individuals earning a living by feeding the demand for white newborns, under the postwar adoption mandate. *Look* sensationally referred to these as "the others." They were the ones who

> run away from home, lose themselves in the cities. . . . A few will take the sleeping-tablet way out. Others will crawl animal-like into hiding, leave their babies in ashcans—dead or alive—depending on the mother's mental condition. But most will hear eventually of the black market . . . a seeming godsend offering food, shelter and release from shame. Only it does not turn out that way.[126]

The story of the black market in babies, captured so vividly by the Kefauver hearings in 1955 and 1956, provides a rare view of the experiences of white unwed mothers who were not broadly middle class. These young women, very often without resources—money, emotional support, or information—were terribly vulnerable to the ploys of black marketeers whose intentions were to capitalize on the experience of the growing number of white girls and women in the postwar years who were conceiving babies outside of marriage, and on the insatiable demand for the babies.

The stories of unwed mothers abused by the baby market reveal how class, gender, and (white) race together created the possibilities to use these girls and women for profit. The black market was supported in these years by a number of social conditions. First of all white unwed girls and women were taking more sexual license for themselves despite prevailing ideas about the value of virginity for marriageable girls and despite legal and cultural proscriptions against abortion and birth control. While bridal pregnancy rates climbed in the 1950s, many males continued to feel free of the need to take responsibility for the consequences of intercourse, including financial responsibility. Parents of unwed mothers were eager to eradicate the illegitimacy experience from their daughters' lives and from their family escutcheon. Some—mostly the poorest—did not have the funds or the information necessary to ally their daughters with maternity home or adoption agency services. Others—some poor and some better off—lacked the information or the willingness to associate themselves and their daughters with agencies, public or private. Of course, many girls and women were on their own, without family support. The new, postwar "unclassed" status of white babies, which rendered all white newborns valuable, contributed also to the vulnerability of these unwed mothers. Cultural sanctions against sexual nonconformity were strong enough, and social pressure on female nonconformists intense enough, to send unwed mothers with few resources into the anonymous marketplace, which offered, simultaneously, protection and danger.

It is important to note that the Kefauver hearings had a specific agenda. Its members and many who they called to testify condemned all independent adoptions and championed licensed adoption agencies as the only legitimate way to handle relinquishment. In general, the subcommittee believed that the state should have a bigger and more carefully safeguarded role in the disposition of illegitimate babies. The testifiers cited so often in this chapter, therefore, were frequently selected because their stories or their point of view supported this agenda. Nevertheless, the unwed mothers and others who testified revealed themselves largely without reference to anyone's concerns but their own. The mix of victims, perpetrators, and experts who testified allows a complex picture of the black market to emerge. This is true despite (and because of) the amount of self-justifying, sermonizing, and outright lying that seemed to have characterized the testimonies. The hearings reveal that operators in the baby market were not, by definition, dangerous because they facilitated adoptions without the benefit of state licensing. They were dangerous simply because they made their living off of young girls and women who were culturally shamed and lacking the resources to protect themselves.

The Professions and Black Marketeering

The locus of concern at the Children's Bureau, in the mass media, and among the professions testifying at the Kefauver hearings, suggests that lawyers and doctors were most often involved in gray and black market adoptions. These professionals often justified their activities with reference to the ever-growing and hard-to-meet demand for white babies and with contempt for the way that licensed agencies conducted their business. A New York lawyer claimed that "a large per cent [of the social agencies] were absolutely no good legally and . . . agencies gave unmarried mothers little advice and often forced them unfairly to care for their children between birth and adoption."[127] Sometimes the offending lawyers were protected by their legal superiors, as when an Ohio probate judge who had jurisdiction in adoptions refused to attend any more meetings of the municipal adoption committee "after an obstetrician suggested he would discover a considerable grey market in babies if he took the opportunity to interview doctors and lawyers."[128]

One unmarried mother from Chicago who became pregnant in 1954 told how she was stopped on the street by Nathan M. Gomberg, an attorney very active in black-market placements. Gomberg asked her if she "had any children to adopt out to let him know." He also said to let him know if she heard of any other pregnant girls who wanted to place out children.[129] Gomberg had hit his mark on the street and ended up paying this unmarried mother $150 for her baby. He received considerably more himself from the adoptive parents. New Yorker Irwin Slater, another lawyer–baby dealer, had a somewhat more elaborate strategy. He advertised for unmarried mothers in Miami, Florida newspapers, and "developed a pool of children there, and brought from New York City prospective adopting couples to Miami where they purchased children for sums of money from $1500 to $3000. Then the children were brought to New York."[130]

Such transactions did not reflect gains for the unwed mother herself. This is illustrated by the following exchange between Mitler, the Kefauver Committee's special counsel, and an unmarried mother, "Miss Green," about the woman's dealings with Gale Marcus, a Chicago lawyer.

Mr. Mitler: Where did you go [on January 31, 1956] with your child?

Miss Green: We went to Gale Marcus' office.

Mr. M: And did he give you money at that time, or any other time?

Miss G: Not at that time, but the next day he gave me $150.

Mr. M: That is the only money you received in the whole course of this placement?

Miss G: Yes.

Mr. M: That was to cover what?

Miss G: That was to cover hospital expenses.

Mr. M: Did you subsequently learn that Mr. Marcus received $3200 for this placement?

Miss G: Yes.

Mr. M: Did Mr. Marcus pay your [medical] bill[s]?

Miss G: No.

Mr. M: Did he pay your expenses during the prenatal period?

Miss G: No, he did not.

Mr. M: So, so far as you are concerned, you just got $150?

Miss G: That's true.[131]

Some operators went to extreme lengths to protect the viability of the deal. For example, Marcus Siegel, a New York City attorney, obtained a signed adoption consent from "Miss Williams" lying in her hospital bed a few days after delivering her baby on June 30, 1950. Immediately after the relinquishment, "Miss Williams" changed her mind and wanted her baby back. (The young woman's doctor had referred her to Marcus Siegel, who came to see her at the hospital and suggested adoption to her.) When the mother went to Siegel and asked for the child back, the lawyer handed her a death certificate and told her that the baby was dead. He went even further, telling "Miss Williams" that he had made arrangements to erect a tombstone for the baby in Lynn, Massachusetts. Several months later, the mother found out, through the New York County District Attorney's Office that the baby had not died. In fact, Siegel had arranged for an infant, who had died in Lynn at the same time that Miss Williams had asked for her child, to be buried under the name and dates of the Williams baby. In the process of finally locating her baby, she discovered that the surrogate court in Hudson, New York, had finalized the adoption only three weeks after the relinquishment, instead of waiting the required six months. The adoptive parents had been instructed to lie about these dates in court.[132]

Doctors sometimes engaged in these activities as well. Black market doctors worked through hospitals, maternity homes, and their private practices to find unwed mothers and negotiate for their babies. Virginia Kinzel, the director of a social services department at a major New York obstetric hospital who was also a member of the New York Committee on Unmarried Mothers and Adoption Services, described the uneasy relationship between social workers and doctors. For social workers, the source of antagonism was their suspicions about the role of doctors in independent adoptions. Doctors, on the other hand, charged that social workers were violating the confidential, protected status of unwed mothers. But Kinzel, drawing on her years of experience with doctors and unwed mothers, countered with the pervasive suspicions about the motives of doctors: "We wonder if some doctors who participate in private adoptions do not raise the issue of confidentiality as a rationale for independent action which they wish to take and for which they seek justification."[133]

Dorothy, an illegitimate mother in the late 1940s, was determined to keep her baby, despite inordinate pressure from her mother and her doctor who she said together "coerced" her to sign the adoptive consent. They told her that if she didn't sign, they would "take her to court to prove her an unfit mother." With Dorothy's mother's consent, the doctor cut the telephone wires in Dorothy's hospital room and told her that she could not take the baby home with her if she didn't have her own money to pay what was owed the hospital and himself.[134]

A letter from a young woman in Los Angeles to a government official described the kind of pressure a doctor could exert on an unwed mother. She wrote, in part,

> I am writing in a last desperate attempt to keep possession of my unborn baby. . . . As you have probably already guessed the baby has no legal father. I am willing to spend the rest of my life paying for this mistake . . . the one thing I cannot do is give up the child. [A doctor] said he would take my case only under one condition and that was to let them have the baby, and if I would they would pay for every expense that should come up. This is probably the easiest solution to the whole thing, but I'd rather die than lose my baby.[135]

Some unwed mothers committed to keeping their babies were not successful in resisting the deals offered by black market doctors. An undercover policewoman attached to the Women's Bureau of the Metropolitan Police Department in Washington, D.C., discovered a single, pregnant woman who was under the care of an obstetrician in the District of Columbia. She had been unable to pay her bills. Consequently, the doctor and his secretary "gave her an alternative to either pay the bill or give up the baby, and she tried to make . . . financial arrangements . . . was unable to, and did finally sign over the baby to be sent out for adoption."[136] Hospitals, too, engaged in this form of pressure. Another unmarried woman in Washington gave her child up to adoptive parents in Maryland, but testified that she did so only because the hospital would not let her have the baby since she could not pay her hospital bill.[137]

The senior judge in the Dade County, Florida, Juvenile Count testified at the Kefauver hearings about the tactics of one doctor in Miami. He told how, one day, a court probation officer was making a routine call and

> She heard a young woman crying. [The girl's mother] said, "That's Mary. She wants to get her baby back and the doctor won't let her have it." [The

probation officer] insisted on talking to her. She told the story that she had agreed to let the doctor take her baby for the services rendered providing she could see the baby and then she could make up her mind after it was born. However, the baby was snatched, as we say, taken immediately upon birth, and she had not been permitted to see it. This inflamed her and angered her and frustrated her. She was in tears and wanted to get the baby back. . . . She said that the doctor would not tell her where it was; that she had never signed any consent and that she wanted the baby back.[138]

A reporter, posing as a prospective adoptive mother in Miami, visited a Dr. Suarez and told him that she wanted a baby. The doctor said,

"Well, when you come around to getting a baby this way, it is going to cost you money." He wrote down the figure of $150. He said, "That is all the welfare people will let us charge, but," he said [implying it would actually cost a great deal more], "I have to take care of these bills. They come to me and they cry and they have a lot of trouble. They are a headache to me and they want me to abort them. I take care of them. I pay $20 a week."[139]

It was stories such as these that motivated Children's Bureau staff to get doctors out of the adoption process. In addition, the Bureau, as the leading advocate of the efficacy of social work in this area, was deeply concerned that the profession would never achieve primacy as long as doctors and lawyers continued to dabble in adoptions, some unscrupulously.[140] Maud Morlock regularly addressed these issues. Always willing to see the good side of people, she acknowledged sympathetically that "[D]octors receive a great deal of psychological satisfaction out of placing children, particularly infants, for adoption."[141] She also regularly sent out warnings to social workers that they must learn to stand united as a profession if they wanted to overcome the contempt or suspicion many doctors felt for casework, and to earn their rightful role.

Free-Lancing in the Black Market

Among black market operators were a number of nonprofessional individuals cashing in on the misfortune of unwed mothers. These people were usually associated with some form of shelter for unmarried mothers. A woman running a home in Texarkana, Texas, for example, boasted to an employee that she had sold 993 babies throughout the United States and that she wanted to make it 1,000 before she died. [142] Investigators of the notorious Tennessee Children's Home Society in the mid-1950s reported to the state governor that

While the financial transaction of Miss [Georgia] Tann [the supervisor] were shocking enough, other facts came to our attention which disturbed us even more. We found that on many occasions babies had been taken from their mothers at the hospitals when only a few hours old and placed in nursing homes in and about Memphis where they were without medical care. Many of these children died."[143]

A young, unmarried woman from Maine, utterly destitute, but determined to keep her child, was unable to pay the ten dollars a week boarding costs for her infant and was told by the people who ran the boarding facility to come up with the money or to give them the baby to put on the adoption market.[144]

A case that dramatically captures the plight of poor, white, unwed mothers was presented at the Kefauver hearings by Mary Grice, an investigative reporter for the *Wichita Beacon*. Grice testified about a woman, "Mrs. T.," who had been in the adoption business since 1951 or 1952. "Mrs. T." warehoused unwed pregnant girls in the basement of her home. "She would have them on cots for prospective adoptive parents [who] would come in and she would take them downstairs, and she would point to the girls and say, 'Point out the girl that you want to be the mother of your child.'" Grice's investigation revealed that "Mrs. T." kept on average seven unmarried mothers in her basement at a time and that she would oversee a number of the deliveries herself in the basement. According to Grice, between 150 and 164 adoptions a year of this sort were taking place in Sedgwick County, Kansas. "Mrs. T." often collaborated with Grace Schauner, a Wichita abortionist. Unmarried pregnant girls and women would first see Schauner. If they decided not to have an abortion, they would be referred to "Mrs. T.," who would "care for them and sell their infants after birth."[145]

"Mrs. T's" girls were the ones who never made it to maternity homes or social service agencies. Because they were poor, they did not have the information or other resources to resist baby market operators. Because they were female (specifically, white females), their socially mandated shame precluded self-protection and motherhood. Because they were white, their babies had market value. This combination of poverty, race, and gender put some white, unwed mothers in a position of extreme vulnerability. These operators developed an array of strategies to establish business relationships with pregnant young women.

It was not always necessary to meet all three conditions of vulnerability. In the mid-1950s, Mae Marshall, proprietor of a facility in Oklahoma for unwed mothers, questioned a potential procurer: "She wanted to know [if I lived in] a college town . . . [and] if I ever knew of any unfortunate girls. She asked me to take her card, and if I found any girls . . . to call her collect or she would come after them." The contact, Mary Jane Dunning, described where Marshall put her girls—"in little long shacks in the back with outside bath," while Marshall herself lived in "a nice home, a modern home, an up-to-date home."[146] While these college girls were probably not without economic resources, their shame and the value of their babies combined to render them vulnerable targets.

A young man reported how one of his business associates badgered him to procure unmarried mothers: "He would hound me about babies, every time I went in to the office, that was all I would hear from him." The recruiter particularly focused on the young man's fraternity contacts at his former college, Florida State University. He asked, " 'Is there any babes that you know that are in trouble that I could take over and give them a few bucks?'. . . [H]e said, 'I need a kid real bad.' "[147]

Some operators placed ads in newspapers. This one appeared in the *Columbus Dispatch* in the Fall of 1960: "*Expectant Mothers*—Vacation in Florida while you wait. Ultra-modern accommodations on oceanfront at reasonable rates." Other operators watched and waited and virtually pounced on the prospect. "One Bronx black market couple learned that the pregnant girls in a shelter run by the New York Foundling Hospital often stopped for sodas at a nearby drugstore. This couple made the drugstore their headquarters, offering one thousand dollars a baby to any girl who would talk to them."[148] Ernest Mitler provided another example from New York City "whereby a man with a criminal record, Michael Cermolla, working with a woman, Margaret Gamble, devised a pattern of approaching unmarried mothers who were living in adoption shelters during the prenatal period, when they visited the corner drugstore, and offering them one thousand dollars to leave the shelter." Mitler produced this story to support his contention that there was so much profit to be had in the baby market that hoodlums and notorious underworld figures were getting involved.[149]

One Chicago lawyer was said to send his clerk to court every time a bastardy case was on the docket, to strike up an acquaintance with the girl who brought the proceeding.[150] A Canadian, Mr. Moyneur, conveyed the flavor of the recruitment project when he described the footwork of several of his associates.

> That was the man and woman that went out, well, out over the town. They watch for a gal who was going to have a baby—"my father musn't know"—"my mother musn't know"—yakity yak—anyways,—well, they are caught, you see. Too late now, they can't do nothing about it so the legman, and some of them was women, you know—the legmen, that was women too, you see. So anyways, they went out and they would snare women like that and bring her down to Sarah's and Sarah, she's cute—she makes with the chops good with them gals.[151]

Indeed, once involved with the black market system, it was difficult for many to extricate themselves. A girl in Phenix City, Alabama, agreed to let the wife of a local doctor take her baby and put it up for adoption. A few days after the birth, she changed her mind, but the doctor's wife said it was too late and took the baby away. A woman in Miami had a similar experience. When she came to collect her baby from the woman who had been caring for it, temporarily, according to the mother, she found that the child was being offered for sale.[152]

Poor, white, unwed mothers were often viewed by marketeers as their property and simply as machinery for producing a valuable, highly marketable commodity. Mae Marshall, who kept unwed mothers in chicken coop–like housing in Oklahoma, had such an otherwise proprietary attitude about "her girls" that it was her regular practice to call the police department if "one of the girls had left her home and was en route to their home and she wanted the girl picked up and brought back."[153]

In the end, if the sale was successful, white, unmarried mothers became no more to their black market agents than a pair of empty arms. One such woman described the end of her motherhood. She came from the hospital with her baby to the agent's office. "At first he told me I would be able to meet the [adoptive parents], and after I signed the papers he told me that I would mostly hand them [the baby] through a door, that I wouldn't get to meet the people."[154] An adoptive father confirmed the use of this practice by reporting that in his case, "The mother brought the child to a door and the mother handed the child to my wife." The door was opened slightly and the mother handed the child through the door to his wife around the door.[155] With that gesture, the market's interest in the white, unwed mother came to an end.

An intruder in the courtroom in Miami, Florida, where a section of the Kefauver hearings was held in November 1955, expressed the frustration of some girls and women who felt they had lost control over the disposition of their illegitimate children. This woman stood up, unbidden, and lectured the men before her in a loud voice. She said,

> Excuse me. I am not leaving no court. . . . You have to carry these children nine months and then you have them taken away by the Catholic Charities, and then they throw you out and drag you all over the street. . . . I'm no drunk, I'm no whore. . . . I gave birth to two children and had them taken away from me. I don't sleep nights thinking about my children. What do you people care? Don't take my picture. You people have no feelings at all. That man [a judge testifying that there are plenty of services available for unwed mothers] is sitting there and lying—lying. These people just take other people's children away from them. All that he has said is a lie. My baby was born . . . and I haven't seen it since. . . . How would you like it? Year after year you have to go to the people . . . and ask them why you can't have your children.[156]

The adoption opportunity was a godsend and a lifesaver for the many girls and women whose sexual "mistakes" could only be redressed by relinquishment. But the assumption that every white unwed mother should put her baby up for adoption, even when she desired otherwise, even without her unfettered cooperation, created problems for many, like the intruder in the courtroom. Charles Bowerman and his associates who conducted one of the most exhaustive and in-depth studies of unwed mothers in the pre–*Roe* era, found "that more of the illegitimate mothers regret relinquishing their children than express remorse at having kept them." The girls and women who expressed regret to Bowerman's team may have been, like some women who have felt conflict and sorrow after aborting a pregnancy, experiencing retrospective anger or regret that circumstances or society did not allow them to have a baby they would have liked to have had. Perhaps for some, giving up the baby didn't accomplish what the mother had hoped or what society promised. Bowerman highlighted this finding among the hundreds the study produced "as a caveat for those who press most often for release of the infant."[157] He was particularly targeting Professors Meyer, Jones, and Borgatta, among the supporting architects of the adoption mandate who had recently claimed "the more realistically the situation is faced, the more likely the girl will relinquish the child."[158] Bowerman and others were concerned that the best interests of all white unwed mothers and their babies were not being served by the social and institutional axiom that all white unwed mothers were not mothers.

Clark Vincent was another such academic architect, but unusual in his commitments to scrupulous methodology and to considering the implications of some of his and others' assumptions. In 1960, Vincent described current disposition practices and offered the following description to his colleagues as a vision of a world in the near future where the state would have unrestrained authority to determine who is a mother.

> If the demand for adoptable infants continues to exceed the supply; if more definitive research . . . substantiates that the majority of unwed mothers who keep their children lack the potential for "good motherhood"; and if there continues to be an emphasis through laws and courts on the "rights of the child" superseding the "rights of the parents"; then it is quite probable that in the near future unwed mothers will be "punished" by having their children taken away from them at birth. Such a policy would not be enacted nor labeled overtly as "punishment." Rather it would be implemented under such pressures and labels as "scientific finding," "the best interests of the child," "rehabilitation goals for the unwed mother," and the "stability of family and society."[159]

Chapter Six

The Disposition of Illegitimate Babies II: A Taxpayers' Issue

Black Unwed Mothers and Their Babies—Three Views

In postwar America there was only one public intention for white unwed mothers and their babies: separate them. Toward black single mothers and their babies, however, there were three broadly different public attitudes. One attitude, often held by middle-of-the-road politicians, social service adminis-trators, and practitioners, contended that blacks had babies out of wedlock because they were Negro, because they were ex-Africans and ex-slaves. Blacks were perceived by this group as irresponsible and amoral, but baby loving. According to this attitude, the state and its institutions and agencies could essentially ignore black breeding patterns since blacks would take care of their children themselves. But if they didn't, they were responsible for their own mess. Adopting Daniel Moynihan's famous phrase from this period, this public attitude toward black illegitimacy will be called "benign neglect" here.

The "punishers" mounted a second response to black mothers and babies. The conservative, racist politicians who championed this position argued simply that the mothers were bad and should be punished. The babies were expendable because they were expensive and undesirable as citizens. Public policies could and should be used to punish black unmarried mothers and their children.

The third way of seeing this group will be called "benevolent reformist." Employees at the United States Children's Bureau and many in the social work community who took this position maintained that black girls and women who had children out of wedlock were just like whites who did the same. Both groups of females were equally disturbed and equally in need of help, particularly in need of social casework. Regarding the baby, this attitude held that black unwed mothers should be accorded every opportunity to place the infant for adoption, just like whites.

Despite the different intentions toward black women and their babies these attitudes represented, proponents of all of them shared some fundamental assumptions. First, they shared the belief that the black illegitimate baby was the product of pathology. This was the case whether it was a pathology grounded in race, as it was for the benign neglecters and the punishers, or in gender, as it was for the benevolent reformers. In addition, all groups felt that the baby's existence justified a negative moral judgment about the mother and the mother-and-baby dyad. The black illegitimate infant was proof of its mother's moral incapacities and, for many, of its own probable tendencies toward depravity. Because of the eager market for white babies, these "desirable" infants were cleared of the charge of inherited, genetic moral taint long before black babies. The benevolent reformers took the black baby's existence as proof of the mother's psychological and maternal incapacities. Her desire to keep her child, therefore, had, for these observers, negative moral implications, as it did in the case of a white unmarried mother.

One shared assumption followed naturally from the fact that public and private institutions and agencies handling black unmarried women and their children were headed and mostly staffed by whites in a white-dominant culture.[1] This was that white politicians and professionals had the right, the responsibility, and the capability to interpret black single pregnancy and to structure the experience of mother and child. So natural that an alternative did not occur to many politicians and professionals in the postwar years, was the willingness to ignore or distort black community standards, values, family mores, and traditions regarding reproduction and child rearing. It is important, in this regard, that it was the construction of black female sexuality and the black woman that were most centrally at issue here. White society has had a long history of defining these subjects in ways that justify white male behavior, denigrate black males, and demobilize white females, while diminishing the humanity of black women.[2] In postwar America, interpreters of black unwed motherhood could boost all of these projects by the way they treated black unmarried mothers and their children.

Proponents of each of the three perspectives agreed that the unwed black mother had, in most cases, to keep her baby. Where they differed was in explaining why this was so. The different answers they provided reflected different strains of racism and carried quite different implications for public policies and practices regarding the black unmarried mother and her child.

The "Benign Neglecters"

The "benign neglecters" began to articulate their position at about the same time that the psychological explanation for white single pregnancy emerged and set black and white unwed mothers in different universes of cause and effect. According to this view, black and white single mothers were different from each other in several ways. When black single girls and women had intercourse, it was a sexual, not a psychological act, and black mothers had "natural affection" for their children, whatever their birth status. The white unwed mother had only neurotic feelings for her out-of-wedlock child.

Ruth Reed, who conducted an extensive study of black illegitimacy in New York in the 1930s, claimed that typically her subject's "natural affection for her child is less likely to be hampered by strong social pressures [and] she is consequently less likely to be willing to give him up."[3] For Reed and her successors who studied black illegitimacy in the 1940s and 1950s, this "natural affection" was defined as a "cultural" characteristic. These investigators created a special meaning for the term "cultural" as it applied to blacks. They used the term to refer to basic personality patterns that derived from a combination of biology and slavery. Thus the "unrestrained sexuality" of black women and their capacity to love the resulting illegitimate children were inbred traits, and unchangeable. It was fruitless for social workers or policy makers to try to alter this reproductive pattern. It was equally foolish to think of separating mother and child, especially since no one but the mother and perhaps her family wanted the baby.

Child development experts supported these contentions. For example, Arnold Gessell wrote in 1943, "It is well known that among the colored race there are many women who are supremely endowed with almost unique emotional equipment which makes their services ideal for infants and young children."[4] Gessell demonstrated how racist sexism could serve a number of purposes at once. If black women were natural mammies, they were perfectly suited to the only job the white middle class wanted to see them occupy: housekeepers and nursemaids for white families. In addition, by becoming mothers, even unwed mothers, black women were simply doing what came naturally. There was no reason for social service workers or policy makers to interfere. It was also important in this regard that the operative concept of "culture" rendered considerations of environment unnecessary. Environment was not a primary factor in shaping female sexual behavior or the mother's relationship to her illegitimate baby. These were determined by "culture." Therefore, since professionals could only have an impact on the immediate situation—and could not penetrate or rearrange black "culture"—it was doubly futile to consider interfering.

Annie Lee Davis of the Children's Bureau who was herself a black, a reformer, and an environmentalist of the Franklin Frazier school,[5] was deeply frustrated by the benign neglecters, as she could see clearly how their position justified the absence of services for black unwed mothers. She complained bitterly and often about this stance. "I am frequently told by Negro and white social workers that Negro unmarried mothers do not give up their babies because unwed motherhood is no threat to them; it is a part of the cultural heritage carried over from the institution of slavery."[6] Davis abhorred this justification for the lack of services—including adoption services—to unwed blacks and understood it as a thin veil over the racist exclusion of these mothers and their children. Davis believed, with Maud Morlock, that many black unwed mothers would have sought social services but stayed away because of fear that the agency would impose its own agenda on them.[7] She recognized that maternity homes excluded blacks and publicly offered this rationale, "Why take a girl in and provide care and service when she is going to keep the child and return to the community with it? What need do these girls have for maternity home service?"[8] She was arguing for the right of black girls to give up their illegitimate babies if they chose.

Additional arguments and strategies to deny services to black unmarried mothers also drew on the benign neglect model. The Public Welfare Department in Cincinnati in the late 1940s claimed that black unwed mothers expressed little interest in placing their babies in temporary foster-care situations while they figured out how to manage, but often gave the baby to a friend. This pattern excused the Welfare Department from developing foster placements or lobbying for the money to support such arrangements. The truth seems to have been that the department's philosophy and regulations made it very difficult for mothers to use the foster-care option. The public welfare staff disapproved of foster care because they believed it created a situation for the infant of divided loyalty. Thus they would only sanction a six-month placement. If, after this period, the mother was not ready to take the child, he or she would be committed, through the Juvenile Court, to Children's Services of the Department of Public Welfare, which meant complete relinquishment by the mother.[9] Seeking out the help of a friend might have been, indeed, a more attractive, less threatening option for these mothers.

Davis cited other instances as well in which the needs of black unwed mothers were denied on "cultural" grounds. She referred to a judge who "refused to appropriate county funds for boarding care for Negro unmarried mothers because he said and believed that Negroes always care for their own children and, therefore, boarding care is not needed." A report to the Children's Bureau in the mid-1940s contained the following statement which excused white officials from providing services to black unwed mothers and their children: "It was the general opinion of the child welfare workers of X County that Negro families care for Negro children when something happens to their parents and that the neighborliness and kindliness of Negro relatives far exceed that of white relatives. Therefore, there is very little need for foster care for dependent Negro children."[10]

Issues regarding blacks and adoption were particularly quickly dismissed by those who counselled neglect. Agencies claimed black mothers didn't want to part with their babies, and, just as important, black couples didn't want to adopt children.[11] Agencies also claimed that blacks were too picky about finding an acceptable child. In Cincinnati again, the Department of Public

Welfare staff explained to a visitor from the U.S. Children's Bureau that there was little demand for black babies for adoption because "when foster parents make such a request they want the child to resemble them in color."[12] Staff members neglected to note that the similar demands of prospective white adoptive parents were well-known headaches to social workers who nevertheless worked hard to honor them.[13]

White policy makers and service providers often pointed to the black grandmother—willing, able, loving, and present—to justify their contentions about the black family taking care of its own and to support their claims that no additional services were necessary. Patricia Garland, a black social worker and a trenchant critic in the mid-1960s of the use of black "culture" to justify the lack of services, found bitter irony in the claim that grandmothers could fill the "service vacuum." Garland noted that when grandmothers rendered such service, they were labeled "matriarchs" and blamed for "faulty personality growth and for maladaptive functioning in children."[14] The mother was similarly placed in a double bind: "She suffers because invalid assumptions [about "Negro culture"] provide the rationale for failure to end the white-non-white disparities in provision of services, and she is then held responsible for the personal and social consequences."[15] Garland demonstrated here how easily observers in the dominant culture could make the transition from respecting the cultural distinctions of a minority group to blaming the group for the consequences of their differences. Both stances excused the dominant culture from responsibility or obligation to black unwed mothers.

The Punishers

As welfare costs were rising and the civil rights movement was gathering force and successes in the late 1950s and early 1960s, the voices of benign neglecters were drowned out by the voices of public officials who insisted that black unmarried mothers and their babies should be punished. One of the earliest and most publicly articulate national champions of this position was Senator Barry Goldwater, who was, at this time, building support for his presidential ambitions. Goldwater put his name and his full support behind an effort to deny welfare benefits to unwed mothers and their babies in Newburgh, New York, in 1961. He described the attempt to control and punish this population "as refreshing as breathing the clean air of my native Arizona."[16]

The punishers drew in part on the "cultural" argument to target both the unwed mother and her baby. They held that black culture was genetically transmitted and that the baby would likely be as great a social liability as its mother. Moreover, they claimed that for a poor black woman to have a baby was an act of selfishness, as well as pathological, and deserved punishment.

Leontine Young, a pillar of the section of the social work community that dealt with unwed mothers, wrote off black single mothers as

> socially disorganized girls who have no standards of their own and little control over their impulses. . . . Becoming an unmarried mother is only one incident in a life history that is largely chaotic. . . . [These girls] grew up in homes characterized by the same lack of social and moral standards as they suffer from.[17]

Young's analysis of black illegitimacy provided policy makers with grounds for ignoring such allegedly endemic behavior or targeting it for punishment. Once the public came to believe that black illegitimacy was not an innocuous social fact but carried a direct and heavy cost to white taxpayers, many whites sanctioned their political representatives to target black unwed mothers and their babies for attack.[18]

In the late summer of 1960, Governor Jimmie H. Davis of Louisiana oversaw the passage of legislation that removed twenty-three thousand illegitimate children from the state's welfare rolls. Ninety-five percent of these children were black. The law read,

> In no instance shall assistance be granted to any person who is living with his or her mother if the mother has had an illegitimate child after a check has been received from the Welfare Department unless and until proof satisfactory to the Parish Board of Public Welfare has been presented showing that the mother has ceased illicit relationship and is maintaining a suitable home.

The state's attorney general announced, as the legislation was enacted, that its provisions were retroactive and applied in all cases.[19] The Louisiana law was similar to many approved by state legislators in the 1950s and early 1960s. The North Carolina legislature, for example, eliminated the requirement for obtaining the mother's consent for putting her child up for adoption, in certain cases, when she was judicially determined to be living out of wedlock. The Louisiana "suitable home" law, however, received a great deal of attention because so many thousands of children were targeted and severed from support in one month, August 1960.[20] It was dramatic politics. A Gallup poll was conducted soon after these events in Louisiana, in an effort to gauge the public's response. It found that "[E]veryone was concerned that children, even if illegitimate, should not be made to suffer and . . . something must be done to care for them—yet, [only] one in ten favored giving aid to further children born to unwed parents who have already produced an out of wedlock child."[21] The editor of the *St. Louis Post-Dispatch* described these results as revealing the "point which brings the warm humanitarianism of many people into violent conflict with their moral indignation [and their] racism."[22]

The Gallup poll and other evidence of support for the Louisiana law suggested that it was acceptable to withhold federal support, or food money, from illegitimate black babies. One prominent social welfare administrator observed in testimony before the U.S. House of Representatives Ways and Means Committee: "In response to the illegitimate child . . . we feel that many people seem to believe that we should deny assistance to the unmarried mother and her child. Perhaps they think that by starving the unmarried mother or starving the child we can improve the morals of the mother."[23] Other dissenters were people who believed it was wrong "to deny food to children because of the sins of the parents."[24] Both groups, however, fell into a trap set by conservative politicians who found it politically profitable to associate black illegitimacy in their constituents' minds with the rising costs of public welfare grants. There were a great many reasons for the increase in the Aid to Dependent Children caseload in the postwar period. These included the basic rise in number of children and number of families, the rise in divorce and in households headed by women because of divorce, separation, desertion, *and* illegitimacy. Between 1953 and 1959, the number of families headed by women rose 12.8 percent while the number of families rose only 8.3 percent.[25] While white sentiment was being whipped up to support punitive measures against black unmarried mothers and their babies because of their "subsidized immorality,"[26] only about 16 percent of nonwhite unwed mothers were receiving Aid to Dependent Children grants.[27] Adoption, which was, of course, not an option for most blacks, was the most important factor in removing white children from would-be ADC families. Of unwed white mothers who kept their children, 30 percent, or nearly twice as large a percentage as blacks, were receiving Aid to Dependent Children grants in 1959.[28] Yet in the mind of large segments of the white public, black unwed mothers were being paid, in welfare coin, to have children. The "suitable home" laws, originally designed, so it was claimed, to protect the interests of children, were now instrumental in stopping those payments. The children in question carried only negative value for the politicians leading the attacks on welfare costs. Thus, these men had no qualms about using black illegitimate children as pawns in their attempt to squash black "disobedience" via morals charges.

In this era, some whites could define black mothers, black children, and the black maternal-child bond as different from and lesser than their white counterparts, even into the 1960s. A member of the department of religion at Princeton University wrote to the *New York Times* about his ideas for handling black unwed mothers and their children, a plan he felt would "satisfy both liberals and conservatives." He wrote,

> Any mother who has more than one illegitimate child would lose all her children and they would be placed under the protection of the local community or the state . . . immediately be put in the care of foster parents . . . [and] be made available for adoption . . . [by] the literally thousands of

childless parents in this country [who would be] more than willing. This procedure would serve as a warning to unmarried mothers with a *minimum penalty for the children*. In fact, both the children and the adoptive parents would benefit from this policy.[29] (italics added)

Paul Harrison, the author of this plan, captured in his letter two central difficulties for the state and consequently for black mothers. First, while many whites were unhappy or enraged about using public funds to support black children in their own homes headed by unwed mothers, even the most threatening southern state governments had to admit there was simply no other place to put them. There was a seriously insufficient supply of foster homes or other facilities available for these children, even the ones judged to live in "unsuitable homes." Moreover, it was far less expensive for the state to contribute (or not) to the child's support at home, through ADC grants, than to pay for his or her maintenance elsewhere.[30] The "suitable home" legislation, therefore, remained largely a strategy for withdrawing support, not children, from the households of unwed mothers. Legislators were more interested in threatening and subduing these women than in accomplishing their expressed aim: improving the moral environment in which these children lived. They were, however, willing to sacrifice the children to accomplish their goals.

Secondly, Harrison, along with many liberals and conservatives, had no trouble perceiving black unmarried mothers as wanton women who didn't care about their children overly much. Politicians repeatedly brought attention to black unmarried mothers as women who had children simply as a business venture,[31] and characterized them as irresponsible in other ways. According to the director of the Citizens Adoption Committee of Los Angeles County, caseworkers were "concerned" about mothers on ADC. "[T]he girls with babies," they claimed, "rent a room or small apartment with ADC money, cannot live on it, are lonely, take the baby to night movies or invite in undesirable persons and are soon worse off than they originally were."[32]

What was apparently not clear to Harrison was that public policies that enforced poverty and shame and permitted black unmarried mothers to be harassed and threatened were centrally instrumental in creating the outcomes Harrison deplored. For example, liberals and conservatives alike were concerned about the rising incidence of illegitimate babies abandoned in hospitals. Yet women who abandoned their babies often did so because of "suitable home" laws, with provisions like the Louisiana law. Such legislation could force women to go to such drastic and tragic lengths to preserve their family's source of support. Ursula Gallagher of the Children's Bureau wrote to a colleague in 1959 about "some unmarried mothers [who try] to conceal the second baby [from the welfare worker] by using an assumed name at the hospital and literally giving the baby away."[33] A casework supervisor at Metropolitan Hospital in New York understood that when unwed black girls and women resorted to abandonment, it was because, "They see their only salvation in leaving the baby in the hospital."[34]

The "Benevolent Reformers"

Led by Annie Lee Davis, many members of the social work community worked unceasingly to convert benign neglecters and punishers into benevolent reformers. Davis was a committed integrationist, dedicated to convincing the white social service establishment that black unmarried mothers needed and deserved the same services as their white counterparts. She was willing to make strong unequivocal statements on behalf of this goal. In 1948, Davis addressed this message to her colleagues: "Within minority groups, unmarried mothers suffer guilt and shame as in the majority group." She added, "I know there are those who will challenge this statement," but Davis insisted, "In the process of adopting the cultural traits of the dominant group in America all groups are striving to be American."[35]

The benevolent reformers were acutely sensitive to the fact that environment and tradition create different meanings for illegitimacy among different groups of people. Their typically integrationist politics shaped their stance toward black unmarried mothers and toward their profession. For example, Annie Lee Davis was determined to convince white public officials and social workers that black unwed mothers were psychologically and morally the equals of whites. Only then would the former be accorded the consideration and the services available to the latter. Ironically, Davis believed that a key aspect of the proof was to establish that blacks were as interested in adoptive placements for their illegitimate babies as whites were urged to be. Davis's task was to convince her colleagues that lack of alternate options alone created the custom and the necessity that blacks keep their illegitimate children.

Annie Lee Davis was not completely unsuccessful in her efforts. A number of the benevolent reformers took the position that it was unacceptable and possibly racist to assume that blacks did not want every opportunity that whites had, including adoption. Maud Morlock consulted with Davis on all matters concerning unmarried mothers and took Davis's position that this population "was interested in adoption if they are given a chance to use it."[36] The problem for Davis and Morlock and other benevolent reformers was that it was extremely difficult for them to suggest that some black single mothers wanted their children and others didn't. It was not simply unwed mothers and their babies at issue, it was the Race. This was, of course, similar to using the blanket diagnosis of all white unwed mothers as psychologically impaired to bolster fraying norms of female sexual purity and family stability. Individual distinctions and intra-group differences were canceled in the interests of larger social goals. This was as true for the reformers as it was for mainstream service providers and the culture at large. For the reformers, constructing an identity between black and white unmarried mothers was the most promising and practical route to social services and social justice. Joseph Reid, chief administrator of the Child Welfare League of America, for example, recommended to Congress in 1956 that black unwed mothers should receive "guidance and counseling." Each such woman should be referred to "a psychiatrist . . . who could counsel with her on what it was in her life that that was causing her to do this sort of thing."[37]

Rose Bernstein, a Children's Bureau insider, chastised public and private agencies for denying appropriate services to blacks. "The structure and function of many . . . agencies," she wrote in 1963, "may be resulting in underservice to a substantial proportion of the unmarried mother population."[38] She was particularly concerned about the "chronic shortage of Negro adoptive homes [which gave] most Negro unmarried mothers . . . little choice but to keep their babies."[39] Similarly, when the Children's Bureau prepared a list of service gaps for unmarried mothers to present to the House of Representatives Appropriations Committee in 1962, one of the two unmet needs for blacks cited was adoptive placements.[40] There is no doubt that there were not sufficient adoption opportunities for blacks who wanted or needed to place their illegitimate babies. But the growing focus on this problem throughout the 1950s and 1960s deflected attention and resources from addressing the needs of the substantial majority of blacks who kept their babies and did so because they wanted to.

According to some reformers, the major obstacle to black adoptions was the paucity of suitable applications from potential adoptive parents. Morlock learned in the late 1940s that the Illinois Children's Home and Aid organization had closed its intake of black babies for adoption because the black couples applying to adopt children did not meet standards on housing and income.[41] Los Angeles adoption agencies did the same in this era.[42] A nineteen-year-old unmarried mother in Baltimore had her application for adoption services rejected in 1959 because the agency had "more negroes than we can handle,"[43] which was not very many. A 1964 study reported that the absent subset was the "right" prospective, black, adoptive parents. According to the study, this group didn't want to adopt illegitimate babies because caring for them would interfere with their status strivings to be full members of the black middle class.[44] Reformers concerned about the lack of adoptive opportunities for black illegitimate babies looked forward to a time when black applicants could offer black illegitimate babies the white family model of postwar affluence and security.

Annie Lee Davis did not believe it was necessary to wait. She was convinced that appropriate black couples were out there, trying to adopt babies. She had some good evidence, too. In October, 1949, *Ebony* magazine ran an article about black adoptions and listed the Children's Bureau as a source of further information. As a result, the Bureau received a flurry of letters from black couples across the country, which Davis collected, excerpted, and passed around to her colleagues to demonstrate the stability and respectability of prospective black adoptive parents.[45]

A man in Alabama, trying to adopt a child wrote, "I am a local insurance man, supervisor for Atlanta Life Insurance Company. My wife is a teacher in the city school system." Another, in Florida, zeroed in on what was important to adoption agencies: "We haven't a home of our own, but we plan to buy soon. We both work, making good. We have a bank account and a postal account." A New Jersey woman was similarly pointed: "I have a seven-room bungalow home, all paid for." From South Carolina, a would-be mother established her credentials: "I am a school teacher and have been teaching for ten years. I make a good salary and my husband is Ex-G.I. and we are really able to give a child the care that any child needs." There were many more such statements from childless black couples seeking babies to adopt. Davis was eager to facilitate the match between these couples and the black girls and women who wanted to place their illegitimate children. In answering the letters sent to the Children's Bureau, she referred the black couples to their state Departments of Public Welfare,[46] even though these public agencies were not always welcoming to potential adoptive parents. But Annie Lee Davis had nothing else to offer them.

To prove that black unmarried mothers wanted to place their babies, reformers cited various kinds of evidence. One study provided the statement of a director of a black maternity home who said that 40 percent of her residents asked about adoption for their babies. This study also pointed out that the number of black babies abandoned in hospitals was "tangible proof" that many unwed blacks did not want their babies.[47] While undoubtedly some blacks did want adoption, this evidence is strikingly weak, since only a minuscule number of black unwed girls and women used maternity homes and these were from the thin strata of the black middle and upper class. As for the abandoned babies, we have seen that their fate was often sealed not by maternal rejection but by desperation. A maternity home and adoption agency in New York City did have evidence that when blacks were in a "relinquishment-oriented" maternity home, the great majority did want to place their babies. "Under such circumstances, where relinquishment was an acceptable form of maternal behavior, the black mothers chose to relinquish their babies almost as frequently as did the [white] mothers."[48]

In the mid-1950s, the report of the State's Attorney's Commission on Adoption in Cook County, Illinois, commented on the adoption situation for black illegitimate children:

> The Commission is aware that at present there are more Negro children available for adoption than there are adopting families. The Commission views this as a temporary situation which is likely to change, as did the situation with white children. Fifty years ago it was difficult to find an adoptive family for a white child. . . . Even though a greater effort is required to find any adopting family for any Negro children, the parties to all adoptions are entitled to the safeguards of careful procedures so as to prevent human tragedies.[49]

Integrationists and reformers in a number of cities began to take the initiative in the late 1940s to address the shortage in adoption placements for black babies. For example, in New York City at this time, Archbishop Spellman opened a drive to encourage black Catholics to provide foster homes for illegitimate babies of their race. In the 1950s the Public Welfare Department in Richmond, Virginia, established a casework unit dealing with black adoptions, as did the same agency in Raleigh, North Carolina, at this time. After having placed only two black babies for adoption in Dayton, Ohio, in 1953, the Family and Children's Service Association of that city hired a full-time black worker to concentrate on black adoptions and, with the help of the Urban League in developing an outreach program, soon placed sixty children in one year.[50] In 1955, the Field Foundation and the New York Fund for Children gave forty-nine thousand dollars to support ADOPT-A-CHILD, an organization that had been initiated in 1953 by black social workers, to place minority children. The Foundation also supported a similar project in Chicago with twenty-five thousand dollars.[51] In the mid-1960s a committee of representatives from a number of Minnesota adoption agencies mounted a two-year "promotion campaign" using newspaper stories about white applicants for "Negro children," speeches to groups, and talks with individual persons to target "room-for-one-more families." The project determined that "community readiness was high" and succeeded in placing twenty black babies in white families. The rationale for the campaign was "that Minnesota's small population of Negroes, already adopting at the same rate as the white population, could not absorb the many Negro children awaiting adoption."[52]

Programs like these were created in many cities, a number under the auspices of the Urban League, which made black adoptions one of its central goals between 1953 and 1958. The League's intention was to increase the number of placements using three strategies. First the League planned to demonstrate the ways that black unmarried mothers were prevented by punitive-minded officials and agencies from expressing a desire to put their babies up for adoption. Second, the League wanted to publicize the existence of black babies without permanent families. Third, it intended to make clear the tactics used by agencies to screen out and discourage black couples trying to adopt babies.[53]

These efforts to improve outreach and agency practices had spotty results. According to Andrew Billingsley, the Urban League project eventually failed because its effect was to strengthen white agencies which "forestalled changes that would have made [them] more specific to the situation of black children."[54] The project was never successful in overcoming adoption agencies' "reluctance to place black babies in black families and black communities that did not meet white middle class standards."[55]

A particularly telling finding and interpretation in a study of adoption agency practices in this era was reported in a Child Welfare League study on black adoptions in 1957:

> About three times as many couples who desired a girl were rejected as were those who desired a boy. The reasons for this are not known but suggest

the possibility that individuals whom the agency finds unacceptable as applicants may gravitate toward the choice of a girl because of some premise which arises out of an unreadiness for parenthood.[56]

The author suggested that a mature reason to prefer a boy might include a father's desire "to carry on the family name," but a woman seeking a "life companion" in a daughter was making a decision on a "neurotic basis," and was rejectable by the agency.

This type of capriciousness by agency personnel continued to characterize the treatment of black couples applying to adopt illegitimate babies into the 1960s. A well-known study published in 1962 examined the experiences of 484 black families in Washington, D.C., and Baltimore who, on the face of it, met all the stringent agency criteria for adoptive parents. Still, a majority did not consummate adoptions because of agency practices, including snooping, excessive red tape, and burdensome requirements.[57] Similarly, another large-scale study from 1963 to 1965 of adoption agency practices in a large eastern metropolitan area produced results that "startled" the investigators: "[T]he proportion of accepted Negro couples was smaller than the percentage among the white group accepted by the agencies."[58] This study encompassed eight agencies, eighty-seven caseworkers, and 398 adoptive-applicant couples.

A direct consequence of these agency practices for the black unwed mother was that even if she did consider placing her child for adoption, she knew that the likelihood that the agency would expeditiously approve a couple as adoptive parents was slim. While a white unwed mother could assume a rapid placement, the black one knew that her child would be forced, in part because of agency practices, to spend months in foster homes or institutions before placement, if that was ever achieved. Billingsley and Giovannoni reported that beyond maintaining their own obstructive practices, adoption agencies neglected to work with schools and hospitals in contact with black unwed mothers to improve referral services between these institutions and the agencies. Agencies feared recruiting black babies when there might not be homes for them. In these ways, at least, the organizations that reformers depended on to provide black unwed mothers services equal to whites, and to make it more possible for society to perceive these blacks in the same way as they saw whites, did not hold up their end. The reformers had their integrationist vision but the institutions of society would not cooperate, even when some black unwed mothers did.

Evidence from the Black Community

The evidence from postwar black communities suggests that in this era, the black mother accepted responsibility for her baby as a matter of course.[59] An experienced social worker in Philadelphia reported that poor, black, single mothers do not feel especially in control of their destiny; the illegitimate births "happen." It goes something like this; there are men and women, they get together, sometimes babies are conceived, you wish you weren't pregnant but when the baby comes you love it and take care of it, because it's your child.[60]

A well-publicized and influential study of ADC recipients in Cook County, Illinois, in the late 1950s aimed to demonstrate that black welfare mothers were not having children in order to get higher welfare grants. The study argued that their reproductive patterns were shaped by lack of access to birth control information and by the impact lack of economic opportunity had on male behavior.[61] The investigators found that

> The typical ADC family . . . consists of a mother and three or four children. The children were born in Illinois, the mother has lived here fifteen years or more. She is between 30 and 35 . . . was born in Mississippi and is Negro. . . . The mother was married and had children by her husband, who deserted. . . . The youngest child is illegitimate. The mother knew the father for more than a year before she became pregnant. The couple thought about marriage, but because the mother was already married, this was impossible. The mother did not want to have another child, but did not know what to do to prevent becoming pregnant. When she learned she was pregnant, she did nothing to prevent having the child. Once the baby was born, she accepted it and loves it.[62]

Studies such as these were directed toward policy makers who favored punishing black single mothers and their children. Some investigators felt it was also necessary to correct the thinking and the practice of benevolent reformers. A study in the mid-1960s cautioned the social work profession: "Social work wisdom is that Negroes keep because there is no place to give the baby up, but the study showed . . . that Negroes did not favor adoption, opportunities or their absence notwithstanding." This study measured twenty-eight attitude differences between whites and blacks associated with agencies for unwed mothers. Findings showed that the issue of disposition of the child was the only one that consistently yielded a difference between black and white respondents, no matter whether they were the unwed mother, her parents, or professional staff. In fact, the blacks revealed their determination to keep mother and child together and the whites their determination to effect separation, "no matter how [the investigator] varied the content of the questions."[63]

In the same period in Cincinnati, several researchers captured the comments of the mothers themselves. Some girls and women focused on the needs of the baby: "An innocent child should not be denied his mother's love."[64] Joyce Ladner's subjects in another midwestern city considered the illegitimate baby as "a child who had the right to be cared for and reared in the community of his parents without stigmatization."[65] Others in the Cincinnati study focused on the strength of their own needs: "I'd grieve myself to death if I let my baby go." A few predicted they would have had nervous breakdowns if they hadn't been allowed to keep their babies. A representative outlook drew on the sanctified status of motherhood: "The Lord suffered for you to have a baby. He will suffer for you to get food for the baby." Still others expressed themselves in forward-looking, practical terms: "You were less apt to have regrets if you kept the baby than if you let him go."[66]

For many black unwed mothers the reasons to keep a baby were simply grounded in an immutable moral code of maternal responsibility. A young black woman said, "Giving a child away is not the sort of thing a good person would do," and a teenager asserted, "My parents wouldn't let me give up the baby for adoption."[67] A Chicago doctor reported as the most typical comment explaining the decision to keep, "You don't give babies to strangers."[68]

Two black women in Philadelphia subscribed to this morality. One said, "I sure don't think much of giving babies up for adoption. The mother mightn't be able to give it the finest and best in the world, but she could find a way like I did. My mother had thirteen heads and it was during the Depression. . . . *She* didn't give us away." The other commented, "If you have a child, bring it up. Take the responsibility. Hard or easy, it's yours."[69]

The central question for all of these black single mothers was how good a mother you were, not whether you were legally married.[70] The overriding stimulus in structuring the personal decisions of these girls and women was a "powerful drive toward family unity, even if the family is not the socially approved one of father-mother and children."[71] In a study of thirty, poor single black mothers, only two told the investigators that they would advise another woman in their situation to give the baby up and both cited difficulties with the welfare office for their reason.[72] The author of the study referred to the "vehemence" of the others about their decisions to keep.[73]

Mignon Sauber and Elaine Rubinstein, who interviewed 321 unmarried mothers in New York City who kept their newborns in 1962 and 1963, found further evidence that it was not simply a lack of options that bound the black unwed mother to her baby. Sixty-six percent of their sample was black and only a minuscule number of these ever considered adoption. In answering the question "Looking back over the past year and a half, if you still had it to do over again, would you still want to keep the baby with you?" 96 percent of these girls and women responded "yes," with additional comments such as, "Because I love him, because he's mine."[74]

Another New York study, this one conducted in 1956 and 1957, interviewed 227 unwed mothers and offered the generalization that when white single mothers used social agencies, they were looking for assistance with placing the baby. When blacks and Puerto Ricans did, they were "obtaining assistance in maintaining the family unit."[75] Similarly, Charles Bowerman, in his North Carolina study, found that four-fifths of the black single mothers felt that the illegitimate baby belonged to the whole family.[76]

Public agencies in many cities tried to engineer the disposition of illegitimate black babies, sometimes pressuring mothers to do one thing, sometimes another. Most often, the mother kept her baby, and did so under the terms she and her family agreed upon. Miss J., for example, was pressured by the Family and Children's Society in Baltimore to place her child for adoption; when Miss J.'s aunt stepped forward and claimed the baby, however, the matter was settled. Again, Miss M. in the same city was counseled by a social worker to give her baby up. But five days after the fourteen-year-old girl received this advice, Miss M.'s mother "informed the social worker that after the family had thought it over, they had decided not to ask for adoption as the [girl's] grandmother is coming North to care for the baby."[77]

One of the first public-private partnerships to address the needs of minority, unwed mothers was sponsored by the Berean Institute in Philadelphia in the late 1950s. The Institute's goal was to teach mothering skills and offer vocational training under one program. The project was unusual because it assumed the mothers would keep their babies (making it unpopular with the Children's Bureau); and it did not assume that the babies would and should be raised by their maternal grandmothers. These assumptions offended the benign neglecters and benevolent reformers alike. The letter below, from the mother of a fourteen-year-old unwed mother, demonstrates the older woman's sense of family oneness as well as her appreciation that the Institute was helping to relieve her of the responsibility of caring for her grandchild.

> I am well pleased with the wonderful work you have put forward for the progress of the girls. It is not only an asset for the girls but also for their babies and the girls' mothers, those that are unable to care for their grandchildren. I, myself, suffer from arthritis and have a nervous condition. . . . I am really thrilled with your method. May God bless you in your undertakings.[78]

An assessment of the Institute's accomplishments put first "the deepened relationship between mother and child." Staff found that the girls no longer expressed their original feeling that "the baby feels more like my mother's than my own."[79] The unwed mother shared her mother's sense of family while she was pleased to develop a deep maternal bond with her child.

By the early 1960s, some practitioners in the social service community were recognizing their responsibility to black unwed mothers and acknowledging their special needs. Still, most had an "uncomfortable feeling" when confronted with girls and women who kept their children.[80] Many caseworkers, interested in offering blacks the same services as whites, found it difficult to alter their negative assessment of the black unwed mother who kept. Throughout Maud Morlock's tenure at the U.S. Children's Bureau, she nurtured a hope that, someday, blacks would feel the stigma of illegitimacy as keenly as whites. She imagined this development would be an impressive signal of "Negro progress."[81] As it was, Morlock simply could not understand why black unwed mothers kept their babies, although she tried to understand and tried to devise programs to support this tradition in the black community, such as temporary foster-care programs for the babies, to give the mothers a chance to get back on their feet. She wrote, "Many Negro mothers went [sic] to keep the child. Some of the Negro mothers return to their own homes which are in deplorable condition. There may have been much illegitimacy in the family but she still wants to keep her child and to take it to her home." At least Morlock grasped the intentions of these women and recognized them as mothers; throughout the period of this study, the white-dominated social work community generally persisted in doubting that any unwed mother could care for her own child. In this vein, Zelina was given a "fair," that is, fairly poor, prognosis by her social worker because of her decision:

> Zelina was an attractive, intelligent, twenty year old Negro girl, business-like. Both she and her mother decided to place the child in adoption. Placement services were explained, but no action was taken. It was revealed that neither the girl nor her mother had wanted adoption but each had been planning what they thought the other wanted. . . . The ambivalence seemed to warrant further casework service, but Zelina refused referral saying that she and her mother could work out their own plans.[82]

Helen Harris Perlman, recognizing the tenacity and inclusiveness of social work attitudes toward girls and women who failed to relinquish, counseled her colleagues in the 1960s, "Even if more opportunities for adoption of Negro babies become possible, there is a strong probability that most Negro mothers—indeed, most unwed mothers—will want to keep their babies."[83] Indeed, blacks sustained traditional practices during the postwar decades, practices that single white mothers came back to after two or three decades of willingly or unwillingly relinquishing their babies. In 1960, when approximately 70 percent of white illegitimate babies were adopted, about 5 percent of such nonwhite babies were placed. Ninety-four percent of black illegitimate babies, on the other hand, lived with their natural parents or relatives, compared with 29 percent of white illegitimate babies.[84]

Conclusion

Charles Bowerman's research team at the University of North Carolina concluded in the early 1960s that one major difference between white and black unwed mothers was that the white girl generally felt that a "new maturity" had come with the experience of conceiving out of wedlock. This was not true for his black subjects. The authors explained the finding this way: "The white subculture demands learning from experience," so the white unwed mother must learn her lesson. The white girl, they went on, "has probably been encouraged to look within herself for the reasons for her mistake because the white subculture stresses individual responsibility for error."[85]

These observations capture a great deal of the intentionality underlying the white culture's treatment of unwed mothers under its adoption mandate. For these girls and women, the "lesson" was twofold: no baby without a husband, and no one is to blame but yourself. Learning the lesson meant stepping on the road to maturity, which was also the road to properly sanctioned maternity and womanhood. The illegitimate child was an encumbrance or an obstacle to following this route. The ability to relinquish was constructed as the first, most crucial step in the right direction.

Joyce Ladner, in her study of black women in the 1960s, dealt with the same issue—the relationship between illegitimacy and maturity. She suggested a strikingly different finding:

> The adolescent Black girl who becomes pregnant out of wedlock changed her self-concept from one who was approaching maturity to one who had attained the status of womanhood. . . . Mothers were quick to say that their daughters had become grown, that they have "done as much as I have done," that is, have had a baby. . . . Mothers begin to respond [to their daughters] as co-equals.[86]

The road to maturity for black unwed mothers was unmediated. Maturity accompanied maternity, the baby's legal status notwithstanding.

Both black and white women in the postwar era were subject to a definition of maturity that depended on motherhood. But the uses of race in the United States in that era combined with the uses of gender in ways that dealt black and white unwed mothers quite different hands. According to social and cultural intentions for the white unwed mother and her baby, the relinquishment was meant to place all scent of taint behind them, and thus restore good value to both. The black unwed mother and her child, triply devalued, had all their troubles before them.

Chapter Seven

The Population Bomb and the Sexual Revolution: Toward Choice

> " 'While the rich in America do whatever it is they do, the poor are begetting children,' says former Assistant Secretary of Labor Daniel Moynihan."
> *The New Republic*
> September 25, 1965

In 1957 when Sally Brown and Brenda Johnson (the two teenagers whose case histories were presented in the Introduction) got pregnant, the repercussions for both girls were humiliating and coercive. Parents, service providers, policy makers, and punitive public attitudes about female nonmarital sexuality and maternity structured what happened to both girls and their babies. Neither the black teenager nor the white had access to options beyond the scenarios prepared for them.

In 1957 the treatment of unwed mothers was not, in general, the subject of public debate, even while the subjects of female premarital sexuality and childbearing, black and white, were of increasing public concern. Public debate was very narrow or absent in part because the vulnerability of unmarried sexually active girls and women was not in doubt; the vulnerability of single *pregnant* females was particularly enforceable. Since the family, service providers, policy makers, and the public could count on this vulnerability as they demanded and arranged for unwed mothers to be sequestered, or ignored, or punished, by race, single pregnant girls and women did not emerge as a population—or populations—of dangerous aggressors against society throughout most of the period of this study.

By the early 1960s, however, public discourse about both black and white nonmarital sexuality and maternity had shifted. It now used a new language that denied the vulnerability of unmarried, sexually active females

205

and transformed these girls and women—both those who were pregnant and those who might become pregnant—into aggressors against a vulnerable society. By 1965, the end point of this study, the white unwed mother had been changed in the public consciousness from a species of mental patient into a sexual revolutionary. The black unwed mother was still portrayed as a participant in an aberrant culture of sexuality and as the taxpayers' nemesis. But at the highest levels of policy discussion, she was increasingly cast as the triggering device affixed to the Population Bomb, USA.

The "sexual revolution" and the "population bomb" were racially specific metaphors of destruction. Their widespread use after 1960 reflected, in part, the hopelessness with which influential segments of society regarded their own capacity to control nonmarital female sexuality and its consequences. The two separate and contemporaneous metaphors also reflected common feelings about the need to fashion explicitly race-specific defenses, even in the face of an overwhelming task. Since the "revolution" and the "bomb" were identified with female sexual behavior, the metaphors also suggested public perception of a terrible new capacity embodied by unmarried girls and women. By virtue of these tropes, unwed mothers, along with all unmarried sexually active females, were assigned apocalyptic importance.[1]

This concluding chapter will describe how these metaphors were gathering focus and significance between 1960 and 1965. They both reflected and created the context in which strange bedfellows allied to support population control for blacks and pregnancy control for whites, as well as a range of social programs—all as antidotes to unacceptable levels of nonmarital, female sexuality and fertility. Whatever moral, ideological, or social intentions separated the members of these alliances, they shared a growing loss of confidence in the belief that nonmarital female sexuality and its consequences could be comprehended, managed, or contained by biological or psychological theory, or regulated by law. They also shared an increasing confidence that technology would be more effective in containing the illegitimacy crisis than an unlikely resurgence of chastity.[2]

Black Unwed Mothers and The Population Bomb

Between 1945 and 1960, public efforts to respond to black illegitimacy took one of three forms, all of which were *ex post facto*. First, various states legislated punitive sanctions against poor women who had illegitimate children. Second, public agencies simply ignored the black unwed mother and her child, or the welfare system grudgingly supported them in the "culture of poverty." Third, the child welfare apparatus in some localities tried to promote a willingness among black unwed mothers to put their illegitimate children up for adoption and tried to develop placements for these babies. None of these efforts influenced the rate of illegitimate pregnancy among black women, although all of them directly or indirectly aimed to demonstrate that unsanctioned sexuality and illegitimate pregnancy carried harsh consequences for black women in the United States.[3]

By the early 1960s, "the punishers" commanded support and political resources in a number of states and cities, but their ability to legislate sanctions against unwed mothers began to meet substantial objections from national politicians, national welfare organizations, some important media, and civil rights activists. The fate of attempts to punish black unwed mothers in Louisiana in 1960 and in Newburgh, New York, in 1961 demonstrated that it was not so easy for localities to move unimpeded in this terrain.[4]

In the wake of the Louisiana and Newburgh failures to sustain state and local autonomy concerning the punitive treatment of poor, black unwed mothers, the public debate about how to respond to high rates of black illegitimate pregnancy struck out in a totally new direction. When oral contraceptives became available in 1960, policy makers, service providers, and concerned citizens had an entirely new option: to support preventative rather than punitive strategies to reduce the black fertility rate. At this point, an array of supporters of pregnancy prevention who usually expressed their project in terms of population control began to present their cases publicly. Population control strategies had the disadvantage of seeming to sanction illicit female sexuality, but the distinct advantage of curtailing fertility *a priori*. William A. Ryan, a representative to the Michigan State House, expressed the dilemma facing a politician: "My bills [prohibiting welfare workers from initiating birth control discussions with clients] are an attempt to draw the line between two dangers . . . excessive illegitimacy at public expense on the one hand, and the idea that the State sanctions sexual promiscuity by providing birth control information to unmarried women on the other."[5]

Increasingly in the early 1960s, politicians and their constituents came to two conclusions; first, that black unmarried women typically have sexual relations, and secondly, that the financial and demographic burdens of illegitimacy were more onerous for society to bear than the moral strain. Illinois State Senator Morgan Findlay, who had opposed a bill to provide birth control to poor unwed women in 1963, said two years later, when he changed sides, "I felt it boiled down to the lesser of two evils, the so-called evil of bringing unwanted children into the world and increasing the public payrolls, or the evil of giving contraceptives to unmarried people." Findlay chose to support birth control for poor, unmarried girls and women because, he said, it was "good for the entire population of the State of Illinois," a decision one national television commentator called "a triumph of pocketbook over principle" that was occurring "almost everywhere" in the United States by 1965.[6]

During the early 1960s, state after state and then the federal government selected oral contraceptives as the method of choice for addressing unacceptably high rates of black illegitimacy. This development represented an instance of remarkably rapid consensus building among groups with distinct views of black illegitimacy. In June 1965, United States Senator Ernest Gruening, chairman of the Senate Subcommittee on Foreign Aid Expenditures of the Committee on Government Operations, opened hearings on S. 1676, which called for offices, staff, and programs in the Department of State and the Department of Health, Education and Welfare to deal with population problems abroad and in the United States. Senator Gruening called hundreds of expert witnesses to offer their perspectives on the nature of the population crisis. The thousands of pages of testimony from these hearings, and the appended magazine and journal articles, books, conference proceedings, radio and television transcripts, newspaper editorials, and political speeches constitute a rich record of the range of thinking of many who could claim membership in the contraceptive alliance.

The most voluble members of this coalition were politicians, demographers, agronomists, and civic leaders concerned about the population bomb. These participants were convinced of the volatile, inexorable relationship between "overpopulation" in the U.S. black community and social chaos. Joining this group were others with at least five different agendas, but all shared the vision that supplying contraceptives to unwed black women was a solution to "overpopulation."

Philip Hauser, a former assistant director of the United States Census Bureau and a prominent demographer from the University of Chicago, dramatically framed his concern about the consequences of postwar fertility rates in terms that set the tone of the hearings. Overpopulation of the cities will, Hauser asserted, "worsen the United States unemployment problem, greatly increase the magnitude of juvenile delinquency, exacerbate already dangerous race tensions . . . greatly increase traffic accidents and fatalities, augment urban congestion and further subvert the traditional American governmental system."[7]

The Gruening hearings began the summer of the uprising in the Watts section of Los Angeles, and many witnesses made the direct connection between black illegitimacy rates and, as James V. Bennett, the former director of the Federal Bureau of Prisons, testified, "the almost insuperable problem of law enforcement in such overpopulated areas as Los Angeles' Watts, New York's Harlem, or Philadelphia's ghettos." Bennett added, "We know that these areas generate severe tensions because of the constantly expanding population pressure which the law, as it is now organized, cannot cope with."[8] By the mid-1960s, the fertility of black women, especially the unmarried, was constructed as an explosive issue, profoundly threatening to the fabric of American life. For many, it was now immaterial whether black women had too many babies because of their biological or their cultural propensities; the point was that they must be stopped.[9]

The idea that cities in the United States were "overpopulated" by hostile, discontent, and dangerous blacks reflected fear of urban rebellions and the perceived threat of the civil rights movement. It also reflected the "realities" of postwar economics and the domestic Cold War in the United States, in which "the runaway inflation of people . . . sustained at starvation levels" was linked with "revolution and communism" abroad and now at home.[10] The population control imperative had come close to the vital center of the fight to sustain democracy in the United States. Thus, many contended that the United States had a responsibility to address its own population crisis if it were to exercise credible leadership in the democratic struggle to defuse the population bomb worldwide. This population control position was distinct from but related to the argument that overpopulation of the inner cities was the chief reason that U.S. "society [was] falling apart."[11] As Secretary of the Interior, Stewart L. Udall, testified, "I think that really for the United States to attempt to lecture or prod other countries around the world on this problem before we have set our own house in order is not proper." Udall's solution was the same: population control by dissemination of contraceptives to black females and other minorities.[12]

Another pair of members of the contraceptive alliance were the tax resisters, those who resented the financial burden associated with illegitimacy and the ADC program, and those who minded most being taxed to support the sin of illegitimacy. Demonstrating the logic of the first group, *The New York Times* explained, "Nationally the illegitimacy rate has tripled since 1940, and the children's aid program, heavily burdened by unwed mothers, has grown to four million cases, costing $1.5 billion. In 1955 there were $639 million [sic]. In short, there is a tax savings in birth control."[13]

The director of public welfare in Mecklenburg County, North Carolina, provided the Gruening hearings with an example of how the savings worked on a local level. He explained that the birth control pills his department had been distributing in large quantities to black women cost the taxpayers about one dollar per package. That one dollar saved taxpayers the monthly cost of supporting "an unwanted child." He said, "I think on quite solid ground, that for every dollar we have spent [on birth control], it resulted in a savings of $25."[14]

President Lyndon Johnson promoted birth control as cost-effective, as well, when he addressed the twentieth anniversary celebration of the United Nations in San Francisco, three days after the Gruening hearings began. At a time when presidential pronouncements on population issues and fertility were rare and very carefully phrased and noted, Johnson recommended, "Let us act on the fact that less than five dollars invested in population control is worth $100 invested in economic growth."[15] These cost-accounting arguments extended the grounds for accusing poor unwed mothers, often black, of consumer violations: an unmarried girl or woman who failed to buy into the contraceptive bargain was forcing society to pay full price for an unwanted item.[16]

Most of the advocates of a federal population control policy were convinced that contraceptives could reduce the birth rate of poor minorities and thus promote the health, safety, and prosperity of American society. Still, there was a distinct group appearing before the Gruening subcommittee who wanted contraceptives to be available to poor and black women because the women themselves might want them and because social justice demanded that if more affluent white women had access to birth control, all women should. Often, however, this "rights" position was quickly confounded by the issue of "duty." Michigan Representative John Conyers, the only black among sixty witnesses to appear in the first round of hearings, for example, cited the influential observations of the National Academy of Sciences in their report, *The Growth of U.S. Population*: "The freedom to limit family size to the number of children wanted when they are wanted is, in our view, a basic human right. The evidence cited in this report shows clearly that most Americans of high income and better education exercise this right, as a matter of course, but that many of the poor and uneducated are in effect deprived of the right."[17] Having established the "right" of black women to access, Conyers went on to associate his support of contraceptives for black women with the argument that fewer black babies would "stabilize and improve the Negro family structure," a structure severely compromised by "the tragedy of unwanted children." Thus, the interest in social justice and the rights of black women to have protected sex lives was eclipsed by the notion that these females had the duty to use birth control if the black community were to be saved from the "disintegrating effects of too many children" and the country as a whole were to be saved from the effects of the population bomb.

In a similar vein, the chairman of the board of the New York Life Insurance Company, R. K. Paynter, Jr., wrote to Senator Gruening in the Fall of 1965 to offer his support for S. 1676: "I believe every family should have the opportunity to 'want' its children. Broadly speaking, today that opportunity is in inverse relation to family income. Would anyone today think of withholding polio shots because the family cannot take its children to a private physician?"[18] Paynter's association of birth control with immunization against a crippling, even deadly virus matched Senator Gruening's own belief that excess population "has a relation to a disease."[19] In this case, birth control became a public health duty of black women; the consequences of ignoring that duty, a virulent epidemic.

The specter of overpopulation, specifically in relation to the super-packed ghetto, was so potent in the mid-1960s that spokespeople from all parts of the contraceptive alliance supported the use of birth control pills and the new IUD, first and foremost, as the obligation, not the right of black women. Conyers and others were careful to spell out their position that "no one, of course, is suggesting that any American citizen be pressured into utilizing any information that would be made available."[20] Still, these policy makers tied the wretched condition of the black community tightly to excess population, implying that women should be protected from the coercion of welfare workers but should not be protected from public blame if they continued to be contraceptively irresponsible.

It is, of course, noteworthy that black women did not have a voice in the public discussion of these issues in the mid-1960s. The discussants, almost exclusively white and male, had and took a great deal of latitude in constructing the importance of birth control for black women. Black women made an appearance at the Gruening hearings exclusively in the descriptions of policy makers—descriptions that stressed how their helplessness and ignorance fueled the population bomb. Senator Joseph Tydings offered a typical assessment: "It is absolutely incredible the number of adult women on welfare rolls who, by reason of their background and their complete lack of parental supervision, their complete lack of education, have had illegitimate children and yet do not really . . . know about the birds and the bees."[21]

It is likewise meaningful to link the advent of oral contraceptives and the IUD as policy options to the emergence of the "population bomb" as a compelling description of the demographics of the ghetto. The point is, for black women the early history of the new contraceptive technology was controlled not by a value-free technological development, or by a discourse of women's rights, but by public discussion that blamed black women for the problems of their community and demands that these women accept measures to halt "excess reproduction." The new reproductive technologies were not publicly sanctioned or offered to black women in a user-friendly mode. The rhetoric promoting their efficacy often had more in common with public justifications of sterilization of black women than it did with discussion of reproductive rights.[22]

As the contraceptive alliance gathered influential proponents in the early 1960s, those who did not join failed, more and more often, to control or even influence policy outcomes. The nonjoiners, like the joiners, represented a variety of perspectives. Prominent and persistent among them were public officials who felt strongly that unmarried mothers, especially teenagers, should not be engaging in sexual relations and should, therefore, not be provided with birth control. Some who took this exclusionary position were Catholics opposed to all contraception. Others were traditionalists upset that governmental bodies were facilitating nonmarital coitus. Some who may have been associated with either or both of these two groups were moralists disgusted by the notion of sex on the loose and by the distribution of birth control materials that could exacerbate the spread of rampant sexuality. Richard B. Nowakowski, a Milwaukee alderman, expressed outrage that federal money had been committed to support five birth control clinics in his city: "We will have 'sexmobiles' moving around the streets passing out birth control to whomever wants it—just like popcorn wagons."[23] In the early 1960s, the contraceptive coalition had to beat back these groups of nonjoiners to establish the eligibility of unwed mothers. The coalition succeeded in this effort in part by invoking the population bomb in the media, in the Gruening hearings, and in other legislative proceedings as an artifact of black illegitimacy rates. By the mid-1960s, the positions of the antis were no longer competitive.

Despite some thirteenth-hour attempts on the federal level to exclude unwed mothers from contraceptive services, the trend was otherwise.[24] The Webster School, a model, federally funded facility for unwed mothers in Washington, D.C., was prohibited by the District's board of education from discussing family planning and the use of contraceptives in the classroom. But by the mid-1960s, the D.C. Department of Public Health was able to provide birth control materials to the school's students, almost all of whom were black, at the six week postpartum examination. Only girls fifteen and younger needed their parents' approval.[25]

In Maryland, a policy statement put in force in the fall of 1962 that excluded unwed welfare clients from birth control services lasted only two and a half years. In the spring of 1965, the policy was changed: any girl or woman on welfare who had had an illegitimate child could receive such services, including those under 16.[26] Similarly, in Illinois and New York, restrictive policies adopted in the first years after the pill became available specifically excluded unwed women, including mothers, from family planning programs. But in 1965, Illinois amended its public assistance code, authorizing birth control information and services to "needy persons who are 15 or more years of age."[27] A year earlier the New York State Social Welfare Board allowed "head of household" status to qualify a welfare mother for birth control services, whereas from 1962 to 1964 only legally married women were so entitled. In 1965, going a step further, the New York state legislature amended its penal code to allow the sale of "devices and materials for the purpose of birth control through pharmacists to any person over the age of 16."[28]

These changes reflected a widespread acknowledgment that teenage girls and older unmarried women were having sex and babies in large numbers and that policy should catch up with reality if the "overpopulation" crisis were to be addressed.[29] The National Academy of Sciences pointed out that "Government statistics show that mothers of approximately forty-one percent of the 245,000 babies born illegitimately in the United States every year are women under nineteen years of age or younger. Thus a large proportion of all illegitimate children are progeny of teenage mothers." The Academy strongly recommended family planning services "to reduce the number of such children."[30]

Thus in the mid-1960s, one effect of the population bomb metaphor was to shift a measure of the expression of public concern about black procreation away from issues of sexuality and focus concern on how "unwanted babies" undermined the possibilities for a healthy and just society. Dr. Leslie Corsa, Jr., the director of the Center for Population Planning in the School of Public Health at the University of Michigan cataloged the considerations behind the recent successes of the contraceptive coalition in these terms: "As public concerns about social, economic, and racial equality, about rising illegitimacy and about higher fertility rates and tax costs of unwanted children among low-income families have heightened, civic and medical leaders have begun to incorporate birth control into existing tax-supported health services."[31] Civic and medical leaders in Whitley County, Kentucky, indeed, determined that "if civilization is to flourish to any extent, we must face the matter of excess babies born out of wedlock" and provide even their unwed mothers with birth control.[32]

Before 1960, seven states, all of them southern, included family planning services as a regular part of public health services.[33] Between 1961 and 1965, approximately twenty-five additional states and the District of Columbia initiated some birth-control services. In 1965 Detroit, Minneapolis, and other cities initiated birth control programs for poor women, whatever their marital status.[34] In what one observer labeled "an epidemic spread of family planning services," the number of local Health Departments providing birth control materials rose from 591 in 1963 to 843 in 1965, which included about 20 percent of the country's local Health Departments.[35] Senator Joseph Tydings, approving of these developments, noted that the crises of overpopulation and social chaos were moving policy makers toward "facing up to it and realizing that any fight against poverty and delinquency must include the ways and means to educate and assist persons in planning a family."[36]

As Tydings indicated, by the early 1960s, birth control was perceived as the prime effective deterrent against the causes of social chaos, including the cause most frequently identified in the 1950s, juvenile delinquency, and the more recently named cause, illegitimacy, leading to overpopulation and poverty. Whereas in the 1950s, boys, as juvenile delinquents, were most often perceived as threatening to the social fabric, now girls, specifically unwed mothers, became not simply breeders of unwanted babies, but bearers of social pathology and of social breakdown. In this period, for the first time, young black girls were identified as a target population for programs and services designed to curtail antisocial, destructive behavior.

"Comprehensive Programs" for Black Unwed Mothers

At this point, the designers of such programs and services became innovators. None of the postwar approaches to black unwed mothers described in Chapter Six—benign neglect, punitive, or benevolent reform—commanded credibility at the federal level by the early 1960s since black illegitimacy rates remained at unacceptably high levels. Ignoring black unwed mothers and their babies did not lower illegitimacy rates or social costs. Nor did punishing them, nor developing casework treatment for black mothers and adoption placements for their babies.

The innovation consisted of a two-pronged attack. In cities across the country, black unwed mothers were presented with the technological solution of birth control pills combined with the vocational solution of community-based "comprehensive" programs against illegitimacy and its destructive social consequences. The new approach situated pathology primarily in the outcome rather than the cause of unwed sexuality. Concerning black women, the social potency of illicit sexuality and conception was in the fact of more illegitimate children to challenge the social fabric. Consistent with this view, public health experts in New York "urged that large-scale rehabilitation programs be undertaken for unmarried mothers [in order to] break the cycle of the out of wedlock child turned into a delinquent who will repeat the parental pattern."[37] The innovation thus did conform to traditional ideas about biological transmission of the taint of illegitimacy, with experts predicting that the sins of the mothers would be replicated.

The technology of birth control could effectively abort the biological consequences of illegitimate sex and thus the transmission of a delinquent culture. In addition, for the first time, social programs aimed to penetrate this culture, through the experiences of black girls and women, and remake both black culture and its female members in a whiter image.[38] This was an interesting departure from the project of benevolent reformers who aimed to elevate the dignity and the opportunities of black unwed mothers by assigning them the neuroses associated with white unwed mothers. Now that blacks were specifically targeted for social programs, rather than construct them as being as disturbed as white unwed mothers were, the intention was to improve them so they could meet the healthy behavior standard of white culture. Project directors in the early 1960s freely acknowledged that black unwed mothers were different from whites. They believed, however, that their projects must eradicate that difference, in the name of deterrence. The Webster School Project in Washington, D.C., which quickly became a model for nearly forty similar projects serving about eight thousand unwed mothers across the country,[39] took what its directors and evaluator called a "middle class approach" to its black clients. The Webster School offered a "behavior modification" program designed "to rehabilitate school-age girls to acceptable social standards," and specifically to "middle class behavior," including the ability to plan for the future and to embrace norms regarding "sexual discipline." The staff also promoted the idea that its students should abdicate the mother role so as to be students and normative adolescents. This last premise endeared the Webster School program to the Children's Bureau's professionals who funded the project and who continued to prefer the position that unwed mothers were not-mothers. But it also put this school and its imitators in a paradoxical relation to another central thrust of programs for black unwed mothers—that the curriculum should be created "in the interests of establishing stable family life values" among black unwed mothers.[40] While recognizing a need to improve the environment of this population, many claimed that a higher purpose still was to "motivate [the girls] to want and appreciate the values of a stable and orderly family life,"[41] and to "accept the family pattern of the prevailing culture: marriage."[42] In attempting to remake black unwed mothers and their culture, the experts often drew on two of the most common strategies of white unwed mothers—relinquishment and marriage—strategies that were often unavailable or unacceptable to black girls and women.

Still, many of the professionals whose projects qualified for federal and state grants were experienced in working with white unwed mothers for whom services had long been available. The literature on unwed motherhood generated by psychiatrists, psychologists, and social workers in the postwar era was the only published guidance available. Consequently many of the projects for blacks were based on theories developed for white maternity home residents. Interest in remaking black girls and women in the image of whites was supported at the level of service delivery by project staff steeped in the theory and treatment of the psychological pathologies of illegitimacy.[43] Even among practitioners who recognized that the treatment of black unwed mothers called for a new combination of "psychiatry and sociology," many persisted in seeing their clients' problems in "intangible" or purely psychological terms, thus expressing their programs' greatest interest in changing the "mentality" of these unwed mothers.[44]

A program in Cleveland required all of its participants to join a therapy group, beginning in 1962. The group was led by a white male psychistrist because the program director "thought that a male psychiatrist would be better than a female because of the characteristically matriarchal families [of the girls]."[45] Another worker in a model program for black unwed mothers in Cleveland diagnosed her clients in the quasi-psychological terms provided by Leontine Young, the prominent social worker who, herself, dismissed blacks as outside the bounds of her categories because of endemic family and community disorganization. The Cleveland worker intrepidly defined the girls in her program as "passive dependents," unable "to see cause and effect" (in the sense that "they failed to see the connection between the sex act and childbirth") and "out of control." This woman, a "specialist" in working with unwed teen mothers, did not see the contradiction between this diagnosis and her determination that, in her own role toward the mothers, she must be "rather active, outgoing, and accepting to convey to the women that I was really interested in them and that I was not there to make judgments." In fact, demonstrating how thoroughly the white "experts" were indoctrinated by the social work literature and little else, she justified her diagnosis of "dependency" on the grounds that many of the girls and women in her program "desire to give their babies to their mothers or women custodians who serve as substitute mothers." Again, following the prescription of Leontine Young and others, prescriptions specifically devised to treat whites,[46] this young woman aimed to wean her clients from dependence on their mothers and other female relatives, inserting herself, instead, as "substitute mother." In this role, she would develop "a trusting relationship with them, setting a good many limits and expectations and helping them to live up to them."[47]

The phenomenon of nonmarital conception consistently stimulated program designers to construct their target population as deficient in the qualities of an ideal type and to mount training programs to redress the deficiency. As white unwed mothers were schooled in maternity homes to assume the grooming and comportment of middle-class femininity and gentility, blacks were trained to be more like whites. As white unwed mothers were pressured to give up their babies so they could sustain the image of normative young womanhood, blacks, many hoped, would advance to the practice of relinquishing their illegitimate babies in a future time, when black culture had been successfully penetrated and rearranged to resemble white culture. A sociologist imagined this future time when, white norms prevailing, black unwed mothers would be blocked from transmitting the values of a delinquent culture to their illegitimate offspring. Under these circumstances, black out-of-wedlock babies would no longer be tinder for the bomb.

> In the historical sense [cultural or racial differences concerning disposition] are almost certainly transitory. With increased secularization of all areas of social life, any subcultural values that may exist . . . are likely to change in the direction of the more general value system. [Regarding] Negroes[,] as secular values become more general and life styles become more homogeneous, it appears that in the long run . . . all unmarried mothers will seek to surrender their babies.[48]

The efforts to reach and educate black unwed mothers became, by 1964, one of many similar thrusts in the name of the Great Society. The Children's Bureau launched a "massive frontal attack" against the social problems resulting from black illegitimacy[49] and oversaw, during the early 1960s, what one high-level employee called "the quiet revolution [in services to black unmarried mothers] which we have developed." He went on, "We cannot keep up with the mail we are receiving as community after community is changing its position in providing services . . . for this group of girls."[50] In the late 1950s only one or two "comprehensive programs" for black unwed mothers existed in the entire country; by the mid-1960s there were more than forty, including at least one program in most major cities.[51] More were in the planning stages.[52] The director of the Erie County, New York, Anti-Poverty Action Committee described local efforts targeting unwed mothers as a "preventative device in the War on Poverty."[53]

As a metaphor providing direction to public policy in the early 1960s, the "population bomb" expressed white fear of the physical and fiscal dangers embodied by blacks in the United States. Most specifically, the bodies of black single mothers became a key symbol of destructiveness. "Unacceptable" rates of black illegitimacy became a powerfully convincing explanation for unacceptable welfare expenditures, unacceptable demographic changes in the big cities of the United States, unacceptable levels of juvenile delinquency and poverty.

The population bomb metaphor structured solutions as well. As the bomb squad dismantles and defuses the bomb, so public policies aimed to address the phenomenon of black illegitimacy. Through exclusion from public grants, through sterilization, through public pressure to use oral contraceptives, black females had constraints put on the explosive potential of their fertility. In a secondary effort, black unwed mothers were trained in "sexual discipline" and other alleged middle-class values so as to extinguish the behaviors threatening to detonate the population bomb.

The Sexual Revolution

Ironically, the sexual discipline of white middle-class single girls and women, so urgently invoked to subdue blacks, was itself a seriously threatened construct by the early 1960s. At that time, academics and the media prepared a salacious feast on the tasty subject of white female sexuality, or the "sexual revolution," and invited the public to sample such morsels as the Radcliffe senior who explained that "Stealing food from the dormitory refrigerator . . . would be more condemned around here than fornicating on the livingroom couch."[54] As the public became fascinated with the sex lives of female college students-as-sex-revolutionaries, white unwed mothers were increasingly considered a subset of a much larger, nearly normative group—white sexually active young women—rather than the discrete, anormative phenomenon they had represented in the 1940s and 1950s. As such, white single pregnant girls and women were less frequently described as neurotic, as pathological, or as in the prewar decades, fallen women.

In the 1940s and 1950s, the white unwed mother was diagnosed as psychologically disordered first because she was pregnant without a husband. Her mental problems were allegedly the product of her parents' neuroses. In distinction, the young woman who had sex, even if she became pregnant, in the early 1960s, was often characterized as rebellious without a husband, not sick. Her behavior was conditioned by peers and social pressures, not parents; her participation in intercourse was decidedly sexual. Before the 1960s, experts counseled that the unwed mother must be constrained, retrained, institutionalized. She was a dependent, a victim, a daughter. By the early 1960s, experts increasingly viewed these girls as beyond the bounds of institutions. Not victims, they were agents of social change. Not daughters, they were "college girls," or "career girls."[55] They were independent, sexualized, and at large. The earlier crop of unwed mothers was, by definition, "not-mothers"; for the later group, even this hard-and-fast certainty was softening.

The shifting of the public image and treatment of white unwed mothers reflected a pervasive shift in the view of the relationship between behavior and the social context in which it occurred. The postwar view of white unwed mothers as mental patients was part of a general belief that nonconformists were aberrant in an otherwise well-functioning society. In fact, the exceptional nature of individual and family pathology that experts associated with the root of unwed motherhood, constituted proof that, as a rule, postwar family life in the United States was healthy.

The prominence of theories of social rather than individual pathology in the 1960s situated the etiology of white unwed pregnancy differently. These theories ascribed sexual nonconformity to social-structural breakdown, a phenomenon that could be traced to the disintegration of values previously guiding the family, youth, and the media.[56] Once the weaknesses of society replaced individual weakness as explanation for white single pregnancy, an individual white unwed mother was—at least in theory—relieved of a great deal of personal culpability. After 1960, many social commentators argued that unwed mothers should not be personally blamed for their situation. Disapproval was trained on society instead. A prominent minister placed the blame for teenage sexuality and pregnancy on the media: "It's simply not fair to subject young people to sensual [movies] and expect them to control emotions which are already at a high pitch." A mother of four teenagers observed, "I know the stock accusation when trouble hits—blame the parents, and while you're at it blame the church. But I don't think our real failure is with the kids; it's in tolerating this filth until it now has the upper hand."[57] Mary Louise Allen, the executive director of the Florence Crittenton Association of America, complained about typical charges against parents of sexually active or pregnant girls as "either 'too domineering' or 'too permissive.' " She explained, "It is my conviction that the vast majority of parents care deeply about their children's welfare and that they make tremendous efforts to guide their children into creative and happy adulthood. It is not the individual parents but society as a whole that is too permissive."[58]

Clark Vincent described the problem this way:

> What would the Martian visitor say about a society that inundates young people with sexual stimuli and then not only castigates them for responding to such stimuli but also denies them the contraceptive means and knowledge whereby they could at least exercise caution? . . . To continue to support a matrix of social practices which serve to instill permissive attitudes toward illicit sexual behavior and at the same time to intensify efforts to decrease illicit pregnancies is to say the least, illogical.[59]

A sociologist who directed a major study of unwed mothers in North Carolina summed up several years of work by asserting that societal attitudes condone youthful sex, "Thus, *in fin*, it really isn't at all difficult to become an unwed mother."[60]

On the one hand, these experts and many others placed a degree of responsibility on "society," thus defining unwed mothers as passive victims of social forces, hardly the stuff of sexual revolutionaries. On the other hand, if "society," not the individual, were the agent responsible for both constructing and destroying social-sexual values and behavior, then young women themselves became, in an interesting sense, free agents able to pursue sexual experimentation, able even to become pregnant without blame. Indeed, one investigator of the attitudes of single pregnant girls noted at this time, "Contemporary unwed mothers, however their feelings may be described, do not seem to feel very guilty."[61]

In a new twist, white unwed mothers were absolved in one sense, but nailed nonetheless. The new charge recognized that society created the context for sexuality, but girls and women who moved freely in that context were at fault. A medical columnist for *Look* expressed his feelings about single pregnant women this way, "Women have more freedom now—are sexual, supposed to experiment but . . . I can't help wishing women had somehow managed to make better use of the emancipation they worked so hard to achieve."[62]

The white unwed mother could be blamed now as an abuser of her free agency, of her emancipation in the context of the so-called sexual revolution. A typical assessment claimed that "The [sexual] revolution . . . has primarily to do with women, and middle class women in particular. They are the ones who have finally come to embrace ways of thinking and behaving that have long been customary for others."[63] An account of the sexual revolution in *Time* placed the typical unwed mother on campus, participating in typical sexual behavior:

> Many girls are still sincere and even lyrical about saving themselves for marriage, but it is becoming a lot harder to hold the line. There is strong pressure not only from the boys but from other girls, many of whom consider a virgin downright square. The loss of virginity, even resulting in pregnancy, is simply no longer considered an American Tragedy.[64]

Newsweek placed all sexually active coeds similarly and suggested they were influential pioneers:

> "We've discarded the idea that the loss of virginity is related to moral degneracy," a husky Ohio State senior explained. . . . The quest of sex on the campus is not just academic. Ultimately, the new morality will have a meaning for American society as a whole: today's campus code may be tomorrow's national morality.[65]

What is extraordinary about this reconstruction and repositioning of the white unwed mother is that contemporary experts now associated her directly with normal-middle class females in a startling break from expert opinion in the immediate past, which strictly isolated the white unwed mother from middle-class standards, values, and behavior.

In the recent past, the white-middle-class-unwed-mother-as-mental-patient had reassured the middle-class public that illegitimate pregnancy marginalized a female. At the same time, that construct threatened the same public by suggesting the vulnerability of families and daughters to the neuroses of the era. After 1960, the white unwed mother as participant in the middle-class sexual revolution remained paradoxically comforting and threatening to the middle-class public, but for new reasons. As a typical single female, she was "safe" because she was "one of our own," a girl with a lot to lose, a girl society was motivated to protect. In 1961, a play about the dilemma of the white unwed mother, produced under the auspices of the Family Service Association of America and presented across the country for professional, charitable, and student audiences, characterized the unwed mother this way:

> Carol Vaughn is attractive, wholesome, and competent. Having grown up in a relatively large community in the Midwest as the daughter of respectable middle-class parents, she fits very well the description of "the girl next door." Liked both at home and at college, she is to all appearances well adjusted to society and her group.[66]

At the same time, the same girl was threatening as a sexual revolutionary. Young women assuming sex lives and becoming pregnant were rendering the familiar middle-class daughter unrecognizable and dangerous. In this vein, society was less motivated to protect her than it was to protect itself from the wages of the sexual revolution. The prime concern, in either case, was not demographic or economic. The concern was, most often, for the health of traditional gender relations and generational relations *within the nuclear family* in the face of the sexualized single girl. As a leading family expert observed in 1960, "The basic reason that societies control sex behavior at all levels is not fear of pregnancy but experience with the intensity and uncontrollability of sex and the resultant social disorganization when social sanctions are not imposed."[67]

Given these views of sex, pregnancy, and the single girl, how were contraceptives viewed in relation to white illegitimate pregnancy after 1960? This was a confusing question for many professionals who had so recently equated nonmarital female sexuality and pregnancy with severe maladjustment. Now these same professionals had the option of prescribing pills to prevent illegitimate pregnancy while facilitating nonmarital sex. One doctor in a university town explained his rationale for routinely prescribing pills to coeds: "It is not that I will feel personally responsible if she gets pregnant. It is that I have it in my power to prevent that eventuality. If you had seen as much grief as I have, you wouldn't hesitate to exercise that power."[68] For this physician, contraceptives did not raise questions of sexual morality or unwanted babies, or social costs, but of emotional stress from which the girls themselves deserved protection. While engaging in a practice that promoted the "sexual revolution" of college girls, this doctor and many others responded to patients as if they were daughters, thus paternalistically deflecting focus from the sex itself and from the potential illegitimate babies, who, in any case, could quickly be taken off the hands of college girls. A New York gynecologist genially described the levels of deception he was willing to countenance in his office. He said that "a fourth of the young ladies who come to him for [contraception] don't have marriage immediately in mind, but he keeps up the pretense; they get embarrassed if you tell them you know. They like to think of us as kindly old idiots."[69]

A Boston doctor explained why he and his colleagues dispensed contraceptives to all who requested them: "I don't know a doctor who demands a marriage license before giving contraceptive advice or prescriptions. The law says 'health reasons' and leaves the interpretation up to our discretion. We proceed on the basis that unmarried women need contraceptive methods for their own and for society's health."[70] Society's health in this view was not so much threatened by the birth of fatherless babies, expensive to taxpayers, as by the birth of independent, sexualized, unmarried females. Doctors dispensing contraceptives to this population often took the position that in the current sexualized environment, since girls couldn't be stopped from having intercourse, the pills could allow them to mask their sex lives. Contraceptives could create a population of sexually active unmarried females who did not get pregnant, a population whose sexuality, therefore, would not be revealed by pregnancy and could only be confirmed by a doctor for sure.

In this sense, oral contraceptives simultaneously provided the last chance to obfuscate the active sex lives of unmarried girls and women and the first opportunity for the sexual freedom that allegedly followed from the freedom from fear of pregnancy. The pill thus became a "declaration of independence"[71] for unmarried females because it held the promise of protecting and liberating them at the same time. As Andrew Hacker observed at the time, "A device like the pill does away with obsessive and irrational feelings about sex and can serve to reduce the illegitimacy rate—which has been rising alarmingly in recent years."[72]

Dismantling the Psychological Explanation

The unmarried girl who became pregnant after 1960 thus became in a sense a fallen revolutionary: she was "liberated" but "unprotected." Her pregnancy became a technical failure, that is, a failure to utilize technology, or a technological breakdown. As such, it was not impossible to blame a pregnancy on neuroses, but somewhat more difficult than in the heyday of the ubiquitous diagnoses. After 1960, it became increasingly problematic to view such a pervasive experience as individually aberrant, particularly when sociologists and service providers had become willing to reconnect individual behavior, including white illegitimate pregnancy, to its social context. One of the most powerful blows against individual explanations of single pregnancy was the notion that white, female, premarital sexual activity in the United

States was an expression of the new, postwar poverty of American culture. In this view, the culture had become bereft of values, with sex preoccupation filling the vacuum.[73] Experts found that many girls engaging in illicit sex felt they had "nothing to lose,"[74] or were experiencing "existential loneliness,"[75] a condition connoting the meaninglessness or normlessness of life. A Radcliffe student claimed that for her generation, sex was "the only way to get close to someone."[76] A political scientist observed, "If Freud was influential a generation go, today's intellectual rationale [for premarital sex] is to be found in existentialism."[77] A three-part article in *Better Homes and Gardens* in this era called "America's Moral Crisis" claimed that female "promiscuity" was "the unhappiness disease." Sexually active girls did not like sex, but "had fled to the vaunted refuge of sex freedom as an escape from reality's problems, just as others like them fled to heroin or marijuana."[78] In this formulation, nonmarital female sexuality was as unnatural and unhealthy as it had been for the postwar psychologists. The difference was that it now resulted from and expressed negative social conditions, not individual and family pathologies. In a related finding, female premarital sex was often associated with an increasing tendency to embrace a "fun morality" that defined "sex as play," an idea very disturbing "even among liberals."[79]

At a time when very conservative estimates counted 300,000 unwed mothers yearly, the "mental patient" explanation for single pregnancy became impractical, if not unbelievable.[80] The annual numbers of illegitimately pregnant teenagers in particular in the mid-1960s would have suggested a critical mass of "illness" that was untenable. For one thing, the constant focus on middle-class female nonmarital sex, in conjunction with these numbers, created the choice of accepting vast numbers of "our daughters" as neurotic or simply giving up the label. Indeed, Rose Bernstein observed, "The extension of unmarried motherhood into our upper and educated classes in sizeable numbers [renders] our former stereotypes less tenable . . . when the phenomenon has invaded our own social class—when the unwed mother must be classified to include the nice girl next door, the college graduate, the physician's or pastor's daughter."[81]

The cost of providing appropriate casework services for neurotic unwed mothers became impractical as well. A service agency for unwed mothers in Hartford, Connecticut, for example, revamped its offerings in the early 1960s for this reason; ever-rising numbers of unmarried mothers together with budget constraints provided motivation for the agency to modify its psychiatric perspective.[82]

As white unmarried mothers themselves felt less guilty about their pregnancies and more able to express their feelings about the services they were offered, more of them rejected psychological explanations and treatment. A study of residents at maternity homes in Queens, New York, and Cincinnati, Ohio, at this time, found that the girls were interested in practicalities not therapy: "The majority of the girls come to a social agency for specific services and tend to withdraw from contact when a plan for the baby has been concluded. . . . Few take kindly to the idea of regular sessions aimed at uncovering pathology."[83] Another study in the early 1960s revealed that unwed mothers reported that they almost never felt any conflict about having had sexual relations, but 90 percent of the sample reported that the "conflicts and problems" they were experiencing "were those created by the pregnancy."[84]

The combination of new social analyses, steadily increasing numbers, and uncooperative unwed mothers caused some commentators to reconsider the bases for the psychological explanations of single pregnancy. Rose Bernstein, in her influential article "Are We Still Stereotyping the Unwed Mother?", suggested that behavior considered evidence of the pathology of unwed mothers "may be appropriate responses to an anxiety-producing situation."[85] Clark Vincent asked his colleagues to consider whether unwed mothers were sick or, like many married mothers, simply sick of unwanted pregnancies.[86] The new question was, to whom should white unwed mothers most aptly be compared. Typically, white unwed mothers had been compared with unmarried white virgins, to demonstrate the psychological or personality differences between these groups.[87] By the early 1960s, some students of illegitimacy began to consider the situation of white unwed mothers alongside of the situation of married mothers, of married women unhappily pregnant, and most often, alongside other sexually active but not pregnant white unmarried girls and women.[88] This last comparison often suggested that unwed mothers were simply unluckier but no less rational than "thousands of other women and girls who by their own admission, engage in illegal coition . . . [without] bearing children."[89]

Unraveling the Adoption Mandate

The trends that lifted white unwed mothers out of the slough of psychiatric diagnoses and allied them with a social movement—the sexual revolution— had a substantial effect on the prevailing assumption that white unwed mothers were not mothers. If unwed mothers were rebels sexually, perhaps they were simply rebels maternally. If unwed mothers had exercised rights to their own sexuality, perhaps they could exercise rights to their own illegitimate children. One analyst sensed a fatal weakness in the generation-long practice of placing white bastard children for adoption:

> Adoption, as it has been institutionalized and practiced in contemporary social work, is . . . a relatively recent development and does not have the support of a long and well-established practice; those who accept it are still not likely to feel as secure in what they are doing as are those who follow the older tradition which kept the child with the mother.[90]

At the same time that white unwed mothers were reconstructed as typical—if rebellious and careless—middle-class girls, the government and service agencies began to pay more attention to the fact that many whites were keeping their illegitimate babies.[91] This followed, in part, from reported declines in the number of unmarried mothers who applied to adoption agencies for assistance.[92] The Department of Health, Education and Welfare, in a dramatic departure from its staunch support of adoption, began to fund projects designed to "determine whether babies were better off with their unmarried mothers or placed for adoption."[93]

A number of studies conducted in the early 1960s highlighted a finding that was either studiously ignored or absent in the two previous decades: that white girls were keeping their babies as part of a rational life plan. One investigator noted "a trend toward women feeling that they can manage the problems of employment and childcare without the assistance of a husband . . . [suggesting] . . . that society is less disapproving than in past years[.]"[94] A study of maternity home residents in the early 1960s determined that unmarried mothers "are less likely to value legal marriage than their parents and are more inclined to value the maternal role than either their parents or the [home] staff."[95] Among a North Carolina study's sample of 461 whites,[96] only one-third placed their babies for adoption, and among the two-thirds who kept were "Many [who] thought their reputation had improved." The investigators drew on an alleged race-neutral American ideal to explain this finding: "Motherhood is so positively viewed within our culture [that] becoming a mother, even an unwed one, can help overcome a bad reputation."[97] The investigators hypothesized that unwed motherhood could provide this sort of positive experience because the illegitimacy stigma had diminished and unwed motherhood carried a reduced "socio-psychological hazard" for girls and their parents.[98]

The studies gave some attention to which white unwed mothers tended to keep their babies and concluded, often in passing, that socioeconomic status, or class, was the determining factor.[99] But in general, the meaningful news about disposition practices had been racial ever since the emergence of the white adoption mandate in the 1940s, and still was. The news—which was not always, in fact, new—was that white unwed mothers were ignoring the mandate more often. What *was* new was the fact that investigators reported this behavior, and did so without classifying the mothers as mentally ill.

The experts' waning allegiance to the psychological explanation of white illegitimate pregnancy and unwed motherhood gave rise to a willingness to record the attitudes and behaviors of the mothers themselves, whose experiences had previously been captured almost exclusively in the language of illness. For the first time in the postwar years, white girls who kept their babies were quoted regarding the "joys" of motherhood and even more often, after 1960, the horrors of relinquishment were aired in public. One unwed mother said, "I thought I knew about grief. I lost my mother. But this was so much worse." She explained that while death was inevitable, "deciding to give up a baby was not a natural act." Other white unwed mothers were similarly presented as rational. A group of unwed mothers in a relinquishment support group in Minnesota shared "the confusion they'd felt as they experienced the joy of creating [a baby] and felt they couldn't express this as people wouldn't understand. One said, 'The five days in the hospital while I cared for my baby were the happiest days of my life.' "[100]

In 1962, in a story calculated to upset readers, *Readers' Digest* printed the oath an unwed mother signed upon legally relinquishing her child: "I do hereby voluntarily, unconditionally, absolutely, and irrevocably surrender the said child. . . . I expressly pledge not to interfere with the care of said child in any way, or allow or encourage anyone else to do so."[101] Reflecting on the experience of unwed mothers who signed, a doctor admitted what no professional would have countenanced only several years earlier. He said, "I have yet to see any women willingly relinquish her child, no matter what she says or how much she hated the father. Giving away a baby, even a baby a girl doesn't want, leaves deep emotional scars."[102] The doctor acknowledged that for white girls, relinquishment might not constitute a psychological cure.

Another doctor observed:

> No one in the technical literature has stressed the heartlessness, the cruelty and the sadism that the pregnant woman so frequently senses . . . when the physician, minister, or lawyer suggests to her that she carry the child to term and then hand it over, never to see it again, to someone else to rear. Thirty-seven of the last forty-four unwillingly pregnant patients referred here for consultation had, before their referral, adamantly rejected all pressure in this direction. All felt exactly the same way about it. . . . [All] objected to farming the child out for adoption. As they termed it, and in exactly the same words, "I'm not an animal." Each asked, "Do you think I could give my baby away after carrying it for nine months? There is a civil rights movement in this country now. *A hundred years ago you could take the babies away from slaves. You can't do that now!* And you can't turn me into the kind of animal that would give my baby away."[103] (italics added)

The new attention to the words and feelings of white unwed mothers reflected their emerging image as normal American girls—sexual and accidentally pregnant. The work of sociologist Ira L. Reiss published in the early and mid-1960s was instrumental in normalizing, contextualizing, and most important, rationalizing the sexual behavior of unmarried girls, a group from which Reiss did not exclude the ones who became pregnant.[104] A strikingly innovative study of unwed mothers in Boston in the mid-1960s confirmed that unwed mothers belonged within Reiss's sample. It found that white unwed mothers in three maternity homes had levels of self-esteem equal to the self-esteem of never-pregnant and single, and married pregnant control populations. The investigator found that the unwed mother "did not see herself as incompetent, neither was she complacent. . . . To a lesser degree she did not feel she was disesteemed, inadequate, worthless, unconcerned, nonaggressive, irrational, unacceptable or uncertain. . . . [She] appeared to be a fairly confident person with an adequate amount of self-esteem or self-worth."[105] In sum, the author found, "All the results of this study pointed to the normality of the unwed mother."[106]

The Boston study was utterly conventional in one sense. Its author selected maternity home residents—broadly middle-class girls—as subjects and thus continued to promote the idea that the experiences of this population could illuminate the experiences of all white unwed mothers. The study was, in fact, consistent with academic, popular, and professional literature, which more than ever relied on studies of middle-class girls.[107] This was the case in part because aggregates of college girls were the most accessible population to study and in part because the public was titillated by the idea of the independent, sexually active middle-class girl. This girl made good copy because she was portrayed as liberated, free of all fear of pregnancy, and willing to sleep with a boy she didn't have plans to marry.[108] Her life was portrayed as governed by a contingent, not an absolute, moral system, which sanctioned premarital sex this way: "With one hundred percent birth control, you are not running the risk of hurting anyone by your behavior and therefore it is not immoral."[109]

The image of this new normative female, simply sexual, and even sexual and pregnant, celebrated the female vanguard of the sexual revolution. At the same time, it masked the shame and sorrow and the stunning lack of resources that still characterized the unwed mothers who had been bypassed by the sexual revolution, or whose lives revealed its limits as a transformative social movement. A nineteen-year-old girl from North Carolina wrote to President Johnson in 1965, several years into the "sexual revolution," in terms that demonstrate the persistence of unwed motherhood as a degraded status. She wrote to the president asking for financial assistance and sympathy:

> I feel as though you will help me, I have seen you on television and your heart seems to go out to anyone that needs you.
>
> The father of my baby, after finding out that I was expecting turned his back on me. And my mother told me that I would have to get out because the house would be too full. . . . I am just so afraid for me and the baby. . . .
>
> If I don't have any money to pay the Doctor, I won't have anyone to deliver my baby and I am so afraid to be alone.[110]

The association of the white unwed mother with the sexual revolution was, in many ways, as distorted as the psychiatric construct it replaced. Yet, in one important sense, it probably improved the experience of the average white unwed mother a great deal. If unmarried white girls were, according to the gospel of the sexual revolution, typically accepting premarital sex as "a perfunctory aspect of the dating system,"[111] then logically, premarital pregnancy could happen to anyone.[112] Paradoxically, by becoming simply a typical American girl, the unwed mother could be allowed a distinctive voice. She could, in fact, become an expert on the subjects of her sexual experience and her single pregnancy. Unwed mothers were freer now to express their anger and their desire not to cooperate with institutions and a society that effaced their feelings. Such girls spoke without fear of being marginalized by a psychiatric diagnosis, as this one: "I hated every pregnant woman I saw. Why should she be able to freely walk around looking so obviously pregnant while I was hiding mine inside a raincoat. I wanted to throw my coat open and yell, 'I am going to have a baby!' Even after all these months, I still hate married pregnant women when I see one on the street."[113]

White unwed mothers became resources, "expert witnesses" for high-school students, other unwed mothers, clergy, medical personnel, professional and church groups. The National Council on Illegitimacy[114] reported in the mid-1960s that when

> a teacher of a Family Life course in a local high school called [a Minnesota maternity home] to ask if we had a tape that could be used to stimulate discussion regarding premarital sex with his teenage students, [twelve former clients] volunteered to tape a discussion on what they would want to tell a high school group based on their own experiences, so that this could be shared with groups.

In another situation, two maternity home veterans made an audiotape for current clients. One woman spoke about the experience of keeping her illegitimate child, the other about relinquishing.[115] The sponsors of these projects honored the unwed mother as expert on her own life and acknowledged the psychological, moral, and logistical viability of a variety of experiences and decisions.

Another aspect of this trend was the recognition that the perspective of professional workers was often not congruent with the perspectives of unwed mothers. In the 1960s, this recognition could be interpreted as an obstacle to effective service rather then as a justification for the professional staff to work harder on transforming their charges. One social worker noted considerable attitude differences between staff and clients, and observed, "The interaction between clients and staff is probably seriously hampered, possibly to the point where it is difficult to create any relationship beyond what is required for dealing with the immediate situation."[116] In light of the practices of the recent past, what is most striking here is simply the acceptance of the idea that unwed mothers had a distinctive and *rational* perspective on their own situation.

Emblematic of the newly and rationally voiced white unwed mother in the 1960s was a young pregnant woman from Massachusetts who wrote for advice, as had so many young women in the past, to the United States Children's Bureau.

> I am feverishly looking for a good, reliable home for unwed mothers. I
> don't want a place to be a recluse for a few months but rather a place with
> stimulating recreation and entertainment. I don't want to be bored and
> depressed during my "waiting period." I would love a place on the seashore
> in a warm climate. I love the outdoors. I hope I'm not asking the impossible.
> I'm just trying to make my impending confinement as happy as possible
> under the conditions.[117]

As bereft of information, and probably other resources, as this single pregnant
woman was, her situation did not deter her from an intention to control her
own experience, even to choose her own destiny.

As a metaphor describing the relationship of white girls to sexuality and to
the community after 1960, the "sexual revolution" had significant implications
for the public perception and treatment of white unwed mothers. It suggested
two related and enduringly oppositional social responses to female sexuality.
The first was an acknowledgment that very large numbers of unmarried white
girls and women were publicly and privately claiming the right to have sex lives,
an enormous change in twentieth-century culture in the United States. The
second was the fear that this claim constituted an upheaval—a profound challenge to traditional gender roles and male sexual prerogatives, in particular.
Since the phenomenon was promoted as a widespread and inclusive transformation, a "revolution," the unmarried girl or woman who became pregnant in the
midst of it became simply one of the crowd. For some white unwed mothers,
being one of many was empowering. Most, however, were swept along in a
sexualized but still profoundly sexist context over which they had little control.
In 1965 these white single pregnant girls and women could be found in maternity homes, on the tables of illegal abortionists, reluctantly taking out marriage
licenses, dealing with black marketeers, in welfare offices, as the heads of the
growing number of single parent households. Despite the considerable advantage of race and often of class, white unwed mothers in the mid-1960s were all
too frequently lost in the crowd.

The Bomb and the Revolution Subdue Unwed Mothers

The population bomb and the sexual revolution apparently helped the
American public to comprehend disturbing new evidence of female sexuality
and fertility, and guided some policy makers' and professionals' attempts to
deal with increasing rates of illegitimacy. But the racially specific approaches
toward sexually active females and unmarried mothers that these constructs
reflected did not have an impact on rates of single pregnancy.

In the early 1960s, Children's Bureau staff recognized how little had
been accomplished in the areas of controlling illegitimacy and serving the
illegitimately pregnant girl or woman, despite decades of trying. The Bureau's
Committee on Services to Unmarried Mothers acknowledged, "It is obvious

that the problems of illegitimacy are not yielding to approaches developed so far."[118] The old institutional methods were becoming dysfunctional or were under attack. Local welfare programs assisting poor unwed mothers used disproportionate resources to determine eligibility and punish clients or would-be clients. Maternity homes were losing their traditional client base and were being forced to reconsider their mission or close. The new, often government-sponsored, comprehensive programs for unwed mothers in urban settings were experimental, small, underfunded, and understaffed, as well as ideologically problematic. This lack of institutional coherence and vision reflected the public response to a social problem that had outgrown established strategies but had not gained additional public sympathy or support. Even the new government-supported birth control programs were not demonstrating a capacity to prevent a significant number of unwanted illicit pregnancies in any large population.[119] At this time, 67 percent of all unwed mothers experiencing a first illegitimate birth were teenagers, the population most excluded from contraceptive services by state laws, despite some liberalizing tendencies in the early 1960s.[120] The reigning metaphors suggested an intense lack of public sympathy for sexually active unmarried females. These metaphors undermined the possibility for female- or mother-centered support for unwed mothers.

Nonetheless, ideas for addressing the increasing rates of illegitimacy and the problems of single pregnant girls and women were not in short supply in the early and middle 1960s, although institutional support for most strategies was not forthcoming. When the Children's Bureau undertook to ask state Welfare Departments what services should be offered to unwed mothers in 1962, one state responded,

> There is a serious need for the development under public auspices on a statewide basis of a service geared specifically to helping unmarried mothers whether they plan to give up their children, are receiving assistance, or are just floundering around without any counsel or direction. . . . Funds are not available to develop such a service, employ staff, or meet any individual costs.[121]

Yet at the same time, the Children's Bureau itself continued to present and analyze the state of services to this population almost solely in terms of the adoption scene for white illegitimate babies.[122] In the Cook County Hospital in Chicago where 40 percent of the live births were illegitimate, the hospital administration decided to abandon its practice of automatically referring unmarried mothers to its social service department because of lack of staff and funds, despite the recognition that these girls and women required social services.[123] Similarly in West Virginia, after an agency for unwed mothers received a "tremendous response" to an outreach campaign, it decided to curtail all efforts to attract new clients because of lack of "facilities and funds."[124] Mary Verner of the Salvation Army suggested that racial stereotyping of unwed mothers remained the biggest obstacle to service delivery when she wrote, "We must not expect our clients to fit the mold of the agency. Instead, we must attempt to change the pattern of our programs to meet the needs of those seeking help."[125]

In 1965, fertile unmarried females, black and white, remained a highly vulnerable population. The fact that the "sexual revolution" and the "population bomb" metaphors were so widely accepted suggests some answers to why the needs of these girls and women continued to be addressed in such a meager and often punitive fashion. The population bomb precisely captured—and also structured—the white public's postwar fears about social instability, economic insecurity, gender insubordination, and black challenges to race hierarchy in the United States. The builders of the population bomb metaphor instructed the white public that the black illegitimacy rate was a profound domestic threat in all these areas because the babies themselves had the potential to fundamentally change American society for the worse. The women producing these babies were of interest to the population controllers of the early and mid-1960s as excessive reproducers. The population bomb suggested simply that the reproduction should be halted, one way or another. Beyond that, the population bomb metaphor offered little to the black unwed mother or to a public considering the relationship between female sexuality and fertility and other social issues.

The sexual revolution, on the other hand, expressed the discovery in the United States, in the twentieth century, of white female sexuality, and to some degree, the public's acceptance of it, via the alleged behavior of middle-class coeds. The association of white unwed mothers with this relatively privileged population undermined the possibility of a sense of social responsibility for the more typical white unwed mother who had few resources,[126] who was not a revolutionary, fallen or otherwise. The public focus on female sexuality as "revolutionary" curtailed discussion of what remained the same for sexually active unmarried girls in a male-dominated society. The public focus on sex in relation to the lives of unmarried girls and women, and in relation to social change, could cancel out the dangers of revolution by sustaining these subjects as titillating and harmless.

Yet both the bomb and the revolution also cast unmarried females, black and white, as aggressors against American society and diminished an appreciation of their true vulnerability, particularly when they became unwed mothers. By constructing unwed mothers as aggressors, the public was justified in meting out punishment, scorn, and disrespect, in racially specific ways.

Finally, the history of the racially specific treatment of unwed mothers after World War II, captured and apotheosized by the prevailing metaphors of the early and mid-1960s, added new grounds for racial separation, racial alienation, and intra-gender hostility between black and white women. This history suggests why the contemporary politics of female fertility continues to be rent by race.

The treatment of unwed mothers in the postwar era demonstrates how female sexuality and fertility and the unwed mother herself have been used in our recent past as proving grounds for theories of race, gender, motherhood, and social stability. In the postwar era, the unwed mother supplied babies to childless couples, took the blame for rising tax bills, symbolized the wages of gender insubordination, was cast as the source of all problems in the black community, was described and treated as mentally ill, frigid, wantonly sexual, and as a typical American girl. The variety of roles unwed mothers were assigned and constrained to fill in our recent past indicates the consistent vulnerability of sexually active, especially pregnant, girls and women without male protection. The variety of roles also illuminates the shifting requirements of a society that depends upon sustaining gender, class, and racial inequality under changing historical conditions.

Throughout the Gruening hearings in the mid-1960s, many testifiers cited a powerful argument to justify federal support of contraceptives: widespread access to contraceptives was the most effective deterrent to widespread abortion.[127] Walter Tobriner, the president of the Board of Commissioners of the District of Columbia, called abortion rates "higher than a healthy society can tolerate";[128] Senator Gruening, himself, referred to abortion as a "desperate act"; and Alan Guttmacher labeled abortion in America as a "serious disease." Guttmacher, president of Planned Parenthood, elaborated, "I feel that the only way to eliminate this hideous problem [of abortion] is by making effective contraceptives available to everyone who needs it and who desires it. . . . If we could have effective, simple methods [of contraception] . . . we could cut down this one million [abortions a year] figure to probably a few hundred thousand."[129] The abortion issue, statistically associated with whites, made a frequent, although race-neutral appearance at the hearings. For the antiabortionists, contraceptives constituted a deterrence weapon, a traditionally appealing concept to defense-minded Americans.

By the mid and late 1960s, however, many experts acknowledged that contraception alone was not functioning well enough as a deterrent either to illegitimate pregnancy or to abortion.[130] Consequently, many policy makers again made a choice, determining that the population bomb and the sexual revolution held more serious repercussions for society than the legalization of abortion. Abortion became an acceptable way to meet an old goal, that is, containing the social consequences of illicit female sexuality and fertility.

The legalization of abortion was a feminist victory; this study, however, offers one explanation of why the time was right in the late 1960s and early 1970s for feminists and other prochoice proponents to prevail. It suggests that the treatment of unwed mothers between 1945 and 1965 was conditioned by a stubbornly persistent public attitude that the unprotected pregnant female is a social resource of sorts. The multiple uses of unwed mothers described here suggests why a pregnant woman's prerogatives have been so hard to establish and sustain.[131]

Notes

Introduction

[1]The stories of Sally and Brenda are composite case histories. Every element of both stories occurs at least once, and most many times, in published and unpublished case records of single, pregnant girls and women who didn't marry or turn to outlaw abortionists in the postwar, pre–*Roe v. Wade* era. I have chosen to provide composite case histories in order to illustrate the stereotypical, if not typical, racially specific cycles of pregnancy, prenatal experience, childbirth, and disposition of the baby. Existing case studies generally did not follow one unwed mother over such a period, as service agencies which employed caseworkers usually addressed special aspects of the ordeal only, for example, the adoption process, or the determination of eligibility for welfare benefits.

[2]Betty Friedan, *The Feminine Mystique* (New York: W.W. Norton, 1963), p. 45.

[3]In the first postwar decade approximately three-quarters of premaritally conceived first births to white and one-third of those to blacks, aged 15–24, were legitimated by marriage. Martin O'Connell and Maurice J. Moore, "The Legitimacy Status of First Births of U. S. Women Aged 15–24, 1939–1978," *Family Planning Perspectives* 12 (January–February 1980):16–25.

[4]Mary Calderone, ed., *Abortion in the United States* (New York: Harper and Brothers, 1958), pp. 92–3, 139; Alan Guttmacher, "Therapeutic Abortion: The Doctor's Dilemma," *Journal of Mt. Sinai Hospital* 21 (1954):111; Lewis Savel, "Adjudication of Therapeutic Abortion and Sterilization," in Edmund W. Overstreet, ed., *Therapeutic Abortion and Sterilization* (New York: Harper and Row, 1964), pp. 14–21.

[5]Calderone, ed., *Therapeutic Abortion*, pp. 86–8.

[6]See, for example, J. G. Moore and J. H. Randall, "Trends in Therapeutic Abortion: A Review of 137 Cases," *American Journal of Obstetrics and Gynecology* 63 (1952):34.

[7]Harry A. Pearce and Harold A. Ott, "Hospital Control of Sterilization and Therapeutic Abortion," *American Journal of Obstetrics and Gynecology* 60 (1950):297; James M. Ingram, H.S.B. Treloar, G. Phillips Thomas, and Edward B. Rood, "Interruption of Pregnancy for Psychiatric Indications—A Suggested Method of Control," *Obstetrics and Gynecology* 29 (1967):251–5.

[8]See, for example, Charles C. Dahlberg, "Abortion," in Ralph Slovenko, ed., *Sexual Behavior and the Law* (Springfield, IL: Charles C. Thomas, 1965), p. 384.

[9]Arthur Mandy, "Reflections of a Gynecologist," in Harold Rosen, ed., *Therapeutic Abortion* (New York: The Julian Press, 1954), p. 291.

[10]Gregory Zillboorg, "The Clinical Issues of Postpartum Psychopathology Reac-

tions," *American Journal of Obstetrics and Gynecology* 73 (1957):305; Roy J. Heffernon and William Lynch, "What Is the Status of Therapeutic Abortion in Modern Obstetrics?", *American Journal of Obstetrics and Gynecology* 66 (1953):337.

[11]Nicholson J. Eastman, "Obstetric Forward," in Rosen, *Therapeutic Abortion*, p. xx.

[12]Theodore Lidz, "Reflections of a Psychiatrist," in Rosen, *Therapeutic Abortion*, p. 279.

[13]Flanders Dunbar, "Abortion and the Abortion Habit," in Rosen, *Therapeutic Abortion*, p. 27.

[14]Mandy, "Reflections," p. 289.

[15]Manfred Guttmacher, "The Legal Status of Therapeutic Abortion," in Rosen, *Therapeutic Abortion*, p. 183. Also see Nanette Davis, *From Crime to Choice: The Transformation of Abortion in America* (Westport, CT: Greenwood Press, 1985), p. 73; Johan W. Eliot, Robert E. Hall, J. Robert Willson, and Carolyn Hauser, "The Obstetrician's View," in Robert E. Hall, ed., *Abortion in a Changing World, vol. 1* (New York: Columbia University Press, 1970), p. 93; Kenneth R. Niswander, "Medical Abortion Practice in the United States," in David T. Smith, ed., *Abortion and the Law* (Cleveland: The Press of Case Western Reserve University, 1967), p. 57.

[16]David C. Wilson, "The Abortion Problem in the General Hospital," in Rosen, *Therapeutic Abortion*, pp. 190–1. Also see Myra Loth and H. Hesseltine, "Therapeutic Abortion at the Chicago Lying-In Hospital," *American Journal of Obstetrics and Gynecology* 72 (1956): 304–11, which reported that 69.4 percent of their sample were sterilized along with abortion. Also relevant are Keith P. Russell, "Changing Indications for Therapeutic Abortion: Twenty Years Experience at Los Angeles County Hospital," *Journal of the American Medical Association,* January 10, 1953, pp. 108–11, which reported an abortion-sterilization rate of 75.6 percent; and Lewis E. Savel, "Adjudication of Therapeutic Abortion and Sterilization," *Clinical Obstetrics and Gynecology* 7 (1964):14–21.

[17]Interview with Marcia Weiland, February 1, 1989.

[18]Jean Thompson, *The House of Tomorrow* (New York: Harper and Row, 1967), pp. 15–16.

[19]Ibid., 72, pp. 152–3.

[20]Leontine Young, *Out of Wedlock* (New York: McGraw-Hill, 1954), p. 216.

[21]Elizabeth Tuttle, "Serving the Unmarried Mother Who Keeps Her Child," *Social Welfare* 43 (October 1962): 415–22.

[22]Mignon Sauber and Elaine Rubinstein, *Experiences of the Unwed Mother As Parent: A Longitudinal Study of Unmarried Mothers Who Keep Their Babies* (New York: Community Council of Greater New York, 1963), p. 63.

[23]Ibid., pp. 127, 129, 116.

[24]Ibid.

[25]Howard Osofsky, *The Pregnant Teenager: A Medical, Educational, and Social Analysis* (Springfield, IL: Charles C. Thomas, 1966), p. 56.

[26]See Winifred Bell, *Aid to Dependent Children* (New York: Columbia University Press, 1965).

[27]On the subject of illegitimacy and family shame at midcentury, see Ernest W. Burgess, *The Family* (New York: The American Book Company, 1953), pp. 186–8, 549–51.

[28]See Jan E. Dizard and Howard Gadlin, *The Minimal Family* (Amherst: University of Massachusetts Press, 1990).

[29]John D'Emilio and Estelle B.Friedman, *Intimate Matters: A History of Sexuality in America* (New York: Harper and Row, 1988) p. 277

[30]See, for example, Elaine Tyler May, *Homeward Bound: American Families in the Cold War Era* (New York: Basic Books, 1988).

[31]D'Emilio and Freedman, *Intimate Matters*, p. 298.

[32]Phillips Cutright, "Illegitimacy in the United States: 1920–1968," in Charles F. Westoff and Robert Parke, Jr., eds., *Demographic and Social Aspects of Population Growth* (Washington, D.C.: Commission on Population Growth and the American Future), p. 384.

[33]Elizabeth Herzog, "Unmarried Mothers: Some Questions to be Answered and Some Answers to be Questioned," *Child Welfare* 41 (October 1962):330–49.

[34]Wyatt C. Jones,"What Are Unmarried Mothers Really Like?", paper presented at the National Conference on Social Welfare, 1960.

[35]Hannah Adams, *Social Services for Unmarried Mothers and Their Children Provided Through Public and Voluntary Child Welfare Agencies*, United States Department of Health, Education and Welfare (Washington, D.C.: Government Printing Office, 1962).

[36]*Illegitimacy and Its Impact on the Aid to Dependent Children Program*, Bureau of Public Assistance, Social Security Administration, U.S. Department of Health, Education and Welfare (Washington, D.C.: Government Printing Office, 1960).

[37]See, for example, Leona Baumgartner to Eleanor Hunt, June 23, 1955, Box 691, file 7–4–3–1–1, Record Group 102, National Archives.

[38]Robert W. Roberts, *The Unwed Mother* (New York: Harper and Row, 1966), Introduction.

[39]Clyde Kiser, Wilson Grabill, Arthur A. Campbell, *Trends and Variations in Fertility in the United States* (Cambridge, MA: Harvard University Press, 1968), chapter 8.

[40]Joan Jacobs Brumberg, " 'Ruined Girls,': Changing Community Response to Illegitimacy in Upstate New York, 1890–1920," *Journal of Social History* 18 (Winter 1984):248–9. Brumberg is writing here about a white population, although she doesn't specify this restriction.

[41]See Michael W. Sedlak, "Young Women and the City: Adolescent Deviance and the Transformation of Educational Policy, 1870–1960," *History of Educational Quarterly* 23 (Spring 1983):1–28.

[42]Brumberg in "Ruined Girls" found that a substantial number of unwed mothers in her late-nineteenth and early-twentieth-century samples put their illegitimate babies up for adoption, a surprising finding. Brumberg notes that the tendency to adoption reported in her article does not mesh with Sedlak's study (see note 21), nor does it mesh with the contention in the present study that wide-scale adoption was a post-World War II innovation. Brumberg does not give a lot of information in her article about the actual disposition of the babies, so it is difficult to discern exactly where and with whom the babies were being placed.

[43]On maternity homes before the Second World War, see, for example, Katherine G. Aiken, "The National Florence Crittenton Mission, 1883–1925; A Case Study of Progressive Reform," Ph.D. dissertation, Washington State University, 1980. Also see Peggy Pacsoe, *Relations of Rescue: The Search of Female Moral Authority in the American West, 1874–1939* (New York: Oxford, 1990) and Regina Kunzel, *The Girl Problem: Evangelicals, Social Workers, and Unmarried Mothers, 1890–1945* (New Haven: Yale University Press, forthcoming).

[44]See, for example, Henry C. Schumacher,M.D., "The Unmarried Mother: A Socio-Psychiatric Viewpoint," *Mental Hygiene* 4 (October 1927):775–82.

[45]Ibid., p. 775.

[46]D'Emilio and Freedman, *Intimate Matters*, p. 234.

[47]Before World War II, unwed mothers were widely considered to be the proper mothers of their bastard children, despite the lack of husbands.

[48]Herbert G. Gutman, "Persistent Myths About the Afro-American Family," in Michael Gordon, ed. *The American Family in Social-Historical Perspective* (New York: St. Martin's Press, 1983),pp. 459–81; and Herbert G. Gutman, *The Black Family in Slavery and Freedom 1750–1925* (New York: Vintage Books, 1976).

[49]E. Franklin Frazier, *The Negro in the United States* (New York: Macmillan, 1949), p. 627.

Chapter One

[1]Lillian Ripple, "Social Work Standards of Unmarried Parenthood as Affected by Contemporary Treatment Formulations," Ph.D. dissertation, University of Chicago, 1953; and Helen H. Perlman, "Unmarried Mothers," in Nathan E. Cohen, ed., *Social Work and Social Problems* (New York: National Association of Social Workers, 1964), p. 301.

[2]After having been a staunch proponent of mandatory breast-feeding for all children, in 1938 the Children's Bureau released a statement suggesting that while breast-feeding was good for a child's health, it could have harmful psychological effects in some situations, including illegitimacy. The statement also praised recent advances in artificial feeding. Soon after this public change of position, the states rescinded breast-feeding legislation. See "Legislation and Regulations Relating to Separation of Babies from Their Mother," *The Child* 3 (July 1938):19–21.

[3]See Philip Wylie, *The Generation of Vipers* (New York: Farrar and Rinehart, Inc., 1942) at the beginning of the period, and Daniel Patrick Moynihan, *The Negro Family: The Case for National Action* (Washington, D.C.: Government Printing Office, 1965), at the end.

[4]Elaine Tyler May, *Homeward Bound: American Families in the Cold War Era* (New York: Basic Books, 1988), p. 96.

[5]Ibid., p. 70.

[6]Ibid., pp. 96, 67.

[7]Leontine Young, "Personality Patterns in Unmarried Mothers," in *Understanding the Psychology of the Unmarried Mother* (New York: Family Service Association of America, 1947), p. 13.

[8]See, for example, Ferdinand Lundberg and Marynia F. Farnham, *Modern Women: The Lost Sex* (New York: Harper and Brothers, 1947), chapter 11.

[9]Sara Edlin, *The Unmarried Mother in Our Society* (New York: Farrar, Straus and Young, 1954),pp. 128–9.

[10]An excellent history of these efforts is Winifred Bell, *Aid to Dependent Children* (New York: Columbia University Press, 1965).

[11]Bell, *Aid to Dependent Children*, p. 188.

[12]See Bell, *Aid to Dependent Children*, and Thomas Littlewood, *The Politics of Population Control* (Notre Dame, IN: Notre Dame University Press, 1977), chapter 7.

[13]"The Current Attack on ADC in Louisiana," September 16, 1960, folder: National Urban League, New York City, Florence Crittenton Association of America Papers

(hereafter cited as FCAA Papers), Social Welfare History Archives, University of Minnesota (hereafter cited as SWHA).

[14]See Joan Jacobs Brumberg, " 'Ruined Girls': Changing Community Responses to Illegitimacy in Upstate New York, 1890–1920," *Journal of Social History* 18 (Winter 1984):262, for a discussion and references to the medical and social work focus in the Progressive Era, on the illegitimate baby, not the mother.

[15] Ripple, "Social Work Standards," p. 300.

[16]Maud Morlock, "Meetings to Discuss Services to Unmarried Mothers," March 20, 1950, Box 455, File 7–4–3–2, Record Group 102, National Archives (hereafter cited as N.A.).

[17]See, for example, Henry J. Meyer, Edgar F. Borgatta, and David Fanshel, "Unwed Mothers' Decisions About Their Babies; An Interim Replication Study," *Child Welfare* 38 (February 1959):5–6; and Stephen Fleck, M.D., "Pregnancy As a Symptom of Adolescent Maladjustment," *International Journal of Social Psychiatry* 2 (Autumn 1956):21.

[18]Young, *Out of Wedlock*, chapter 5, p. 80.

[19]See Chapter Two.

[20]In 1960, 79 percent of all children adopted by a nonrelative were born to single girls and women. See "Material Prepared for House Appropriations Committee," January 1962, Box 893, file 7–4–3–0, Record Group 102, N.A.

[21]Janice P. Montague, "Acceptance or Denial—The Therapeutic Use of the Mother-Baby Relationship," paper presented at the Florence Crittenton Association of America Northeast Conference, 1964.

[22]Helen H. Perlman, "Unmarried Mothers, Immorality and the ADC," paper presented at Annual Conference of Florence Crittenton Association of American, in conjunction with the National Conference on Social Welfare, 1963.

[23]See, for example, Mary Jane Sherfey, M.D.,"The Evolution of the Nature of Female Sexuality in Relation to Psychoanalytic Theory," *Journal of the American Psychoanalytic Association* 14 (January 1966):121. Mary Beth Norton draws on John Demos's analysis of seventeenth-century witchcraft episodes in New England to make the point that, "Attention to the antithesis of maternity is, of course, precisely what one would anticipate in a society in which motherhood had taken on such significance." Mary Beth Norton, "The Evolution of White Women's Experience in Early America," *American Historical Review* 89 (June 1984):611. The same point could be made about the social construction of unwed motherhood as the "antithesis of maternity" in an era that was committed to the "glorification" of motherhood.

[24]See Thomas M. Shapiro, *Population Control Politics: Women, Sterilization and Reproductive Choice* (Philadelphia: Temple University Press, 1985), chapter 1.

[25]Ibid., 25, and Littlewood, *The Politics of Population Control,* p. 177.

[26]A social work theorist of the era noted that ,"[W]hite [illegitimate], physically healthy babies are considered by many to be a social boon, an asset. . . .Sometimes social workers in adoption agencies have facetiously suggested setting up social provisions for 'more baby breeding.' " Helen H. Perlman, "Unmarried Mothers," p. 274.

[27]In the 1950s, the surviving old guard of service providers, such as Dr. Robert Barrett, retired head of the National Florence Crittenton Mission, were deeply uncomfortable with newer institutional policies and practices mandating adoption of illegitimate infants. In 1952, Dr. Barrett wrote to Virgil Payne, the first national director of the newly formed Florence Crittenton Association of America, "Personally, I feel very badly that a girl in our Homes shall not be given every opportunity and help to keep her baby if she wants to. Often a girl who has made up her mind to give up her baby

feels different when the baby comes and her mother's instinct is aroused. Not to give her that chance seems a cruel and unnatural proceedings [sic]." Robert Barrett to Virgil Payne, December 23, 1952, folder 3:25, National Florence Crittenton Mission Papers, SWHA. Ironically, the most forward-looking maternity home administrators felt the same way. Mrs. Lillian Bye, executive director of the Crittenton-Hastings House in Boston, appealed publicly for "another look at the modern policy of putting nearly all children born to unmarried mothers out for adoption." She asked, "Are we doing the right thing. . .[pressuring] a young woman to give up her baby?" *Boston Globe,* March 31, 1959.

[28]Maud Morlock, June 11, 1952, Box 456, File 7–4–3–1, Record Group 102, N.A.

[29]Eighty percent more children were adopted in 1944 than in 1953; 50 percent of all children adopted were born out of wedlock, a 55 percent increase since 1944. Chief, Social Statistics Section to Martha Eliot, February 10, 1955, Box 689, File 7–4–0–3, Record Group 102, N.A. Also see Mary Beth Weinstein, "Markets, Black and Gray, in Babies," *New York Times Magazine,* November 27, 1955, p. 12.

[30]Ruth Pagan to Louise Noble, October 15, 1956, Box 691, File 7–4–3–1–1, Record Group 102, N.A.

[31]Lillian Bye to Sibley Higgenbotham, August 8, 1958, Box 894, File 7–4–3–1–1, Record Group 102, N.A.

[32]"Material Prepared for House Appropriations Committee," January 1962.

[33]See, for example, Maud Morlock to Executive Secretary, Council of Community Agencies, Nashville, August 11, 1949, Box 454, File 7–4–0–6, N.A.; Maud Morlock to Jane Wrieden, Salvation Army, September 28, 1951, File 7–4–2–1, Box 455, N.A.; Annie Lee Davis, "Attitudes Toward Minority Groups: Their Effect on Social Services for Unmarried Mothers," paper presented at National Conference on Social Welfare, 1948; "Memo to Executive Committee, Division of Family and Child Welfare from Committee on Services to Unmarried Mothers," January 31, 1958, FCAA Papers, Box 7, Folder: Committee on Services to Unmarried Mothers, Welfare Council of Metropolitan Chicago, SWHA.

[34]Hazel McCalley, "The Community Looks at Illegitimacy," FCAA Papers, Box 3, Folder: FCAA Annual 11th, 1960–61, SWHA.

[35]"Minutes of Ad Hoc Committee on Services to Unmarried Mothers, Division of Family and Child Welfare, Welfare Council of Metropolitan Chicago," April 17, 1961, FCAA Papers, File: "Other Organizations," SWHA.

[36]Ursula Gallagher to Mrs. Hynning, September 17, 1959, Box 983, File 7–4–3–0, Record Group 102, N.A.

[37]Lillian Dinniman, "Meeting the Needs for Services to Unmarried Mothers," paper presented at the Midwest Area Conference of the Florence Crittenton Association of America, 1964.

[38]A government report published in 1960 noted that, "It appears that the non-white population is supporting and caring for as many as 1.2 million illegitimate children without public assistance funds." *Illegitimacy and Its Impact on the Aid to Dependent Children Program: Implications for Federal and State Administrators,* Public Assistance Report No. 41, U.S. Department of Health, Education and Welfare (Washington, D.C.: Government Printing Office, 1960), p. 36.

[39]Ursula Gallagher, September 17, 1959, Box 893, File 7–4–3–0, Record Group 102, N.A.

[40]Maud Morlock to Dwight Ferguson, November 19, 1951, Box 456, File 7–4–3–1–1, Record Group 102, N.A.

[41]Leontine Young, "Is Money Our Trouble?", paper presented at the National Conference on Social Welfare, 1953.

[42]Ursula Gallagher to Mary Louise Pyle, December 3, 1959, Box 893, File 7–4–3–0, Record Group 102, N.A.

[43]The founding of *Playboy* magazine in 1953, its subsequent popularity and imitators, and the assumption concerning children as "mother's products" implicit in the most successful childcare manual of the era, *Baby and Child Care*, by Dr. Spock, are the two most obvious manifestations of this trend. See Nancy P. Weiss, "Mother, The Invention of Necessity," *American Quarterly* (Winter 1977):519–46.

[44]See, for example, *New York Times*, August 28, 1960, which quotes Louisiana governor Jimmie H. Davis justifying the recent state legislation targeting "those who make it their business to produce illegitimate children."

[45]*The New York Times*, March 4, 1958.

[46]U.S. Congress, House of Representatives, Committee on Ways and Means, *Hearings on the Public Assistance Titles of the Social Security Act, April 12, 13, 16, 19, 20, 1956* (84th Congress, 2d sess., [Washington, D.C.: Government Printing Office, 1965]), p. 60.

[47]*Atlanta Constitution*, January 25, 1951.

[48]"A Study of Negro Adoptions," *Child Welfare* 38 (February 1959):33, quoting David Fanshel, *A Study in Negro Adoptions* (New York: Child Welfare League of America, 1957). "In moving from white to Negro adoptions we are moving from what economists would call a 'seller's market' . . . to a 'buyer's market.' "

[49]See, for example, Lydia Hylton, "Trends in Adoption," *Child Welfare* 44 (February 1966):377–86. Hylton cites the figures 182 white applicants for every one hundred white infants in the mid-1960s, although higher ratios obtained earlier in the period of this study. In 1960, a government report claimed that in some communities, there were ten suitable applicants for every white infant. *Illegitimacy and Its Impact*," p. 28.

[50]*Arkansas Gazette*, September 1, 1959.

[51]*New York Times*, July 7, 1961.

[52]*New York Times*, August 9, 1959. In late 1958, average monthly family grants in the ADC program were $99.83 nationally, but in the south, ranged between $27.09 in Alabama and $67.73 in Texas, Bell, *Aid to Dependent Children*, p. 224.

[53] *Facts, Fallacies and the Future: A Study of the ADC Program of Cook County, Illinois* (New York: Greenleigh Associates, 1960), p. 29.

[54] McCalley, "The Community Looks at Illegitimacy."

[55]Florida Department of Public Welfare, "Suitable Home Law" (Jacksonville, 1962), pp. 25–6, quoted in Bell, *Aid to Dependent Children*, p. 132.

[56]Clark Vincent, "Illegitimacy and Value Dilemmas," *Christian Century* 80 (June 19, 1963):806.

[57] *Illegitimacy and Its Impact*, p. 28.

[58]Katherine B. Oettinger, "Current Concerns of the Children's Bureau," *Children* 5 (May–June 1958):123–8.

[59]John H. Hall, "An Experimental Program for Unmarried Mothers," *Child Welfare* 30 (May, 1951):14.

[60]Alice Lake, "Why Young Girls Sell Their Babies," *Cosmopolitan*, December 1956, p. 45ff.

[61]Lena Heyman to Genevieve Griffin, January 3, 1963, Box 1038, File 7–4–3–0, Record Group 102, N.A.

[62]"Letters," *Ladies' Home Journal*, March 1958, pp. 4, 53.

[63]Irene M. Josselyn, "The Unmarried Mother," in Ralph Slovenko, ed., *Sexual Behavior and the Law* (Springfield, IL: Charles Thomas, 1965), p. 376.

[64]See, for example, Ruth Butcher and Marion Robinson, *Girls and Women Who Become Unmarried Mothers*, (New York: Public Affairs Commission, 1958).

[65]Maud Morlock, "Field Report, Texas, 1950," Box 455, File 7–4–0–7–4, Record Group 102, N.A.

[66]See Patricia Garland, "Teenage Illegitimacy in the Urban Ghetto," in *Unmarried Parenthood: Clues to Agency and Community Action* (New York: National Council on Illegitimacy, 1967), pp. 24–39.

[67]Margaret Thornhill, "Problems of Repeated Out-of-Wedlock Pregnancies," *Child Welfare* 38 (June 1959): 1.

[68]Edwin Schur, *Labeling Women Deviant: Gender, Stigma and Social Control* (Philadelphia: Temple University Press, 1983), p. 44.

[69]See, for example, Leontine Young, *Out of Wedlock*, chapter 2. On the other hand, Mignon Sauber and Elaine Rubinstein, who conducted a comprehensive and methodologically sophisticated study of unmarried mothers in New York in the early 1960s, showed that more than 80 percent of the girls had known the father for at least a year before the birth of the baby, and 60 percent were in touch eighteen months later. Mignon Sauber and Elaine Rubinstein, *Experience of the Unwed Mother as a Parent* (New York: Community Council of Greater New York, 1965).

[70]*New York Times*, August 9, 1959.

[71] Wylie, *The Generation of Vipers*, p. 195.

[72]See, for example, Mary Rall, "Conference on Work with Unmarried Mothers, Phoenix," Box 454, File 7–4–0–4, Record Group 102, N.A.

[73]Maud Morlock to Ruth Pagan, February 5, 1952, Box 455, File 7–4–2–2, Record Group 102, N.A.

[74]Elizabeth Herzog to Harry Roberts, December 14, 1959, Box 892, File 7–4–0–1, Record Group 102, N.A.

[75]The Children's Bureau did fund a major project in California in 1963 that studied services for and characteristics of unmarried fathers. This project, however, targeted a relatively elite group of young men, socioeconomically. Among the findings of this study was that 50 percent of the fathers saw the female whom they had impregnated as the aggressor, sexually. Reuben Pannor, et al, *The Unmarried Father: New Approaches for Helping Unmarried Young Parents* (New York: Springer Publishing Company, 1971), p. 71.

[76]Rose Bernstein, *Helping Unmarried Mothers* (New York: Association Press, 1971), p. 161.

[77]Katherine T. Kinkead, "The Lonely Time," *The New Yorker*, January 20, 1951, p. 33.

[78]Ibid., p. 155.

[79] Bell, *Aid to Dependent Children*, pp. 81–4.

[80]*Chicago Sun-Times*, April 27, 1950.

[81]Robert Viet Sherwin, "The Law and Sexual Relationships," *Journal of Social Issues* 22 (April 1966):113–14

[82]Harold Rosen, "The Emotionally Sick Pregnant Woman," in Harold Rosen, ed., *Therapeutic Abortion* (New York: Julian Press, 1954), pp. 235–6. Also see, for example,

A. S. Levine, "The Problem of Psychiatric Disturbances in Relation to Therapeutic Abortion," *Albert Einstein Medical Center Journal* 6 (1958):73–8.

[83]See, for example, Sidney Bolter, "The Psychiatrist's Role in Therapeutic Abortion: The Unwitting Accomplice," *American Journal of Psychiatry* 119 (September 1962): 312–16 and J. V. O'Sullivan and L. Fairchild, "The Case Against Termination on Psychiatric Grounds," *Mental Health* 20 (Autumn 1960):97–101.

[84]About one out of eight women who first married between 1955 and 1959 were pregnant when they became brides. Clyde V. Kiser, Wilson H. Grabil, and Arthur A. Campbell, *Trends and Variations in Fertility in the United States* (Cambridge, MA: Harvard University Press, 1968), p. 134.

[85]In 1990, a prominent antichoice bumper sticker slogan reads, "Adoption: The Non-Violent Alternative."

[86]See Chapter Seven.

Chapter Two

[1]David Glass to Julius Paul, October 11, 1958; quoted in Julius Paul, "The Return of Punitive Sterilization Proposals," *Law and Society Review* 3 (August 1968):89.

[2]See, for example, *Illegitimacy and Its Impact on the Aid to Dependent Children Program: Implications for Federal and State Administrators,* Bureau of Public Assistance, Department of Health, Education and Welfare (Washington, D.C.: Government Printing Office, 1960), pp. 52-3.

[3]Mimi Abramovitz, *Regulating the Lives of Women: Social Policy from Colonial Times to the Present* (Boston: South End Press, 1988). Abramovitz compares the midtwentieth century attack on ADC with the attacks in 1820 and 1870 on outdoor relief, p. 320.

[4]See, for example, Taylor Branch, *Parting the Waters: America in the King Years, 1954-1963* (New York: Simon and Schuster, 1989).

[5]Jacqueline Jones, *Labor of Love, Labor of Sorrow: Black Women, Work and the Family From Slavery to the Present* (New York, Vintage Books: 1986), p. 288.

[6]Ira Reiss, "Pre-marital Sexual Permissiveness Among Negroes and Whites," *American Sociological Review* 2 (October 1964):688-97.

[7]See, for example, Jacquelyn Dowd Hall, " 'The Mind That Burns in Each Body': Women, Rape and Racial Violence," in Ann Snitow, Christine Stansell and Sharon Thompson, eds., *Powers of Desire: The Politics of Sexuality* (New York: Monthly Review Press, 1983), p. 329.

[8]Barbara Omolade, "Hearts of Darkness," in *Powers of Desire*, pp. 351-2.

[9]Herbert Gutman, "Marital and Sexual Norms Among Slave Women," in Nancy Cott and Elizabeth Pleck, eds., *A Heritage of Her Own: Toward a Social History of American Women* (New York: Simon and Schuster, 1979), p. 305.

[10]Carl Degler, *Autobiographical Accounts of Negro Ex-Slaves* (Nashville: Fisk University Press, 1968), p. 1.

[11]Omolade, "Hearts of Darkness," p. 354.

[12] *New York Times*, December 29, 1956.

[13]U.S. Congress, House, District of Columbia Committee, Investigation of Public School Conditions; *Hearings Before the Special Subcommittee to Investigate Public School Standards and Conditions and Juvenile Delinquency in the District of Columbia,* September

19-October 1, 1956 (84th Cong., 2d sess. [Washington, D.C.: Government Printing Office, 1956]), p. 1.

[14]Ibid., p. 76.

[15]Ibid., pp. 132, 123, 43, 61.

[16]*New York Times*, December 29, 1956.

[17]See Joseph L. Morrison, "Illegitimacy Sterilization and Racism: A North Carolina Case History," *Social Service Review* 36 (March 1965): 1-10.

[18]*Richmond News Leader*, March 22, 1957.

[19]Morrison, "Illegitimacy, Sterilization, and Racism," p. 4.

[20] *New York Times*, June 15, 1960.

[21] "Chicago Committee on Services to Unmarried Parents, Minutes, March 5, 1959,"Florence Crittenton Association of America Papers, (hereafter cited as FCAA Papers), File: Chicago Committee on Services to Unmarried Parents, Box 7, Social Welfare History Archives, University of Minnesota (hereafter cited as SWHA).

[22]"Unwed Mothers—even experts are stumped about how to treat them," *Journal of Housing* 11 (Spring 1959):290.

[23]Ibid.; also see "Litigation Forces Review of Public Housing Prohibition Against Families with Illegitimate Children," *Welfare Law Bulletin* 8 (May 1967):3, and "Public Housing Prohibition Against Families with Illegitimate Children," *Welfare Law Bulletin* 9 (July 1967):7.

[24]Mignon Sauber and Janice Paneth, "Unwed Mothers Who Keep Their Children: Research and Implications," in *Proceedings of the National Conference of Social Welfare* (New York: Family Service Association of America, 1965), p. 103.

[25]*New York Times*, December 10, 1965.

[26]Mignon Sauber and Elaine Rubinstein, *Experiences of the Unwed Mother as a Parent* (New York: Community Council of Greater New York, 1965), p. 68-9.

[27]Richmond, Virginia, to President Truman, 1949, Box 457, File 7-4-3-1-4, Record Group 102, National Archives (hereafter cited as N.A.).

[28]Lelia Bowden, "Report of a Panel Discussion on the Hospital Experience of the Unmarried Mother, March 25, 1958," FCAA Papers, Box 7, File: Community Council of Greater New York, 1958, SWHA. Also see Katherine Oettinger, "The Most Profound Challenge," *Children* 12 (November-December 1965):214, in which the chief of the Children's Bureau noted that in the first nine months of 1964, in New York City, 443 well babies were "left in hospitals by mothers who simply walked out because they had no way of caring for them."

[29]*New York Times*, December 10, 1965.

[30]See, for example, Theodore White, *The Making of the President 1964* (New York: Antheneum Publishers, 1965), pp. 227-30.

[31]Julius Horwitz, "The Arithmetic of Delinquency," *New York Times Magazine*, January 31, 1965, p. 12ff.

[32]M. Elaine Burgess and Daniel O. Price, *An American Dependency Challenge* (Chicago: American Public Welfare Association, 1963), pp. 42, 147. To some extent, exclusionary public policies discussed in this chapter probably accounted for some of the decline for blacks. There was also a slight decline in black illegitimacy rates at this time. See *Trends in Illegitimacy in the United States, 1940-1965*, Department of Health, Education and Welfare (Washington, D.C.: Government Printing Office, February, 1968), p. 5. See Michael Katz, *The Undeserving Poor: From the War on Poverty to the War on Welfare* (New York: Pantheon, 1989), p. 48, for a discussion of policy

initiatives during this period which caused fluctuations in the ADC numbers, independent of the number of eligible poor in the population.

[33]Margaret Thornhill, "Problems of Repeated Out of Wedlock Pregnancies," *Child Welfare* 38 (June 1959):2.

[34]Philadelphia to President Truman, 1948, Box 166, File 7-4-3-1-4, Record Group 102, N.A.

[35]Maud Morlock to Sister Mary Assisium, New York Foundling Hospital, February 2, 1950, Box 455, File 7-4-3-0, Record Group 102, N.A.

[36]Norfolk, Virginia, to the Children's Bureau, March 6, 1948, Box 166, File 7-4-3-1-4, Record Group 102, N.A.

[37]Greenwood, Mississippi, to Washington, December, 1949, Box 457, File 7-4-3-1-4, Record Group 102, N.A.

[38]Baltimore to the Children's Bureau, n.d., Box 457, File 7-4-3-1-4, Record Group 102, N.A.

[39]See, for example, Maud Morlock to Executive Secretary, Council of Community Agencies, Nashville, August 1, 1949, Box 454, File 7-4-0-6, Record Group 102, N.A.

[40]Maud Morlock to Jane Wrieden, September 28, 1951, Box 455, File 7-4-3-1-1, Record Group 102, N.A.

[41]Sauber and Rubinstein, *Experiences of the Unwed Mother*, p. 136.

[42]Renee Berg, "A Study of A Group of Unwed Mothers Receiving ADC," D.S.W. dissertation, University of Pennsylvania, 1962, p. 80.

[43]Ibid., p. 34.

[44]Ibid., p. 82.

[45]*Chicago Tribune*, May 3, 1962.

[46]*Buffalo Courier Express*, December 5, 1957.

[47]See, for example, Winifred Bell, *Aid to Dependent Children* (New York: Columbia University Press, 1965).

[48]Berg, "A Study of A Group of Unwed Mothers," pp. 77-8.

[49]Bell, *Aid to Dependent Children*, is the best source on the efforts of many state legislatures to save money in this way.

[50]*Atlanta Constitution*, January 25, 1951.

[51]Morrison, "Illegitimacy, Sterilization and Racism," p. 3.

[52]See Charles Reich, "Searching Homes of Public Assistant Recipients: The Issues Under the Social Security Act," *Social Service Review* 37 (December 1963):328-39.

[53]This assumption suggests another example of the association in the minds of whites between black women, sex, and money.

[54]*Phoenix Gazette*, May 21, 1962.

[55]*New York Times*, July 20, 1961

[56]Hodding Carter to Julius Paul, September 26, 1958, quoted in Julius Paul, "The Return of Punitive Sterilization Proposals," p. 89.

[57]Helen H. Perlman, "Unmarried Mothers, Immorality and the ADC Program," paper presented at the Annual Conference of the Florence Crittenton Association of America, National Conference on Social Welfare, 1963.

[58]Howard Osofsky, *The Pregnant Teenager: A Medical, Educational and Social Analysis* (Springfield, IL: Charles C. Thomas Publishers, 1966), p. 88.

[59]*Washington Post*, January 27, 1965.

[60]Meg Greenfield, " 'The Welfare Chiselers' of Newburgh, New York," *The Reporter*, August 17, 1961, p. 39.

[61] White, *The Making of the President 1964* , chapter 8.

[62]Morrison, "Illegitimacy, Sterilization and Racism," p. 1.

[63] Paul, "The Return of Punitive Sterilization Proposals," p. 97.

[64]Ibid., p. 90.

[65]Joseph McD. Mitchell, "The Revolt in Newburgh," quoted in Lucy Komisar, *Down and Out in the USA* (New York: New Viewpoints, 1974), p. 86.

[66]Julius Paul reviews the terms of the debates in each state involved. See Paul, "The Return of Punitive Sterilization Proposals."

[67]Frank R. Breul, "Public Welfare: Safeguard or Free Ride?", *University of Chicago Magazine*, January 1962, p. 22.

[68]See the discussion in Chapter Seven concerning the relationship between the "population bomb" metaphor and democracy.

[69]Paul, "The Return of Sterilization Proposals," p. 81.

[70]Ibid.

[71]Morrison, "Illegitimacy, Sterilization and Racism," p. 5.

[72]Jewel Handy Gresham, "The Politics of Family in America," *The Nation*, July 24-31, 1989, p. 118.

[73]See Thomas Shapiro, *Population Control Politics: Women, Sterilization and Reproductive Choice* (Philadelphia: Temple University Press, 1985); Gerald C. Wright, "Racism and the Availability of Family Planning Services in the United States," *Social Forces* 56 (June 1978):1087-98; and Martha C. Ward, *Poor Women, Powerful Men: America's Great Experiment in Family Planning* (Boulder, CO: Westview Press, 1986). Racially specific sterilization practices did not end when technologically advanced methods of birth control became available. See Rosalind Pollack Petchesky, " 'Reproductive Choice' in the Contemporary United States: A Social Analysis of Female Sterilization," in Karen Michaelson, ed., *And the Poor Get Children* (New York: Monthly Review Press, 1981), pp. 50-88.

[74]*Washington Post*, January 27, 1965.

[75]*Illegitimacy and Its Impact* , p. 28.

[76]Joan Younger, "The Unmarried Mother," *Ladies' Home Journal*, June 1947, p. 107.

[77]Myrtle Robertson Byrd to Katherine Oettinger, April 9, 1957, Box 691, File 7-4-3-1-1, Record Group 102, N.A.

[78]See Bell, *Aid to Dependent Children*; and Abramovitz, *Regulating the Lives of Women*, p. 323.

[79]Mary Lois Pyles to Ursula Gallagher, July 13, 1960, Box 893, File 7-4-3-1, Record Group 102, N.A.

[80]Helen H. Perlman, "Unmarried Mothers," in Nathan E. Cohen, ed., *Social Work and Social Problems* (New York: National Association of Social Work, Inc., 1964), p. 305.

[81]*Detroit Free Press*, November 22, 1961

[82]Paul, "The Return of Punitive Sterilization Proposals," p. 93.

[83]See Horwitz, "The Arithmetic of Delinquency," in which he advocated institutionalizing all slum children because "It seems clear that [proper mothering] can be provided only in an institution," p. 55.

[84]Maud Morlock, Field Report, Texas, 1948, Box 165, File 7-4-3-1-1, Record Group 102, N.A.

[85]E. Franklin Frazier, *The Negro Family in the United States* (Chicago: University of Chicago Press, 1939).

[86]Ibid., p. 345

[87]Ibid., p. 347.

[88]Ibid., p. 343.

[89]Ibid., p. 348.

[90]Ibid., p. 343.

[91]See Deborah Gray White, *Ar'n't I A Woman: Female Slaves in the Plantation South* (New York: W.W. Norton, 1985), p. 166, for discussion of additional "worms" in Frazier's analysis.

[92]See Gunnar Myrdal, *The American Dilemma* (New York: Harper and Brothers, 1944); also see Katz, *The Undeserving Poor*.

[93]Annie Lee Davis to Babette Block, October 3, 1950, Box 455, File 7-4-2-1, Record Group 102, N.A.

[94]See, for example, White, *The Making of the President 1964*, chapter 8.

[95]Annie Lee Davis, "Attitudes Toward Minority Groups: Their Effect on Social Services for Unmarried Mothers," *The Child* 13 (1948):82-5.

[96]Annie Lee Davis to Babette Block, July 22, 1949, Box 455, File 7-4-2-1, Record Group 102, N.A.

[97]Ibid.

[98] Davis to Block, October 3, 1950.

[99]Annie Lee Davis to Amelia Schultz, June 11, 1947, Box 165, File 7-4-2-1, Record Group 102, N.A.

[100]Davis, "Attitudes Toward Minority Groups."

[101]Davis to Block, October 3, 1950.

[102]Ibid.

[103]Elizabeth Herzog and Hylan Lewis, "Priorities in Research on Unmarried Mothers," in *Research Perspectives on the Unmarried Mother* (New York: Child Welfare League of America, 1962), p. 35.

[104]Davis, "Attitudes Toward Minority Groups."

[105]Bess Williams, "Summary Remarks, San Francisco," February 20, 1951, Box 454, File 7-4-0-4, Record Group 102, N.A.

[106]*Facts, Fallacies and Future—A Study of the ADC Program of Cook County, Illinois* (New York: Greenleigh Associates, 1960), Introduction.

[107]A'Lelia Josephine Osili and Frieda Alice Parker, *A Study of Fifty Unmarried Negro Mothers in Pending and Active Aid to Dependent Children Cases in Marion County Department of Public Welfare* (Indianapolis: Marion County Department of Public Welfare, 1957).

[108]Barbara Griswold, Kermit Wiltse, and Robert Roberts, "Illegitimate Recidivism Among AFDC Clients," in *Unmarried Parenthood: Clues to Agency and Community Action* (New York: National Council on Illegitimacy, 1967), p. 20. Julius Horwitz in "The Arithmetic of Delinquency" also describes the typical black unwed mother as a mental patient.

[109]Patricia Garland, "Teenage Illegitimacy in Urban Ghettos," in *Unmarried Parenthood: Clues to Agency and Community Action*, p. 31.

[110]Davis to Block, October 3, 1950.

[111]Davis to Block, July 22, 1949.

[112]See Bell, *Aid to Dependent Children*. Also see Frances Fox-Piven and Richard A. Cloward, *Regulating the Poor: The Functions of Public Welfare* (New York: Vintage, 1972), p. 245.

[113]See *Social Service Review* 35 (June 1961):207-9 and 210-14 for text of "Decision of the Commissioner of Social Security in the Matter of the Louisiana Plan for Aid to Dependent Children Under Title IV of the Social Security Act"; and "Memorandum for the Commissioner of Social Security from the Secretary of Health, Education and Welfare."

[114]*Illegitimacy and Its Impact*, p. 3.

[115]See Bell, *Aid to Dependent Children*, pp. 211-2 for a comprehensive list of ADC/illegitimacy studies. See, also, *Children* 6 (July-August 1959):157, for a report on a South Dakota study, one of many. "Charged with looking into the increase in illegitimacy in relation to the aid-to-dependent-children program, a committee of South Dakota's legislative Research Council reported last fall that it had found no causal relationship between the two. . . .[T]he committee recommended against legislation that would place specific restrictions on the the amount of payments that mothers of illegitimate children might receive. . . ."

[116]Charles E. Bowerman, Donald Irish, and Hallowell Pope, *Unwed Motherhood: Personal and Social Consequences* (Chapel Hill: University of North Carolina, 1966), p. 368; see "Virginia League of Local Welfare Executives, Bulletin no.31," December 29, 1951, American Public Welfare Association Papers, Box 34, File 34:9, SWHA. This issue was still being addressed in the same terms in the late 1970s. For example, a study published in 1977 found that "neither the level of AFDC benefits nor AFDC acceptance rate appear to serve as economic incentives to out-of-wedlock child-bearing. . . ." Kristin Moore and Steven Caldwell, "The Effect of Government Policies on Out of Wedlock Sex and Pregnancy," *Family Planning Perspectives* 9 (July-August 1977):164.

[117]*New York Times*, November 19, 1959.

[118]Davis, "Attitudes Toward Minority Groups."

[119]U.S. Department of Health, Education and Welfare, "A Multidisciplinary Approach to a School-Centered Rehabilitation Program for Pregnant School-Aged Girls in Washington, D.C.: A Summary Report," by Elizabeth Goodman and Fabola M.L. Gill, Child Welfare Demonstration Grant No. D-130 (Washington D.C.: Government Printing Office: 1966), p. 14. It is interesting that the project directors, advocating a psychological approach to the treatment of unwed motherhood, never mention race in their project report. Project evaluators and the press did make it clear that the clientele was black.

[120]Ibid., "Evaluation Section".

[121]Davis, "Attitudes Toward Minority Groups"; also see Chapter Six.

[122]Maud Morlock, Field Report, Texas, 1950, Box 455, File 7-4-0-7-4, Record Group 102, N.A.

[123]Annie Lee Davis to Edith Lauer, April 28, 1948, Box 165, File 7-4-3-1-1, Record Group 102, N.A.

[124] See Marie Brown to Maud Morlock, April 5, 1951; Maud Morlock to Dwight Ferguson, November 2, 1950; Maud Morlock to Dwight Ferguson, May 2, 1950, Box 456, File 7-4-3-1-1, Record Group 102, N.A. In 1949, Ruth Pagan, the Salvation Army's consultant on women's programs, wrote to Maud Morlock about the Army's home in Cleveland, noting, "You will recall our Home there was opened at the request

of a certain group of Negro women." March 17, 1949, Box 456, File 7-4-3-1-1, Record Group 102, N.A.

[125]At this time, the Talbert Home was completely out of money and about to be closed permanently. It had just been denied funding for a project "specially beamed to help teenage unmarried pregnancies in multiproblem families," to be administered under the auspices of the Salvation Army. The Army was committed to providing services for blacks in the Central Hough area, nonetheless, and decided, apparently with community approval, to save services for blacks by amalgamating this all-black program with their integrated, though largely white, Booth Home. The woman who became the superintendent of the two merged programs, Mary Verner (later the third Consultant on Women's Programs for the Army) reported that when the decision was made to join the programs and move the black girls over to the Booth Home, the black girls "showed substantial concern . . . about integration," which Verner interpreted, insensitively, as "evidence of fear of change," a quasi-psychological diagnosis of the sort many practitioners felt free to impose on unwed mothers at this time. By the 1960s some white liberal practitioners applied such diagnoses as freely to blacks as to whites. Mary Verner, "Effective Techniques of Communication with and Rehabilitation of Hard-to-Reach Out-of-Wedlock Families," paper presented at the Annual Meeting of the National Conference on Social Welfare, May 1963.

[126]Mrs. Revelle to Mrs Ketcham, n.d. (early 1950s), National Florence Crittenton Mission Papers (hereafter cited as NFCM), Box 3, File 20, SWHA.

[127]Annie Lee Davis to Louis Noble, n.d. (late 1940s), Box 165, File 7-4-3-1-1, Record Group 102, N.A.

[128]Maud Morlock, Field Report, Ohio, 1950, Box 455, File 7-4-3-0, Record Group 102, N.A.

[129]Annie Lee (Davis) Sandusky to Ursula Gallagher and Maud Morlock, June 27, 1958, Box 894, File 7-4-3-1-1, Record Group 102, N.A.

[130]Maud Morlock, Field Report, Chicago, 1947, Box 164, File 7-4-0-7-6, Record Group 102, N.A.

[131]Mrs. Eugene Revelle, Field Secretary's Report, October 1952, NFCM Papers, Box 3, File 25, SWHA.

[132]*Report of Services, 1960* (Chicago: Florence Crittenton Association of America, 1960).

[133]*Maternity Home Directory* (Cleveland: National Association on Services to Unmarried Parents, 1960), pp. 17, 24, 43, 57, 129.

[134]Robert Barrett to Mrs. Revelle, June 22, 1954, NFCM Papers, Box 1, File 4, SWHA.

[135]Mrs. Arthur Heuberer to Virgil Payne, November 13, 1956; and Virgil Payne to Mrs. Arthur Heuberer, November 16, 1956, FCAA Papers, Box 2, File: "Executive Committee," SWHA.

[136] Heuberer to Payne, November 13, 1956. The Salvation Army maintained integrated maternity homes throughout this period. See, for example, Maud Morlock, Field Report, Jersey City, 1948, Box 165, File 7-4-3-1, Record Group 102, N.A. The FCAA faced the issue as a national organization for the first time in the early postwar period when its affiliates in southern states were reluctant to sign the national charter governing the restructured organization because they feared they would be "compelled to take Negroes in their homes," Robert S. Barrett to Mrs. Eugene Revelle, December 30, 1949. NFCM Papers, Box 3, File 20, SWHA.

[137]Morlock, Field Report, Ohio, 1949.

[138]Maud Morlock to Christine Mulbach, May 16, 1955, Box 691, File 7-4-3-1-1, Record Group 102, N.A.

[139]Maud Morlock, Field Report, Kentucky, 1948, Box 165, File 7-4-3-1-1, Record Group 102, N.A.

[140]Morlock, Field Report, Ohio, 1949.

[141]Mrs. Helen K. Anderson, "Whom We Serve," paper presented at the Southern Area Conference, Florence Crittenton Association of America, 1964.

[142]Robbie Patterson to Reba B. Smith, May 7, 1947, NFCM Papers, Box 7, File 74, SWHA.

[143] (Davis) Sandusky to Gallagher, June 27, 1958.

[144]Ursula Gallagher to Dwight Ferguson, March 21, 1960, Box 893, File 7-4-3-1, Record Group 102, N.A.

[145]Jane Wrieden to Maud Morlock, n.d. (c. 1948), Box 456, File 7-4-3-1-1, Record Group 102, N.A.

[146]Maud Morlock, Field Report, Jersey City, 1948, Box 165, File 7-4-3-1-1, Record Group 102, N.A.

[147] Ibid.

[148]Marian Bowman to Maud Morlock, November 7, 1951, Box 456, File 7-4-3-1-1, Record Group 102, N.A.

[149]Mrs. Eugene Revelle to Mrs. Esther M. Ulrich, December 9, 1949, NFCM Papers, Box 3, File 20, SWHA.

[150]Ruth Pagan to Maud Morlock, March 17, 1949, Box 456, File 7-4-3-1-1, Record Group 102, N.A.

[151]Carolyn Sollis, Report of Consultant/Executive Director's Report, 1961-62, FCAA Papers, Box 2, File: FCAA Executive Director's Reports, 1959-62, SWHA.

[152]Meeting of Executive Committee, Minutes, March 19-20, 1961, FCAA Papers, Box 2, File Executive Committee, SWHA.

[153]Morlock, Field Report, Chicago, 1947; and Maud Morlock, Field Report, New York, 1948, Box 165, File 7-4-3-1-1, Record Group 102, N.A.

[154]Grace Knox to Reba B. Smith, April 12, 1949, FCHM Papers, Box 8, File 88, SWHA.

[155]Morlock, Field Report, Texas, 1950.

[156]Ibid.

[157]Ibid.

[158]Executive Committee Meeting, March 28-30, 1962, FCAA Papers, Box 2, File: Executive Committee Meetings, SWHA.

[159]See Chapter Four.

[160]Ursula Gallagher to Dwight Ferguson , March 21, 1960.

[161]See, for example, William Rashbaum, Janice Paneth, Helen Behr and Martin Greenberg, "Use of Social Services by Unmarried Mothers," *Children* 10 (January-February 1963):11-16; and Blanche Bernstein and Mignon Sauber, *Deterrents to Early Prenatal Care and Social Services Among Women Women Pregnant Out of Wedlock*, (Albany: New York State Department of Social Welfare, April 1961).

[162]Morrison, "Illegitimacy, Sterilization and Racism," p. 10.

[163]Raleigh Hobson to Kate Helms, June 11, 1962, Box 893, File 7-4-3-0, Record Group 102, N.A.

[164]See for example, Sauber and Rubinstein, *Experiences of the Unwed Mother As a*

Parent, pp. 129-33; and Ursula Gallagher, Field Report, New York City, 1958, Box 892, File 7-4-0-4, Record Group 102, N.A.

[165]See, for example, Rose Bernstein, "Are We Still Stereotyping the Unmarried Mother?", *Social Work* 5 (July 1960):22-38.

[166]See Michael Katz, *The Undeserving Poor.*

[167]Clark Vincent, *Unmarried Mothers* (Glencoe, IL: The Free Press, 1961), p. 20.

[168]See, for example, Herzog and Lewis, "Priorities in Research."

[169]Elizabeth Herzog to Mignon Sauber, May 27, 1960, Box 892, File 7-4-0-3, Record Group 102, N.A.

[170]See Katz, *The Undeserving Poor,* chapters 1-3.

[171]Ibid. Katz demonstrates that the identification of such characteristics was not always meant by culture of poverty theorists to suggest inhering, biological imperatives, but the theory was often interpreted this way nonetheless. In the same way, theorists often intended for culture of poverty to clearly distinguish class behavior from racial behavior, but when the theory was interpreted, such distinctions were often ignored.

[172]Elizabeth Herzog, "Unmarried Mothers: Some Questions to Be Answered and Some Answers to Be Questioned," *Child Welfare* 41 (October 1962):347.

[173]Elizabeth Herzog, "Some Assumptions About the Poor," *Social Service Review* 37 (December 1963):394.

[174]See the special issue on sexuality of the *Journal of Social Issues* 22 (April 1964), ed. Ira Reiss, "The Sexual Renaissance in America." Also see Chapter Seven.

[175]Studies also sometimes denied blacks a distinctive decision-making process by finding that black women simply supported white, middle-class norms. See, for example, Joseph Hines, "Some Reactions to a Hypothetical Premarital Pregnancy by 100 Negro College Girls," *Journal of Marriage and the Family* 26 (August 1964):344. Despite Hines's claim, his data does not demonstrate this similarity.

[176]Herzog, "Some Assumptions About the Poor," pp. 398-9.

[177]Ibid., p. 399.

[178]Herzog and Lewis, "Priorities in Research," p. 37.

[179]Ibid.

[180]See, for example, "Samuel H. Lowrie, "Early Marriage: Premarital Pregnancy and Associated Factors," *Journal of Marriage and the Family* 27 (February 1965):48-55; Harold T. Christensen and Hanna H. Meissner, "Studies in Child Spacing III - Premarital Pregnancy As a Factor in Divorce," *American Sociological Review* 18 (December 1953): 641-4; Harold T. Christensen and Bette B. Rubinstein, "Pre-marital Pregnancy and Divorce: A Follow-up Study by the Interview Method," *Marriage and Family Living* 18 (May 1956):114-23.

[181]Berg, "A Study of a Group of Unwed Mothers," p. 57.

[182]Ibid., p. 75.

[183]See Daniel Patrick Moynihan, *The Negro Family: The Case for National Action* (Washington, D.C.: Government Printing Office, 1965) and Lee Rainwater and William Yancey, *The Moynihan Report and the Politics of Controversy* (Cambridge, MA: MIT Press, 1969).

[184]See, for example, Bowerman, *Unwed Motherhood,* p. 146.

[185]Berg, "A Study of a Group of Unwed Mothers," p. 96.

[186]Bowerman, p. 312.

[187]Ellery Reed and Ruth Latimer, *A Study of Unmarried Mothers Who Kept Their Babies* (Cincinnati: Social Welfare Research, Inc., 1963), Casework Section, p. 2.

[188]Herzog, "Some Assumptions About the Poor," p. 400.

[189]Reed and Latimer, *A Study of Unmarried Mothers*, Casework Section, p. 2.

[190]Ibid.

[191]Perlman, "Unmarried Mothers," p. 303.

[192]Sauber and Paneth, "Unwed Mothers Who Keep Their Children," p. 97.

[193]St. Clair Drake and Horace R. Clayton, *Black Metropolis: A Study of Negro Life in a Northern City* (New York: Harcourt Brace & Co., 1945), p. 592.

[194]Berg, "A Study of a Group of Unwed Mothers," p. 32.

[195]Ibid., p. 109.

[196]Reed and Latimer, "A Study of Unmarried Mothers," Casework Section, p. 2.

[197]Patricia Knapp and Sophie T. Cambria, "The Attitudes of Negro Unmarried Mothers Toward Illegitimacy," *Smith College Studies in Social Work* 17 (September 1946-June 1947):188.

[198]Deborah Shapiro, "Attitudes, Values, and Unmarried Motherhood," in *Unmarried Parenthood: Clues to Agency and Community Action* (New York: National Council on Illegitimacy, 1967), pp. 58-61.

[199]*Children* 11 (November-December 1964):240.

[200]Shapiro, "Attitudes, Values, and Unmarried Motherhood," p. 61.

[201]Sauber and Rubinstein, "Experiences of the Unwed Mother As Parent," pp. 135-8.

[202]Berg, "A Study of a Group of Unwed Mothers," p. 88.

[203]Sauber and Rubinstein, "Experiences of the Unwed Mother As Parent," p. 133.

[204]Perlman, "Unmarried Mothers," p. 319.

[205]Gresham, "The Politics of the Family," p. 117.

[206]Lynda Birke, *Women, Feminism and Biology: The Feminist Challenge* (New York: Methuen, 1986), pp. 34-5.

[207]Gresham, "The Politics of the Family," p. 120.

[208]Quoted in Salim Muwakkil, "Black Family's Ills Provoke New Concern," *In These Times*, June 12-25, 1985, p. 6.

[209]Melvin Zelnick and John Kanter, "U.S.: Exploratory Studies of Negro Fertility—Factors Relating to Illegitimacy," *Studies in Family Planning* 1 (December 1970):7. Interestingly, the authors do note on the following page that "Compared with a white girl of the same age, a Black girl finds it harder to get a job that will support her; she lacks the residential options open to whites, and she may be concerned about the discrimination she will encounter on leaving home."

[210]See Osfosky, *The Pregnant Teenager*, which explains that more blacks left school than whites and argues that school officials "urge earlier departure and quicker exclusion of blacks." Moreover, when a black girl left school, it was generally a permanent departure, whereas white girls tended to leave temporarily; pp. 63, 322.

Chapter Three

[1]This chapter first appeared in *Frontiers*, vol. 11, nos. 2 & 3, and is reprinted with permission of the *Frontiers* Editorial Collective. Nancy Mann was extraordinarily helpful in the preparation of this essay.

[2]Theorists and practitioners dealing with white single pregnancy did not generally take class differences into account. This was typical of social analysis in the postwar period and also reflects the fact that anybody's white baby had become valuable on the adoption market.

[3]See, for example, Ruth I. Workum, "Problems of the Unmarried Mother and Her Child," *Child Welfare League of America Bulletin* 11 (May 1924):1–13; W. E. McClure and Bronett Goldberg, "Intelligence of the Unmarried Mother," *The Psychological Clinic* 18 (May–June 1929):119–27; Charlotte Lowe, "Intelligence and Social Background of the Unmarried Mother," *Mental Hygiene* 4 (October 1927):783–94.

[4]See Michael Sedlak, "Young Women and the City: Adolescent Deviance and the Transformation of Educational Policy, 1870–1960," *History of Education Quarterly* 23 (Spring 1983):1–28 for a good description of the intentions and programs of the evangelical "rescue homes" sheltering unwed mothers in the late–19th and early–20th centuries. Also see Peggy Pascoe, *Relations of Rescue: The Search for Moral Authority in the American West, 1974–1939* (New York: Oxford, 1990) and Regina G. Kunzel, *The Girl Problem: Evangelicals, Social Workers, and Unmarried Mothers, 1890–1945* (New Haven: Yale University Press, forthcoming).

[5]Philip Solomon, M.D., and Morris Ward Kilgore, M.D., "The Psychiatric Case Conference in a Maternity Home Setting," American Protestant Hospital Association Conference, Salvation Army Session Papers, 1965, Accession No. 82–1, Salvation Army Archives.

[6]Jane E. Wrieden, "The Meaning of the Maternity Home," *Children* 3 (January– February 1956):24.

[7]Ibid., p. 22.

[8]James P. Cattell, M.D., "Psychodynamic and Clinical Observations in a Group of Unmarried Mothers," *American Journal of Psychiatry* 111 (November 1954):337–42.

[9]Edmund Pollock, "An Investigation into Certain Personality Characteristics of Unmarried Mothers," Ph.D. dissertation, New York University, 1957, p. 4.

[10]Harry G. Gianakon, M.D., "Ego Factors in the Separation of Unwed Mothers and Child," in *Casework Papers 1960* (New York: Family Service Association of America, 1960), p. 60.

[11]See, for example, Irene Phrydas, M.D., "Emotional Problems of the Unmarried Pregnant Girl and the Patterns of Denial Before and During Pregnancy," paper presented at the Southern Area Conference of the Florence Crittenton Association of America, Chattanooga, 1964, in *Papers from Midwestern, Southern and Western Area Conferences (1),* (Chicago: Florence Crittenton Association of America, 1964); Leontine Young, *Out of Wedlock* (New York: McGraw Hill, 1954), p. 35; and Stephen Fleck, M.D., "Pregnancy As a Symptom of Adolescent Maladjustment," *International Journal of Social Psychiatry* 2 (Autumn 1956):120–1.

[12] Young, *Out of Wedlock*, p. 31.

[13]Helene Deutsch, *The Psychology of Women*: vol. 2, *Motherhood* (New York: Grune and Stratton, 1945), p. 366.

[14] Fleck, "Pregnancy As a Symptom," p. 128.

[15] Pollock, "An Investigation into Certain Personality Characteristics," p. 55. Pollock cites an unpublished paper by Dr. Ner Littner as evidence.

[16]Cattell, in his study of fifty-four unmarried mothers, found that seventeen were schizophrenic; of those, seven were pseudo-neurotic and ten exhibited other types of schizophrenia. Thirty displayed character disorders, seven neurotic reactions such as anxiety (both depressive and conversion).

[17]See, for example, Fleck, "Pregnancy As a Symptom," pp. 126–7; Sara Edlin, *The Unmarried Mother in Our Society* (New York: Farrar, Straus, and Young, 1954), p. 86; Marcel Heiman, M.D., "Out of Wedlock Pregnancy in Adolescence," in *Casework Papers 1960* (New York: Family Service Association of America, 1960), pp. 65–74; Young, *Out of Wedlock*, p. 51; Pollock, "An Investigation into Certain Personality Characteristics," p. 140.

[18] Fleck, "Pregnancy as a Symptom," p. 129.

[19]Ibid., p. 123; and Edlin, *The Unmarried Mother*, p. 86.

[20]See, for example, Wayne E. Henderson, "An Investigation of the Unwed Mother's Relationships with Important People in Early Life and Cross Sectionally," Ph.D. dissertation, University of Tennessee, 1962.

[21]Gender confusion, or the alleged tendency of white, middle-class women to deny or reject their femininity, was a central preoccupation of psychiatrists in the postwar years. See Robert P. Odenwald, M.D., *The Disappearing Sexes: Sexual Behavior in the United States and the Emergence of Uni-Sex* (New York: Random House, 1965); and Barbara Ehrenreich and Deirdre English, *For Her Own Good: 150 Years of the Experts' Advice to Women* (New York: Doubleday 1979), chapter 8 for a discussion of the midcentury "epidemic of unwomanliness."

[22]Pollock, "An Investigation into Certain Personality Characteristics," p. 2.

[23]Fleck, "Pregnancy As a Symptom," p. 126.

[24]Catherine Donnell and Selma Glick, "Background Factors in One Hundred Cases of Jewish Unmarried Mothers," *The Jewish Social Service Quarterly* 29 (Winter 1952):152–60.

[25]Jane Judge, "Casework with the Unmarried Mother in a Family Agency," *Social Casework* 32 (January 1951):7–15.

[26]It is interesting to note that in the pre–*Roe* era, parents were much more easily blamed than they are today. Contemporary laws mandating parental notification for teenagers' abortions ignore the variable of abusive parental behavior.

[27]James Cattell, "Psychodynamic and Clinical Observations," p. 98.

[28]Katheryn M. Nielsen and Rocco L. Motto, "Some Observations on Family Constellations and Personality Patterns of Young Unmarried Mothers," *American Journal of Orthopsychiatry* 33 (July 1963):741.

[29]Miriam Powell, "Illegitimate Pregnancy in Emotionally Disturbed Girls," *Smith College Studies in Social Work* 19 (June 1949):171–9.

[30]Frances H. Scherz, " 'Taking Sides' in the Unmarried Mother's Conflict," in *Understanding the Psychology of the Unmarried Mother* (New York: Family Service Association of America, 1947), p. 22.

[31]Babette Block to Editor of the *Ladies' Home Journal*, March 29, 1949, Box 456, File 7–4–3–1, Record Group 102, National Archives (hereafter cited as N.A.).

[32]Ursula Gallagher, Field Report, September 8, 1958, Box 893, File 7–4–3–0, Record Group 102, N.A.

[33]Elaine Tyler May, *Homeward Bound: American Families in the Cold War Era* (New York: Basic Books, 1988), p. 96.

[34]Maud Morlock to Frances Whitefield, March 9, 1955, Box 691, File 7–4–3–1–1, Record Group 102, N.A.; Fleck, "Pregnancy As a Symptom," p. 126. Fleck found that "maternal rejection is more important in itself [as a source of illegitimate pregnancy] than the loss of the father through death or divorce, high as that incidence is."

[35]Fleck, p. 21.

[36]Leontine Young, "Personality Patterns in Unmarried Mothers," in *Understanding*

the Psychology of the Unmarried Mother" (New York: Family Service Association of America, 1947). Young wrote, "The girls dominated by their mothers . . . seemed to reduce the man to the position of a tool, a kind of biological accessory without reality or meaning as a person," p. 13.

[37]Jane Goldsmith, "The Unmarried Mother's Search for Standards," *Social Casework* 38 (February 1957):69.

[38]Babette Block, "The Unmarried Mother—Is She Different?" in *Understanding the Psychology of the Unmarried Mother* (New York: Family Service Association of America, 1947), p. 6.

[39]Scherz, " 'Taking Sides,' " pp. 22–3.

[40]In a variation on this family metaphor, Helen H. Perlman, professor of social work at the University of Chicago, wrote in 1959, "Mothered by sociology, with psychiatry as a father figure, social casework has passed through a number of developmental stages before reaching its present mature status." "Social Casework Today," *Public Welfare* 17 (April 1959): 51ff.

[41]See, for example, Clifford R. Adams, "Can You Control Your Daughter?" *Ladies' Home Journal* December 1956, p. 45ff.; Goodrich C. Schauffler, "Today It Could Be Your Daughter," *Ladies' Home Journal,* January 1958, p. 43ff.; Virgil G. Damon, "My Daughter Is in Trouble," *Look,* August 14, 1962, pp. 26–35. The *Ladies' Home Journal* had approximately five million subscriptions in 1955.

[42]See Ferdinand Lundberg and Marynia F.Farnham, *Modern Woman: The Lost Sex* (New York: Harper and Brothers, 1947) for a full discussion of these dangers.

[43]Heiman, "Out of Wedlock Pregnancy in Adolescence," pp. 67, 70.

[44]"We're Not Alone," *True Story,* September 1959, p. 86.

[45]Heiman, "Out of Wedlock Pregnancy," p. 67.

[46]Viola Bernard, "The Needs of Unmarried Parents and Their Children As Seen by a Psychiatrist," paper presented at meeting of the National Conference of Social Work, Atlantic City, NJ, 1948.

[47]Heiman, "Out of Wedlock Pregnancy," p. 68.

[48]The psychoanalytic explanations contained apparent contradictions which the model could nevertheless encompass. For example, sexually active girls were most often frigid; girls had out-of-wedlock babies as an expression of love and/or hatred for their own mothers; unmarried girls and women for whom pregnancy was so disastrous had easier pregnancies than married women.

[49]Young, *Out of Wedlock,* pp. 28–30.

[50]Deutsch, *The Psychology of Women,* vol. 2, p. 377.

[51]See Margaret Hickey, "Not Just a Place to Hide," *Ladies' Home Journal,* August 1958, pp. 23–4, 26, for a description of a Florence Crittenton Home in Cleveland.

[52]Jean Thompson, *The House of Tomorrow* (New York: Harper and Row, 1967), is a breathtaking personal account of life in a California Salvation Army maternity home around 1960.

[53]Young, *Out of Wedlock,* p. 36.

[54]Block, "The Unmarried Mother—Is She Different?" p. 6.

[55]Interview with Frances Whitefield, September 20, 1989. Also see Hannah Adams to Jules Saltman, March 29, 1966, Box 1038, File 7–4–6–0, Record Group 102, N.A. The Los Angeles study cited above found that "over 90% of the girls that were served placed their children for adoption." Neilsen and Motto, "Some Observations," p. 741.

[56]The attempts of state legislatures in the postwar period to disqualify black single mothers from ADC benefits for their children included threats to remove illegitimate children from their mothers' custody. These attempts reflect how far state authorities were willing to go to define, in terms to suit their own fiscal and race agenda, who was a mother.

[57]Jonathan Rinehart, "Mothers Without Joy," *Saturday Evening Post*, March 23, 1963, p. 30.

[58]Thompson, *The House of Tomorrow*, pp. 167–8.

[59]Young, "The Unmarried Mother's Decision About Her Baby," pp. 19–20.

[60]Young, *Out of Wedlock*, p. 216.

[61]Maud Morlock, Field Report, New York, 1948, Box 165, File 7–4–3–1–1, Record Group 102, N.A.

[62]Donnell and Glick, "Background Factors in One Hundred Cases," pp. 159–60.

[63]See the *Directory of Maternity Homes* (Cleveland: National Association on Services to Unmarried Parents, 1960). A typical entry describes the daily program of the Vanderburgh Christian Home in Evansville, Indiana, which "includes sewing, typing, crafts, games, piano, radio, record player and television," p. 35.

[64]Morlock, Field Report.

[65]William Masters, M.D., "What Does the Physician Desire for the Social Agencies by Way of Service for the Unmarried Mother?" n.d., Box 691, File 7–4–3–1–1, Record Group 102, N.A.

[66]See, for example, "Psychiatric Complications: A Psychoanalytic View of Pregnancy," in *Medical, Surgical and Gynecological Complications of Pregnancy*, Joseph J. Rovinsky and Alan F. Guttmacher, eds. (Baltimore: Williams and Wilkins, 1965), p. 481.

[67]See, for example, Cattell, "Psychodynamic and Clinical Observations," in which the psychiatrist claims that only the schizophrenics in his study kept their babies; the more normal mothers put their babies up for adoption.

[68]Block, "The Unmarried Mother—Is She Different?" p. 4.

[69]Edlin, *The Unmarried Mother*, p. 54.

[70]Solomon and Kilgore, "Psychiatric Case Conference," pp. 14–15.

[71]See Rose Bernstein, "Are We Still Stereotyping Unmarried Mothers?" *Social Work* 5 (July 1960):22–38.

[72]Rose Bernstein, "Gaps in Services to Unmarried Mothers," *Children* 10 (March–April 1963):53.

[73]See Elizabeth Herzog, "Unmarried Mothers: Some Questions to Be Answered and Some Answers to Be Questioned," *Child Welfare* 41 (October 1962):339–49.

[74]A good example of the new literature is Howard J. Osofsky, *The Pregnant Teenager: A Medical, Educational and Social Analysis* (Springfield, IL: Charles C. Thomas, 1966).

[75]Young, *Out of Wedlock*, p. 8.

[76]See Philip Wylie, *Generation of Vipers* (New York: Farrar and Rinehart, Inc., 1942), chapter 11; also Betty Friedan, *The Feminine Mystique* (New York: W.W. Norton, 1963), p. 189.

[77]See Rose Bernstein, "Unmarried Parents," *Encyclopedia of Social Work*, 15th issue (New York: National Association of Social Workers, 1965), pp. 797–801.

[78]See Lundberg and Farnham, *Modern Woman*, Deutsch, *The Psychology of Women*, and Harold Rosen, ed., *Therapeutic Abortion* (New York: Julian Press, 1954). One of the psychiatrist contributors to the Rosen volume asserted that a woman who has had

an abortion will be in a "state of dis-ease." He added, "She will become an unpleasant person to live with and possibly lose her glamour as a wife. She will gradually lose conviction in playing a feminine role." p. 27.

[79]See Lundberg and Farnham, *Modern Woman*, for the most extended discussion of midcentury neuroses and frustration as the wages of feminism, among American women dissatisfied with subordinate domesticity. See also, Robert Coughlan, "Changing Roles in Modern Marriage," *Life*, December 24, 1956, p. 109ff.

[80]See May, *Homeward Bound* for a brilliant analysis of the role of women in preserving and sustaining the family in the postwar era.

[81]See Martin O'Connell and Maurice J. Moore, "The Legitimacy Status of First Births to U.S. Women Ages 15–24, 1939–1978," in *Family Planning Perspectives* 12 (January–February 1980):16–25; Joseph Schachter and Mary McCarthy, Vital Statistics, Special Reports, "Illegitimate Births: U.S. 1938–1957," U.S. Government Document (Washington, D.C.: Government Printing Office, 1960); Clyde Kiser, Wilson Grabill and Arthur Campbell, eds., *Trends and Variations in Fertility in the United States* (Cambridge, MA: Harvard University Press, 1968), chapter 8; Alice Clague and Stephanie Ventura, *Trends in Illegitimacy: United States - 1940–1965* (U.S. National Center for Health Statistics: 1968). Also see Dr. Kinsey's statement in 1958: "There is a much higher percentage of girls in the U.S. who are having premarital intercourse today than was true forty years ago." Mary Calderone, ed., *Abortion in the United States* (New York: Harper and Brothers, 1958), p. 53.

[82]See, for example, Marie N. Robinson, M.D., *The Power of Sexual Surrender* (New York: Signet Books, 1959). See also Ehrenreich and English, *For Her Own Good*, pp. 243–5.

[83]See, for example, Dr. David Goodman, *A Parent's Guide to the Emotional Needs of Children* (New York: Hawthorne Books, 1959), p. 64.

Chapter Four

[1]Alice McDermott, *That Night* (New York: Harper and Row, 1987), p. 90.

[2]Rosalind Pollack Petchesky, *Abortion and Woman's Choice: The State, Sexuality and Reproductive Freedom*, rev. ed. (Boston: Northeastern University Press, 1990), p. 209.

[3]Hannah Adams to Jules Saltman, March 29, 1966, Box 1038, File 7–4–0–6, Record Group 102, National Archives (hereafter cited as N.A.).

[4]In 1957, the official number of unwed mothers was 200,000; in 1965, the number was approximately 300,000; of those, 123,000 were white and 167,000 were non-white. See Arthur A. Campbell and James D. Cowhig, "The Incidence of Illegitimacy in the United States," *Welfare in Review* 5 (May 1967):3–5, Table 2.

[5]See "NASUP, Some Notes on History or Plans," January 1963, Child Welfare League of America Papers (hereafter cited as CWLA), Box 48, File 48:1, Social Welfare History Archives, University of Minnesota (hereafter cited as SWHA).

[6]*Everywoman*, August 1955, pp. 16–17, 50.

[7]See Benjamin Spock, M.D., *The Common Sense Book of Baby and Child Care* (New York: Duell, Sloan and Pearce, 1946).

[8]See Robert Ruark, "The Flapper's Children," *Collier's*, December 28, 1946. p. 18ff.

[9]Maud Morlock to Leona Massoth, January 2, 1955, Box 690, File 7–4–3–1–1, Record Group 102, N.A.

[10]Joan Jacobs Brumberg, " 'Ruined Girls': Changing Community Responses to

Illegitimacy in Upstate New York, 1890–1920," *Journal of Social History* 18 (Winter 1984):268, n. 32.

[11]See, for example, Jean Thompson, *The House of Tomorrow* (New York: Harper and Row, 1967).

[12]Maud Morlock and Hillary Campbell, *Maternity Homes for Unmarried Mothers: A Community Service*, United States Children's Bureau Publication No. 309 (Washington, D.C.: Government Printing Office, 1946).

[13]Katherine T. Kinkead, "The Lonely Time," *The New Yorker*, January 20, 1951, p. 38; also see Sara Edlin, *The Unmarried Mother in Our Society* (New York: Farrar, Straus and Young, 1954), chapter 1. Edlin explains that when she first came to the Lakeview Maternity Home in 1912, the home's charge was to provide a shelter "where [the unwed mother's] mother love and responsibility could be awakened, where a strong moral influence could be at work and where she could be trained industrially. . . ."

[14]Quoted in Brumberg, " 'Ruined Girls,' " p. 260.

[15]"Group Work and Recreation in Maternity Homes for Unmarried Mothers," prepared by the National Committee on Services to Unmarried Parents, in Cooperation with the Staff of the United States Children's Bureau," 1947, Box 165, File 7–4–3–1–1, Record Group 102, N.A.

[16]Maud Morlock to Jane Wrieden, March 14, 1955, Box 691, File 7–4–3–1–1, Record Group 102, N.A.

[17]See, for example, Maud Morlock to Regional Child Welfare Representatives, June 11, 1952, Box 456, File 7–4–3–1–1; also see Maud Morlock to Roberta Morgan, February 26, 1953, Box 690, File 7–4–3–0, Record Group 102, N.A.

[18]Joan Younger, "The Unwed Mother," *Ladies' Home Journal*, June 1947, p. 102.

[19]Maud Morlock, Field Report, Delaware, 1951, Box 455, File 7–4–0–3, Record Group 102, N.A.

[20]"I Am an Unwed Mother," 1949, Box 454, File 7–4–0, Record Group 102, N.A.

[21]See Charles Bowerman, Donald Irish, and Hallowell Pope, *Unwed Motherhood: Personal and Social Consequences* (Chapel Hill: Institute for Research in Social Science, University of North Carolina, 1966), p. 297.

[22]East Orange, New Jersey to President Truman, June 3, 1947, Box 166, File 7–4–3–1–4, Record Group 102, N.A.

[23]Ruth Pagan, "The Citizen, the Girl, the Problem," paper presented at the Institute on Unwed Parenthood, Riverside, California, November 1952, Child Welfare League of America Papers (hereafter cited as CWLA), Box 47, File 47:4, SWHA.

[24]*Florence Crittenton Bulletin, Los Angeles*, 23 (Fall 1964), Florence Crittenton Association of America Papers (hereafter cited as FCAA Papers), Box 6, File: Member Agencies Newsletters, 1965), SWHA.

[25]G.R. to Mary Haworth, Box 457, File 7–4–3–1–4, Record Group 102, N.A.

[26]"We're Not Alone," *True Story*, September 1959, p. 49.

[27]Mary Louise Allen as told to Eleanor Harris, "What Can We Do About America's Teenagers?" *McCall's*, November 1963, p. 40ff.

[28]Thompson, *The House of Tomorrow*, p. 17.

[29]"We're Not Alone," p. 48.

[30]Of 21,201 maternity home residents queried in the mid-1960s, 47 percent were students at the time of pregnancy. Lucille Grow, *Unwed Mothers Served by Voluntary*

Agencies: Data Collection Project for Agencies Serving Unmarried Mothers, United States Department of Health, Education and Welfare, 1967.

[31] Maud Morlock, Field Report, Chicago, 1947, Box 164, File 7–4–0–7–6, Record Group 102, N.A.

[32] Ursula Gallagher to Jeanette Harris, October 6, 1961, Box 895, File 7–4–3–1, Record Group 102, N.A. Also see Jerry Kelly, "The School and Unmarried Mothers," *Children* 10 (March–April 1963):60–4.

[33] Gallagher to Harris, October 6, 1961.

[34] *U.S. News and World Report*, July 12, 1957, p. 68.

[35] In the mid-1960s, data was collected on the family incomes of just over five thousand maternity home residents. About 32 percent had incomes of $8,501 or higher; 32 percent had incomes between $5,500 and $8,500; 29 percent between $2,501 and $5,499. Grow, *Unwed Mothers Served by Voluntary Agencies*, p. 35.

[36] Ruth Pagan, "The Citizen, the Girl, the Problem."

[37] Babette Block, "A Philosophy of Community Services for the Unmarried Mother," paper presented at the Institute on Unwed Parenthood, Riverside, California, November 1952, CWLA Papers, Box 47, File 47:4, SWHA.

[38] Case Records, Midwestern Maternity Home, case no. 330, Salvation Army Archives.

[39] Sister Margaret Mary, D.C., "Contributions of Social Work to Services for Unmarried Parents," in *Effective Services for Unmarried Parents and Their Children* (New York: National Council on Illegitimacy, 1968).

[40] Kinkead, "The Lonely Time," p. 44.

[41] San Francisco to President Truman, October 22, 1947, Box 166, File 7–4–3–1–4, Record Group 102, N.A.

[42] Cleveland to Washington, 1949, Box 457, File 7–4–3–1–4, Record Group 102, N.A.

[43] Pittsburgh to Washington, December 20, 1948, Box 166, File 7–4–3–1–4, Record Group 102, N.A.

[44] Pennsylvania to the Children's Bureau, 1949, Box 457, File 7–4–3–1–4, Record Group 102, N.A.

[45] Maud Morlock to Leontine Young, January 4, 1949, Box 455, File 7–4–0–7–3, Record Group 102, N.A.

[46] "Proposal to Establish Individualized Information and Referral Service for Unmarried Parents," January 12, 1965, National Association on Services to Unmarried Parents Papers, (hereafter cited as NASUP), SWHA.

[47] Des Moines to the Children's Bureau, July 16 ,1945, Box 166, File 7–4–3–1–4, Record Group 102, N.A.

[48] Connecticut to the Children's Bureau, November 11, 1949, Box 457, File 7–4–3–1–4, Record Group 102, N.A.

[49] See Table 17, "Source of Referral of Unwed Mothers to Maternity Homes and to Other Social Agencies," in Grow, *Unwed Mothers Served by Voluntary Agencies*; also see Maud Morlock, Field Report, Jersey City, 1948, Box 165, File 7–4–3–1–1, Record Group 102, N.A.; Ellery F. Reed and Ruth Latimer, *A Study of Unmarried Mothers Who Kept Their Babies* (Cincinnati: Social Welfare Research, Inc., 1963); interview with Frances Whitefield, September 20, 1989.

[50] Maud Morlock, Field Report, Colorado, 1947, Box 165, File 7–4–3–1–1; Maud

Morlock to Reverend G. H. Bechtold, n.d., Box 166, File 7–4–3–1–1, Record Group 102, N.A.

[51]Margaret McCall to Maud Morlock, June 27, 1945, Box 166, File 7–4–3–1–4, Record Group 102, N.A.

[52]Maud Morlock, "Memo of Conference with Ruth Pagan," November 1949, Box 452, File 7–4–3–1–1, Record Group 102, N.A.

[53]Maud Morlock, Field Report, New York, 1948, Box 165, File 7–4–3–1–1, Record Group 102, N.A.; *New York Times*, March 23, 1955.

[54]Betty Woodward to Ursula Gallagher, November 10, 1958, Box 894, File 7–4–3–1–1, Record Group 102, N.A.

[55]Thompson, *The House of Tomorrow*, p. 135.

[56]"Florence Crittenton Association, Program Plan submitted to Department of Health, Education and Welfare for Demonstration Grant," September 22, 1961, Box 894, File 7–4–3–1–1, Record Group 102, N.A.

[57]Mary Louise Allen, "Executive Director's Report, 1961–62," FCAA Papers, Box 2, File: Executive Director Reports 1959–62, SWHA.

[58]Interview with Jennie Phelps, September 19, 1989.

[59]Aileen Werton, "Some Thoughts on the Reassessment of Services in a Maternity Home," paper presented at the Western Area Conference of FCAA, November 6, 1964, in *FCAA Papers from Midwestern, Southern and Western Area Conferences,* 1964 (1) (Chicago: Florence Crittenton Association of America, 1964).

[60]Grow, *Unwed Mothers Served by Voluntary Agencies*, Table 38A. Eighty percent of the residents under the age of twenty-one had been living with their parents at the time they got pregnant, p. 26. The median age for residents was 18.9; for whites it was 19.1, for nonwhites, 17.7, p. 9.

[61]Ibid., p. 36.

[62]See, for example, Morlock, Field Report, Colorado, 1947; Kinkead, "The Lonely Time," p. 32.

[63]Morlock, Field Report, Ohio, 1949.

[64]Grow, *Unwed Mothers Served by Voluntary Agencies,* p. 64.

[65]Leora Connor, "Maternity Home Budget; Workshop 2," paper presented at FCAA Northeast Conference, 1964; also see Mrs. Forrest Bennett, "Expansion of Maternity Home Services," paper delivered at the FCAA Midwestern Area Conference, 1964. Mrs. Bennett wrote, "We used to be able only to accept as adoptive parents those who could be generous financially with the Home. Now the Community Chest helps. We charge $2.00 a day board, $125.00 for maternity care within the Community Chest area, $150.00 within the state, $225.00 out of state. We assume the cost if a girl can't pay."

[66]Morlock, Field Report, Texas, 1950.

[67]Morlock, Field Report, Ohio, 1950.

[68]This was a continuation of the traditional practice of mixing all types of "wayward girls" in one institution. See Michael Sedlak, "Young Women and the City: Adolescent Deviance and the Transformation of Educational Policy, 1870–1960," *History of Education Quarterly* 23 (Spring 1983):3–7.

[69]Maud Morlock to Assistant Executive Director, Baltimore Council of Social Agencies, 1944, Box 165, File 7–4–2–1, Record Group 102, N.A.

[70]Ibid.

[71]In 1945, Dr. Robert Barrett, reporting on twenty years as president of the National

Florence Crittenton Mission, wrote, "Perhaps we will have to give up our maternity work. . . . National and state authorities are constantly encroaching upon our field with requirements that make our operations difficult at times. Officials from community chests from which our Homes receive a large part of their funds for maintenance sometimes interfere in our management on matters over which they have no control." "Report of National Florence Crittenton Mission, 1925–1945," Box 166, Folder 7–4–3–1–1, Record Group 102, N.A.

[72]Mary Louise Allen, Field Secretary's Report, October, 1952, FCAA Papers, Box 4, File: Field Secretary's Reports, SWHA.

[73]Mrs. John Cragoe to Mary Louise Allen, December 15, 1959, FCAA Papers, Box 5, File: FCAA Member Agencies Circles, SWHA.

[74]Morlock, Field Report, Ohio, 1950.

[75]Mrs. John Cragoe, "The Role of Adjunct Groups." FCAA Papers, Box 2, File: Executive Director's Memos, 1959-1962," SHWA.

[76]See Mary Louise Allen to Mrs. John Cragoe, December 15, 1959, and the *Crittenton Chronicle* 9 (March 1965), FCAA Papers, Box 6, File: Member Agencies, Newsletters, 1965, SWHA.

[77]"Florence Crittenton Fund Raising Projects," FCAA Papers, Box 5, File: FCAA Member Agencies Circles, SWHA; Helene Nemschoff, "How Can Auxiliaries, Circles, and Other Voluntary Groups Strengthen and Extend Their Effectiveness?" paper presented at the Western Area Conference of FCAA, October 6, 1964, in *FCAA Papers from Midwestern, Southern and Western Area Conferences,* 1964 (1) (Chicago: Florence Crittenton Association of America, 1964).

[78]In John Patrick Diggins's study of the middle decades of the twentieth century, the author notes the rising rates of premarital pregnancy in the United States in the 1940s: "Homes for unwed mothers grew to be a thriving business." John Patrick Diggins, *The Proud Decades: America in War and Peace, 1941-1960* (New York: W.W. Norton, 1988), p. 24. This is far from the truth, although the market for white, illegitimate babies was, indeed, brisk, as demonstrated in Chapter Five of this book.

[79]New York to the Children's Bureau, 1950, Box 457, File 7–4–3–1–4, Record Group 102, N.A.

[80]Boston to the Children's Bureau, December 8, 1949. Box 487, File 7–4–3–1–4, Record Group 102, N.A.

[81]See, for example, Ruth Pagan to Maud Morlock, December 7, 1949, Maud Morlock to Christine Mulbach, June 29, 1951, Box 457, File 7–4–3–1–4; John Winters to Mary Lois Pyles, January 26, 1962, Box 894, File 7–4–3–1–1, Record Group 102, N.A.

[82]Maud Morlock to Tennessee Children's Home, January 20, 1950, Box 456, File 7–4–3–1–1, Record Group 102, N.A.

[83]Mildred Arnold to Kentucky, 1949, Box 457, File 7–4–3–1–4, Record Group 102, N.A.

[84]See Beth L. Bailey, *From Front Porch to Back Seat: Courtship in Twentieth-Century America* (Baltimore: The Johns Hopkins University Press, 1988), chapter 7.

[85]Ibid., p. 77.

[86]Kinkead, "The Lonely Time," p. 37.

[87]Thompson, *The House of Tomorrow,* p. 23.

[88]Adelaide Delorme, "Group Living: A General Component of Treatment in a Residential Treatment Program," paper delivered at the National Conference on Social

Work, 1961, FCAA Papers, Box 3, Folder: FCAA Eleventh Annual Conference, 1960–61, SWHA.

[89]*Behind the Fence*, May 1965 and October 1965, FCAA Papers, Box 6, File: Member Agencies Newletters, 1965, SWHA.

[90]Morlock, Field Report, Ohio, 1949.

[91]Ibid.

[92]Morlock, Field Report, Jersey City, 1948.

[93]Morlock, Field Report, Texas, 1950.

[94]Morlock, Field Report, Kentucky, 1948.

[95]King's Daughters Home, Natchez, Mississippi, brochure, n.d., Box 894, File 7–4–3–1–1, Record Group 102, N.A.

[96]"Slide Script," June 26, 1956, FCAA Papers, Box 6, File: FCAA Public Relations—Slide Scripts, SWHA.

[97]Thompson, *The House of Tomorrow*, p. 47.

[98]Ibid., p. 67.

[99]Interview with Jennie Phelps.

[100]See Ruth I. Pierce, *Single and Pregnant* (Boston: Beacon Press, 1971), p. 62; also Rose Bernstein, *Helping the Unmarried Mother* (New York: Association Press, 1971), p. 179. Jennie Phelps estimated that in this era, about 30 to 35 percent of the residents used aliases. Also see Maud Morlock to Ruth Gay, February 7, 1956, Box 691, File 7–4–3–1–1, Record Group 102, N.A., in which Morlock discussed the "name" issue.

[101]Kinkead, "The Lonely Time," p. 40.

[102]*The Home Front*, no. 5, March 1965, FCAA Papers, Box 6, File: Member Agencies Newsletters, 1965, SWHA.

[103]Thompson, *The House of Tomorrow*, pp. 120–1.

[104]"Child Welfare League-Children's Bureau Conference, notes," January 19, 1951, Box 456, File 7–4–3–1–1, Record Group 102, N.A.

[105]In a Children's Bureau newsletter in the early 1940s, a maternity home superintendent wrote, "In my annual report last year to the Board, I reviewed the policies of the home for the past ten years showing the changes we have made in an effort to meet the immediate needs. By the time I had finished the report, the newer Board members were in stitches over the funny things we did a short time ago. It just didn't seem possible." *United States Children's Bureau Newsletter*, no. 18, June 1942, CWLA Papers, Box 49, File: 49:2, SWHA.

[106]Morlock, Field Report, Texas, 1950.

[107]Maud Morlock to Bess Williams, June 4, 1947, Box 126, File 7–4–3–1–1 ; also see Maud Morlock to Child Welfare Representatives, September 29, 1950, in which Morlock wrote, "When I came the the Children's Bureau in 1936 . . . many [maternity homes] thought it was their responsibility to see incoming and outgoing mail. . . . No modern homes open mail now." Box 456, File 7–4–3–1–1, Record Group 102, N.A.; also see *United States Children's Bureau Newsletter Eleven on Problems Associated with Birth Out-of-Wedlock*, April 1, 1940, in which the director of the Toledo Florence Crittenton Association wrote that between 1931 and 1939, censoring of girls' mail ceased, resulting "in a finer relationship between girls and staff." CWLA Papers, Box 49, File 49:2, SWHA.

[108]Morlock, Field Report, Ohio, 1950. The director of this home told Morlock that many of her girls did return as employees because the home was "a safe place and girls are afraid to work outside."

[109]Morlock, Field Report, New York, 1948.

[110]Morlock to Child Welfare Representatives, September 29, 1950.

[111]Morlock, Field Report, Colorado, 1947.

[112]"Group Work and Recreation in Maternity Homes for Unmarried Mothers," FCAA Papers, Box 49, File 49:1, SWHA.

[113]Morlock, Field Report, Jersey City, 1948.

[114]Morlock, Field Report, Kentucky, 1948.

[115]Morlock, Field Report, New York, 1948.

[116]"Volunteers of America, Maternity Home, Guidelines," n.d. (late 1940s), Box 165, File 7–4–3–0, Record Group 102, N.A.

[117]Board member of Ingleside Home to Maud Morlock, September 7, 1952, Box 456, File 7–4–3–1–3, Record Group 102, N.A.

[118]See, for example, Morlock, Field Report, Ohio, 1949.

[119]Mrs. Forrest Bennett, "Expansion of Maternity Home Services."

[120]"Report of meeting between Major Cox and Miss Vogel," August, 1950, Box 456, File 7–4–3–1–1, Record Group 102, N.A.

[121]Jeanette Harris to Maud Morlock and Ursula Gallagher, September 7, 1956. Box 690, File 7–4–3–1–1, Record Group 102, N.A.

[122]Ursula Gallagher to Wilber Schmidt, July 1, 1959, Box 894, File 7–4–3–1–1, Record Group 102, N.A.

[123]See, for example, Rose Bernstein, *Helping Unmarried Mothers*, p. 150.

[124]Babette Block to Editor of the *Ladies' Home Journal*, March 29, 1949, Box 456, File 7–4–3–1–1, Record Group 102, N.A.

[125]Morlock, Field Report, Ohio, 1949.

[126]Morlock, Field Report, Kentucky, 1948.

[127]Morlock, Field Report, Ohio, 1949.

[128]Babette Block, "A Philosophy of Community Service for the Unmarried Mother."

[129]Howard J. Osofsky, M.D., *The Pregnant Teenager: A Medical, Educational and Social Analysis* (Springfield, IL: Charles C. Thomas, 1966), p. 54.

[130]*Directory of Maternity Homes* (Cleveland: National Association on Services to Unmarried Parents, 1960). See, for example, p. 108.

[131]Interview with Jennie Phelps.

[132]Morlock, Field Report, Jersey City, 1948.

[133]Mrs. Comus Young, "Round Table Discussion—Public Relations," FCAA Papers, Box 4, File: "Southern Regional Conference, 1959, Panel Discussions," SWHA.

[134]Jonathan Rinehart, "Mothers Without Joy," *Saturday Evening Post*, March 23, 1963, p. 33.

[135]Major Norman E. Sampson, "The Small Speciality Hospital, Home and Related Institutions,"Accession no. 82–1, Salvation Army Archives.

[136]See, for example, Morlock, Field Report, Kentucky, 1948.

[137]"Report of Proposed Boarding Home Program for Young, Adolescent Unmarried Mothers by Women's Service Division, Chicago," n.d., Box 894, File 7–4–3–1–1, Record Group 102, N.A.

[138]Interview with Jennie Phelps.

[139]Maud Morlock to Lois Biefelt, April 17, 1953, Box 691, File 7–4–3–1–1, Record Group 102, N.A.

[140]*Directory of Maternity Homes*, pp. 43, 124, 133, 145, 149.

[141]Morlock, Field Report, Texas, 1950.

[142]"Slide Script," June 26, 1956, FCAA Papers.

[143]*Directory of Maternity Homes*, p. 97.

[144]See, for example, Morlock, Field Report, Texas, 1950; Helen K. Anderson, "Values Emanating from a New Structure of a Maternity Home Council," FCAA Papers, Box 95, File: Florence Crittenton Homes of America/FCAA, SWHA.

[145]Morlock, Field Report, Kentucky, 1948; Morlock, Field Report, Ohio, 1949; Morlock, Field Report, Texas, 1950.

[146]Grow, *Unwed Mothers Served by Voluntary Agencies*, p. 22.

[147]Lawrence Derthick, "Elimination of Roadblocks in Educating School-Age Unmarried Mothers," June 1960, FCAA Papers, Box 95, File: Florence Crittenton Homes of America, SWHA.

[148]Morlock, Field Report, Texas, 1950.

[149]Osofsky, *The Pregnant Teenager*, p. 76.

[150]Derthick, "Elimination of Roadblocks."

[151]Director of Special Education Division of Curriculum and Instruction, State Board of Education, Trenton, "Eliminating Roadblocks in Educating School-Age Unmarried Mothers," FCAA Papers, Box 95, File: Florence Crittenton Homes of America, SWHA.

[152]Derthick, "Elimination of Roadblocks."

[153]Jane Wrieden to Mildred Arnold, December 18, 1959, Box 894, File 7–4–3–1–1, Record Group 102, N.A.

[154]Grow, *Unwed Mothers Served by Voluntary Agencies*, pp. 65–9.

[155]Ibid., p. 69.

[156]Morlock, Field Report, Ohio, 1950.

[157]"Field Secretary's Report," October 1952, National Florence Crittenton Mission Papers, (hereafter cited as NFCM), Box 3, Folder 25, SWHA.

[158]Morlock, Field Report, Texas, 1950.

[159]Ursula Gallagher, Field Report, New York, 1958, Box 892, File 7–4–0–4, Record Group 102, N.A.

[160]Kinkead, "The Lonely Time," p. 29.

[161]"Group Work and Recreation in Maternity Homes for Unmarried Mothers."

[162]Isabelle Walters to Maud Morlock, April 29, 1949, Box 456, File 7–4–3–1–1, Record Group 102, N.A.

[163]Maud Morlock to Mary Lois Pyles, August 15, 1955, Box 690, File 7–4–3–1–1, Record Group 102, N.A.

[164]See, for example, Margaret McCall to Maud Morlock, June 27, 1945, Box 166, File 7–4–3–1–4, Record Group 102, N.A. McCall wrote, "We now have a new social worker on the staff. . . . It certainly is a tremendous help and I think we have you to thank, as I think it is the result of your visit here."

[165]Martha Steinmetz, "Role Playing in a Maternity Home," *Children* 11 (March–April 1964): pp. 61–4.

[166]Dr. Bernard L. Busfield, M.D., "Recognition and Management of Emotional Factors in Repeated Out-of-Wedlock Pregnancies," paper presented at the FCAA Northeast Conference, 1964.

[167]Lillian Bye to Sibley Higginbotham, August 8, 1958, Box 894, File 7–4–3–1–1, Record Group 102, N.A.

[168]Thompson, *The House of Tomorrow*, p. 37.

[169]Marion K. Sanders, "Social Work: A Profession Chases Its Tail," *Harper's*, March 1957, p. 56ff.

[170]Carrie Green, "Dynamics in Repeated Illegitimate Pregnancies—Workers' Attitudes," NASUP Papers, Box CWLA 47, File 47:4, SWHA.

[171] Younger, "The Unwed Mother," p. 105.

[172]Quoted in Block, "A Philosophy of Community Service."

[173] Rinehart, "Mothers Without Joy," p. 29.

[174]U.S. Congress, Senate, Judiciary Committee, *Hearings Before the Subcommittee to Investigate Juvenile Delinquency, Interstate Adoption Practices,* July 15–16, 1955, (84th Congress, 1st sess. [Washington, D.C.: Government Printing Office, 1955]), p. 206.

[175]Edlin, *The Unmarried Mother in Our Society*, p. 53.

[176]Thompson, *The House of Tomorrow*, p. 122.

[177]Ibid., p. 104.

[178]Edlin, *The Unmarried Mother in Our Society*, pp. 68–9.

[179]See, for example, Kinkead, "The Lonely Time," p. 36.

[180]Ibid., p. 40.

[181]Interview with Frances Whitefield.

[182]Salvation Army Case Records, Midwestern Maternity Home, case no. 339, Salvation Army Archives.

[183]Interview with Frances Whitefield.

[184]Director of St. Faith's Home in Tarrytown, New York; quoted in Kinkead, "The Lonely Time," p. 36.

[185]Wisconsin to the Children's Bureau, 1949, Box 457, File 7–4–3–1–4, Record Group 102, N.A.

[186]Rinehart, "Mothers Without Joy," p. 30.

[187]"Salvation Army Women's Social Service Unmarried Parenthood Program—Statistical Report, 1953," Box 689, File 7–4–0–3, Record Group 102, N.A.

[188]Mary Lynch Crockett, "Examination of Services to the Unmarried Mother in Relation to Age of Adoption Placement of the Baby," June 9, 1960, FCAA Papers, Box 95, File: FCAA 1960–1965, SWHA.

[189]Rinehart, "Mothers Without Joy," p. 32.

[190]Ibid.

[191]*The Home Front*, March 1965, FCAA Papers, Box 6, File: Member Agencies Newsletters, 1965, SWHA.

[192]Crockett, "Examination of Services to Unmarried Mothers."

[193]Quoted in Kinkead, "The Lonely Time," p. 38.

[194]Jane Wrieden, "The Meaning of the Maternity Home," *Children* 3 (January–February 1956):25.

[195]Thompson, *The House of Tomorrow*, p. 142.

[196]Wrieden, *"The Meaning of the Maternity Home"*; Thompson, *The House of Tomorrow*, p. 150.

[197]Maud Morlock to Elinor Mullen, March 8, 1949, Box 456, File 7–4–3–1–3, Record Group 102, N.A.

[198]Thompson, *The House of Tomorrow*, p. 164.

[199]Ibid., p. 133.

[200]Ibid., pp. 117–18.

[201]Wrieden, "The Meaning of the Maternity Home."

[202]Thompson, *The House of Tomorrow*, p. 30.

[203]Wrieden, "The Meaning of the Maternity Home," p. 26.

[204]Ruth Reed, *The Illegitimate Family in New York City: Its Treatment by Social and Health Agencies* (Columbia University Press, 1934), p. 61.

[205]Sheltering Arms to Maud Morlock, February 24, 1949. Box 456, File 7–4–3–1–2, Record Group 102, N.A.

[206]Jeanette Harris to Ursula Gallagher, October 6, 1961, Box 893, File 7–4–3–1, Record Group 102, N.A.

[207]Thompson, *The House of Tomorrow*, pp. 136–7.

[208]Maud Morlock to Miriam Hurwich, December 16, 1944.

[209]Mrs. Forest Bennett, "Expansion of Maternity Home Services."

[210]FCAA Papers, Box 6, File: Member Agencies Newletters, 1965.

[211]Mary Louise Allen to Nina Sittler Dorrance, August 28, 1959, FCAA Papers, Box 6, File: FCAA Public Relations—True Story, SWHA.

[212]"Paper Written by Chairman of the National Council on Services to Unmarried Parents for National Conference on Social Work, San Francisco, 1947," Box 165, File 7–4–3–1–1, Record Group 102, N.A.

[213]Marjorie K. Stapf, "A Descriptive Study of the Role of the Social Group Worker in a Home for Unmarried Mothers," M. S.W. thesis, University of Minnesota, 1951, p. 52.

[214]Mary Louise Allen, "What Can We Do?" p. 51.

[215]Interview with Jennie Phelps.

[216]Kinkead, "The Lonely Time," p. 42.

[217]Thompson, *The House of Tomorrow*, pp. 146, 101.

[218]Morlock, Field Report, Ohio, 1950.

[219]"Commission on the Historical Role of the Salvation Army, 1955–1959," Accession no. 82–1, Salvation Army Archives.

[220]Edlin, *The Unmarried Mother*, p. 80.

[221]Interview with Jennie Phelps.

[222]Interview with Lee Anne Bell, July 17, 1989; also Thompson, *The House of Tomorrow*.

[223]"Report of a meeting between Major Cox and Miss Vogel."

[224]Thompson, *The House of Tomorrow*, p. 99.

[225]*Florence Crittenton Anchorage*, FCAA Papers, Box 6, File: Member Agencies Newsletters, 1965, SWHA.

[226]Rinehart, "Mothers Without Joy," p. 30.

[227]Norfolk newspaper clipping, n.d., NFCM Papers, Box 8, File 91, SWHA; Kinkead, "The Lonely Time," p. 41.

[228]Janice P. Montague, "Acceptance or Denial—the Therapeutic Use of the Mother/Baby Relationship," paper delivered at the FCAA Northeast Conference, 1964.

[229]Thompson, *The House of Tomorrow*, pp. 138, 178.

[230]For a report on present-day maternity homes, see "Anti-Abortion Revival: Homes for Unwed Mothers," *New York Times*, July 23, 1989.

[231]Kinkead, "The Lonely Time," p. 46.

Chapter Five

[1]*New York Times*, June 5, 1955; See also Percy Kammerer, *The Unmarried Mother* (Boston: Little, Brown, 1918) and Dorothea Andrews to *Reader's Digest*, September 27, 1951, Box 454, File 7–4–0, Record Group 102, National Archives (hereafter cited as N.A.).

[2]Maud Morlock and Hilary Campbell, *Maternity Homes for Unmarried Mothers: A Community Service*, Children's Bureau Publication no. 309 (Washington, D.C.: Government Printing Office, 1946).

[3]Maryland passed such a law in 1919 and Wisconsin in 1922. It was claimed that these laws would reduce high infant mortality rates, although they were never shown to do so. Maternity home residents were targeted, since this group was considered most likely, in its search for secrecy, to abandon its babies.

[4]Elza Virginia Dahlgren, "Attitudes of a Group of Unmarried Mothers Toward the Minnesota Three Months Nursing Regulation and Its Application," M.A. thesis, University of Minnesota, 1940.

[5]Maud Morlock, "Field Report, Ohio," 1949, Box 455, File 7–4–3–0, Record Group 102, N.A.

[6]Katherine T. Kinkead, "The Lonely Time," *The New Yorker*, January 20, 1951, p. 38.

[7]Maud Morlock, "Field Report, New Jersey," 1948, Box 165, File 7–4–3–1–1, Record Group 102, N.A.

[8]National Florence Crittenton Mission Papers, (hereafter cited as NFCM), File: "Poetry and Memorabilia," Social Welfare History Archives, University of Minnesota (hereafter cited as SWHA).

[9]"Essential Differences Between Unmarried and Married Mothers," no author, c. 1939, Child Welfare League of America Papers (hereafter cited as CWLA Papers) 49:1, SWHA.

[10]These ideas lingered on into the early postwar period. A 1945 article about illegitimacy noted, "For neither food nor money can change her basic misfortune, nor her child's: both will be forevermore objects of curiosity and suspicion, and victims of fear and deceit." Some unwed mothers internalized this attitude. A journalist reported the feelings of a typical one who did: "Despite her doctor's assurance that [the baby] was a fine healthy boy, she was afraid that his illegitimacy would mark him in some way—a fear that she said most of the [maternity home] girls shared." Joan Younger, "The Unwed Mother," *Ladies' Home Journal*, June 1947, p. 43; Kinkead, "The Lonely time," p. 45.

[11]See Kammerer, *The Unmarried Mother*.

[12]Even though many studies published in this era claimed that rates of illicit coition were not rising in the postwar era, the fact that the illegitimacy rates and illegal abortion rates were higher than ever suggests otherwise. See, for example, Alfred C. Kinsey, Wardell B. Pomeroy, Cylde E. Martin, and Paul H. Gebhard, *Sexual Behavior in the Human Female* (Philadelphia: W.B. Saunders Company, 1953), chapter 8. By 1958 Dr. Kinsey acknowledged that nonmarital intercourse rates for females had risen

significantly since the early part of the twentieth century. Mary Calderone, ed., *Abortion in the United States* (New York: Harper and Row, 1958), p. 53.

[13]See, for example, Florence Clothier, "Psychological Implications of Unmarried Parenthood," *American Journal of Orthopsychiatry* 13 (July 1943):531–49. Also see Chapter Three.

[14]See Viviana A. Zelizer, *Pricing the Priceless Child: The Changing Social Value of Children* (New York: Basic Books, 1985) for an interesting discussion of related issues.

[15]See for example, Mary Lynch Crockett, "An Examination of Services to the Unmarried Mother in Relation to Age at Adoption Placement of the Baby," *Casework Papers, 1960* (New York: Columbia University Press), pp. 75–85.

[16]Jeanette Harris to Maud Morlock, September 7, 1956, Box 690, File 7–4–3–1–1, Record Group 102, N.A.

[17]The policy makers and practitioners ushering these new postwar ideas into practice, and the old guard holding on to their venerable beliefs, took serious note of the changes. Dr. Robert Barrett, for twenty years the president of the National Florence Crittenton Mission, noted in 1945, "Professional social workers often are not interested in our religious training. Some of our most sincere friends do not believe in our policy of keeping mother and child together." A year later, Maud Morlock of the United States Children's Bureau, wrote to a colleague that the moves toward casework and adoption represented, "a long step from where we were a few years ago. I am sure Mrs. Reba Smith [Dr. Barrett's sister and a principal in the NFCM] is somewhat bewildered when she thinks of the new practices." Robert Barrett, "Report of the National Florence Crittenton Mission, 1925–1945," July 23, 1945, Box 166, File 7–4–3–1–1; Maud Morlock to Miss Wood, April 11, 1946, Box 165, File 7–4–3–1–1, Record Group 102, N.A.

[18]Ruth L. Butcher and Marion O. Robinson, *Girls and Women Who Become Unmarried Mothers* (New York: Public Affairs Committee, 1959), p. 22.

[19]Charles Bowerman, Donald Irish, and Hallowell Pope, *Unwed Motherhood: Personal and Social Consequences* (Chapel Hill: Institute for Research in Social Science, University of North Carolina, 1966), p. 165.

[20]See Henry Meyer, Wyatt Jones, and Edgar Borgatta, "The Decision by Unmarried Mothers to Keep or Surrender Their Babies," *Marriage and Family Living* 1 (April 1956):103–9, and Henry Meyer, Edgar Borgatta, and David Fanshel, "Unwed Mothers' Decisions About Their Babies: An Interim Replication Study," *Child Welfare* 38 (February 1959):1–6.

[21]Janice P. Montague, "Acceptance or Denial—the Therapeutic Uses of the Mother/Baby Relationship," paper presented at the Florence Crittenton Association of America Northeast Conference, 1964.

[22] Crockett, "Examination of Services."

[23]It wasn't always so easy for the unwed mother to accept the new way of thinking. One described how the single pregnant girls and women sharing a maternity home residence with her vacillated in the early postwar years: "Except for two girls who cared so little about their babies that they were already thinking about dates, all twenty of us at [the home] wanted to keep our babies, and we used to talk about how we could manage it. Only eight of us finally did." Kinkead, "The Lonely Time," p. 44.

[24]Marybeth Weinstein, "Markets, Black and Gray, in Babies" *New York Times Magazine*, November 27, 1955, p. 20.

[25]Winston Ehrmann, "Illegitimacy in Florida II: Social and Psychological Aspects of Illegitimacy," *Eugenics Quarterly* 3 (December 1956):227.

[26]Miss Wood to Field Consultants, November 1, 1945, Box 166, File 7–4–3–1–4, Record Group 102, N.A.

[27]"Commission on the Historical Role of the Salvation Army Maternity Home and Hospital," 1956, Accession no. 82–1, Salvation Army Archives, New York City.

[28]Leontine Young, "Is Money Our Trouble?" paper presented at the National Conference on Social Work, Cleveland, 1953.

[29]*New York Times*, June 5, 1955.

[30]Chief, Social Statistics Section, to Martha Eliot, February 10, 1955, Box 689, File 7–4–3–0, Record Group 102, N.A.

[31]See Meyer, Borgatta, and Fanshel, "Unwed Mothers' Decision."

[32]Mary Louise Allen to Jane Wrieden, Florence Crittenton Association of America Papers (hereafter cited as FCAA Papers), Box 2, File: FCAA, Executive Director, Memos 1959–62, SWHA.

[33]See, for example, Katherine Brownell Oettinger, "Current Concerns of the Children's Bureau," *Children* 5 (May–June 1958):123–8.

[34]*New York Times*, November 28, 1944.

[35]Lawrence Cole to Maud Morlock, August 27, 1954, Box 691, File 7–4–3–1–1, Record Group 102, N.A.

[36]Mary Rall, "Conference on Work with Unmarried Mothers," Phoenix, February 7, 1949, Box 165, File 7–4–3–1–1, Record Group 102, N.A.

[37]Maud Morlock, "Field Report, Kentucky," 1948, Box 165, File 7–4–3–1–1, Record Group 102, N.A.

[38]For an example of an expression of this perspective, see Justine Wise Polier, "Illegitimate!" *Woman's Home Companion*, August 1947, p. 39.

[39] Dalhgren, "Attitudes of a Group of Unmarried Mothers," pp. 109–10.

[40]Frances H. Sherz, " 'Taking Sides' in the Unmarried Mother's Conflict," in *Understanding the Psychology of the Unmarried Mother* (New York: Family Service Association of America, 1945–47), pp. 21–5.

[41]Leontine Young, "The Unmarried Mother's Decision About Her Baby," in *Understanding the Psychology of the Unmarried Mother* (New York: Family Service Association of America, 1945–47), p. 14.

[42]*Ibid.*

[43]Sherz, " 'Taking Sides.' " See also, Sylvia Oshlag, "Surrendering a Child for Adoption," in *Understanding the Psychology of the Unmarried Mother* (New York: Family Service Association of America, 1945–47), pp. 25–32. This is reminiscent of Mrs. Roman Castavet's famous advice to Rosemary Woodhouse in *Rosemary's Baby*.

[44]Dr. Robert Barrett to Grace Knox, January 26, 1947, NFCM Papers, Box 8, File 88, SWHA.

[45]U.S. Congress, Senate, Judiciary Committee, *Hearings Before the Subcommittee to Investigate Juvenile Delinquency, Interstate Adoption Practices*, July 15–16, 1955 (84th Congress, 1st sess. [Washington, D.C.: Government Printing Office, 1955]), p. 200.

[46]Maud Morlock, "Field Report, Ohio," 1949.

[47]Nebraska Division of Child Welfare, 1950, Box 457, File 7–4–3–1–4, Record Group 102, N.A.

[48]Helen Witmer to George Wyman, March 26, 1956, Box 689, File 7–4–0–6, Record Group 102, N.A.

[49]Kinkead, "The Lonely Time," p. 30.

[50]Maud Morlock, "Field Report, Texas," 1950, Box 455, File 7–4–0–7–4, Record Group 102, N.A.

[51]CWLA Papers, Box 14, 14:8, SWHA.

[52]*Children* 9 (March–April 1962):47.

[53]Two documents that illuminate this resentment are "Meeting to Discuss Services to Unmarried Mothers, Dallas," March 2, 1950, Box 455, File 7–4–3–0, Record Group 102, N.A., and Morris Wessel, M.D., "A Physician Looks at Professional Services for Unmarried Mothers," paper presented at the Annual Conference of the Florence Crittenton Association of America, New York, 1962.

[54]Glenn Strand and William Larson, "Five Professions View the Unmarried Parent," *International Journal of Psychiatry* 6 (Autumn 1960):269–76.

[55]In 1955, government statistics indicated that 42 percent of adopted out-of-wed-lock babies were placed by social agencies; 37 percent were placed independently. Chief, Social Statistics Section, to Martha Eliot, February 10, 1955.

[56]Leontine Young, "The Responsibility of Social Work in Changing Community Attitudes," paper presented at National Conference of Social Work, Atlantic City, 1948.

[57]See U.S. Congress, Senate, Judiciary Committee, *Hearings Before the Subcommittee to Investigate Juvenile Delinquency, Interstate Adoption Practices, Miami Florida*, November 14–15, 1955, (84th Congress, lst sess. [Washington, D.C.: Government Printing Office, 1956]), p. 250 ; and Maud Morlock, "Field Report, Wilmington Delaware," 1951, Box 455, File 7–4–3–0, Record Group 102, N.A.

[58]*Hearings*, Interstate Adoption Practices, July 15–16, 1955, p. 206.

[59]Maud Morlock, "Field Report, New York," 1948, Box 165, File 7–4–3–1–1, Record Group 102, N.A.

[60]*Directory of Maternity Homes* (Cleveland: National Association on Services to Unmarried Parents, 1960).

[61]Ibid.

[62]Maud Morlock, "Field Report, Texas," 1950.

[63]Bernice R. Brower, "What Shall I Do with My Baby?" *The Child* 12 (April 1948):167.

[64]Interview with Jennie Phelps, September 19, 1989.

[65]Jean Thompson, *The House of Tomorrow* (New York: Harper and Row, 1967), p. 135.

[66]Jeanette Harris to Maud Morlock and Ursula Gallagher, September 7, 1956, Box 690, File 7–4–3–1–1, Record Group 102, N.A.

[67]Maud Morlock, "Field Report, New York," 1948.

[68]Ibid.

[69]Lotte Levi to Ursula Gallagher, July 24, 1962, Box 894, File 7–4–3–1–1, Record Group 102, N.A.

[70]"Meeting to Discuss Services to Unmarried Mothers, Dallas," March 20, 1950.

[71]Sara Edlin, *The Unwed Mother in Our Society* (New York: Farrar, Straus and Young, 1954), p. 175.

[72]Maud Morlock, "State and Local Planning of Services for Unmarried Mothers," n.d., c. 1946, FCAA Papers, 49:1, SWHA.

[73]"Meeting to Discuss Services to Unmarried Mothers, Dallas," March 20, 1950.

[74]FCAA Papers, Box 6, File: Member Agency Newsletters, 1965, SWHA.

[75] Adelaide DeLorme, "Group Living: A General Component of Treatment in a Residential Treatment Program," FCAA Papers, Box 2, File: FCAA Eleventh Annual Conference 1960–61, SWHA.

[76] Carol Kerry, "Approaches to Better Agency and Community Services for Unmarried Parents," in *Unmarried Parenthood: Clues to Agency and Community Action* (New York: National Council on Illegitimacy, 1967), p. 70.

[77] Interview with Florence Whitefield, September 20, 1989.

[78] See Chapter Four.

[79] Anne Ford, paper presented at the FCAA Northeast Conference, 1964.

[80] U.S. Congress, House, Ways and Means Committee, *Hearings on Public Assistance Titles of the Social Security Act*, April 12, 13, 16, 19, 20, 1956 (84th Congress, 2d sess. [Washington, D.C.: Government Printing Office, 1956]), p. 103.

[81] Ibid., p. 55.

[82] *Hearings, Interstate Adoption Practices*, July 15–16, 1955, p. 191.

[83] *Hearings, Interstate Adoption Practices, Miami, Florida*, November 14–15, 1955, p. 156.

[84] Ibid., p. 169.

[85] U.S. Congress, Senate, Judiciary Committee, *Hearing Before the Subcommittee to Investigate Juvenile Delinquency, Commercial Child Adoption Practices*, May 16, 1956, (84th Congress, 2d sess.[Washington, D.C.: Government Printing Office, 1956]), p. 6.

[86] *Standards for Services to Unmarried Parents* (New York: Child Welfare League of America, 1960), pp. 1–2.

[87] *Hearings, Interstate Adoption Practices*, July 15–16, 1955, p. 205.

[88] *Hearings, Interstate Adoption Practices, Miami, Florida*, November 14–15, 1955, p. 244.

[89] Lucy Freeman, "Biennial Conference: Round-Up Report," *Public Welfare* 14 (January 1956):20.

[90] *Hearings, Commercial Child Adoption Practices*, May 16, 1956, p. 69.

[91] *New York Times*, July 10, 1958.

[92] *Cleveland Plain Dealer* , March 10, 1953.

[93] Bess Williams to Maud Morlock, March 29, 1950, Box 457, File 7–4–3–3–7, Record Group 102, N.A.

[94] Maud Morlock, "Field Report, Ohio," 1949.

[95] Dorothy Allen to Kate Helms, April 5, 1962, Box 893, File 7–4–3–0, Record Group 102, N.A.

[96] Mrs. Forrest Bennett, "Expansion of Maternity Home Services," paper presented at the Midwest Area Conference, FCAA, 1964.

[97] U.S. Congress, Senate, Committee on the Judiciary, Subcommittee to Investigate Juvenile Delinquency in the United States, (84th Congress, 2d sess.), Unpublished Hearing, May 11, 1956. See Maud Morlock, "Field Report, Texas," 1950, for evidence that the Texas State Department of Public Welfare had found the Gladney home seriously below standard in this era.

[98] See, for example, Oettinger, "Current Concerns."

[99] *Hearings, Interstate Adoption Practices,* July 15–16, 1955, p. 236.

[100] Ibid.

[101] Ibid., p. 207.

[102]Ibid.

[103]Garnet Larsen to Bob Brieland, April 24, 1956, Box 689, File 7–4–0–6, Record Group 102, N.A.

[104]*Hearings, Interstate Adoption Practices*, July 15–16, 1955, p. 73.

[105]Irene Josselyn, M.D., "Some Defenses Seen in the Unmarried Mother," n.d., CWLA Papers, 47:4, SWHA.

[106]Texas to President Truman, Box 457, File 7–4–3–3–4, 1951, Record Group 102, N.A.

[107]Leontine Young, "Is Money Our Trouble?" paper presented at the National Conference of Social Workers, Cleveland, 1953.

[108]*Hearings, Interstate Adoption Practices*, July 15–16, 1955, p. 203.

[109]Ibid., p. 110; see also Maud Morlock to Miss Wood, June 6, 1946, Box 165, File 7–4–3–0, Record Group 102, N.A.

[110]*Hearings, Interstate Adoption Practices*, July 15–16, 1955, p. 111.

[111]Duluth, Minnesota, to Governor Luther Youngdahl, August 2, 1950, and to President Truman, August 14, 1950 Box 457, File 7–4–3–3–4, Record Group 102, N.A.

[112]Mildred Arnold to Duluth, Minnesota, August 21, 1950, Box 457, File 7–4–3–3–4, Record Group 102, N.A.

[113]Sterling, Colorado, to Mrs. Lenroot, November 21, 1949, Box 457, File 7–4–3–3–7, Record Group 102, N.A.

[114]*Hearings, Commercial Child Adoption Practices*, May 16, 1956, p. 86.

[115]Harriet Gates Oman, "Giving Up a Baby," *The Survey* 88 (January 1952):14. Also see Catherine MacKenzie, "Black Market in Babies, Too," *New York Times Magazine*, February 18, 1945, 5ff, which cites the "minimum standards of the Child Welfare League of America." These included the provision "that the baby's mother is given time to make up her mind and helped to make plans if she wants to keep him." Also relevant is Ruth Reed's observation in the 1930s that "young unmarried mothers who at first were eager to surrender their infants for adoption find themselves, after a few weeks assocation with the child, of a contrary opinion and grateful to those who have made such a period of reflection possible. These workers have seen instances when a hasty decision as to the separation of mother and child has resulted in much unhappiness for the young woman and fruitless efforts on her part to recover possession of the child." Ruth Reed, *The Illegitimate Family in New York City: Its Treatment by Social and Health Agencies* (Westport, CT: 1971; originally published by Columbia University Press, 1934), p. 60. Regarding the situation in the 1950s, see Hester B. Curtis and Alberta de Rongé, "Medical and Social Care for Unmarried Mothers," *Children* 4 (September–October 1957):174–80.

[116]Advance, Arkansas, to Children's Bureau, 1950, Box 457, File 7–4–3–1–4, Record Group 102, N.A. See also Babette Block to Maud Morlock, February 7, 1951, in which the director of Chicago's central agency for unmarried mothers favorably describes a forced relinquishment endorsed at the highest administrative levels.

[117]*Hearings, Interstate Adoption Practices,* July 15–16, 1955, p. 195. This home and its nefarious practices were the subject of the Ophra Winfrey Show, June 20, 1991, during which adults who had been victims of this home as children appeared.

[118]Often the court claimed that the mother abandoned her infant at the hospital.

[119]*Hearings, Interstate Adoption Practices, Miami, Florida*, November 14–15, 1955, p. 61.

[120]Ibid., p. 77.

[121]Ibid., p. 120.

[122]Ibid., pp. 131–2.

[123]Ibid., pp. 116–17.

[124]*Hearings, Interstate Adoption Practices*, July 15–16, 1955, p. 206.

[125]Clark Vincent, "The Adoption Market and the Unmarried Mother's Baby," *Marriage and Family Living* 18 (May 1956):124–7; Clark Vincent to Helen Witmer, May 7, 1956, Box 689, File 7–4–0–6, Record Group 102, N.A.

[126]Dan C. Fowler, "The Problem of Unwed Mothers," *Look*, July 29, 1949, p. 33.

[127]*New York Times*, July 10, 1958.

[128]Maud Morlock, "Field Report, Ohio," 1949.

[129]*Hearings, Interstate Adoption Practices*, July 15–16, 1955, p. 184.

[130]Ibid., p. 9

[131]*Hearings, Commercial Child Adoption Practices*, May 16, 1956, p. 37.

[132]*Hearings, Interstate Adoption Practices*, July 15–16, 1955, p. 111.

[133]Virginia Kinzel, "Confidentiality of Recording on Medical Charts," n.d., Box 892, File 7–4–0–4, Record Group 102, N.A.

[134]Brower, "What Shall I Do with My Baby?" p. 167.

[135]Los Angeles to the Children's Bureau, February 12, 1949, Box 457, File 7–4–3–1–4, Record Group 102, N.A.

[136]*Hearings, Commercial Child Adoption Practices*, May 16, 1956, p. 110.

[137]Ibid., p. 115.

[138]*Hearings, Interstate Adoption Practices, Miami, Florida*, November 14–15, 1955, p. 242.

[139]Ibid., p. 186.

[140]Maud Morlock noted in regret in a memo in 1949 that a very fine and effective maternity home in Boise, Idaho, was in danger of closing because of underuse. "Reduction in demand," she observed, "was not due to a decline in illegitimate pregnancy but . . . to attorneys placing babies and providing care for girls in hospitals." Maud Morlock, "Memo of Conference with Ruth Pagan," November, 1949, Box 456, File 7–4–3–1–1, Record Group 102, N.A.

[141]"Meeting to Discuss Services to Unmarried Mothers, Dallas," March 20, 1950, Box 455, File 7–4–5–0, Record Group 102, N.A.

[142]U.S. Congress, Juvenile Delinquency Subcommittee, Unpublished Hearing, May 11, 1956.

[143]*Hearings, Interstate Adoption Practices*, July 15–16, 1955, Appendix, p. 221.

[144]Augusta, Maine, to Children's Bureau, October 28, 1949, Box 457, File 7–4–3–1–4, Record Group 102, N.A.

[145]*Hearings, Interstate Adoption Practices, Miami, Florida*, November 14–15, 1955, pp. 54–6.

[146]*Hearings, Interstate Adoption Practices*, July 15–16, 1955, pp. 99–100.

[147]U.S. Congress, Senate, Committee on the Judiciary, Subcommittee to Investigate Juvenile Delinquency in the United States (84th Congress, 2d sess.), Unpublished Testimony, May 16, 1956, pp. 67–71.

[148]Alice Lake, "Why Girls Sell Their Babies," *Cosmopolitan*, December 1956, pp. 42ff.

[149]*Hearings, Commercial Child Adoption Practices*, May 16, 1956, pp. 13, 19.

[150]Lake, "Why Girls Sell."

[151]*Hearings, Interstate Adoption Practices*, July 15–6, 1955, pp. 52–3.

[152]*Hearings, Interstate Adoption Practices, Miami, Florida*, November 14–15, 1955, pp. 192–3.

[153]*Hearings, Interstate Adoption Practices*, July 15–16, 1955, pp. 99–100.

[154]*Hearings, Commercial Child Adoption Practices*, May 16, 1956, p. 28.

[155]U.S. Congress, Juvenile Delinquency Subcommittee, Hearings, Unpublished Testimony, May 16, 1956.

[156]*Hearings, Interstate Adoption Practices, Miami, Florida*, November 14–15, 1955, p. 245.

[157] Bowerman, *Unwed Motherhood*, p. 236.

[158]Meyer, Jones, and Borgatta, "The Decision by Unmarried Mothers."

[159]Clark Vincent, "Unwed Mothers and the Adoption Market: Psychological and Familial Factors," *Journal of Marriage and Family Living* 22 (May 1960):118.

Chapter Six

[1]This includes public school systems, health and welfare departments, hospitals, adoption agencies, and integrated maternity homes, but does not refer to the few black maternity homes or to organizations based in the black community, such as churches.

[2]See, for example, Jacquelyn Dowd Hall, " 'The Mind That Burns in Each Body': Women, Rape, and Racial Violence," in *Powers of Desire: The Politics of Sexuality*, Ann Snitow, Christine Stansell, and Sharon Thompson, eds. (New York: Monthly Review Press, 1988), pp. 328–49.

[3]Ruth Reed, *The Illegitimate Family in New York City: Its Treatment by Social and Health Agencies* (New York: Columbia University Press, 1934), p. 202.

[4]Arnold Gessell and Frances L. Ilg, *Infant and Child in the Culture of Today* (New York: Harper and Co., 1943), p. 273.

[5]See Chapter Two.

[6]Annie Lee Davis, "Attitudes Toward Minority Groups: Their Effect on Services for Unmarried Mothers," *The Child* 13 (December 1948):82–5; also see Maud Morlock to Jane Wrieden, September 28, 1951, Box 455, File 7–4–2–1, Record Group 102, National Archives (hereafter referred to as N.A.).

[7]Maud Morlock, "Field Report, Texas," 1950, Box 455, File 7–4–0–7–4, Record Group 102, N.A.

[8]Annie Lee (Davis) Sandusky to Ursula Gallagher, June 27, 1958, Box 894, File 7–4–3–1–1, Record Group 102, N.A.

[9]Maud Morlock, "Field Report, Ohio," 1949, Box 455, File 7–4–3–0, Record Group 102, N.A.

[10]Davis, "Attitudes Toward Minority Groups."

[11]See, for example, Andrew Billingsley and Jeanne Giovannoni, *Children of the Storm* (New York: Harcourt, Brace and Jovanovich, 1972), p. 142.

[12]Maud Morlock, "Field Report, Ohio," 1949.

[13]See, for example, Trudy Bradley, "An Exploration of Caseworkers' Perceptions of Adoption Applicants," *Child Welfare* 45 (October 1966):433–43.

[14]Patricia Garland, "Illegitimacy—a Special Minority-Group Problem in Urban Areas," *Child Welfare* 45 (February 1966):84.

[15]Ibid.

[16] *New York Times*, July 8, 1961.

[17]Leontine Young, *Out of Wedlock* (New York: McGraw-Hill, 1954), pp. 87–8.

[18] During the period considered here, black women in the south were among the first in the United States targeted to receive publicly subsidized birth control, sterilization, and abortion services. See Chapter Two.

[19]*New York Times*, August 18, 1960.

[20]See Winifred Bell, *Aid to Dependent Children* (New York: Columbia University Press, 1965), chapter 9.

[21]*St. Louis Post-Dispatch*, August 8, 1961.

[22]Ibid. Rosalind Petchesky has noted astutely, "Denying poor women access to abortion, thus forcing them to have children they do not want, and restricting their reproductive capacity through coercive measures such as sterilization abuse, would seem to be contradictory policies. Yet . . . these ambiguities are inherent in a society geared historically to the need to control both its 'relative surplus population' and the sexual and reproductive maneuverability of women. These goals hang in an uneasy tension and may be tentatively worked out differently at different times or in different regions." *Abortion and Woman's Choice: The State, Sexuality and Reproductive Freedom*, rev. ed. (Boston: Northeastern University Press, 1990), pp. 160–1.

[23]U.S. Congress, House, Committee on Ways and Means, *Hearings on Public Assistance Titles of the Social Security Act*, April 12, 13, 16, 19, 20, 1956 (84th Congress, 2d sess. [Washington, D.C.: Government Printing Office, 1956]), p. 52.

[24]*Milwaukee Journal*, August 9, 1961.

[25]*Illegitimacy and Its Impact on the ADC Program*, Bureau of Public Assistance, Social Security Administration (Washington, D.C.: Government Printing Office, 1960), p. 30.

[26]*Buffalo Courier Express*, December 5, 1957.

[27]*Illegitimacy and Its Impact*, p. 36.

[28]Ibid.

[29]*New York Times*, August 1, 1961.

[30]*Illegitimacy and Its Impact* , p. 57; also see *Hearings on Public Assistance Titles*, April 12, 13, 16, 19, 20, 1956, p. 55.

[31]See Chapter One.

[32]Mary Stanton to Maud Morlock, November 21, 1951. Box 456, File 7–4–3–1–3, Record Group 102, N.A.

[33]Ursula Gallagher to Mrs. Hymning, September 17, 1959, Box 893, File 7–4–3–0, Record Group 102, N.A.

[34]"Report of Panel Discussion on the Hospital Experience of the Unmarried Mother," March 25, 1958, FCAA Papers, Box 7, File: Community Council of Greater New York, 1958, Social Welfare History Archives, University of Minnesota (hereafter cited as SWHA).

[35]Davis, "Attitudes Toward Minority Groups."

[36]Maud Morlock, "Field Report, Chicago," 1947, Box 164, File 7–4–0–7–6, Record Group 102, N.A.

[37]*Hearing, Public Assistance Titles*, April 12, 13, 16, 19, 20, 1956, p. 59. Also see Ernest E. Jorden, "A Study of the Social and Maternal Responsibility of a Group of Negro Unwed Mothers," Ed.D. dissertation, University of Pennsylvania, 1969.

[38]Rose Bernstein, "Gaps in Services to Unmarried Mothers," *Children* 10 (March–April 1963):50.

[39]Ibid.,p. 51.

[40]"Material Prepared for House Appropriations Committee, January 1962," Box 893, File 7–4–3–0, Record Group 102, N.A. The other unmet need was equally narrowly focused: maternity homes for Negro unwed mothers.

[41]See, for example, Maud Morlock, "Field Report, Chicago," 1947.

[42]Billingsley and Giovannoni, *Children of the Storm*, p. 141.

[43]University of Maryland, Baltimore Project, 1959, Box 893, File 7–4–3–1, Record Group 102, N.A.

[44]See, for example, Seaton W. Manning, "The Changing Negro Family: Implications for the Adoption of Children," *Child Welfare* 43 (November 1964):480–5.

[45]Annie Lee Davis to Staff, Social Service Division, March, 1949, Box 455, File 7–4–2–1, Record Group 102, N.A.

[46]Ibid.

[47]Elizabeth Herzog and Rose Bernstein, "Why So Few Negro Adoptions?" *Children* 12 (January–February 1965):14.

[48]Billingsley and Giovannoni, *Children of the Storm*, p. 203.

[49]U.S. Congress, Senate, Judiciary Committee, *Hearings Before the Subcommittee to Investigate Juvenile Delinquency on Commercial Child Adoption Practices*, May 16, 1956 (84th Congress, 2d sess. [Washington, D.C.: Government Printing Office, 1956]), p. 88. Embedded not so deeply in this statement are the justifications for benign neglect: the situation will change on its own; and the charge to social agencies not to give black babies to "unqualified" couples.

[50]Marie W. Daugherty, Hortense Few, and Margaret Muller, "Achieving Adoption for Sixty Children," *Child Welfare* 37 (October 1958):7–11.

[51]Also see "Agency Sponsors Contest on Ways of Interesting More Colored Families in Adoption," *Child Welfare* 31 (January 1952).

[52]"Interracial Adoptions," *Children* 12 (November–December 1965):247.

[53]Billingsley and Giovannoni, *Children of the Storm*, p. 142.

[54]Ibid., p. 156.

[55]Ibid., p. 167.

[56]David Fanshel, *A Study in Negro Adoption* (New York: Child Welfare League of America, 1957), p. 51.

[57]Leila C. Deasey and Olive W. Quinn, "The Urban Negro and Adoption of Children," *Child Welfare* 41 (November 1962):400–407.

[58]Bradley, "An Exploration of Caseworkers' Perceptions," p. 435.

[59]Elizabeth Tuttle, "Serving the Unmarried Mother Who Keeps Her Child," *Social Welfare* 43 (October 1962):418.

[60]Renée M. Berg, "A Study of a Group of Unwed Mothers Receiving ADC," D. S. W. dissertation, University of Pennsylvania School of Social Work, 1962, p. 55.

[61]See *Facts, Fallacies and Future—a Study of the ADC Program of Cook County, Illinois* (New York: Greenleigh Associates, 1960), pp. 19–20; 552 out of 619 mothers of illegitimate children in this study did not want another child, but had no information about how to prevent conception.

[62]Ibid., pp. 5–6.

[63]Deborah Shapiro, "Attitudes, Values, and Unmarried Motherhood," in *Unmarried*

Parenthood: Clues to Agency and Community Action (New York: National Council on Illegitimacy, 1967), p. 60.

[64]Ellery Reed and Ruth Latimer, *A Study of Unmarried Mothers Who Kept Their Babies* (Cincinnati: Social Welfare Research, Inc., 1963), p. 72.

[65]Joyce Ladner, *Tomorrow's Tomorrow: The Black Woman* (New York: Doubleday, 1971), pp. 2, 8. Also see Carol Stack, *All Our Kin: Strategies for Survival in a Black Community*, (New York: Random House, 1974), especially chapter 5: "Child-Keeping: 'Gimme a Little Sugar.' "

[66] Reed and Latimer, *A Study of Unmarried Mothers*, p. 72.

[67] Shapiro, "Attitudes and Values," p. 61.

[68]Harold Visotsky, M.D., "A Program for Unwed Pregnant Adolescents in Chicago," paper presented at the American Orthopsychiatry Association Annual Meeting, New York, 1965.

[69]Renée Berg, "Utilizing the Strengths of Unwed Mothers in the AFDC Program," *Child Welfare* 43 (July 1964):337.

[70]Ibid.

[71]Berg, "A Study of a Group of Unwed Mothers," p. 96.

[72]Ibid., p. 93.

[73]Ibid., p. 95.

[74]Mignon Sauber and Elaine Rubinstein, *Experiences of the Unwed Mother as Parent: A Longitudinal Study of Unmarried Mothers Who Keep Their Babies* (New York: Community Council of Greater New York, 1963), p. 63.

[75]William Rashbaum, M.D., Janice Paneth, Helen Rehr, and Martin Greenberg, "Use of Social Services by Unmarried Mothers," *Children* 10 (January–February 1963):14.

[76]Charles Bowerman, Donald Irish, and Hallowell Pope, *Unwed Motherhood: Personal and Social Consequences* (Chapel Hill: Institute for Research in Social Science, University of North Carolina, 1966), p. 261.

[77]University of Maryland, Baltimore Project, 1959.

[78]*A Positive Approach to Unmarried Mothers; Parental-Vocational Education Program of the Berean Institute* (Philadelphia: Berean Institute, 1959).

[79]Ibid.

[80] Tuttle, "Serving the Unmarried Mother," p. 415.

[81]See, for example, Maud Morlock, Field Report, Texas, 1950, Box 455, 7–4–0–7–4, Record Group 102, N.A.

[82]Elizabeth V. Parker, "Unmarried Mothers at New Haven Hospital: A Study of 30 Unmarried Mothers Who Took Their Children Home," M.A. thesis, University of Minnesota, 1947, pp. 43–4.

[83]Helen Harris Perlman, "Observations on Services and Research," in *Unmarried Parenthood: Clues to Agency and Community Action* (New York: National Council on Illegitimacy, 1967), p. 41.

[84]Lena Heyman, Children's Bureau Division of Research, to Genevieve Griffin, January 3, 1963, Box 1038, File 7–4–0–3, Record Group 102, N.A. Also see National Association on Services to Unmarried Parents Newsletter, vol. 7., June 1965, NASUP Papers, SWHA.

[85]Bowerman, *Unwed Motherhood*, p. 329.

[86]Ladner, *Tomorrow's Tomorrow*, pp. 214–15. Also see Shapiro, "Attitudes, Values," pp. 52–63.

Chapter Seven

[1] See Elaine Tyler May, *Homeward Bound: American Families in the Cold War Era* (New York: Basic Books, 1988), chapter 4, "Explosive Issues: Sex, Women and the Bomb," which explores "the connection of the unleashing of the bomb with the unleashing of sex." May argues that anxiety about "out of control sexuality" in the postwar era was focused on women.

[2] In October 1965, 122 agencies serving unwed mothers of both races began to use one "data collection" form, facilitating the routine collection, processing, and distribution of comparable data on unwed mothers through one, single vehicle. The interest in this technologically based, quantitative project contrasts with the "need to understand" that governed projects in the 1940s and 1950s.

[3] See *Illegitimacy and Its Impact on the ADC Program*, Bureau of Public Assistance, Social Security Administration, Department of Labor (Washington, D.C.: Government Printing Office, 1960), pp. 5–6; and Phillips Cutright, "Illegitimacy in the United States: 1920–1968," in Charles F. Westoff and Robert Parke, Jr., eds. *Demographic and Social Aspects of Population Growth* (Washington, D.C.: Commission on Population Growth and the American Future), p. 384.

[4] See Winifred Bell, *Aid to Dependent Children* (New York: Columbia University Press, 1965); Lucy Komisar, *Down and Out in the USA* (New York: New Viewpoints, 1974); and *New York Times*, December 2 and 16, 1960, and August 19 and December 20, 1961.

[5] *Detroit News*, April 8, 1965. Agency policies and legislative efforts in this era forbidding professionals from discussing contraception with poor women—and the ultimate failure of these bans—have a special resonance and relevance in 1991, with the Supreme Court's decision, *Rust v. Sullivan*, banning doctors in federally-funded family planning clinics from providing information about abortion to the approximately 4.5 million low-income women in the U.S. who are clients of these healthcare facilities. It is also fruitful to view the activities of the Louisiana state legislature in the summer of 1991—during which it outlawed abortion and mandated stiff jail sentences for doctors who perform this procedure—in the context of the activities of the same legislature in the summer of 1960, when it voted to remove all illegitimate children from the state's welfare rolls.

[6] U.S. Congress, Senate, Committee on Government Operations, Subcommittee on Foreign Aid Expenditures; *Population Crisis: Hearings on S. 1676, A Bill to Reorganize the Department of State and the Department of Health, Education and Welfare*, August 31, September 8, 15, 22, 1965, part 3-B (89th Cong., 1st sess. [Washington, D.C.: Government Printing Office, 1966]), pp. 1974–86.

[7] Ibid., part 3-A, pp. 1540–1. Hauser was clearly an activist liberal scholar in these years. Nicholas Lemann notes that in 1964 Philip Hauser "wrote a report attacking segregation in [Chicago], and afterward had to be put under the kind of twenty-four hour police guard that previously had been necessary only for black families who moved into white neighborhoods." See *The Promised Land: The Great Black Migration and How it Changed America* (New York: Knopf, 1991), p. 237.

[8] Ibid., p. 1414.

[9] See Ibid., pp. 1153–70, which includes the testimony of the Honorable Marriner Eccles, who called the overpopulation problem "more explosive than the bomb," and linked the problem in the United States to "the growth of the colored population [at a rate] about forty percent greater than that of the white population." Also see Ibid., part 1, p. 44, the testimony of Senator Joseph Tydings of Maryland; and J. Edgar

Hoover, *Crime in the United States* (Washington, D.C.: Government Printing Office, 1965), p. 3. Hoover wrote, "A relation is indicated between population growth and the crime rate inasmuch as those areas having the fastest growing populations generally are reporting the highest crime rates."

[10]*Population Crisis*, part 2-B, p. 1155.

[11]Ibid., p. 1168.

[12]Udall oversaw the first nonexperimental foray of the federal government into the business of distributing contraceptives and arranging for distribution "on demand on the Indian reservations, and among our 'native' population, in Alaska and in the Trust Territories." *Population Crisis*, part 2-A, p. 959. See also Udall, Stewart L., "A time bomb called population." Remarks in the House. *Congressional Record* [daily edition] vol. 111, July 29, 1965, pp. 6472–75.

[13]*New York Times*, March 28, 1965.

[14]*Population Crisis*, part 3-B, p. 1773.

[15]Ibid., p. 1662.

[16]See John R. Birmingham to Ernest Gruening, Ibid., part 4, p. 2042, and "Economic Impact—Birth Control Seen as an Investment Tool," *Washington Post*, September 19, 1965. See Chapter One.

[17]*Population Crisis*, part 2-A, pp. 796–7.

[18]Ibid., part 4, p. 2336.

[19]Ibid., part 2-A, p. 799.

[20]Ibid., p. 798.

[21]Ibid., part 1, p. 361.

[22]See Chapter Two.

[23]*New York Times*, March 28, 1965.

[24]On April 1, 1965, Representative Paul Todd (Dem., Michigan) introduced H.R. 7072, which stipulated that "no program under the act could provide contraceptive devices or drugs to unmarried women or women not living with their husbands." *Population Crisis*, part 1, p. 125. A month earlier, the Office of Equal Opportunity issued a statement of policy guidance for family planning groups. The statement proscribed the following activities: providing contraceptives to unmarried mothers, advertising birth control services, drugs, and equipment, abortions, and sterilization. Ibid., part 2-A, p. 741.

[25]Elizabeth Herzog to Lester Kirkendall, March 29, 1967, Box 1169, File 7–4–3–1, Record Group 102, National Archives (hereafter cited as N.A.).

[26]Raleigh Hobson to Directors, Local Welfare Departments, April 20, 1965, in *Population Crisis*, part 4, p. 2104.

[27]Otto Kerner to Ernest Gruening, June 22, 1965, Ibid., p. 2057, also pp. 2062–3.

[28]Ibid., part 3-B, pp. 1784–5.

[29]At the end of 1964, the American Medical Association's trustees moved to end its official "neutral" policy on birth control, backing dissemination of contraceptive data and devices by doctors to patients requiring them. See *New York Times*, December 2, 1964.

[30]*The Growth of U.S. Population* (Washington, D.C.: National Academy of Sciences, Publication no. 1279, 1965), chapter 2.

[31]Leslie Corsa, Jr., M.D., "Family Planning Programs in the United States," paper

presented at the World Population Conference, Belgrade, Yugoslavia, September 1965.

[32]"Family Planning Activities in Kentucky," *Population Crisis*, part 4, p. 2093.

[33]Alabama, Florida, Georgia, Mississippi, North Carolina, South Carolina, and Virginia. In this era, however, public sale of male contraceptives was still tightly controlled. In Maryland, for example, it was illegal to sell contraceptives in vending machines, except in liquor stores. In Mississippi, the sale, distribution, advertisement, and display of all contraceptives was illegal; however, in 1962 a law was introduced in the Mississippi state legislature that would have imposed criminal penalities on any woman who had had an illegitimate child and who did not thereafter go to a planned parenthood clinic. Harriet Pipel, "Sex vs. the Law: A Study in Hypocrisy," *Harper's*, January 1965, pp. 35ff.

[34]See *New York Times*, March 7, March 28, May 27, November 2, 1965.

[35]*Population Crisis*, part 2-B, pp. 1183–96.

[36]Ibid., part 1, p. 362.

[37]*New York Times*, November 2, 1960.

[38]See U.S. Department of Health, Education and Welfare, *A Multidisciplinary Approach to a School-Centered Rehabilitation Program for Pregnant School-Aged Girls in Washington, D.C.: A Summary Report*, by Elizabeth M. Goodman and Fabola M.L. Gill, Child Welfare Demonstration Grant No. D–130 (Washington, D.C.: 1966).

[39]Philip Holman to Dorothea Andrews, October 25, 1967, Box 1169, File 7–4–0, Record Group 102, N.A.

[40]P. Frederick DelliQuardri to Mary Switzer, December 17, 1968, Box 1169, File 7–4–3–1–4, Record Group 102, N.A.

[41]Jean Pakter, M.D., et al, "Out-of-Wedlock Births in New York City: II—Medical Aspects," *American Journal of Public Health* 51 (June 1961):862.

[42]William Rashbaum, M.D., "Use of Social Services by Unmarried Mothers," *Children* 10 (January–February 1963):16.

[43]See, for example, Elizabeth Tuttle, "Serving the Unmarried Mother Who Keeps Her Child," *Social Casework* 43 (October 1962):415–22.

[44]Ibid.

[45]Mary Verner, "Effective Techniques of Communication with and Rehabilitation of Hard-to-Reach Out-of-Wedlock Families," paper presented at the National Conference on Social Welfare, 1963. Also see American Social Hygiene Association (ASHA) Papers, Boxes 120 and 122, SWHA. These contain some sketchy but interesting information about the Tri-City Project, mounted by the ASHA in the late 1950s to study illegitimacy in Washington, Baltimore, and Richmond. Part of this project involved collaboration between Howard University, the D.C. Freedman's Hospital, and the D.C. Departments of Public Health and Public Welfare. At one point, representatives of these institutions planned to interview three hundred "Negro girls . . . in the attempt to discover the social, cultural and personality factors that lead teenagers to such sexual behavior as resulted in their illegitimacy."

[46]See Chapter Three.

[47]Sarah J. Short, "Effective Techniques of Communication with and Rehabilitation of 'Hard to Reach' Out of Wedlock Families," paper presented at the National Conference on Social Welfare, 1963.

[48]Wyatt C. Jones, "Correlates of Social Deviance: A Study of Unmarried Mothers," Ph.D. dissertation, New York University, 1965, p. 108.

[49]National Association on Services to Unmarried Parents Papers, NASUP Newslet-

ter 4 (September 1964), Social Welare History Archives, University of Minnesota (hereafter cited as SWHA).

[50]Charles Gershenson to the Secretary, December 17, 1968, Box 1169, File 7–4–3–1–4, Record Group 102, N.A.

[51]See, for example, Grace A. Day, "A Program for Teenage Unmarried Mothers," *American Journal of Public Health* 55 (1965):978–81; Mattie K. Wright, "Comprehensive Services for Adolescent Unwed Mothers," *Children* 13 (1966):174; Mildred Berl, "An Interim School Program for Unwed Mothers," *Child Welfare* 39 (January 1960):22–4; "A Training and Rehabilitation Center for Young and Unwed Mothers," *New York Times Magazine*, March 3, 1967; also see *Children* 15 (January–February 1968) for a survey of special programs offered throughout the United States.

[52]Katherine B. Oettinger to Marion Obenhaus, June 8, 1967, Box 1169, File 7–4–0–7, Record Group 102, N.A. Also see "Comprehensive Programs for School-Age Pregnant Girls, 1968," Box 1169, File 7–4–3–1–4, and Charles Gershenson to Regional Child Welfare Representatives, August 16, 1968, Box 1169, File 7–4–3–1–4, Record Group 102, N.A.

[53]C.A. Peters to Elizabeth Herzog, August 16, 1965, Box 1039, File 7–4–3–1–1, Record Group 102, N.A.

[54]"The Morals Revolution on the U.S. Campus," *Newsweek*, April 6, 1964, p. 52. Academic studies and the mass media provided safer forums for airing this perspective than individual expression. The University of Illinois fired Professor Leo F. Koch for writing the following letter to the *Daily Illini* in March 1960. "With modern contraceptives and medical advice readily available at the nearest drugstore, or at least a family physician, there is no valid reason why sexual intercourse should not be condoned among those sufficiently mature to engage in it without social consequences and without violating their own codes of morality and ethics. . . .[M]utually satisfying sexual experience would eliminate the need for many hours of frustrating petting and lead to much happier and longer lasting marriages among younger men and women." The American Association of University Professors censored the University of Illinois for firing Professor Koch who lost all of his court appeals, up to the Illinois State Supreme Court, which refused to consider the appeal. *New York Times*, April 27, 1963.

[55]See Helen Gurley Brown, *Sex and the Single Girl* (New York: Bernard Geis, 1962).

[56]See, for example, Clark Vincent, *The Unmarried Mother* (Glencoe, IL: The Free Press, 1961).

[57]Marjorie Holmes, "A Mother Speaks Up for Censorship," *Today's Health* (January 1962), p. 67.

[58]Mary Louise Allen as told to Eleanor Harris, "What Can We Do About America's Unwed Teenage Mothers?" *McCall's*, November 1963, p. 40.

[59]Clark Vincent, "Illegitimacy and Value Dilemmas," *Christian Century*, June 19, 1963, p. 804.

[60]Charles Bowerman, Donald P. Irish, and Hollowell Pope, *Unwed Mothers: Personal and Social Consequences* (Chapel Hill: Institute for Research in Social Science, University of North Carolina), p. 392.

[61]Deborah Shapiro, "Social Distance and Illegitimacy: A Comparative Study of Attitudes and Values," D.S.W. dissertation, Columbia University, 1966, p. 129. Also see Katheryn M. Nielsen and Rocco L. Motto, "Some Observations on Family Constellations and Personality Patterns of Young Unmarried Mothers," *American Journal of Orthopsychiatry* 33 (July 1963):741. Nielsen and Motto found that "In assessing [maternity home residents'] feelings over the fact of their pregnancy, repeat-

edly it was found that they felt no guilt in the sense of having overstepped cultural mores."

[62]Virgil G. Damon, M.D., and Isabelle Taves, "My Daughter Is in Trouble," *Look*, August 8, 1962, p. 26.

[63]Andrew Hacker, "The Pill and Morality," *New York Times Magazine*, November 21, 1965, p. 140.

[64]"The Second Sexual Revolution," *Time*, January 24, 1964, p. 57.

[65]"The Morals Revolution," *Newsweek*, p. 52.

[66]Barbara Kay Davidson, *The Sweet Potato Vine* (New York: Family Service Association of America, 1961).

[67]Thomas S. Poffenberger, "Individual Choice in Adolescent Premarital Sex Behavior," *Marriage and Family Living* 22 (November 1960):327.

[68]Hacker, "The Pill," p. 32.

[69]Gloria Steinem, "The Moral Disarmament of Betty Coed," *Esquire* , September, 1962, pp. 153–4.

[70]Ibid., p. 153.

[71]"The Morals Revolution," p. 54.

[72]Hacker, "The Pill," p. 140.

[73]Thomas S. Poffenberger, "The Control of Adolescent Premarital Coitus: An Attempt at Clarification of the Problem," *Marriage and Family Living* 24 (August 1962):258.

[74]Helen H. Perlman, "Unmarried Mothers, Immorality and the ADC Program," paper presented at the Annual Conference of the Florence Crittenton Association of America, Cleveland, Ohio, 1963.

[75]Hacker, "The Pill," p. 139.

[76]"The Morals Revolution," p. 56.

[77]Hacker, "The Pill," p. 139.

[78]Howard Whitman, "The Slavery of Sex Freedom," *Better Homes and Gardens*, June 1957, pp. 172, 218.

[79]Nelson Foote, "Sex As Play," in Jerome Himmelhoch and Sylvia Fleis Fava, eds., *Sexual Behavior in American Society* (New York: W.W. Norton, 1955), pp. 237–43.

[80]Ira Reiss, "The Sexual Renaissance: A Summary and Analysis," *Journal of Social Issues* 22 (April 1966):127.

[81]Rose Bernstein, "Are We Still Stereotyping the Unmarried Mother?", *Social Work* 5 (July 1960):108.

[82]"Collaboration of Agencies in Serving Unmarried Mothers: Who Does What When?" *1964 Florence Crittenton Association of America Northeast Conference Papers* (Chicago: FCAA, 1964), pp. 93–100.

[83]Shapiro, p. 27.

[84]Lillian E. Taylor, "Social Attitudes Toward Sexual Behavior and Illegitimacy," in *Illegitimacy: Data and Findings for Prevention, Treatment and Policy Formation* (New York: The National Council on Illegitimacy, 1965), p. 26. See, in comparison, Evelyn M. Duvall's book, the most popular teenage sex manual of the postwar years, *Facts of Life and Love for Teenagers* (New York: Association Press, 1956), chapter 4, "Sex Problems and Promises," pp. 83–106.

[85]Bernstein, p. 110.

[86]Vincent, "Illegitimacy and Value Dilemmas," p. 804.

[87]See, for example, Vincent, *Unmarried Mothers.*

[88]Robert Bell, "Parent-Child Conflict in Sexual Values," *Journal of Social Issues* 22 (April 1966):34–44. See also Gertrude Barker, "Self-Esteem of the Unwed Mother," Ed.D. dissertation, Boston University, 1967.

[89]Perlman, "Unmarried Mothers," p. 9.

[90]Shapiro, pp. 253–4. See also Rollo Barnes to Ursula Gallagher, April 13, 1965, Box 1038, File 7–4–0–7, Record Group 102, N.A., concerning the vulnerability of the adoption mandate from another direction, the claims of the unwed father.

[91]See, for example, a high-level Children's Bureau employee's congressional testimony in 1961, which broke from the usual exclusive focus on the adoption solution: "Adoption statistics show that more than one-half of all children adopted each year in the United States are illegitimate. The estimated number of adoptions of illegitimate children—over 50,000 in 1959—is in the proportion of about one out of four illegitimate births during the year. Very few illegitimate children live in institutions. According to the best estimates, more than two out of three live with their own parents or relatives." U.S. Congress, House, Appropriations Committee, Subcommittee on Departments of Labor, Health, Education and Welfare and Related Agencies' Appropriations for 1962, *Hearings Before the Subcommittee of the Committee on Appropriations*, (87th Congress, 1st sess. [Washington, D.C.: U.S. Government Printing Office, 1961]), p. 610. The first reference I have found to this trend, articulated by social service professionals, occurred in a 1957 newsletter of the National Association on Services to Unmarried Parents: "An interesting phenomenon of the Association's sessions [at the annual, national social workers' conference] was the overflow crowd turning out for the session on 'The Unmarried Mother who Keeps Her Child.' Scheduled in a charming room limited to 175, the meeting turned away another 75–100." NASUP Newsletter, August 1957, National Association on Services to Unmarried Parents (NASUP) Papers, File: Newsletters 1956–1965, SWHA.

[92]See, for example, Barbara Smith to Ursula Gallagher, February 19, 1968, Box 1169, File 7–4–0–3, Record Group 102, N.A.

[93]NASUP Newsletter, April, 1962, NASUP Papers, File: NASUP Newsletters 1956–1965, SWHA.

[94]Kathryn Koehler to Mary Watts, June 12, 1962, Box 892, File 7–4–0–6, Record Group 102, N.A.

[95]Shapiro, p. 380; Bowerman, p. 211.

[96]The Bowerman study also included 619 Blacks.

[97]Bowerman, p. 314.

[98]Ibid., pp. 211, 306.

[99]Shapiro, p. 383.

[100]*National Council on Illegitimacy Newsletter*, Fall 1967, Box 1170, File 7–4–3–1–1, Record Group 102, N.A.

[101]Abbie Blair, "Goodbye, Stephen," *Readers' Digest*, August 1962, p. 39.

[102]Damon and Taves, "My Daughter Is in Trouble," p. 28.

[103]In going for consultation with this doctor, pregnant women were seeking permission to obtain therapeutic abortions. They did not want to be forced, as they saw it, according to the doctor, to have babies they didn't want; nor did they want to be forced to carry babies to term and give them up for adoption. Harold Rosen, "Pyschiatric Implications of Abortion: A Case Study in Hypocrisy," in David T. Smith, ed., *Abortion and the Law* (Cleveland: Press of Case Western Reserve University, 1967), p. 94.

[104]See, in particular, Ira L. Reiss, *Premarital Sexual Standards in America* (Glencoe, IL: The Free Press, 1960), and Ira L. Reiss, *The Social Context of Pre-Marital and Sexual Permissiveness* (New York: Holt, Rinehart and Winston, 1967).

[105]Barker, p. 123.

[106]Ibid., p. 134.

[107]See Kenneth L. Cannon and Richard Long, "Premarital Sexual Behavior in the Sixties," *Journal of Marriage and the Family* 33 (February 1971):36–47; Paul A. Walters, "Promiscuity in Adolescence," *American Journal of Orthopsychiatry* 35(July, 1965): 670–5; Dana L. Farnsworth, "Sexual Morality and the Dilemma of the Colleges," *American Journal of Orthopsychiatry* 35 (July 1965):676–81.

[108]See, for example, Robert R. Bell and Jay B. Chaskes, "Premarital Sexual Experience Among Coeds, 1958 and 1968," *Journal of Marriage and the Family* 32 (February 1970):81–3.

[109]Steinem, p. 155.

[110]High Point, North Carolina to President Johnson, November 16, 1965, Box 1038, File 7–4–3–1, Record Group 102, N.A.

[111]Bertrand Y. Glassberg, "Sexual Behavior Patterns in Contemporary Youth Culture—Implications for Later Marriage," *Journal of Marriage and the Family* 27 (May 1965):190–2.

[112]Shapiro explained that unmarried mothers and their parents subscribed to the view that "this can happen to anyone" in part because it was "a socially well-supported defense." She went on, "Popular literature and communications media support it; current television dramas, for example, usually portray an unmarried mother as a young, sincere, confused, but 'nice' girl who is the victim of strong, but understandable, emotions. Furthermore, reassuring social workers often quite literally say, 'This can happen to anyone,' to unmarried mothers and their parents," pp. 149–50.

[113]*National Council on Illegitimacy Newsletter*, Fall 1967.

[114]Formerly the National Association on Services to Unmarried Parents.

[115]*National Council on Illegitimacy Newsletter*, Fall 1967.

[116]Shapiro, p. 393.

[117]Pittsfield, Massachusettes, to the Children's Bureau, January 15, 1969, Box 1169, File 7–4–3–1, Record Group 102, N.A.

[118]Ursula Gallagher to Mrs. Oettinger, October 27, 1961, Box 893, File 7–4–3–1, Record Group 102, N.A.

[119]See Cutright, "Illegitimacy in the United States 1920–1968," p. 426. Cutright noted, "The present contraceptive-only program is not likely to reduce illegitimate births greatly because it is often a post-partum program limited to maternity patients, while nearly three-fourths of white and over half of non-white illegitimate births are first births. Services of the present program are located in areas and facilities serving the poor while 40% of white and 20% of non-white illegitimate births are to women who are not poor. Most state laws create age barriers and thus remove 30% of white and 40% of non-white unwed mothers from preventitive services because they become pregnant before reaching age 18," p. 382.

[120]Phillips Cutright, "Illegitimacy: Myths, Causes and Cures," *Family Planing Perspectives* 3 (January 1971):46

[121]U. S. Congress, House of Representatives, *Hearings Before the Subcommittee of the Committee on Appropriations*, (87th Congress, 1st sess. [Washington, D.C.: Government Printing Office, 1962]), p. 750.

[122]Ibid., "Report on the Problem of Unwed Mothers Supplied by Dr. Katherine Bain, Deputy Chief, Children's Bureau," pp. 747–51.

[123]Ursula Gallagher, Field Report, Chicago, 1959, Box 894, File 7–4–3–1–1, Record Group 102, N.A.

[124]Dorothy Allen to Kate Helms, April 5, 1962, Box 893, File 7–4–3–0, Record Group 102, N.A.

[125]Mary E. Verner, "Administrative Concepts in Comprehensive Services for Unmarried Parents," in *Unmarried Parenthood: Clues to Agency and Community Action* (New York: National Council on Illegitimacy, 1967), p. 46.

[126]According to Cutright, about 60 percent of white unwed mothers were poor. See footnote 107.

[127]This argument was often made in the postwar era. See, for example, Mary Calderone, ed., *Abortion in the United States* (New York: Harper and Brothers, 1958), chapter 8.

[128]*Population Crisis*, part 2-B, p. 1060.

[129]Ibid, p. 975.

[130] See Cutright, "Illegitimacy, Myths, Causes and Cures."

[131]Ibid., p. 45.

Bibliography

Bibliography

Peter Laslett has done a great deal to define the social meaning of illegitimacy and to promote scholarship in this field.[1] Laslett has maintained that "When you study illegitimacy, you study marriage, succession to property, status, the mechanisms and effectiveness of social control, relations of ruling elites with the masses of society, of dominant with dominated classes." Reminding scholars of one of the fundamental purposes of studying deviance, in this case, illegitimacy, Laslett draws attention to this paradox: "[B]reaches of social rules do not necessarily weaken those rules, and under certain circumstances can even serve to strengthen them. Understanding social regulations, moreover, has to proceed to a large extent by the consideration of what happens when such regulation is defied."[2]

Recent historical studies of nonmarital pregnancy in the United States have appeared within the context of social histories dealing with the family, women, and the history of sexuality.[3] For the most part, these studies of illegitimate pregnancy in the past have focused on the measurement and causes of premarital pregnancy: how many cases can be documented in a particular locality during a particular historical period and what social, economic, religious, and political conditions existed to promote or restrain behaviors leading to pregnancy outside of marriage? The studies have largely been concerned with matching the changing rates of illegitimacy, as an index of changing sexual behavior, with changes in the structures of society. Following the work of Edward Shorter, historians of illegitimacy in America have used the illegitimacy rate as a test of the ability of institutions to exercise social control and the ability and willingness of individuals to exercise self-control, in the context of modernization.[4] To a more limited extent, these studies have explored the social significance of illegitimate pregnancy in the past by considering the consequences for the parties involved: which social institution was responsible for leveling what sort of sanction against which offenders?

Several exceptional historical studies lead the discussion of nonmarital pregnancy in new directions, and specifically focus on the community, institutional and legal responses to illegitimacy. Michael Grossberg's work on illegitimacy deals principally with bastards in relationship to the construction of family law in the nineteenth century.[5] In this context, Grossberg offers rich material on changing assumptions concerning the composition of the family between the eighteenth and early-twentieth centuries and on the continuous debates in legal and reform communities about which entity the law must protect first, the individual or the family. Grossberg provides historical, legal perspective on the disposition of illegitimate babies, on treatment of putative fathers, and on the social concerns that tilted the law against the unwed mother and her child over the course of the nineteenth century, and into the twentieth. Joan Jacobs Brumberg's impressive essay on the way illegitimacy was handled in an upstate New York community at the turn of the century assesses the consequences of out-of-wedlock pregnancy for young white girls and the role of family and community in constructing these consequences.[6] These studies illuminate processes by which unwed motherhood is socially constructed. They focus on the sources and content and consequences of the public response to illegitimacy. Brumberg, especially, considers how the private experience of unwed motherhood interacts with public opinion and community strategies. *Wake Up Little Susie* is an allied effort.

Laurel Ulrich's brilliant new book, *A Midwife's Tale: The Life of Martha Ballard Based on Her Diary 1785–1812*, provides some of the public and private meanings of unwed motherhood in New England at the end of the eighteenth and beginning of the nineteenth centuries.[7] Ulrich finds that "There is no evidence that in rural communities women who bore children out of wedlock were either ruined or abandoned as early novels would suggest," despite what the author calls "a broad community-based system" of social-sexual control.[8] Indeed, her evidence shows that "single mothers typically remained with their families of origin and eventually married;"[9] that both parents were responsible for the child born out of wedlock; and that "sexual activity was connected with a comprehensive transition to adulthood, to good citizenship and economic activity."[10]

Without suggesting that life in Hallowell, Maine, two hundred years ago was a Golden Age for illegitimate mothers, it is evident that in the near absence of race and class divisions, this community's supportive impulse toward its own unwed mothers was substantially different from the mid-twentieth century treatment of girls and women in this situation. Interestingly, the construction of unwed motherhood in Hallowell does resemble the construction that Joyce Ladner has suggested governed illegitimacy in the black community during the period of this study. Ladner, for example, explains that the community accepted mother and child, marital status notwithstanding: "There is something about the child-bearing experience that [the community feel[s] enhances maturity. . . . It is the time when the girl learns first hand the same thing that her mother has experienced."[11] Ladner makes no claims that unwed motherhood was validated by the community's expectations that the father would assume financial responsibility for the out-of-wedlock child or that both unwed parents would assume adult roles of "economic productivity" upon the birth of their child. Where racism and economic discrimination have been imposed upon the community, and thwart the community's potential for accepting and incorporating unwed mothers and their children, some expectations are not sustainable.

Clearly the presence or absence of the web of racism was not the only factor shaping the experiences of unwed mothers in eighteenth-century Maine and in the towns and cities of the United States in the mid-twentieth century. Nevertheless, the fact that a white unwed mother in eighteenth-century Maine faced an ordeal that had, in some important respects, more in common with a black girl than with a white one during the period of the present study, suggests just how plastic public policies and community attitudes toward unwed motherhood and race—and their relation to each other—have been in the history of American society.

The race-specific "public polices" to which this study refers include, as is customary, the laws, regulations, and funding patterns initiated and implemented by governmental entities, and to the ends these actions support. While the United States Children's Bureau was not itself a *policy-making* entity, the statements of its employees are often cited in this study as evidence of the government's policy position regarding the treatment of black and white unmarried mothers. The Bureau had a number of functions which made it a central force in shaping governmental, institutional, and public responses to single pregnancy. It set definitions, and clarified and interpreted issues and programs regarding unmarried mothers. The Children's Bureau's constituencies paid attention to its changing interpretations of single pregnancy and to its changing conceptions of appropriate practices.

The professionals at the Children's Bureau concerned with unmarried mothers in the postwar years were a deeply humanitarian group who deplored the public's generally punitive reaction to unwed mothers, black and white, preferring "understanding" and "rehabilitation" for all girls and women who had gone wrong, but could be saved. The staff worked within the framework of race-specific policies and practices emerging in the 1940s, and fully established after that. The Consultant on Services for Unmarried Mothers visited and evaluated public, private, and voluntary programs around the nation; made recommendations regarding licensing and funding of programs and agencies; lobbied and testified before Congress; published newsletters; sponsored conferences; delivered countless keynote addresses on policy matters; published articles; spoke to the press; worked with the media to develop TV shows, movies, and other educational materials; corresponded directly with unmarried mothers who wrote for advice; acted as consultant to and served on the boards of national organizations concerned with illegitimacy. In short, the Consultant on Services for Unmarried Mothers in the Children's Bureau was *the* responsible individual in the United States government in this area.

She, and her colleagues, spoke for the federal government while sometimes opposing the policies and practices of state governments. In general, the Children's Bureau staff supported and promoted an integrationist vision while at the same time acknowledging the need to bolster racially specific approaches to single pregnancy: social work/adoption programs for whites and welfare services for blacks.

The papers of Maud Morlock and Ursula Gallagher, who successively held the position Consultant on Services for Unmarried Mothers at the Children's Bureau between the late 1930s and the late 1960s, are the most important source of information about the federal government's policies, programs, and perspectives regarding unwed mothers. These papers are also a wonderful source of information about the content of programs across the country as both Morlock and Gallagher were in regular correspondence with practitioners in all parts of the United States. Both women wrote rich and lengthy reports for the files on all their numerous and frequent visits to local agencies over the years. In addition, these files, held by the National Archives, contain correspondence among professionals concerned with unwed pregnancy within the Children's Bureau and between Children's Bureau employees and employees of other federal agencies with related missions. Finally, the Morlock-Gallagher files contain a treasure trove of letters from single pregnant girls and women who, in their desperation, turned to anonymous government officials for information and assistance they were unable to find elsewhere. As far as I have been able to ascertain, this portion of Record Group 102 of the National Archives has not previously been used for research purposes.

A number of other federal government sources have been very useful in preparing this study. At odds, in a sense, with the Children's Bureau efforts, which were heavily geared to the needs of the stereotypical white unwed mother, were the reports prepared by the Bureau of Public Assistance, the National Office of Vital Statistics, and other agencies within the Department of Health, Education and Welfare that reported statistical information regarding illegitimacy by race and evaluated government support programs for unmarried parents. Interestingly, these government reports repeatedly revealed data that could have called into question the thrust of the work of government and voluntary agencies so deeply concerned with providing good maternity home care and adoption services for white unwed mothers. For example, *Illegitimacy and Its Impact on the Aid to Dependent Children Program: Implications for Federal and State Administrators*, a 1960 Social Security Administration publication, argued that not all white unwed mothers were middle class, nor were all black unwed mothers ADC recipients. It argued, indeed, for an end to racially specific treatment of unmarried mothers; however, as long as white babies were in increasing demand by postwar couples desiring to create or augment their families, and as long as some blacks contributed to the rising cost of the ADC program to U.S. taxpayers, racially specific treatment of these girls and women was widespread.

The final major federal government sources for this study were congressional hearings, both House and Senate, on such subjects as adoption abuse, welfare reform, civil rights, and the population explosion, all of which involved unwed mothers. These various hearings provided some of the most interesting, complex, and contentious voices for the study, as each hearing was addressed by many individuals with differing and competing interests. Most participants accepted the invitation to make a strong case for their personal or organizational agendas.

Complementing the government sources were materials from a number of private, voluntary agencies. The Social Welfare History Archives at the University of Minnesota holds rich and rarely used sets of relevant papers, especially the papers of the Florence Crittenton Mission, the Florence Crittenton Association of America, the Child Welfare League of America, Family Services Association of America, and the National Association on Services to Unmarried Parents, later called the National Council on Illegitimacy. Each of these organizations was centrally or exclusively concerned with providing services to unmarried, pregnant girls and women in the postwar era. The papers of all of them reflect a similar viewpoint. Between 1945 and the late 1950s, these agencies focused on constructing, advocating, and providing maternity home and adoption services for the girl defined by this study as the stereotypical white unwed mother. Beginning in the late 1950s, all of these agencies began to concern themselves with the situation of the black unwed mother as well, defining her typically as a poor ADC recipient who kept her child.

The employees and consultants to the Children's Bureau and to all of the agencies named immediately above wrote and published frequently on the subject of illegitimate pregnancy in the postwar era, along with other practitioners and academics. The following journals are representative of many in the fields of social work, public health, psychiatry and psychology, and medicine that featured such articles during this period which were sources for this book: *Children* (a Children's Bureau publication), *Child Welfare*, *Social Casework*, *Social Service Review*, *Journal of Orthopsychiatry*, *Public Welfare*, *American Journal of Nursing*, *American Journal of Obstetrics and Gynecology*. Academic studies of premarital sexuality and pregnancy appeared regularly in such journals as the *American Sociological Review*, *American Journal of Sociology*, and the *Journal of Marriage and Family Living*. The study draws on these and very influential book-length studies of illegitimate pregnancy published in the postwar era. The most prominent studies of the era were *Out of Wedlock* by Leontine Young, *Unmarried Mothers* by Clark Vincent, and *Unmarried Mothers in Our Society* by Sara Edlin. The mass media also covered the rising illegitimacy rate regularly. It was an especially popular subject for readers of the *Ladies' Home Journal* and other mass circulation women's magazines. Stories in these magazines were usually more human-interest-oriented, though no less racially specific, than the social work/public health material.

What is extraordinary about this collection of sources, prepared by social workers and other mental health professionals, medical practitioners, and academics, is the utter lack of contentiousness among authors within and across fields of expertise. The public, professional discussion of unwed mothers in the postwar era is a case study of the pervasive and persuasive power of consensus in this period, which lasted, in the case of unwed mothers, until the early 1960s.

Despite the polite consensus within and between various professional communities, politicians and municipal and state governments were engaged in a great deal of controversial rhetoric, as well as legislative efforts, during this period regarding public support for unwed mothers and their children. These episodes were reported and editorialized in *The New York Times* and the local and national press.

Notes

[1] Peter Laslett, *Family Life and Illicit Love in Earlier Generations* (Cambridge, England: Cambridge University Press, 1977); Peter Laslett, Karla Oosterveen, and Richard M. Smith, eds., *Bastardy and Its Comparative Perspective* (Cambridge, MA: Harvard University Press, 1980).

[2] Laslett, et al, eds., *Bastardy*, p. 3.

[3] See, for example, Daniel Scott Smith and Michael Hindus, "Premarital Pregnancy in America 1640–1971," *Journal of Interdisciplinary History* 5 (Spring 1975):537–70; Robert V. Wells, "Illegitimacy and Bridal Pregnancy in Colonial America" and Daniel Scott Smith, "The Long Cycle in American Illegitimacy and Prenuptial Pregnancy," both in Laslett et al, eds., *Bastardy*, pp. 351–61 and 362–78; Daniel Scott Smith, "The Dating of the American Sexual Revolution: Evidence and Interpretation," in Michael Gordon, ed., *The American Family in Socio-Historical Perspective* (New York: St. Martin's Press, 1978); Maris Vinovskis, "Adolescent Sexuality, Pregnancy and Childbearing in America: Some Preliminary Speculations," in Jane Lancaster and Beatrix Hamburg, eds., *School Age Pregnancy and Parenthood: Biosocial Dimensions* (New York: 1986), pp. 303–22; and Phillips Cutright, "The Teenage Sexual Revolution and the Myth of the Abstinent Past," *Family Planning Perspectives* 4 (January 1972):24–31.

[4] Edward Shorter, "Illegitimacy, Sexual Revolution, and Social Change in Modern Europe," *Journal of Interdisciplinary History* 2 (Autumn 1971):237–72.

[5] Michael Grossberg, *Governing the Health: Law and the Family in Nineteenth Century America* (Chapel Hill: University of North Carolina Press, 1985), chapter 6. Also see Mimi Abramovitz, *Regulating the Lives of Women: Social Welfare Policy from Colonial Times to the Present* (Boston: South End Press, 1988).

[6] Joan Jacobs Brumberg, "'Ruined Girls': Changing Community Responses to Illegitimacy in Upstate New York, 1890–1920," *Journal of Social History* 18 (Winter 1984):247–72.

[7] Laurel Thatcher Ulrich, *A Midwife's Tale: The Life of Martha Ballard Based on Her Diary 1785–1812* (New York: Knopf, 1990), pp. 147–60.

[8] Ibid., pp. 149, 153.

[9]Ibid., p. 157.

[10]Ibid., p. 158.

[11]Joyce A. Ladner, *Tomorrow's Tomorrow: The Black Woman* (New York: Doubleday, 1973), pp. 212–15.

Bibliography

Books and Pamphlets

Abramovitz, Mimi. *Regulating the Lives of Women: Social Welfare Policy from Colonial Times to the Present*. Boston: South End Press, 1988.

Bailey, Beth. *From Front Porch to Back Seat: Courtship in Twentieth-Century America*. Baltimore: The Johns Hopkins University Press, 1988.

Barnard, Jessie, ed. *Annals of the American Academy of Political and Social Science* 338 (November 1961). Special Issue: "Teen-Age Culture."

Bell, Robert R. *Premarital Sex in a Changing Society*. Englewood Cliffs, NJ: Prentice Hall, Inc., 1966.

Bell, Winifred. *Aid to Dependent Children*. New York: Columbia University Press, 1965.

Bergler, Edmund, and William S. Kroger. *Kinsey's Myth of Female Sexuality*. New York: Grune and Stratton, 1954.

Bernstein, Blanche, and Mignon Sauber. *Deterrents to Early Prenatal Care and Social Services Among Women Pregnant Out of Wedlock*. Albany: New York State Department of Social Welfare, 1961.

Bernstein, Rose. *Helping the Unmarried Mother*. New York: Association Press, 1971.

Biestek, Felix P. *The Casework Relationship*. Chicago: Loyola University Press, 1957.

Billingsley, Andrew, and Jeanne Giovannoni. *Children of the Storm*. New York: Harcourt, Brace, Jovanovich, 1972.

Birke, Lynda. *Women, Feminism and Biology: The Feminist Challenge*. New York: Methuen, 1986.

Blackwell, Gordon W., and Raymond Gould. *Future Citizens All*. Chicago: American Public Welfare Association, 1952.

Bowerman, Charles E., Donald Irish, and Hallowell Pope. *Unwed Motherhood: Personal and Social Consequences*. Chapel Hill, N.C.: Institute for Research in Social Science, University of North Carolina, 1966.

Branch, Taylor. *Parting the Waters: America in the King Years 1954–1963*. New York: Simon and Schuster, 1989.

Brown, Helen Gurley. *Sex and the Single Girl*. New York: Bernard Geis, 1962.

Burgess, M. Elaine, and Daniel O. Price. *An American Dependency Challenge*. Chicago: American Public Welfare Association, 1963.

Butcher, Ruth L., and Marion O. Robinson. *The Unmarried Mother*. New York: Public Affairs Pamphlet No. 25, 1959.

Calderone, Mary S., ed. *Abortion in the United States; A Conference Sponsored by the Planned Parenthood Federation of America*. New York: Harper and Brothers, 1958.

Carlson, B. *Illegitimacy . . . Who Pays?* Hartford, CT.: *The Hartfold Courant*, 1960. (A compilation of eight articles that appeared in the *Hartford Courant* in 1960.)

D'Emilio, John, and Estelle Freedman. *Intimate Matters: A History of Sexuality in America*. New York: Harper and Row, 1988.

Davidson, Barbara Kay. *The Sweet Potato Vine*. New York: Family Service Association of America, 1961.

Degler, Carl. *Autobiographical Accounts of Negro Ex-Slaves*. Nashville: Fisk University Press, 1968.

Delliquardri, Fred. *A Public Agency Looks at Its Services to the Unmarried Mother*. White Plains, NY: National Association on Services to Unmarried Parents, 1959.

Deutsch, Helene. *The Psychology of Women:* vol. 2, *Motherhood*. New York: Grune and Stratton, 1945.

Diggins, John Patrick. *The Proud Decades: America in War and Peace, 1941–1960*. New York: W.W. Norton, 1988.

Directory of Catholic Maternity Homes, 1963. Washington, D.C.: Association of Catholic Maternity Homes—National Conference of Catholic Charities, 1963.

Dizard, Jan E., and Howard Gadlin. *The Minimal Family*. Amherst: University of Massachusetts Press, 1990.

Drake, St. Clair, and Horace R. Clayton. *Black Metropolis: A Study of Negro Life in a Northern City*. New York: Harcourt Brace and Co., 1945.

Duvall, Evelyn M. *Facts of Life and Love for Teenagers*. New York: Association Press, 1956.

Edlin, Sara. *The Unmarried Mother in Our Society*. New York: Farrar, Straus and Young, 1954.

Effective Services for Unmarried Parents and Their Children. New York: National Council on Illegitimacy, 1968.

Ehrenreich, Barbara, and Dierdre English. *For Her Own Good: 150 Years of the Experts' Advice to Women*. New York: Doubleday, 1979.

Ehrenreich, Barbara, Elizabeth Hess and Gloria Jacobs. *Re-Making Love: The Feminization of Sex*. Garden City: Doubleday and Co., 1986.

Ehrmann, Winston. *Premarital Dating Behavior*. New York: Henry Holt, 1959.

Ellis, Albert, ed. *Sex Life of the American Woman and the Kinsey Report*. New York: Greenberg, 1954.

Facts, Fallacies and Future: A Study of the ADC Program of Cook County, Illinois. New York: Greenleigh Associates, 1960.

Fanshel, David. *A Study in Negro Adoption*. New York: Child Welfare League of America, 1957.

Florence Crittenton Association of America Papers from Midwest, Southern and Western Area Conferences, 1964. Chicago: Florence Crittenton Association of America, 1964.

Frazier, E. Franklin. *The Negro Family in the United States*. Chicago: University of Chicago Press, 1939.

Friedan, Betty. *The Feminine Mystique*. New York: W.W. Norton, 1963.

Gebhard, Paul H., Wardell B. Pomoroy, Clyde E.Martin, and Cornelia V. Christenson. *Pregnancy, Birth and Abortion*. New York: Harper and Bros., 1958.

Geddes, Donald Porter, ed. *An Analysis of the Kinsey Reports on Sexual Behavior in the Human Male and Female*. New York: New American Library, 1954.

Gessell, Arnold, and Frances L. Ilg. *Infant and Child in the Culture of Today*. New York: Harper and Co., 1943.

Gilbert, James. *Another Chance: Postwar America, 1954–1985*. Chicago: Dorsey Press, 1986.

Gill, Derek. *Illegitimacy, Sexuality and the Status of Women*. Oxford, England: Basil Blackwell, 1977.

Goodman, David. *A Parent's Guide to the Emotional Needs of Children*. New York: Hawthorne Books, 1959.

Greenwald, Harold. *The Call Girl: A Social and Analytical Study*. New York: Ballantine Books, 1958.

Grossberg, Michael. *Governing the Hearth: Law and the Family in Nineteenth Century America*. Chapel Hill: University of North Carolina Press, 1985.

Gutman, Herbert G. *The Black Family in Slavery and Freedom 1750–1925*. New York: Vintage Books, 1976.

Hartley, Shirley Foster. *Illegitimacy*. Berkeley: University of California Press, 1975.

Hauser, Philip M., ed. *The Population Dilemma*. Englewood Cliffs, NJ: Prentice-Hall, 1963.

Himmelhoch, Jerome, and Sylvia Fleis Fava, eds. *Sexual Behavior in American Society: An Appraisal of the First Two Kinsey Reports*. New York: W.W. Norton, 1955.

Hunt, Morton M. *The Natural History of Love*. New York: Alfred A. Knopf, 1959.

Illegitimacy in Richmond, Virginia 1910–1955. Richmond, VA: Department of Public Welfare, 1957.

Isaac, Rael Jean, and Joseph Spenser. *Adopting a Child Today*. New York: Harper and Row, 1965.

Jones, Elise F., et al. *Teenage Pregnancy in Industrialized Countries*. New Haven: Yale University Press, 1986.

Jones, Jacqueline. *Labor of Love, Labor of Sorrow: Black Women, Work and the Family from Slavery to the Present*. New York: Vintage Books, 1986.

Kaledin, Eugenia. *American Women in the 1950s: Mothers and More*. Boston: Twayne Publishers, 1984.

Kammerer, Percy G. *The Unmarried Mother: A Study of Five Hundred Cases*. Boston: Little Brown, 1918.

Katz, Michael. *The Undeserving Poor: From the War on Poverty to the War on Welfare*. New York: Pantheon, 1989.

Kinsey, Alfred, Wardell B. Pomeroy, Clyde E. Martin, and Paul H. Gebhard. *Sexual Behavior in the Human Female*. Philadelphia: W.B. Saunders Company, 1953.

Kirkendall, Lester. *Too Young to Marry?* Public Affairs Pamphlet No. 236. New York: Public Affairs Committee, 1957.

———. *Premarital Intercourse and Interpersonal Relationships*. New York: The Julian Press, 1961.

Kiser, Clyde, Wilson H. Grabil, and Arthur A. Campbell. *Trends and Variations in Fertility in the United States*. Cambridge, MA: Harvard University Press, 1968.

Komisar, Lucy. *Down and Out in the USA*. New York: New Viewpoints, 1974.

Konopka, Gisela. *Group Work in the Institution: The Modern Challenge*. New York: William Morrow, 1954.

Kunzel, Regina G. *The Girl Problem: Evangelicals, Social Workers, and Unmarried Mothers, 1890–1945*. New Haven: Yale University Press, forthcoming.

Kraus, Harry D. *Illegitimacy: Law and Social Policy*. Indianapolis: Bobbs-Merrill, 1971.

Ladner, Joyce. *Tomorrow's Tomorrow: The Black Woman*. New York: Doubleday, 1973.

Laslett, Peter, Karla Oosterveen, and Richard M. Smith, eds. *Bastardy and Its Comparative History*. Cambridge, MA: Harvard University Press, 1980.

Laslett, Peter. *Family Life and Illict Love in Earlier Generations.* Cambridge, England: Cambridge University Press, 1977.

Lemann, Nicholas. *The Promised Land: The Great Migration and How it Changed America.* New York: Knopf, 1991.

Lifton, Robert Jay, ed. *The Woman in America: A Timely Appraisal.* Boston: Beacon Press, 1965.

Littlewood, Thomas B. *The Politics of Population Control.* Notre Dame, IN: University of Notre Dame Press, 1977.

Lundberg, Ferdinand, and Marynia F. Farnham. *Modern Woman: The Lost Sex.* New York: Harper and Brothers, 1947.

Mannes, Marya. *More in Anger.* Philadelphia: Lippincott, 1958.

Maternity Homes Directory of 1960. Cleveland, OH: National Association on Services to Unmarried Parents, 1960.

May, Elaine Tyler. *Homeward Bound: American Families in the Cold War Era.* New York: Basic Books, 1988.

McDermott, Alice. *That Night.* New York: Harper and Row, 1987.

Merton, Robert K. *Social Theory and Social Structure.* Glencoe, IL: The Free Press, 1951.

Metalious, Grace. *Peyton Place.* New York: Julian Messner, 1956.

Michaelson, Kate, ed. *And the Poor Get Children: Radical Perspectives on Population Policy.* New York: Monthly Review Press, 1984.

Miller, Douglas T., and Marion Nowak. *The Fifties: The Way We Really Were.* Garden City, NY: Doubleday, 1977.

Myrdal, Gunnar. *The American Dilemma.* New York: Harper and Brothers, 1944.

Odenwald, Robert P. *The Disappearing Sexes: Sexual Behavior in the United States and the Emergence of Uni-Sex.* New York: Random House, 1965.

Ooms, Theodora, ed. *Teenage Pregnancy in a Family Context: Implications for Policy.* Philadelphia: Temple University Press, 1981.

Osili, A'Lelia Josephine, and Frieda Alice Parker. *A Study of Fifty Unmarried Negro Mothers in Pending and Active Aid to Dependent Children Cases in Marion County Department of Public Welfare.* Indianapolis: Marion Country Department of Public Welfare, 1957.

Osofsky, Howard J. *The Pregnant Teenager: A Medical, Educational and Social Analysis.* Springfield, IL: Charles C. Thomas, 1966.

Pannor, Reuben. *The Unmarried Father: New Approaches for Helping Unmarried Young Parents.* New York: Springer Publishing Co., 1971.

Pascoe, Peggy. *Relations of Rescue: The Search for Female Moral Authority in the American West, 1874–1939.* New York: Oxford University Press, 1990.

Peck, Ellen, and Judith Senderowitz. *Pronatalism: The Myth of Mom and Apple Pie.* New York: Thomas Y. Crowell, 1974.

Petchesky, Rosalind Pollack. *Abortion and Woman's Choice: The State, Sexuality and Reproductive Freedom.* Boston: Northeastern University Press, 1990.

Pierce, Ruth I. *Single and Pregnant.* Boston: Beacon Press, 1971.

Piven, Frances Fox, and Richard Cloward. *Regulating the Poor: The Functions of Public Welfare.* New York: Random House, 1971.

Positive Approach to Unmarried Mothers: Parental Vocational Educational Program of the Berean Institute. Philadephia: The Berean Institute, 1959.

Rainwater, Lee, and William Yancey. *The Moynihan Report and the Politics of Controversy*. Cambridge, MA: MIT Press, 1969.

Reed, Ellery F., and Ruth Latimer. *A Study of Unmarried Mothers Who Kept Their Babies*. Cincinnati: Social Welfare Research, Inc., 1963.

Reed, Ruth. *The Illegitimate Family in New York City: Its Treatment by Social and Health Agencies*. New York: Columbia University Press, 1934.

Reiss, Ira L. *Premarital Sexual Standards in America*. Glencoe, IL: The Free Press, 1960.

———. *The Social Context of Pre-Marital Sexual Permissiveness*. New York: Holt, Rinehart and Winston, 1967.

———. ed. *Journal of Social Issues* 22 (April 1966). Special Issue: "The Sexual Renaissance in America."

Rheingold, Joseph. *The Fear of Being a Woman: A Theory of Maternal Destructiveness*. New York: Grune and Stratton, 1964.

Roberts, Robert W., ed. *The Unwed Mother*. New York: Harper and Row, 1966.

Robinson, Marie N. *The Power of Sexual Surrender*. New York: Signet Books, 1959.

Rosen, Harold, ed. *Therapeutic Abortion*. New York: The Julian Press, 1954.

Rothman, Ellen K. *Hands and Hearts: A History of Courtship in America*. New York: Basic Books, 1984.

Rovinsky, Joseph J., and Alan F. Guttmacher, eds. *Medical, Surgical and Gynecological Complications of Pregnancy*. Baltimore: Williams and Wilkins, 1965.

Sauber, Mignon, and Elaine Rubinstein. *Experiences of the Unwed Mother as Parent: A Longitudinal Study of Unmarried Mothers Who Keep Their Babies*. New York: Community Council of Greater New York, 1965.

Schur, Edwin M. *Labeling Women Deviant: Gender, Stigma and Social Control*. Philadelphia: Temple University Press, 1983.

Services to and Characteristics of Unwed Mothers, Based on Florence Crittenton Association of America Two-Year Reporting Project, 1961–1962. Chicago: Florence Crittenton Association of America, 1963.

Services to Ummarried Mothers. New York: Child Welfare League of America, 1958.

Shapiro, Thomas M. *Population Control Politics: Women, Sterilization and Reproductive Choice*. Philadelphia: Temple University Press, 1985.

Sorokin, Pitirim A. *The American Sex Revolution*. Boston: Porter Sargent, 1956.

Spock, Benjamin. *The Common Sense Book of Baby and Child Care*. New York: Duell, Sloan and Pearce, 1946.

Stack, Carol. *All Our Kin: Strategies for Survival in a Black Community*. New York: Harper and Row, 1974.

Standards for Services to Unmarried Parents. New York: Child Welfare League of America, 1960.

Staples, Robert. *The Black Family: Essays and Studies*. Belmont, CA: Wadsworth, 1971.

Szasz, Thomas. *The Myth of Mental Illness*. New York: Harper and Row, 1974.

Teichman, Jenny. *Illegitimacy: An Examination of Bastardy*. Ithaca, NY: Cornell University Press, 1982.

Terkelsen, Helen. *Counseling the Unwed Mother*. Englewood Cliffs, NJ: Prentice-Hall, 1964.

The Double Jeopardy, The Triple Crisis—Illegitimacy Today. New York: National Council on Illegitimacy, 1969.

The Problem of Births Out of Wedlock. Raleigh: North Carolina Conference for Social Services, 1959.

Thompson, Jean. *The House of Tomorrow.* New York: Harper and Row, 1967.

Ulrich, Laurel Thatcher. *A Midwife's Tale: The Life of Martha Ballard Based on Her Diary 1785–1812.* New York: Knopf, 1990.

Understanding the Psychology of the Unmarried Mothers. New York: Family Service Association of America, 1948.

Unmarried Parenthood: Clues to Agency and Community Action. New York: National Council on Illegitimacy, 1967.

Vincent, Clark E. *Unmarried Mothers.* Glencoe, IL: The Free Press, 1961.

Ward, Martha C. *Poor Women, Powerful Men: America's Great Experiment in Family Planning.* Boulder, CO: Westview Press, 1986.

Weeks, Jeffrey. *Sex, Politics and Society: The Regulation of Sexuality Since 1800.* London: Longman, 1981.

Welpton, Pascal Kidder, Arthur H. Campbell, and John E. Patterson. *Fertility and Family Planning in the United States.* Princeton: Princeton University Press, 1966.

White, Deborah Gray. *Ar'n't I a Woman?: Female Slaves in the Plantation South.* New York: W.W. Norton, 1985.

White, Theodore H. *The Making of the President 1964.* New York: Atheneum, 1965.

Wylie, Philip. *Generation of Vipers.* New York: Farrar and Rinehart, Inc., 1942.

Young, Leontine. *Out of Wedlock.* New York: McGraw-Hill, 1954.

Zelizer, Viviana A. *Pricing the Priceless Child: The Changing Social Value of Children.* New York: Basic Books, 1985.

Government Documents

Adams, Hannah. *Social Services for Unmarried Mothers and Their Children Provided Through Public and Voluntary Child Welfare Agencies.* U.S. Department of Health, Education and Welfare, Washington, D.C.: Government Printing Office, 1962.

Choate, Reba E., and Ursula M. Gallagher. *Unmarried Parents: A Guide for the Development of Services in Public Welfare.* Bureau of Public Assistance, Report No. 45. U.S. Department of Health, Education and Welfare, Washington, D.C.: Government Printing Office, 1961.

Clague, Alice, and Stephanie Ventura. *Trends in Illegitimacy: United States—1940–1965.* Washington, D.C.: U.S. National Center for Health Statistics, 1968.

Golden Anniversary White House Conference on Children and Youth, 1960. Washington, D.C.: Government Printing Office, 1960.

Goodman, Elizabeth M., and Fabola M.L. Gill. *A Multi-Disciplinary Approach to a School-Centered Rehabilitation Program for Pregnant School-Aged Girls in Washington, D.C.: A Summary Report.* U.S. Department of Health, Education and Welfare, Washington, D.C. Government Printing Office, 1966.

Grow, Lucille. *Unwed Mothers Served by Voluntary Agencies: Data Collection Project for Agencies Serving Unmarried Mothers.* U.S. Department of Health, Education and Welfare. Washington, D.C.: Government Printing Office, 1967.

Herzog, Elizabeth, and Rose Bernstein. *Health Services for Unmarried Mothers.* U.S. Department of Health, Education and Welfare, Washington, D.C.: Government Printing Office, 1964.

Hoover, J. Edgar. *Crime in the United States.* FBI, U.S. Department of Justice, Washington, D.C.: Government Printing Office, 1965.

Illegitimacy and Its Impact on the Aid to Dependent Children Program: Implications for Federal and State Administrators. Bureau of Public Assistance, Social Security Administration, U.S. Department of Health, Education and Welfare. Washington, D.C.: Government Printing Office, 1960.

Kaplan, Saul. "Support from Absent Fathers of Children Receiving ADC." Public Assistance Report No. 41, U.S. Department of Health, Education and Welfare. Washington, D.C.: Government Printing Office, 1955.

Legislative Guides for the Termination of Parental Rights and Responsibilities and the Adoption of Children. Children's Bureau Publication No. 394, Social Security Administration, U.S. Department of Health, Education, and Welfare, Washington, D.C.: Government Printing Office, 1961.

Morlock, Maud, and Hilary Campbell. *Maternity Homes for Unmarried Mothers: A Community Service.* Children's Bureau. Publication No. 309. Department of Labor, Washington, D.C.: Government Printing Office, 1946.

Morlock, Maud. *The Community's Responsibility for the Child Born Out of Wedlock.* Children's Bureau, U.S. Department of Health , Education, and Welfare, mimeo, 1959.

Moynihan, Daniel Patrick. *The Negro Family: The Case for National Action.* Washington, D.C.: Government Printing Office, 1965.

Oettinger, Katherine Brownell. *The Unmarried Mother.* U.S. Department of Health, Education and Welfare, Washington, D.C.: Government Printing Office, 1959.

Schachter, Joseph, and Mary McCarthy. *Illegitimate Births: United States 1938–1957, Vital Statistics—Special Report.* National Office of Vital Statistics, U.S. Department of Health, Education and Welfare, Washington, D.C.: Government Printing Office, 1960.

Shapiro, Sam. "Illegitimate Births, 1938–1947." *Vital Statistics Reports, Selected Studies,* 33 (February 15, 1950).

The Problem of Births Out of Wedlock: A Preliminary Report. Raleigh, NC: North Carolina Conference for Social Service, 1959.

Thompson, C. Mildred. "Yesterday, Today, Tomorrow: A Chapter in the History of Freedom, 1848–1948," *The American Woman, Her Changing Role: Worker, Homemaker, Citizen.* United States Department of Labor, Woman's Bureau Bulletin No. 224. Washington, D.C.: Government Printing Office, 1948, pp. 42–51.

U. S. Congress, Senate, *Judiciary Committee, Hearings Before Subcommittee to Investigate Juvenile Delinquency, Interstate Adoption Practices, July 15–16, 1955* (84th Cong., 1st sess. [Washington, D.C.: Government Printing Office, 1955]).

U.S. Congress, House, District of Columbia Committee, Investigation of Public School Conditions; *Hearings Before Special Subcommittee to Investigate Public School Standards and Conditions and Juvenile Delinquency in the District of Columbia, September 19–October 1, 1956* (84th Cong., 2d sess. [Washington, D.C.: Government Printing Office, 1956]).

U.S. Congress, House, Ways and Means Committee, *Hearings on Public Assistance Titles of the Social Security Act, April 12, 13, 16, 19, 20, 1956* (84th Cong., 2d sess. [Washington, D.C.: Government Printing Office, 1956]).

U.S. Congress, Senate, Judiciary Committee, *Hearings Before the Subcommittee to Investigate Juvenile Delinquency, Commerical Child Adoption Practices, May 16, 1956* (84th Cong., 2d sess.[Washington, D.C.: Government Printing Office, 1956]).

U.S. Congress, Senate, Judiciary Committee, *Hearings Before the Subcommittee to Investigate Juvenile Delinquency, Interstate Adoption Practices, Miami, Florida, Novem-*

ber 14–15, 1956 (84th Cong., 1st sess. [Washington, D.C.: Government Printing Office, 1956]).

U.S. Congress, Senate, Committee on the Judiciary, Subcommittee to Investigate Juvenile Delinquency, Unpublished Hearing, May 11, 1956 (84th Cong., 2d sess.).

U.S. Congress, Senate, Committee on the Judiciary, Subcommittee to Investigate Juvenile Delinquency, Unpublished Hearing, May 16, 1956 (84th Cong., 2d sess.).

U.S. Congress, House, Appropriations Committee, Subcommittee on Departments of Labor, Health, Education and Welfare and Related Agencies' Appropriations for 1962, *Hearings Before the Subcommittee of the Committee on Appropriations* (87th Cong., 1st sess. [Washington, D.C.: Government Printing Office, 1961]).

U.S. Congress, Senate, Committee on Finance, *Hearings on the Public Assistance Act of 1962, May 14, 15, 16, 17, 1962.* (87th Cong., 2d sess. [Washington, D.C.: Government Printing Office, 1962]).

U.S. Congress, Senate, Committee on Government Operations, Subcommittee on Foreign aid Expenditures; *Population Crisis: Hearings on S. 1676, A Bill to Reorganize the Department of Health, Education and Welfare, August 31, September 8, 15, 22, 1965, Parts 1–4* (89th Cong., 1st sess. [Washington, D.C.: Government Printing Office, 1966]).

Articles

Adams, Clifford R. "Can You Control Your Daughter?" *Ladies' Home Journal*, December 1956, p. 45ff.

———. "Unwed Mother." *Ladies' Home Journal*, February 1962, 46ff.

Adams, Hannah M., and Ursula M. Gallagher. "Some Facts and Observations About Illegitimacy." *Children* 10 (March–April 1963):43–8.

Adams, Hannah M. "Two Studies of Unmarried Mothers in New York City." *Children* 8 (September–October 1961):184–8.

"ADC" *Children* 6 (July–August 1959):157.

"Agency Sponsors Contest on Ways of Interesting More Colored Families in Adoption." *Child Welfare* 31 (January 1952).

Allen, Mary Louise, as told to Eleanor Harris. "What Can We Do About America's Unwed Teenage Mothers?" *McCall's*, November 1963, p. 40ff.

Allen, Mary Louise. "Standards for Services to Unmarried Parents by the Child Welfare League of America." *Social Service Review* 35 (June 1961):228–9.

Amidon, B. "Frontline Officer: Door of Hope in Jersey City." *Survey Graphic*, October 1948, p. 43ff.

Anderson, Ursula M., Rachel Jenss, William E. Mosher, and Virginia Richter. "The Medical, Social and Educational Implications of the Increase in Out-of-Wedlock Births." *American Journal of Public Health* 56 (November 1966):1866–73.

Bell, Daniel. "New Phase in Negro Leadership." *New York Times Magazine*, May 31, 1964, p. 31ff.

Bell, Robert R., and Jay B. Chaskes. "Pre-marital Sexual Experience Among Coeds, 1958 and 1968." *Journal of Marriage and the Family* 32 (February 1970):81–4.

Bell, Robert. "Parent-Child Conflict in Sexual Values." *Journal of Social Issues* 22 (April 1966):34–44.

Berg, Renée. "Utilizing the Strengths of Unwed Mothers in the AFDC Program." *Child Welfare* 43 (July 1964):333–9.

Bernard, Viola. "Psychodynamics of Unmarried Motherhood in Early Adolescence." *The Nervous Child* 4 (October 1944):26–45.

Bernstein, Bernice L. "Law As an Instrument of Justice for Unwed Parents." In *Unmarried Parenthood: Clues to Agency and Community Action.* New York: National Council on Illegitimacy, 1967, pp. 81–6.

Bernstein, Rose. "Are We Still Stereotyping the Unmarried Mother?" *Social Work* 5 (July 1960):22–8.

————. "Gaps in Services to Unmarried Mothers." *Children* 10(March–April, 1963): 49–54.

————. "Perspectives on Services for Teenage Unmarried Mothers." *Child Welfare* 43 (January 1964):5–13.

————. "The Maternal Role in the Treatment of Unmarried Mothers." *Social Work* 8 (January 1963):58.

————. "Unmarried Parents." *Encyclopedia of Social Work.* 15th issue. New York: National Association of Social Workers, 1965, pp. 797–801.

Blair, Abbie. "Goodbye, Stephen." *Readers' Digest.* August 1962, p. 53ff.

Block, Babette. "The Unmarried Mother—Is She Different?" In *Understanding the Psychology of the Unmarried Mother.* New York: Family Service Association of America, 1945–47.

Bonan, Ferdinand. "Psychoanalytic Implications in Treating Ummarried Mothers with Narcissistic Characteristic Structure." *Social Casework* 44 (June 1963):323–5.

Boole, Lucille. "The Hospital and Unmarried Mothers." *Children* 3 (November–December 1956):208–12.

Bowman, Karl M., O. Spurgeon English, Manfred S. Guttmacher, Alfred Kinsey, Karl A.Meninger, Norman Reider, and Robert W. Laidlaw. "Psychiatric Implications of Surveys on Sexual Behavior." *The Psychoanalytic Review* 43 (October 1955):471–500.

Bowman, Lola. "The Unmarried Mother Who Is a Minor." *Child Welfare* 37 (October 1958):13–18.

Bradley, Trudy. "An Exploration of Caseworkers' Perception of Adoption Applicants." *Child Welfare* 45 (October 1966):433–43.

Brenner, Clifford. "Illegitimacy and Aid to Dependent Children." *Public Welfare* 8 (October 1950):174–8.

Breul, Frank R. "Public Welfare: Safeguard or Free Ride?" *University of Chicago Magazine,* January 1962, pp. 19–23.

Brienes, Wini. "The 1950s: Gender and Social Science." *ISS* 56 (1986):69–92.

Brower, Bernice R. "What Shall I Do with My Baby?" *The Child* 12 (April 1948):166–9.

Brumberg, Joan Jacobs. " 'Ruined girls': Changing Community Responses to Illegitimacy in Upstate New York, 1890–1920." *Journal of Social History* 18 (Winter 1984):247–72.

Byrne, Kathryne. "How a Nurse Can Help an Unmarried Mother." *American Journal of Nursing* 45 (October 1945):796–8.

Campbell, Arthur A., and James D. Cowhig. "The Incidence of Illegitimacy in the United States." *Welfare in Review* 5 (May 1967):3–5.

Cannon, Kenneth L., and Richard Long. "Premarital Sexual Behavior in the Sixties." *Journal of Marriage and the Family* 33 (February 1971):36–49.

Cantril, Hadley. "Sex Without Love." *The Nation,* October 10, 1953, pp. 294–6.

Cattell, James P. "Psychodynamic and Clinical Observations in a Group of Unmarried Mothers." *American Journal of Psychiatry* 111 (November 1954):337–42.

Christensen, Harold T., and Bette B. Rubinstein. "Pre-marital Pregnancy and Divorce: A Follow-up Study by the Interview Method." *Marriage and Family Living* 18 (May 1956):114–23.

Christensen, Harold T. and Hanna H. Meissner. "Studies in Child Spacing III—Premarital Pregnancy As a Factor in Divorce." *American Sociological Review* 18 (December 1953):641–4.

Christoph, Father Van F. "The Changing Role of the Father." *The Coordinator* 5 (September 1956):24–8.

Clothier, Florence. "Problems in the Placement of Illegitimate Chldren." *Child Welfare League of America Bulletin*. 20 (March 1941):1–3, 8.

———. "Problems of Illegitimacy As They Concern the Worker in the Field of Adoption." *Mental Hygiene* 25 (October 1941):576–90.

———. "Psychological Implications of Unmarried Parenthood." *American Journal of Orthopsychiatry* 13 (July 1943):531–49.

———. "The Unmarried Mother of School Age As Seen by a Psychiatrist." *Mental Hygiene* 39 (1955):631–46.

Coffino, Frances. "Helping a Mother Surrender Her Child for Adoption." *Child Welfare* 39 (February 1960):25–8.

Coughlan, Robert. "Changing Roles in Modern Marriage." *Life*, December 24, 1956, p. 109ff.

Crockett, Mary Lynch. "Examination of Services to the Unmarried Mother in Relation to Age of Adoption Placement of the Baby." *Casework Papers 1960*. New York: Family Services Association of America, 1960, pp. 75–85.

Curtis, Hester, and Alberta de Ronge. "Medical and Social Care for Unmarried Mothers." *Children* 4 (September–October 1957):174–80.

Cutright, Phillips. "Illegitimacy in the United States: 1920–1968." In Charles F. Westoff and Robert Parke, Jr., eds., *Demographic and Social Aspects of Population Growth*. Washington, D.C.: Commission on Population Growth and the American Future.

———. "Illegitimacy: Myths, Causes and Cures." *Family Planning Perspectives* 3 (January 1971):26–48.

———. "The Teenage Sexual Revolution and the Myth of the Abstinent Past." *Family Planning Perspectives* 4 (1972):24–31.

Damon, Virgil G., and Isabelle Taves. "My Daughter Is in Trouble." *Look*, August 14, 1962, p. 23ff.

Daniels, Bernice J. "Significant Considerations in Placing Negro Infants for Adoption." *Child Welfare* 29 (January 1950):8–9, 11.

Daugherty, Marie W., Hortense Few, and Margaret Muller. "Achieving Adoption for Sixty Children." *Child Welfare* 37(October, 1958): 7–11.

Davis, Annie Lee. "Attitudes Toward Minority Groups: Their Effect on Social Services for Unmarried Mothers." *The Child* 13 (December 1948):82–5.

Davis, Kinsley. "Illegitimacy and the Social Structure." *American Journal of Sociology* 45 (September 1939):215–33.

Deasey, Leila C., and Olive W. Quinn. "The Urban Negro and Adoption of Children." *Child Welfare* 41 (November 1962): 400–407.

"Decision of the Commissioner of Social Security in the Matter of the Louisiana Plan for Aid to Dependent Children Under Title IV of the Social Security Act." *Social Service Review* 35 (June 1961):207–9.

Donnell, Catherine, and Selma Glick. "Background Factors in One Hundred Cases of Jewish Unmarried Mothers." *The Jewish Social Service Quarterly* 29 (Winter 1952):152–60.

Dudley, Katherine. "A Referral Service for Unmarried Mothers." *The Family* 20 (October 1939):200–2.

Ehrmann, Winston. "Illegitimacy in Florida II: Social and Psychological Aspects of Illegitimacy." *Eugenics Quarterly* 3 (December 1956):223–7.

Farnsworth, Dana L. "Sexual Morality and the Dilemma of the Colleges." *American Journal of Orthopsychiatry* 35 (July 1965):676–81.

Fleck, Stephen. "Pregnancy As a Symptom of Adolescent Maladjustment." *International Journal of Social Psychiatry* 2 (Autumn 1956):118–31.

Foote, Nelson. "Sex As Play." *Social Problems* 1 (August 1954):154–63.

"Four Hundred Thousand Babies Left Behind." *U.S. News and World Report*, September 23, 1955, pp. 53–4.

Fowler, Dan C. "The Problem of Unwed Mothers." *Look*, July 29, 1949, p. 30ff.

Frazier, E. Franklin. "An Analysis of Statistics on Negro Illegitimacy." *Social Forces* 11 (1932):249–57.

Freedgood, Anne G. "Dr. Kinsey's Second Sex." *Harper's*, September 1953, pp. 21–7.

Freedman, Estelle B. " 'Uncontrolled Desires': The Response to the Sexual Psychopath, 1920–1960." *Journal of American History* 74 (June 1989):83–108.

Freedman, Mervin. "The Sexual Behavior of American College Women: An Empirical Study and an Historical Survey." *Merrill Palmer Quarterly* 11 (January 1965):33–48.

Friedman, Helen. "The Mother-Daughter Relationship: Its Potential in Treatment of the Young Unwed Mother." *Social Casework* 42 (October 1966):502–6.

Furie, Sidney. "Birth Control and the Lower-Class Unmarried Mother." *Social Work* 11 (January 1966):42–9.

Futterman, Samuel, and Jean Livermore. "Putative Fathers." *Journal of Social Casework* 28 (May, 1947): 174–8.

Gallagher, Ursula M. "What of the Unmarried Parent?" *Journal of Home Economics* 55 (June 1963):401–5.

Garland, Patricia. "Illegitimacy: A Special Minority Group Problem in Urban Areas." *Child Welfare* 45 (February 1966):81–8, 100.

———. "Teenage Illegitimacy in Urban Ghettos." In *Unmarried Parenthood: Clue to Agency and Community Action*. New York: National Council of Illegitimacy, 1967, pp. 24–39.

———. "The Community's Part in Preventing Illegitimacy." *Children* 10 (March–April 1963):71–5.

Gianakon, Harry G. "Ego Factors in the Separation of Unwed Mother and Child." *Casework Papers 1960*. New York: Family Service Association of America, 1960, pp. 58–64.

Glassberg, Bertrand Y. "Sexual Behavior Patterns in Contemporary Youth Culture— Implications for Later Marriage." *Journal of Marriage and the Family* 27 (May 1965):190–2.

Goldsmith, Jane K. "The Unmarried Mother's Search for Standards." *Social Casework* 38 (February 1957):69–74.

Goldstein, Sidney, and Kurt B. Mayer. "Illegitimacy: Residence and Status." *Social Problems* 12 (September 1965):428–36.

Goode, William J. "Illegitimacy in the Caribbean Social Structure." *American Sociological Review* 25 (February 1960):21–30.

Goodman, Elizabeth. "Trends and Goals in Schooling for Pregnant Girls and Teenage Mothers." In *Effective Services for Unmarried Parents and Their Children*. New York: National Council on Illegitimacy, pp. 77–8.

Gray, Paul H. "Conscience, Guilt, and the Unwed Mother." *The Journal of Pastoral Care* 13 (1959):164–70.

Green, Wade. "Federal Birth Control: Progress Without Policy." *The Reporter,* November 18, 1965, pp. 35–7.

Greenfield, Meg. " 'The Welfare Chiselers' of Newburgh, New York." *The Reporter,* August 17, 1961, pp. 37–40.

Gresham, Jewell Handy. "The Politics of Family in America." *The Nation,* July 24–31, 1989, p. 116ff.

Griswold, Barbara, Kermit Wiltse, and Robert Roberts. "Illegitimacy Recidivism Among AFDC Clients." In *Unmarried Parenthood: Clues to Agency and Community Action*. New York: National Council on Illegitimacy, 1967.

Gross, Leonard. "Are We Paying an Illegitimacy Bonus?" *Saturday Evening Post,* January 30, 1960, p. 30ff.

"Guide for Collaboration of Physician, Social Worker and Lawyer in Helping the Unmarried Mother and Her Child." *Children* 14 (May–June 1967):111–2.

Gutman, Herbert. "Marital and Sexual Norms Among Slave Women." In Nancy Cott and Elizabeth Pleck, eds., *A Heritage of Her Own: Toward a Social History of American Women*. New York: Simon and Schuster, 1979.

Hacker, Andrew. "The Pill and Morality." *New York Times Magazine,* November 21, 1965, p. 32ff.

Hall, Jacquelyn Dowd. " 'The Mind That Burns in Each Body': Women, Rape, and Racial Violence." In Ann Snitow, Christine Stansell, and Sharon Thompson, eds., *Powers of Desire: The Politics of Sexuality*. New York: Monthly Review Press, 1983, pp. 328–49.

Hall, John H. "An Experimental Program for Unmarried Mothers." *Child Welfare* 30 (May 1951):12–14.

Hartwick, Elizabeth. "The American Woman As Snow Queen." In Chandler Brossard, ed., *The Scene Before You: A New Approach to American Culture*. New York: Rinehart and Co., 1955.

Heiman, Marcel. "Out of Wedlock Pregnancy." *Casework Papers 1960* New York: Family Service Association of America, 1960, pp. 65–74.

Hertz, Hilda, and Sue W. Little. "The Unmarried Negro Mothers in a Southern Urban Community: A Study of Attitudes Toward Illegitimacy." *Social Forces* 23 (October 1944):73–9.

Hertz, Richard C. "The Effect of Jewish Culture Upon the Problem of Unmarried Motherhood." *Jewish Social Service Quarterly* 29 (December 1952):164–7.

Herzog, Elizabeth, and Rose Bernstein. "Why So Few Negro Adoptions?" *Children* 12 (January–February 1965):14–15.

Herzog, Elizabeth, and Hylan Lewis. "Priorities in Research on Unmarried Mothers."

In Leontine Young, ed., *Research Perspectives on Unmarried Mothers*. New York: Child Welfare League of America, 1962.

Herzog, Elizabeth. "Some Assumptions About the Poor." *Social Service Review* 26 (December 1963):389–402.

———. "The Chronic Revolution: Births Out of Wedlock." *Clinical Pediatrics* 5 (February 1966):130.

———. Unmarried Mothers: Some Questions to Be Answered and Some Answers to be Questioned. *Child Welfare* 41 (October 1962):339–49.

Hickey, Margaret. "Not Just a Place to Hide." *Ladies' Home Journal,* August, 1958, p. 23ff.

———. "Unmarried Mothers: Salvation Army Care." *Ladies' Home Journal,* June, 1949, p. 23ff.

Hildebrand, Catherine. "Casework with Different Kinds of Unmarried Mothers." *Child Welfare* 43 (January 1963):21–7.

Hines, Joseph S. "Some Reactions to a Hypothetical Premarital Pregnancy by 100 Negro College Women." *Journal of Marriage and the Family* 26 (August 1964):344–7.

Holmes, Marjorie. "A Mother Speaks Up for Censorship." *Today's Health,* January 1958, p. 51ff.

"Homes Needed for 10,000 Brown Orphans." *Ebony,* October 1948, p. 19ff.

Horowitz, Julius. "The Arithmetic of Delinquency." *The New York Times,* January 31, 1965, p. 12ff.

Howard, Marian. "Comprehensive Service Programs for School-Age Pregnant Girls." *Children* 15 (September–October 1968):193–7.

Hutchinson, Betty. "Unmarried Mothers As Patients of a Psychiatric Clinic." *Smith College Studies in Social Work* 19 (February 1949):102–3.

"Illegitimacy—a Growing Problem for the Taxpayer." *U.S. News and World Report,* April 20, 1959, p. 86ff.

"Interracial Adoptions." *Children* 12 (November–December 1965): p. 247.

Jackman, Norman, Richard O'Toole, and Gilbert Geis. "The Self-Image of the Prostitute." *The Sociological Quarterly* 4 (Spring 1963):150–61.

Jaffee, Frederick S. "Family Planning, Public Policy and Intervention Strategy." *Journal of Social Issues* 23 (1967):145–63.

Johnson, Nancy. "A Few Comments on Unmarried Mothers." *Social Casework* 37 (December 1956):504–7.

Josselyn, Irene M. "The Unmarried Mother." In Ralph Slovenko, ed., *Sexual Behavior and the Law*. Springfield, IL: Charles C. Thomas, 1965.

Judge, Jane. "Casework with the Unmarried Mother in a Family Agency." *Social Casework* 32 (January 1951):7–15.

Kasanin, J., and S. Handschin. "Psychodynamic Factors in Illegitimacy." *American Journal of Orthopsychiatry* 11 (January 1941):66–85.

Katz, Sanford. "Legal Protections for the Unmarried Mother and Her Child." *Children* 10 (March–April 1963):55–9.

Kelly, Jerry. "The School and Unmarried Mothers." *Children* 10 (March–April 1963):60–4.

Kenyon, G. L. "Illegitimate Children for Sale." *American Mercury,* April 1957, p. 27ff.

Khlentzos, Michael T., and Mary A. Pagliaro. "Observations from Psychotherapy with Unwed Mothers." *American Journal of Orthopsychiatry* 35 (July 1965): pp. 779–86.

King, Charles E. "The Negro Maternal Family: A Product of an Economic and Cultural System." *Social Forces* 24 (October 1945):100–4.

Kinkead, Katherine T. "The Lonely Time." *The New Yorker*, January 20, 1951, p. 29ff.

Kirkendall, Lester A., O. Hobart Mowrer, and Thomas Poffenberger. "Sex Education of Adolescents: An Exchange." *Marriage and Family Living* 22 (November 1960): pp. 317–32.

Knapp, Patricia, and Sophie T. Cambria. "The Attitudes of Negro Unmarried Mothers Toward Illegitimacy." *Smith College Studies in Social Work* 17 (September 1946–June 1947):185–203.

Kronick, Jane. "An Assessment of Research Knowledge Concerning the Unmarried Mother." In Leontine Young, ed., *Research Perspectives on the Unmarried Mothers*. New York: Child Welfare League of America, 1962, pp. 233–51.

Lake, Alice. "Why Young Girls Sell Their Babies." *Cosmopolitan*, December 1956, p. 45ff.

Latimer, Ruth, and Florence Startsman. "The Role of the Maternity Home Social Worker in the Prevention of Illegitimacy." *Mental Hygiene* 47 (July 1963) pp. 470–6.

Latimer, Ruth. "How to Wreck the Baby Racket." *American Mercury*, September 1957, p. 19ff.

"Legislation and Regulations Relating to Separation of Babies from their Mothers." *The Child* 3 (July 1938):19–21.

Levy, Dorothy. "A Follow-up Study of Unmarried Mothers." *Social Casework* 36 (January 1955):27–33.

Liebow, Elliot. "Attitudes Toward Marriage and Family Among Black Males in Tally's Corner." *The Milbank Memorial Fund Quarterly* 48 (April 1970):151–80.

Linkoski, L. Douglas. "Using the Maternity Home Milieu to Facilitate Casework Treatment of the Unmarried Mothers." *Child Welfare* 43 (January 1964):28–31.

"Litigation Forces Review of Public Housing Prohibition Against Families with Illegitimate Children." *Welfare Law Bulletin* 8 (May 1967):3.

Lowe, Charlotte. "Intelligence and Social Background of the Unmarried Mother." *Mental Hygiene* 1(October 1927):783–94.

Lowrie, Samuel H. "Early Marriage: Pre-marital Pregnancy and Associated Factors." *Journal of Marriage and the Family* 27 (February 1965):48–55.

Lunbeck, Elizabeth. "A New Generation of Women: Progressive Psychiatrists and the Hypersexual Female." *Feminist Studies* 13 (Fall 1987):513–43.

Lynch, Elizabeth I., and Alice E. Mertz. "Adoptive Placement of Infants Directly from the Hospital." *Social Casework* 36 (December 1955):450–7.

MacKenzie, Catherine. "Black Market in Babies, Too." *New York Times Magazine*, February 18, 1945, p. 5ff.

Malinowski, Bronislaw. "Parenthood—the Basis of Social Structure." In V.F. Calterton and S.D. Schmalhausen, eds., *The New Generation*. New York: Macauley, 1930, pp. 130–46.

Manning, Seaton W. "The Changing Negro Family: Implications for the Adoption of Children." *Child Welfare* 43 (November 1964):480–5.

Maranell, Gary M., Richard A. Dodder, and David F. Mitchell. "Social Class and Premarital Sexual Permissiveness: A Subsequent Test." *Journal of Marriage and the Family* 32 (February 1970):85–8.

Martz, Helen E. "Illegitimacy and Dependency." *Health, Education and Welfare Indicators*. September 1963.

McClure, W. E., and Bronett Goldberg. "Intelligence of the Unmarried Mother." *The Psychological Clinic* 18 (May–June 1929):119–27.

McGinley, Phyllis. "The Fearful Aspects of Too-Early Dating." *Good Housekeeping*, April 1956, p. 60ff.

Mead, Margaret. "Sex on the Campus: The Real Issue." *Redbook*, October 1962, p. 6ff.

"Memorandum for the Commissioner of Social Security from the Secretary of Health, Education and Welfare." *Social Service Review* 35 (June 1961):210–14.

Meyer, Henry J. "Problems in Developing Research on the Unmarried Mother." In Leontine Young, ed., *Research Perspectives on the Unmarried Mother*. New York: Child Welfare League of America, 1962.

Meyer, Henry J., Edgar F. Borgatta, and David Fanshel. "Unwed Mothers' Decisions About Their Babies; An Interim Replication Study." *Child Welfare* 38 (February 1959):5–6.

Meyer, Henry, Wyatt Jones, and Edgar F. Borgatta. "The Decision by Unmarried Mothers to Keep or Surrender Their Babies." *Marriage and Family Living* 18 (April 1956):103–9.

Monahan, Thomas. "Illegitimacy in the United States." *Eugenics Quarterly* 7 (September 1960):133–47.

Moore, Kristin, and Steven Caldwell. "The Effect of Government Policies on Out of Wedlock Sex and Pregnancies." *Family Planning Perspectives* 9 (July–August 1977):164–9.

Morlock, Maud. "Babies on the Market." *Survey* 86 (March 1945):67–9.

———. "Babies Wanted." *Trained Nurse* 115 (July 1945):17–21.

Morrison, Joseph L. "Illegitimacy, Sterilization and Racism: A North Carolina Case History." *Social Service Review* 34 (March 1965):1–10.

Mueller, K. H., and F. C. Myers. "Married Girls and Unmarried Mothers in the High Schools." *Journal of the National Association of Women Deans and Counselors* 28 (Spring 1965):120–5.

Muwakkil, Salim. "Black Family's Ills Provoke New Concern." *In These Times*, June 12–25, 1985, p. 6.

Nielson, Katheryn M., and Rocco L. Motto. "Some Observations on Family Constellations and Personality Patterns of Young Unmarried Mothers." *American Journal of Orthopsychiatry* 35 (July 1965):740–3.

Norton, Mary Beth. "The Evolution of White Women's Experience in Early America." *American Historical Review* 89 (June 1984):593–619.

Nowak, Marion. "How to Be a Woman: Theories of Female Education in the 1950s." *Journal of Popular Culture* 9 (Summer 1975):77–83.

O'Connell, Martin, and Maurice J. Moore. "The Legitimacy Status of First Births to U.S. Women Ages 15–24, 1939–1978." *Family Planning Perspectives* 12 (January–February 1980):16–25.

O'Connell, Martin. "Comparative Estimates of Teenage Illegitimacy in the U.S. 1940–44 to 1970–74." *Demography* 17 (February 1980):13–23.

Oettinger, Katherine Brownell. "Current Concerns of the Children's Bureau." *Children* 5 (May–June 1958):123–8.

Oman, Harriet G. "Giving Up A Baby." *Survey* 88 (January 1952):14–17.

Omolade, Barbara. "Hearts of Darkness." In Ann Snitow, Christine Stansell, and Sharon Thompson, eds., *Powers of Desire: The Politics of Sexuality*. New York: Monthly Review Press, 1983, pp. 350–67.

Oshlag, Sylvia. "Surrendering a Child for Adoption." In *Understanding the Psychology of the Unmarried Mother*. New York: Family Service Association of America, 1945–47.

Pakter, Jean, and Frieda Nelson. "The Unmarried Mother and Her Child: The Problems and Challenges." In *Illegitimacy: Data and Findings for Prevention, Treatment and Policy Formation*. New York: National Council on Illegitimacy, 1965.

Pakter, Jean, Henry J. Rosner, Harold Jacobziner, and Frieda Greenstein. "Out-of-Wedlock Births in New York City: I—Sociologic Aspects." *American Journal of Public Health* 51 (May 1961):683–96.

———. "Out-of-Wedlock Births in New York City: II—Medical Aspects." *American Journal of Public Health* 51 (June 1961):846–65.

Pannor, Reuben. "Casework Service for Unmarried Fathers." *Children* 10 (March–April 1963):65–70.

Parsons, Lois. "Homes for Unmarried Mothers Develop Leisure Time Programs." *The Child* 12 (October 1947):54–63.

Parton, M. "Sometimes Life Just Happens." *Ladies' Home Journal*, October 1962, p. 28ff.

Paul, Julius. "The Return of Punitive Sterilization Proposals: Current Attacks on Illegitimacy and the AFDC Program." *Law and Society Review* 3 (August 1968):77–106.

Pearson, John S., and Phyllis L. Amacher. "Intelligence Test Results and Observations of Personality Disorder Among 3,594 Unwed Mothers in Minnesota." *Journal of Clinical Psychology* 12 (January 1956):16–21.

Perlman, Helen H. "Unmarried Mothers." In Nathan E. Cohen, ed., *Social Work and Social Problems*. New York: National Association of Social Work, 1964.

Pipel, Harriet. "Sex vs. the Law." *Harper's*, January 1965, p. 35ff.

Poffenberger, Thomas, Richard H. Klemer, Ira L. Reiss, Walter R. Stokes, Lester A. Kirkendall, and Blaine M. Porter. "Premarital Sexual Behavior: A Symposium." *Marriage and Family Living* 24 (August 1962):254–78.

Poffenberger, Thomas. "Individual Choice in Adolescent Premarital Sex Behavior." *Marriage and Family Living* 22 (November 1960): 324–9.

Polier, Justine Wise. "Illegitimate!" *Woman's Home Companion*, August 1947, p. 32ff.

Pope, Hallowell, and Dean D. Knudsen. "Premarital Sexual Norms, the Family, and Social Change." *Journal of Marriage and the Family* 27 (August 1965):314–23.

Porter, Amy. "Sex in Our High Schools." *Collier's*, December 4, 1948, p. 13ff.

Powell, Miriam. "Illegitimate Pregnancy in Emotionally Disturbed Girls." *Smith College Studies in Social Work* 19 (June 1949):171–9.

"Pregnancies Grow in Washington Schools." *U.S. News and World Report*, July 12, 1957, p. 66ff.

"Projects." *Children* 11 (November–December 1964):240.

"Public Housing Prohibitions Against Families with Illegitimate Children." *Welfare Law Bulletin* 9 (July 1967):7.

Rall, M. E. "Casework with the Minor Unmarried Mother and Her Family." *Social Casework* 39 (November 1958):494–502.

Rashbaum, William, Janice Paneth, and Martin Greenberg. "Use of Social Services by Unmarried Mothers." *Children* 10 (January–February 1963):11–16.

Raskin, A. H. "Newburgh Lessons for the Nation." *New York Times Magazine*, December 17, 1961, p. 7ff.

Reed, Ellery F. "Unmarried Mothers Who Kept Their Babies." *Children* 12 (May–June 1965):118–19.

Reich, Charles. "Searching Homes of Public Assistance Recipients: The Issues Under the Social Security Act." *Social Service Review* 37 (December 1963):328–39.

Reid, Joseph H. "Editorial Comments." *Child Welfare* 38 (June 1959):16–17.

Reider, Norman. "The Unmarried Father." *American Journal of Orthopsychiatry* 18 (April 1948):230–7.

Reiss, Albert J. "Sex Offenses: The Marginal Status of the Adolescent." *Law and Contemporary Problems* 25 (Spring 1960):309–33.

Reiss, Ira L. "Pre-marital Sexual Permissiveness Among Negroes and Whites." *American Sociological Review* 29 (October 1964):688–97.

———. "Sexual Codes in Teen Age Culture." *Annals of the American Academy of Political and Social Science* 338 (November 1961):53–62.

———. "Social Class and Pre-marital Sexual Permissiveness: A Reexamination." *American Sociological Review* 30 (October 1965):747–56.

———. "The Scaling of Pre-marital Sexual Permissiveness." *Journal of Marriage and the Family* 26 (May 1964):188–98.

Richardson, Anne. "Evaluation of a Public School Program for Pregnant Girls." Washington, D.C.: Bureau of Social Science Research, Inc., 1966.

Riesman, David. "Permissiveness and Sex Roles." *Marriage and Family Living* 21 (August 1959):211–17.

Rindfleisch, Roberta. "Administration of Unmarried Mothers Services." *Child Welfare* 36 (December 1957):23–8.

Rinehart, Jonathan. "Mothers Without Joy." *Saturday Evening Post*, March 23, 1963, p. 29ff.

Ross, Helen. "The Meaning of Motherhood to the Unmarried Mother." *Casework Papers*. New York: Family Service Association of America, 1955.

Ruark, Robert. "The Flapper's Children." *Collier's*, December 28, 1946, p. 18ff.

Sanders, Marion K. "Social Work: A Profession Chases Its Tail." *Harper's*, March 1957, p. 56ff.

Sauber, Mignon, and Janice Paneth. "Unwed Mothers Who Keep Their Children: Research and Implications." *Proceedings of the National Conference on Social Welfare*. New York: Family Service Association of America, 1965.

Schauffler, Goodrich C. "Today It Could Be Your Daughter." *Ladies' Home Journal*, January 1958, p. 43ff.

Scherz, Frances H. " 'Taking Sides' in the Unmarried Mother's Conflict." In *Understanding the Psychology of the Unmarried Mother*. New York: Family Service Association of America, 1945–47.

Schlossman, Steven, and Stephanie Wallach. "The Crime of Precocious Sexuality: Female Juvenile Delinquency in the Progressive Era." *Harvard Educational Review* 48 (February 1978):65–94.

Schmideberg, Melitta. "Psychiatric-Social Factors in Young Unmarried Mothers." *Social Casework* 32 (January 1951):3–7.

Schottland, Charles I. "The Nature of Services in Public Assistance." *Casework Papers 1959*.New York: Family Service Association of America, 1959.

Schumacher, Henry C. "The Unmarried Mother: A Socio-Psychiatric Viewpoint." *Mental Hygiene* 4 (October 1927):775–82.

Schurch, Martha. "A State Program for Minor Unmarried Mothers." *Child Welfare* 38 (October 1959):5–11.

Sedlak, Michael W. "Young Women and the City: Adolescent Deviance and the Transformation of Educational Policy, 1870–1960." *History of Education Quarterly* 23 (Spring 1983):1–28.

Shaffer, Helen. "The Rise in Illegitimacy." *Editorial Research Report No. 15*. Washington, D.C.: Editorial Research Reports, 1959, pp. 285–302.

Shapiro, Deborah. "Attitudes, Values, and Unmarried Motherhood." *Unmarried Parenthood: Clues to Agency and Community Action*. New York: National Council on Illegitimacy, 1967, pp. 52–63.

Sherfey, Mary Jane. "The Evolution and Nature of Female Sexuality in Relation to Psychoanalytic Theory." *Journal of the American Psychoanalytic Association* 14 (January 1966):28–128.

Shlakman,Vera. "Unmarried Parenthood: An Approach to Social Policy." *Social Casework* 42 (October 1966):494–501.

Shoenberg, Carl. "The Expanding Nature and Purpose of the Maternity Home." *Child Welfare* 43 (January 1964):14–19, 27.

Shorter, Edward. "Illegitimacy, Sexual Revolution, and Social Change in Modern Europe." *Journal of Interdisciplinary History* 2 (Autumn 1971):237–72.

Smith, Daniel Scott, and Michael S. Hindus. "Pre-marital Pregnancy in America 1640–1971: Overview and Interpretation." *Interdisciplinary History* 5 (Spring 1975):537–70.

Smith, Daniel Scott. "The Dating of the American Sexual Revolution: Evidence and Interpretation." In Michael Gordon, ed., *The American Family in Social-Historical Perspective*. New York: St. Martin's Press, 1978.

Steinem, Gloria. "The Moral Disarmament of Betty Coed." *Esquire*, September 1962, p. 97ff.

Steinmetz, Martha A. "Role Playing in a Maternity Home." *Children* 11 (March–April 1964): 61.

Stine, Oscar C. "School-Leaving Due to Pregnancy in an Urban Adolescent Population." *American Journal of Public Health* 54 (January 1964).

Strand, Glenn and William Larson. "Five Professions View the Unmarried Parent." *International Journal of Psychiatry* 6 (Autumn 1960):269–76.

Taylor, Lillian E. "Social Attitudes Toward Sexual Behavior and Illegitimacy." In *Illegitimacy: Data and Findings for Prevention, Treatment and Policy Formation*. New York: National Council on Illegitimacy, 1965.

Teele, James, and William Schnidt. "Illegitimacy and Race." In Clyde V. Kiser, ed., *Demographic Aspects of the Black Community*. Proceedings of the 43d Conference of the Milbank Memorial Fund, New York, October 28–30, 1969, p. 127–95.

"The 'Suitable Home Requirement.' " *Social Service Review* 35 (June 1961):203–6.

"The Morals Revolution on the U.S. Campus." *Newsweek*, April 6, 1964, p. 52ff.

"The Second Sexual Revolution." *Time*, January 24, 1964, p. 54ff.

"The Terrifying Ordeal of the Unwed Mother." *True Confessions*, November 1949.

Thornhill, Margaret. "Problems of Repeated Out of Wedlock Pregnancies." *Child Welfare* 38 (June 1959):1–4.

Trout, Louise K. "Services to Unmarried Mothers." *Child Welfare* 35 (February 1956):21–6.

Tuttle, Elizabeth. "Serving the Unmarried Mother Who Keeps Her Child." *Social Casework* 43 (October 1962):415–22.

"Unwed Mothers—even experts are stumped about how to treat them." *Journal of Housing* 16 (Spring 1959):289–90.

Valien, Preston, and Alberta Fitzgerald. "Attitudes of the Negro Mother Toward Birth Control." *American Journal of Sociology* 55 (November 1949):279–83.

Verner, Mary. "Administrative Concepts in Comprehensive Services for Unmarried Parents." In *Unmarried Parenthood: Clues to Agency and Community Action.* New York: National Council on Illegitimacy, 1967.

Vincent, Clark. "Illegitimacy and Value Dilemmas." *Christian Century* 80 (June 19, 1963):801–4.

———. "Illegitimacy in the Next Decade: Trends and Implications." *Child Welfare* 43 (December 1964):513–20.

———. "Teenage Unwed Mothers in American Society." *Journal of Social Issues* 22 (April 1966):22–33.

———. "The Adoption Market and the Unwed Mother's Baby." *Marriage and Family Living* 18 (May 1956):124–7.

———. "Unwed Mothers and the Adoption Market: Psychological and Familial Factors." *Marriage and Family Living* 22 (May 1960):112–18.

Vinovskis, Maris. "Adolescent Sexuality, Pregnancy and Childbearing in America: Some Preliminary Speculations." In Jane B. Lancaster and Beatrix A. Hamburg, eds., *School-Age Pregnancy and Parenthood: Biosocial Dimensions.* New York: Aldine de Gruyter: 1986, pp. 303–22.

———. "An Epidemic of Adolescent Pregnancy? Some Historical Considerations." *Journal of Family History* 6 (Summer 1981):205–30.

Walters, Paul A. "Prosmiscuity in Adolescence." *American Journal of Orthopsychiatry* 35 (July 1965):670–5.

Wattenberg, Ben J., and Richard M. Scammon. "Our Population: The Statistical Explosion." *The Reporter*, March 25, 1965, pp. 40–1.

"We're Not Alone." *True Story*, September 1959, p. 47ff.

Weinstein, Marybeth. "Markets, Black and Gray, in Babies." *New York Times Magazine*, November 27, 1955, p. 12ff.

"When Is Love Wrong?" *Ladies' Home Journal*, December 1957, p. 6ff.

"Where One Birth in Five Is Out of Wedlock." *U.S. News and World Report*, April 4, 1958, p. 101.

White, Glenn Matthew. "Teenage Illegitimate Pregnancy: Why Does It Happen?" *Ladies' Home Journal*, August 1958.

———. "The Truth About Illegitimacy." *Ladies' Home Journal*, December 1960.

Whitman, Howard. "America's Moral Crisis: The Slavery of Sex Freedom." *Better Homes and Gardens*, June, 1957. p. 59ff.

———. "Youth and the Natural Urge." *Better Homes and Gardens*, July 1957, p. 43ff.

———. "Don't Let Them Scoff at Marriage." *Better Homes and Gardens*, August 1957, p. 58ff.

Whyte, William F. "A Slum Sex Code." *American Journal of Sociology* 49 (July 1943):24–31.

Windle, Charles. "Factors in the Passage of Sterilization Legislation: The Case of Virginia." *Public Opinion Quarterly* 29 (Summer 1965):306–14.

Wolfenstein, Martha. "The Emergence of Fun Morality." *Journal of Social Issues* 7 (1951):15–25.

Workum, Ruth I. "Problems of the Unmarried Mother and Her Child." *Child Welfare League of America Bulletin* 11 (May 1924):1–13.

Wrieden, Jane. "The Meaning of the Maternity Home." *Children* 3 (January–February 1956), pp. 23–6.

———. "To Strengthen Maternity Home Service for Unmarried Mothers: I." *The Child* 16 (August–September 1951): p. 5ff.

———. "To Strengthen Maternity Home Service for Unmarried Mothers: II" *The Child* 16 (October 1951): p. 28ff.

Wright, Gerald C. "Racism and the Availability of Family Planning Services in the United States." *Social Forces* 56 (June 1978): pp. 1087–98.

Young, Leontine. "Personality Patterns in Unmarried Mothers." In *Understanding the Psychology of the Unmarried Mother*. New York: Family Service Association of America, 1945–47.

———. "The Unmarried Mother's Decision About Her Baby." In *Understanding the Psychology of the Unmarried Mother*. New York: Family Service Association of America, 1945–47.

———. "Unmarried Mother: Problems of Financial Support." *Social Casework* 35 (March 1954):99–104.

Younger, Joan. "The Unwed Mother." *Ladies' Home Journal,* June 1947.

Zelnick, Melvin, and John F. Kanter. "U.S.: Exploratory Studies of Negro Fertility—Factors Relating to Illegitimacy." *Studies in Family Planning* 1 (December 1970):5–9.

Dissertations and Theses

Aiken, Katherine G. "The National Florence Crittenton Mission, 1883–1925: A Case Study of Progressive Reform." Ph.D. dissertation, Washington State University, 1980.

Barker, Gertrude F. "Self-Esteem of the Unwed Mother." Ed.D. dissertation, Boston University, 1967.

Berg, Renée. "A Study of a Group of Unwed Mothers Receiving Aid to Dependent Children." D.S.W. dissertation, University of Pennsylvania, 1962.

Bieber, Toby Bennett. "A Comparison Study of Negro Wed and Unwed Mothers." Ph.D. dissertation, Columbia University, 1963.

Costigan, Barbara Hansen. "The Unmarried Mother—Her Decision Regarding Adoption." D.S.W. dissertation, University of Southern California, 1964.

Dalgren, Elza Virginia. "Attitudes of a Group of Unmarried Mothers Toward the Minnesota Three Months Nursing Regulations and Its Application." M.A. thesis, University of Minnesota, 1940.

Edens, Lester William. "An Analysis of Certain Socio-Psychological Characteristics of Unwed Mothers Referred to Private Agenices in Washington and Idaho." Ed.D. dissertation, University of Idaho, 1964.

Hawkinson, Helen. "The Relationship of the Unmarried Mother to Her Parents As a Factor in Her Problem of Illegitimate Pregnancy." M.A. thesis, University of Minnesota, 1949.

Jones, Wyatt C. "Correlates of Social Deviance: A Study of Unmarried Mothers." Ph.D. dissertation, New York University, 1965.

Jordan, Ernest E. "A Study of the Social and Maternal Responsibilities of a Group of Negro Unwed Mothers." Ed.D. dissertation, University of Pennsylvania, 1969.

Julian, Joyce P. "Comparison of the Selected Background Factors of One Hundred and Ten Unmarried Mothers Who Retained or Surrendered Their Children, Known to Hennepin County Welfare Board During 1957." M.A. thesis, University of Minnesota, 1959.

Maxwell, Ethel H. "A Study of the Social Attitudes of Negro Unmarried Mothers Who Have Retained Custody of Their Children Known to the Child Welfare Division of the Ramsey County Welfare Board." M.A. thesis, University of Minnesota, 1939.

McIntyre, Jennie J. "Illegitimacy: A Case of Stretched Values?" Ph.D. dissertation, Florida State University, 1965.

Parker, Elizabeth V. "Unmarried Mothers at New Haven Hospital: A Study of Thirty Unmarried Mothers Who Took Their Children Home." M.A. thesis, University of Minnesota, 1947.

Pollock, Edmund. "An Investigation into Certain Personality Characteristics of Unmarried Mothers." Ph.D. dissertation, New York University, 1957.

Pratt, William. "A Study of Marriages Involving Pre-marital Pregnancies." Ph.D. dissertation, University of Michigan, 1965.

Ripple, Lillian. "Social Work Studies of Unmarried Parenthood As Affected by Contemporary Treatment Formulations: 1920–1940." Ph.D. dissertation, University of Chicago, 1953.

Shapiro, Deborah. "Social Distance and Illegitimacy: A Comparative Study of Attitudes and Values." D.S.W. dissertation, Columbia University, 1966.

Stapf, Marjorie K. "A Descriptive Study of the Role of the Social Group Worker in a Home for Unmarried Mothers." M.S.W. thesis, University of Minnesota, 1951.

Tangadahl, Thorfin N. "A Study of the Specialized Work with Alleged, Acknowledged, and Adjudicated Fathers in the Hennepin Country Welfare Board's Unmarried Mothers Program." M.A. thesis, University of Minnesota, 1946.

Archives

The National Archives. Washington D.C., Children's Bureau Papers, Record Group 102.

The Salvation Army Archives. New York, New York.

Social Welfare History Archives. University of Minnesota, Minneapolis, Minnesota.

The papers of the following organizations:

National Association on Services to Unmarried Parents
National Council on Illegitimacy
Child Welfare League of America
Family Service Association of America
Florence Crittenton Association of America

Florence Crittenton Mission
Travellers' Aid Association of America

Newspapers

Many newspapers were consulted for this study. All articles from the *New York Times*, 1940–70, concerning the subjects of the study were sources. The footnotes provide detailed information about individual articles in this and other newspapers.

Index

Abortion 4, 19, 54, 63, 89, 97, 99, 100, 137, 152, 167, 172, 178, 186 231; illegal 4, 15, 21, 23, 56, 58, 98, 101, 163, 167, 228; legalization of 39–40, 231; and sterilization 5; therapeutic 4; therapeutic and unwed mothers 37

Abortion debates 19, 99, 102

Academic studies 8, 35, 51, 63, 75, 78, 80–1, 90, 171, 174, 217, 224, 225

Adelphi University 88

ADOPT-A-CHILD 198

Adoption 6, 26, 186; agencies 28, 171–2, 178–9; agencies and exclusionary practices 199; black babies 57, 63; blacks 196–9, 202; and courts 165–7; decline of 224; government support of 26–27, 159; independent 3, 163; pressure to 27; prewar practices 149; and psychiatric theory 96, 152; and reform 153–4; as rehabilitation 17, 26, 152; and the rich 167

Adoption caseworkers: and abuse 173–5; and conservatism 171; and hostility 171

Adoption mandate 12, 152–61; and abuse 164–86; and caseworkers 156–8; as coercive 155, 163–4, 172; critiques of 26; and "defective children" 170; dissipation of 224; and lack of services 160, 170; and maternity homes 114; as racist 156; and social agencies 158–61; and women's vulnerability 155, 167; weaknesses of 155, 223

Adoptive parents 31–3, 191, 196–7

Aid to Dependent Children (ADC) 22, 29, 30, 31, 34, 56, 65; as black-identified program 42, 49; black recipients 8, 18; and denial of benefits 37; as incentive for illegitimacy 30, 34, 42, 80; perceived as failure 42; resistance to (see Taxpayers' hostility) 42, 56; and rising expenditures 42, 193; statistics and racial differential 49; typical recipient 8, 200; and white recipients 42, 49, 193

Alabama 196

Allen, Mary Louise 109, 155, 218

Altgeld Gardens Murray Homes Management Company 47

American Journal of Psychiatry 88

American Public Welfare Association 159

Anti-choice movement 40

Arnold, Mildred 117, 130, 173

Atlanta 138

Atlanta Life Insurance Company 196

Atlanta School of Social Work 73

Augusta, Georgia 175–6

Auletta, Ken 84

Baltimore 196, 199

Baltimore Family and Children's Society 202

Banfield, Stone 56

Barrett, Robert 68, 122, 158

Bennett, James V. 208

Berean Institute 202

Bernard, Viola 94

Bernstein, Rose 98, 196, 222–3

7, 172, 174; and ostracism 33, 85, 89–90, 93, 100, 155; and parents' responses to 1, 136–7; and pregnancy disorders 89; as psychotic 88; as rebellious 217; and refusal to relinquish 33, 224–5; and rehabilitation 33; and self-blame 5–6, 137; and the "sexual revolution" 206, 217–21, 230; and shame 24; and social agencies 10; and stigma 89, 134, 155, 171; as witch 90
Unwed pregnancy: black, as typical 18; as subversive 21
Urban League 23, 198

Verner, Mary 229
Vincent, Clark 31, 76, 177, 186, 218, 223
Virginia 22, 56, 65
Virginia Commission to Study Problems Relating to Children Born Out of Wedlock 55
Virginia General Assembly 56
Virginity 105, 108, 151, 178, 219, 223
Volunteers of America 124

Walters, Isabelle 129, 131
Washington, D.C. 45, 60, 65, 78, 81, 181, 199, 212–13
Washington, D.C., Board of Commissioners 231
Washington, D.C., Board of Education 212
Washington, D.C. Department of Public Health 212
Washington, D.C. Metropolitan Police, Women's Bureau 181
Washington Post 57
Watts uprising 208
Webster School 212, 214
Welfare: agencies 3, 7, 12–13, 228, 229; costs 8, 24, 42, 49 ; eligibility

51–2; and "midnight raids" 52; payments 31, 216; policies 7, 36; policies, exclusionary 24, 45, 50–2; workers 2, 27
Wesley, Mrs. Carter 74
Westchester County (New York) 143, 161
West Virginia 229
White family imperative 20, 25, 26, 101, 149, 154, 157, 166
White supremacy 24, 34, 38, 43, 60
White, Theodore, H. 55
Whitley County (Kentucky) 213
Wichita Beacon 183
Williams, Bess 63
Wilmington 141
Williams, John Bell 45
Wisconsin 33, 124, 137
Woman's Life 134
Womanhood 14, 38, 80, 95; definitions of 16
Women: as consumer experts 29; hostility toward 56; and sexual decision-making 102, 178; single 21–22, 35
Women's bodies: black, as political terrain 19, 41, 45–59; as commodities 29
Women's magazines 1, 108
Women's movement 99
Woodward, Harry A. 165, 175–6
World War II 154
Wrieden, Jane E. 70–71, 87, 116, 123, 126–7, 130, 140
Wright, Helen R. 133

Young, Leontine 6, 24, 28, 89, 92, 96, 99, 113, 160, 172, 192, 215
YWCA 71
Youth Consultation Services 12

Zoar Home, Allenson, Pennsylvania 128